Shojo Beat

Skip·Beat!

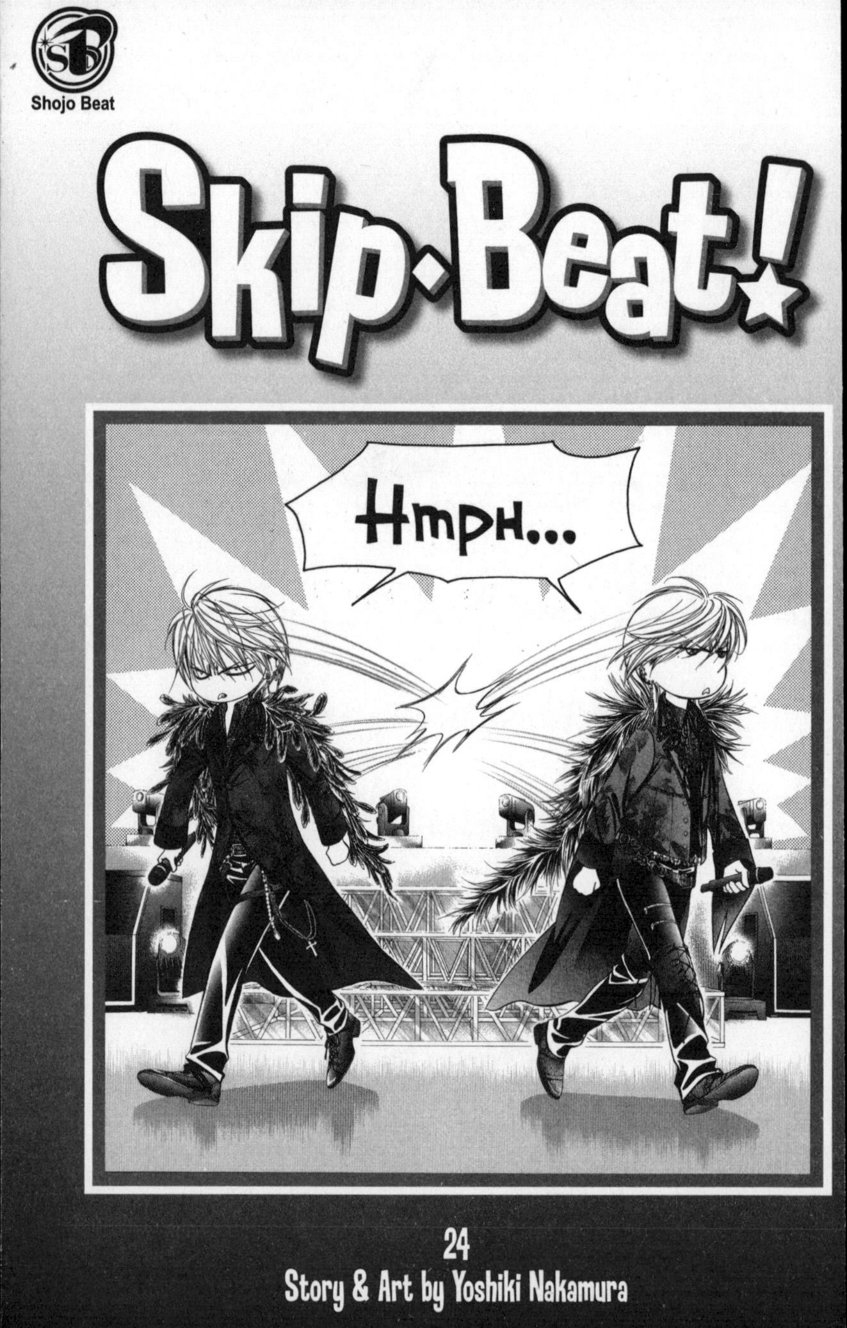
Hmph...

24

Story & Art by Yoshiki Nakamura

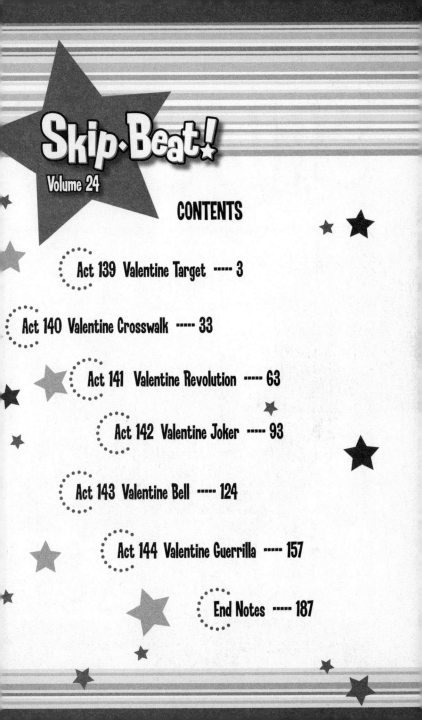

Skip·Beat!

Volume 24

CONTENTS

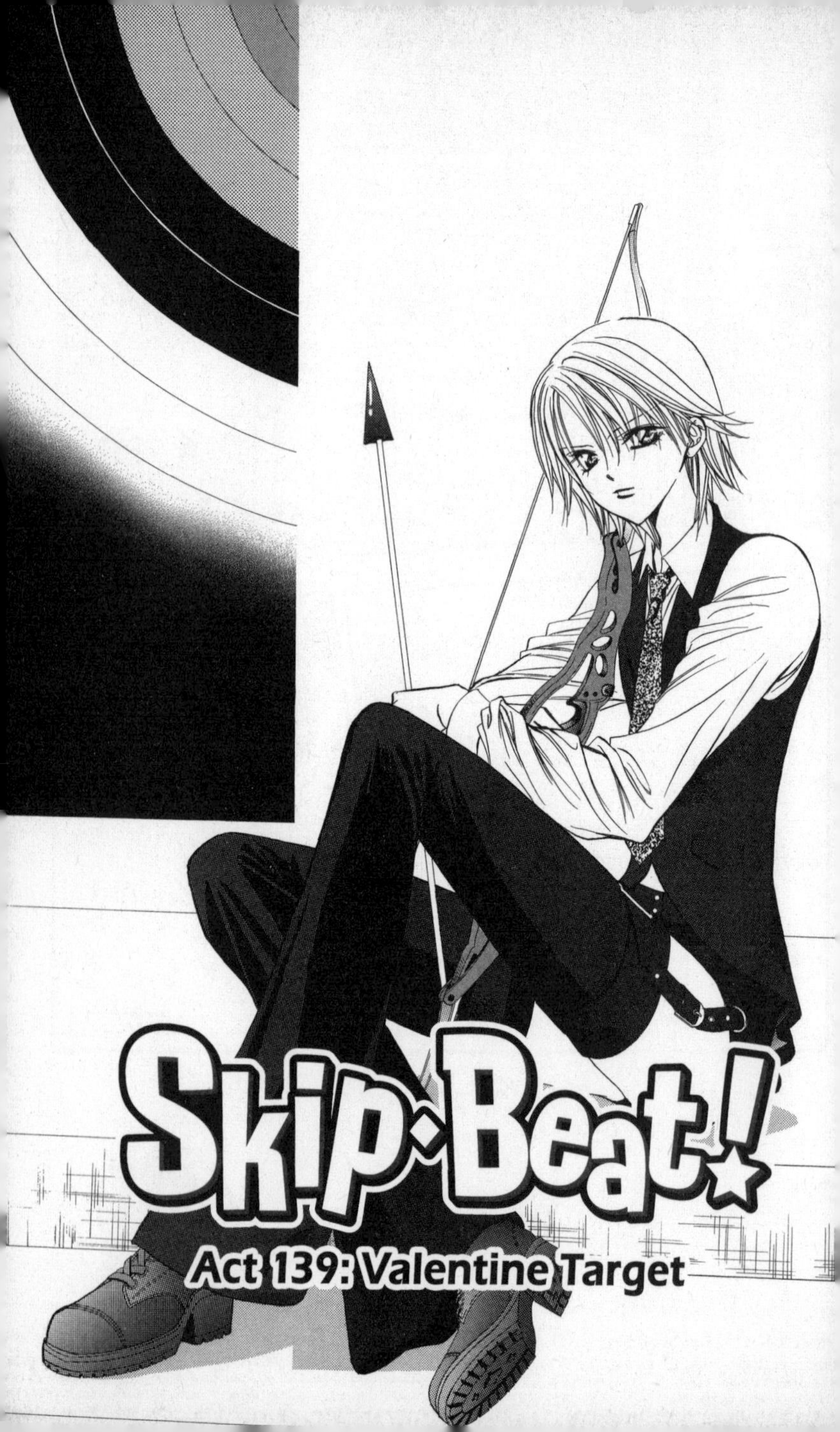
Skip·Beat!
Act 139: Valentine Target

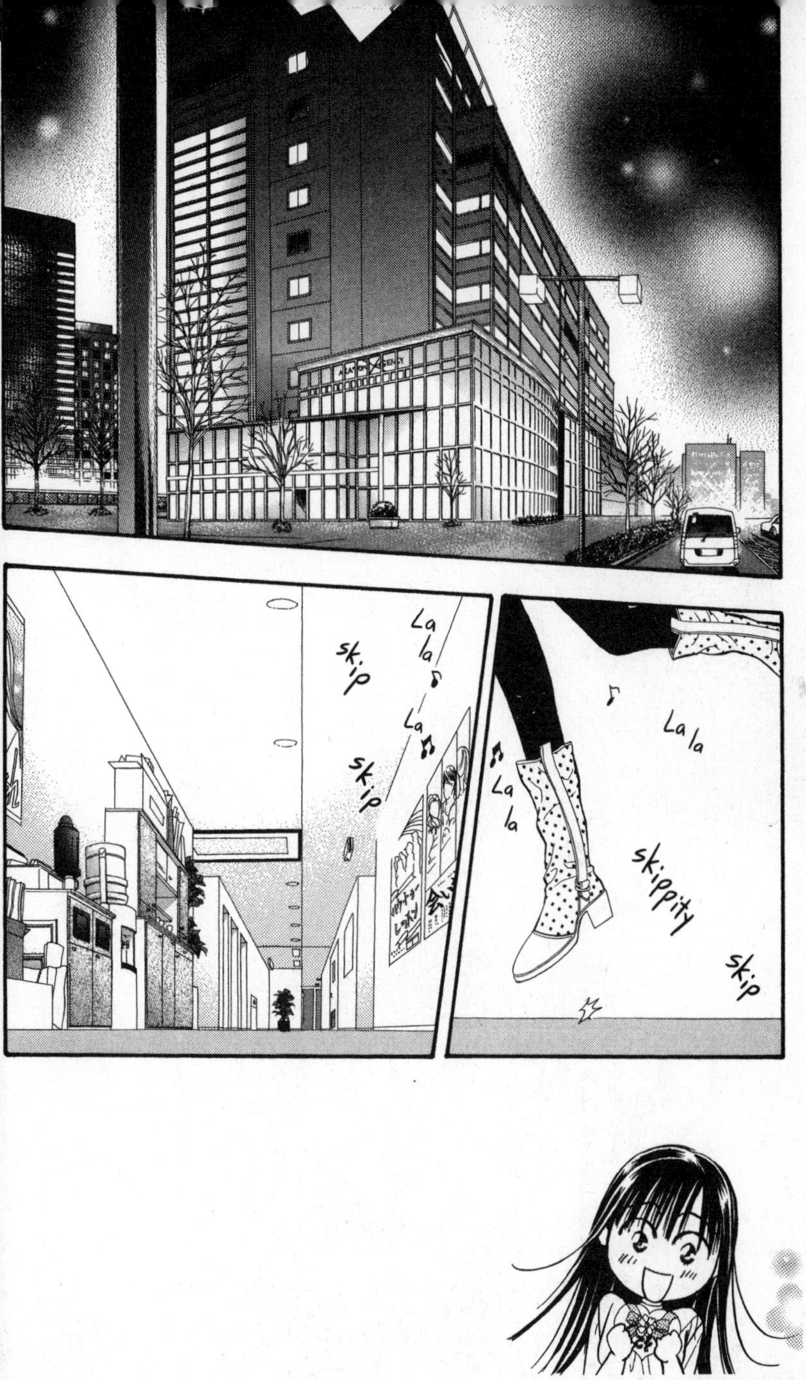
La la
La la
skippity
skip
La la
skip
La
skip

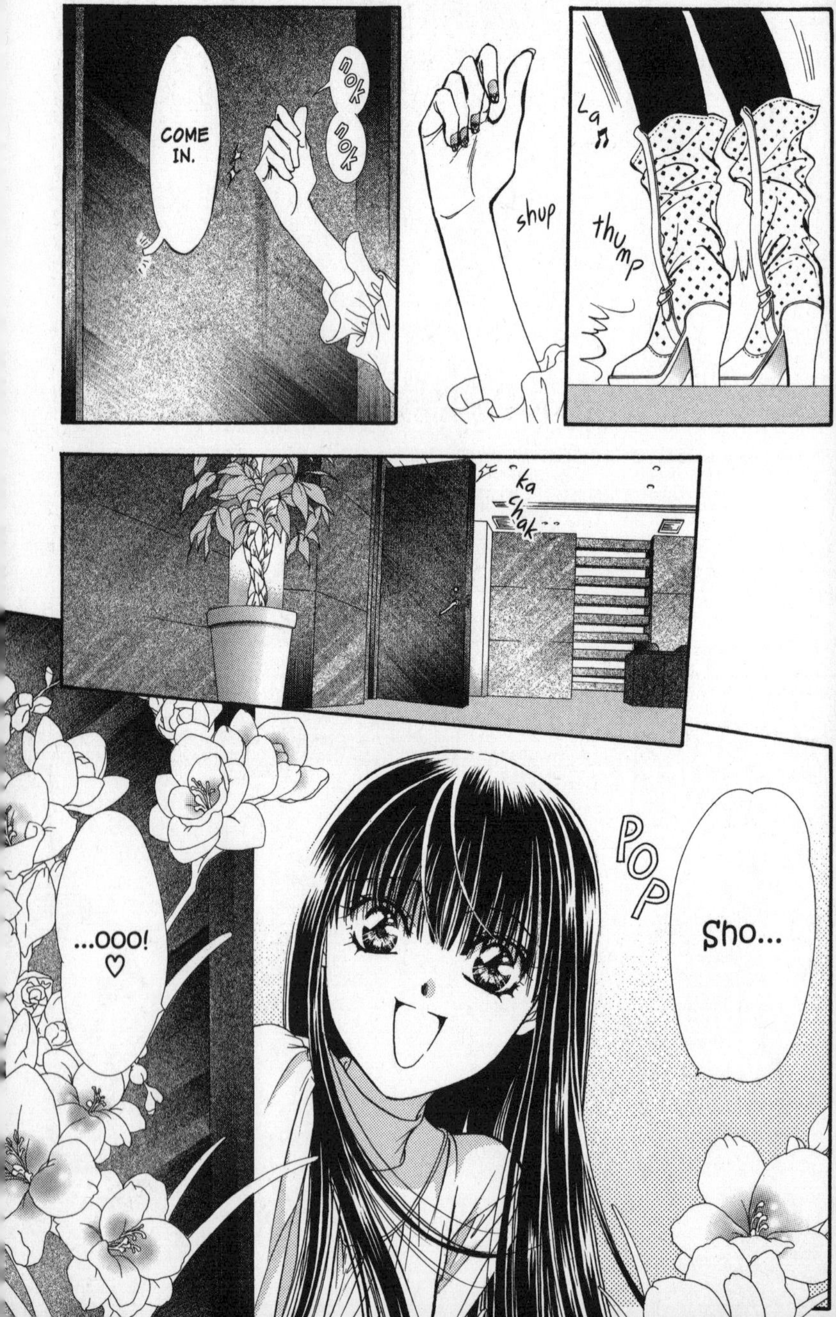
La♪
thump
shup
nok nok
COME IN.
ka chak
POP
Sho...
...OOO! ♡

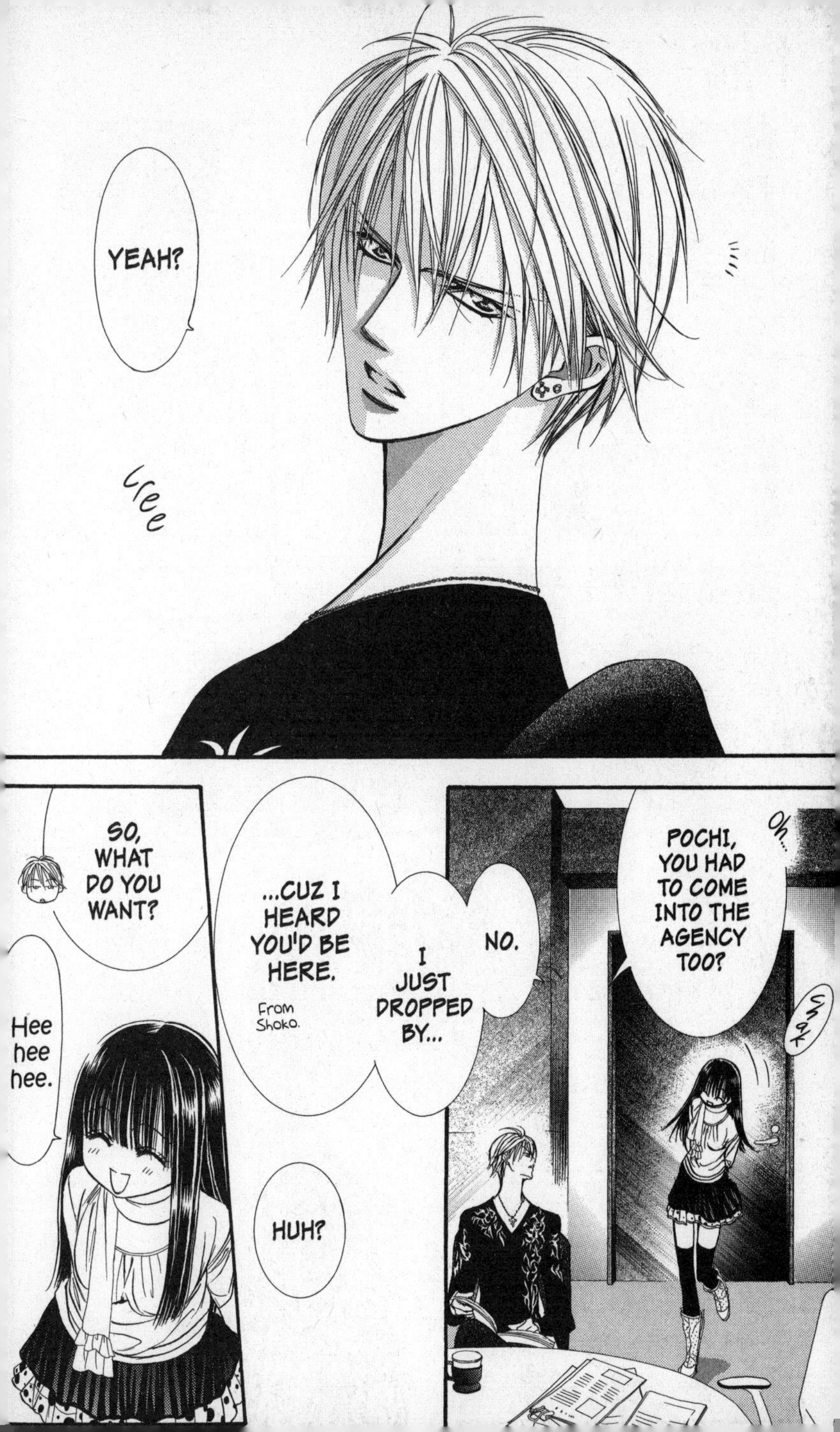
YEAH?
Oh...
POCHI, YOU HAD TO COME INTO THE AGENCY TOO?
NO.
I JUST DROPPED BY...
...CUZ I HEARD YOU'D BE HERE.
From Shoko.
HUH?
SO, WHAT DO YOU WANT?
Hee hee hee.

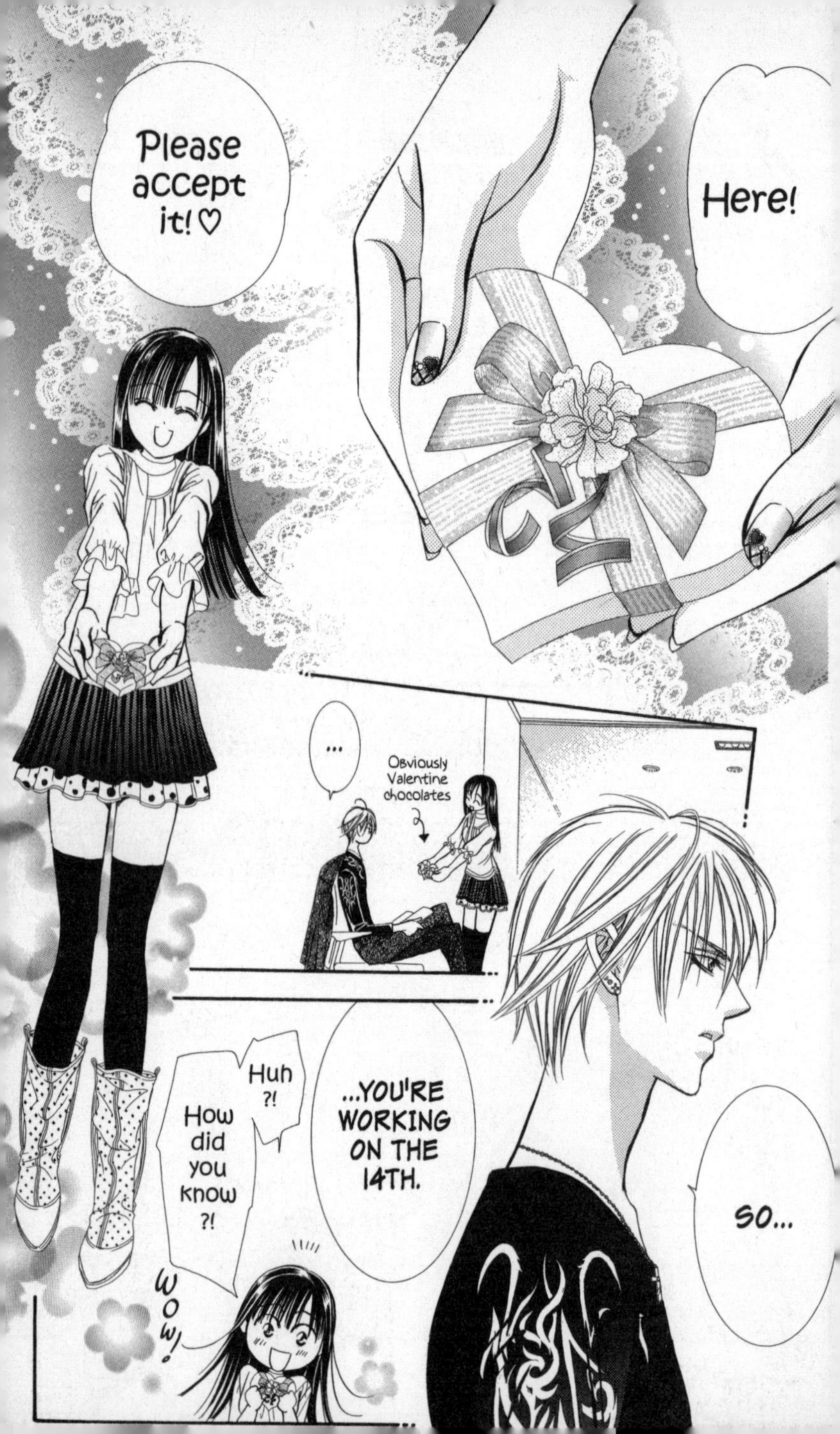
Here!
Please accept it!♡
...
Obviously Valentine chocolates
So...
...YOU'RE WORKING ON THE 14TH.
Huh?!
How did you know?!
WOW!

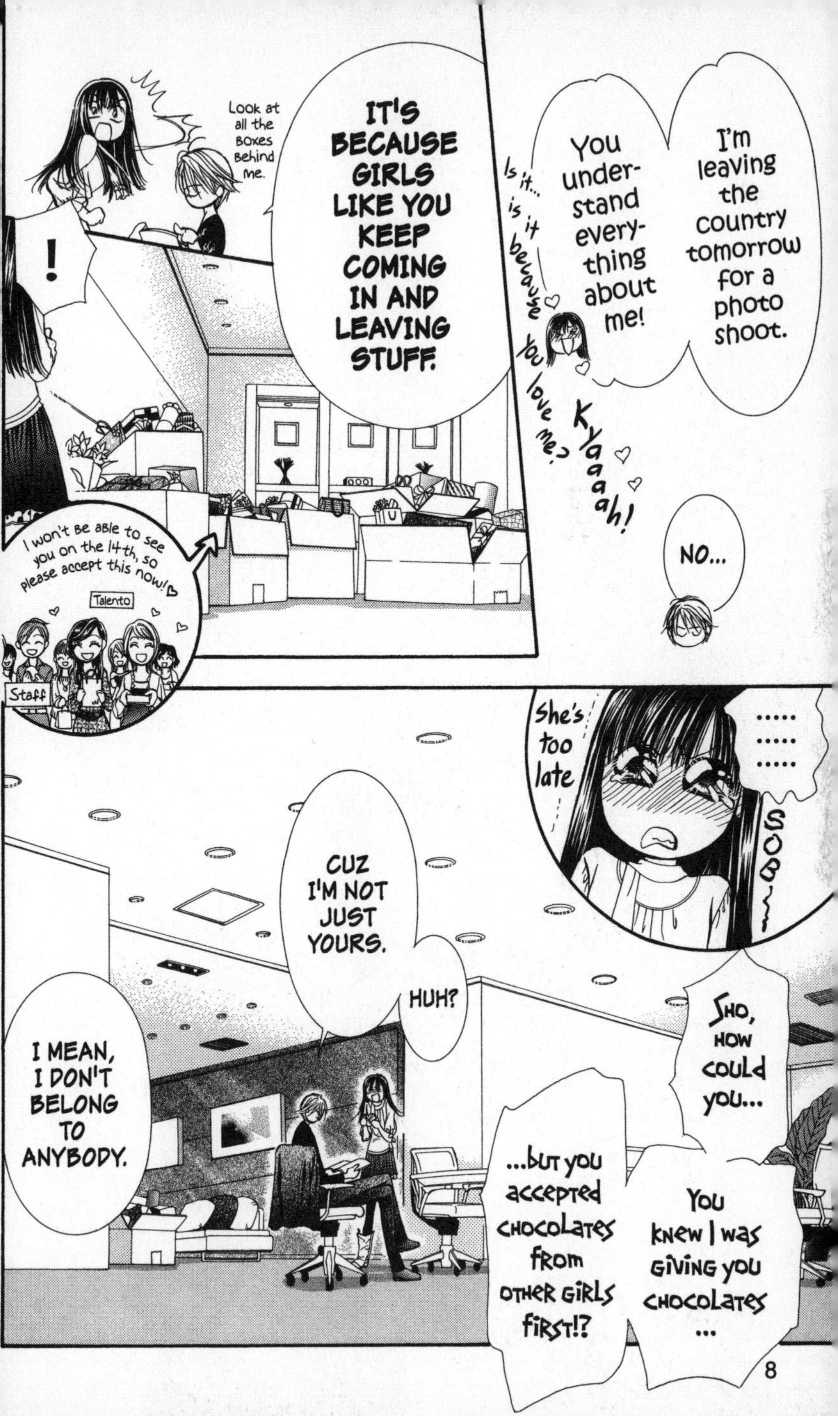
I'm leaving the country tomorrow for a photo shoot.
You under-stand every-thing about me!
Is it... is it because you love me?
Kyaaaah!
NO...
IT'S BECAUSE GIRLS LIKE YOU KEEP COMING IN AND LEAVING STUFF.
Look at all the Boxes Behind me.
!
I won't be able to see you on the 14th, so please accept this now!
Talento
Staff
......
......
......
She's too late
SOB
Sho, how could you...
You knew I was giving you chocolates...
...but you accepted chocolates from other girls first!?
CUZ I'M NOT JUST YOURS.
HUH?
I MEAN, I DON'T BELONG TO ANYBODY.

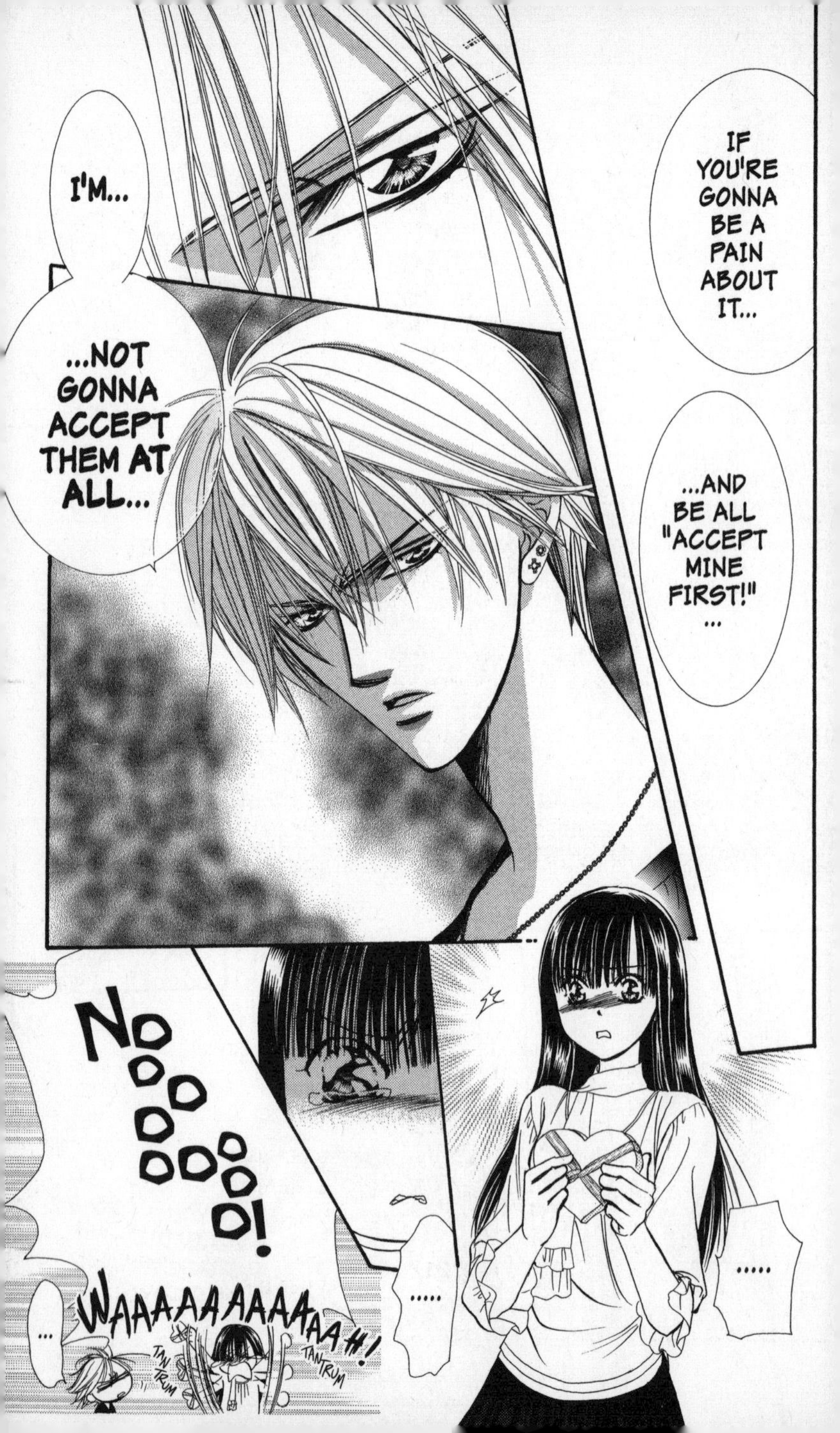

IF YOU'RE GONNA BE A PAIN ABOUT IT...
...AND BE ALL "ACCEPT MINE FIRST!" ...
I'M...
...NOT GONNA ACCEPT THEM AT ALL...
.....
.....
NOOOOOOOOO!
WAAAAAAAAAAAAH!
TANTRUM
TAN TRUM
...

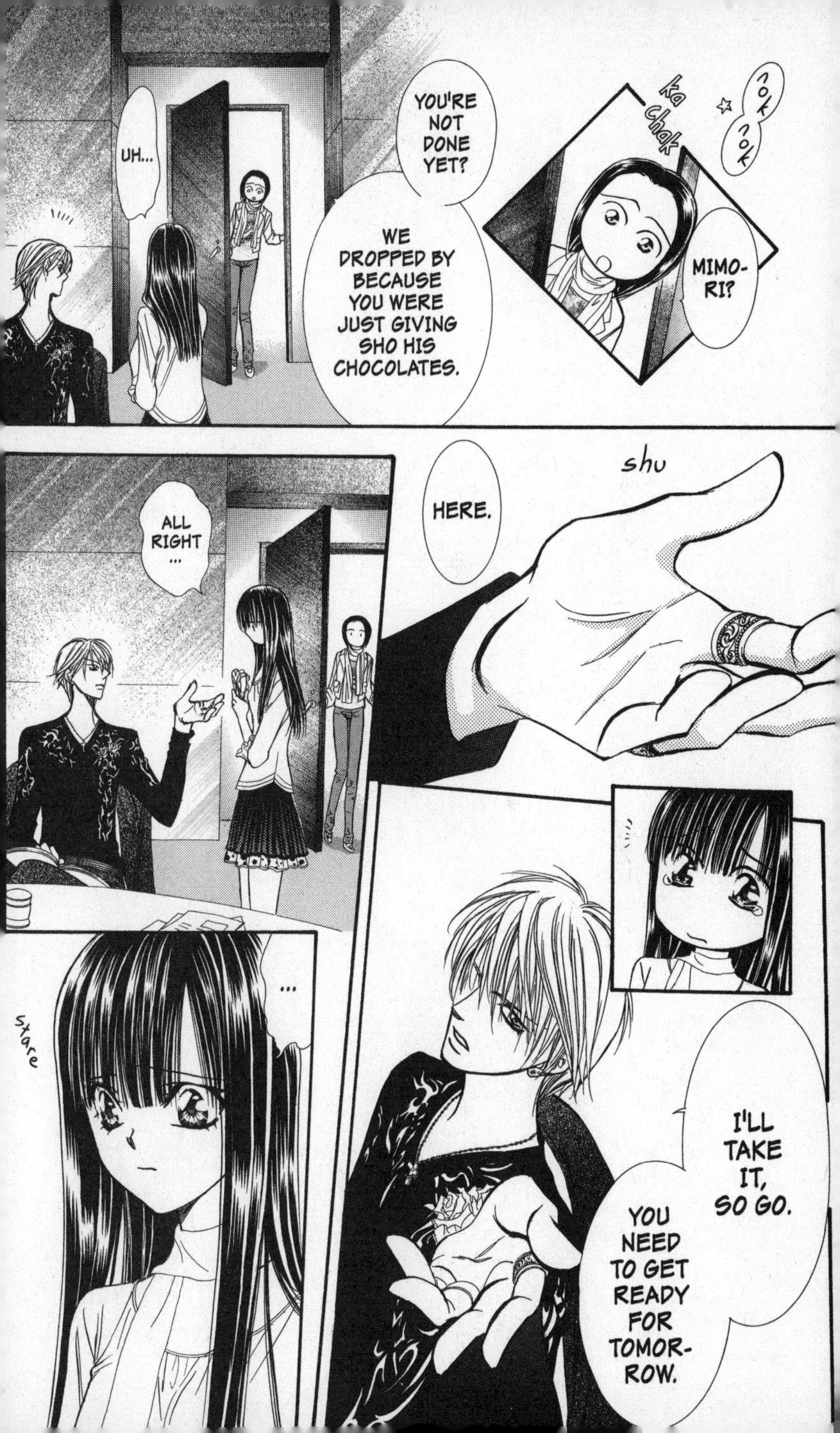

nok nok
ka chak
MIMORI?
YOU'RE NOT DONE YET?
WE DROPPED BY BECAUSE YOU WERE JUST GIVING SHO HIS CHOCOLATES.
UH...
shu
HERE.
ALL RIGHT ...
I'LL TAKE IT, SO GO.
YOU NEED TO GET READY FOR TOMORROW.
...
stare

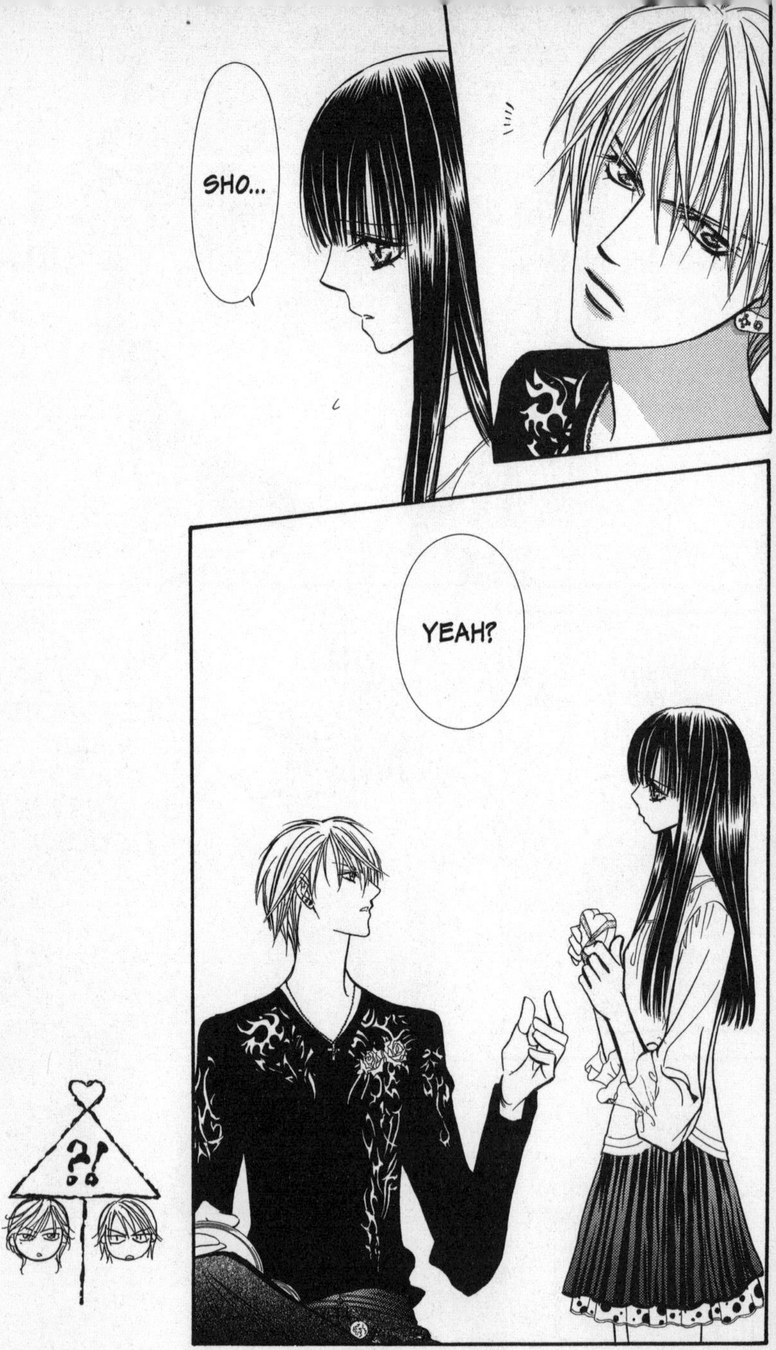
SHO...
YEAH?
?!

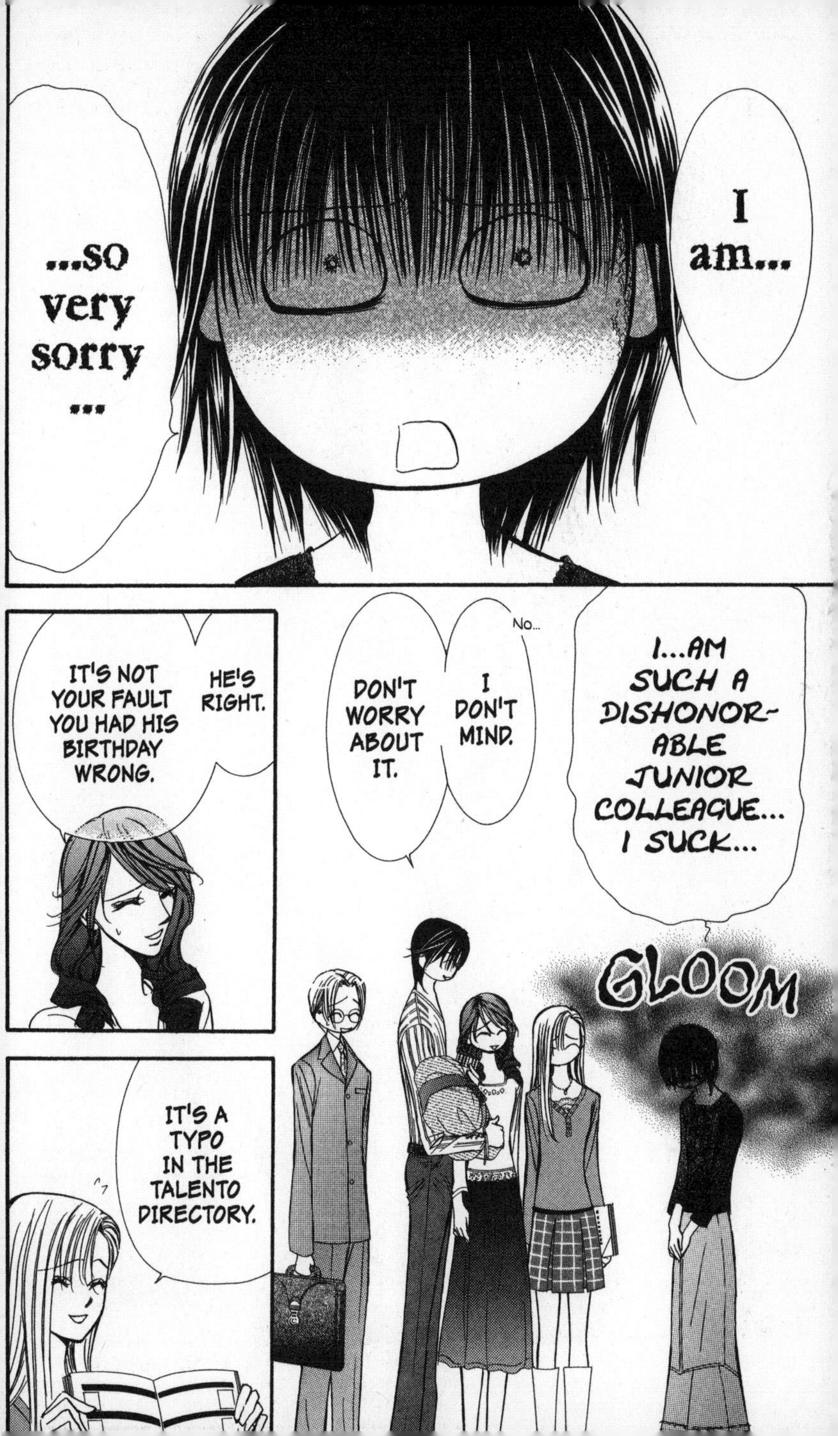
I am...
...so very sorry...
I...AM SUCH A DISHONORABLE JUNIOR COLLEAGUE... I SUCK...
GLOOM
No...
I DON'T MIND.
DON'T WORRY ABOUT IT.
HE'S RIGHT.
IT'S NOT YOUR FAULT YOU HAD HIS BIRTHDAY WRONG.
IT'S A TYPO IN THE TALENTO DIRECTORY.

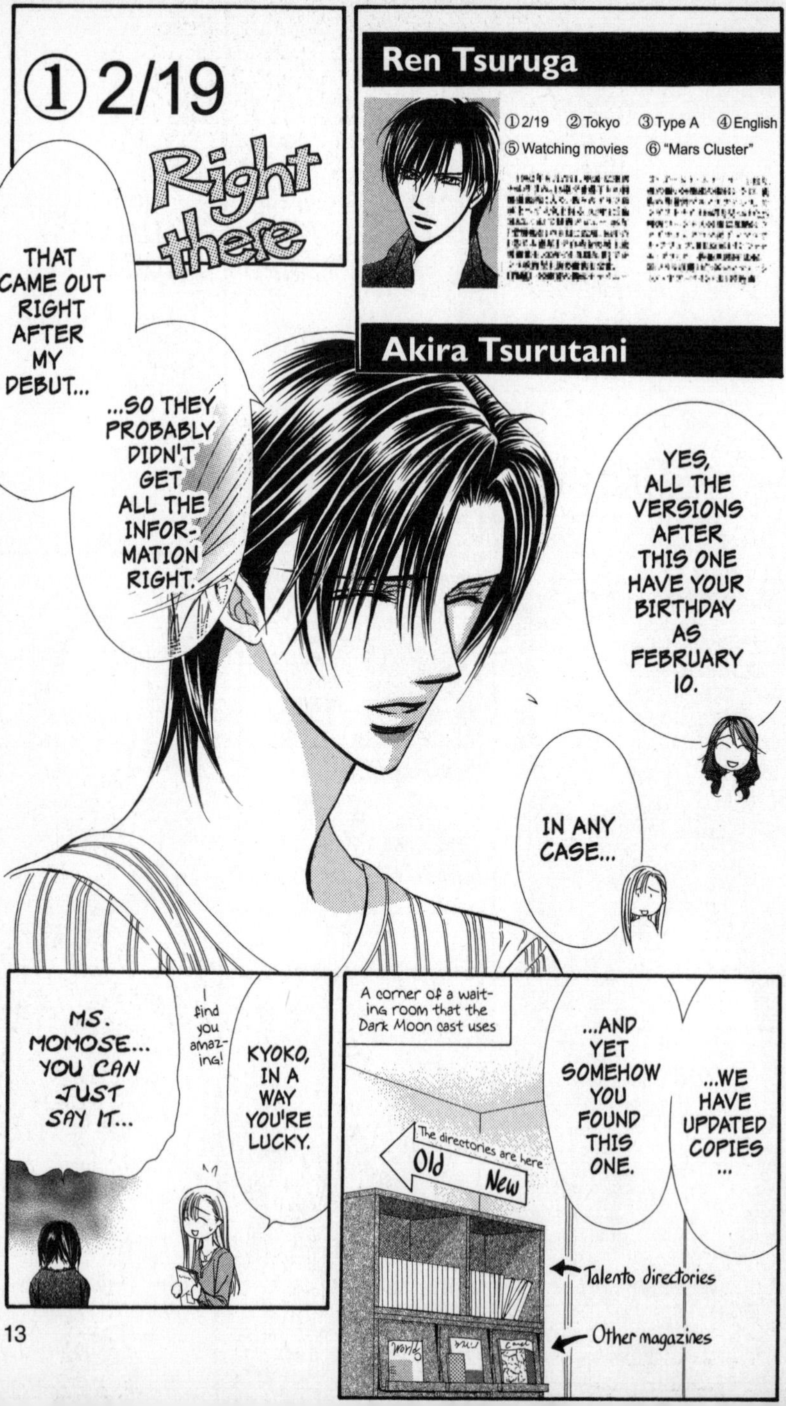
Ren Tsuruga
①2/19 ②Tokyo ③Type A ④English
⑤Watching movies ⑥"Mars Cluster"
Akira Tsurutani
① 2/19
Right there
THAT CAME OUT RIGHT AFTER MY DEBUT...
...SO THEY PROBABLY DIDN'T GET ALL THE INFORMATION RIGHT.
YES, ALL THE VERSIONS AFTER THIS ONE HAVE YOUR BIRTHDAY AS FEBRUARY 10.
IN ANY CASE...
A corner of a waiting room that the Dark Moon cast uses
...WE HAVE UPDATED COPIES...
...AND YET SOMEHOW YOU FOUND THIS ONE.
The directories are here
Old
New
Talento directories
Other magazines
KYOKO, IN A WAY YOU'RE LUCKY.
I find you amazing!
MS. MOMOSE... YOU CAN JUST SAY IT...

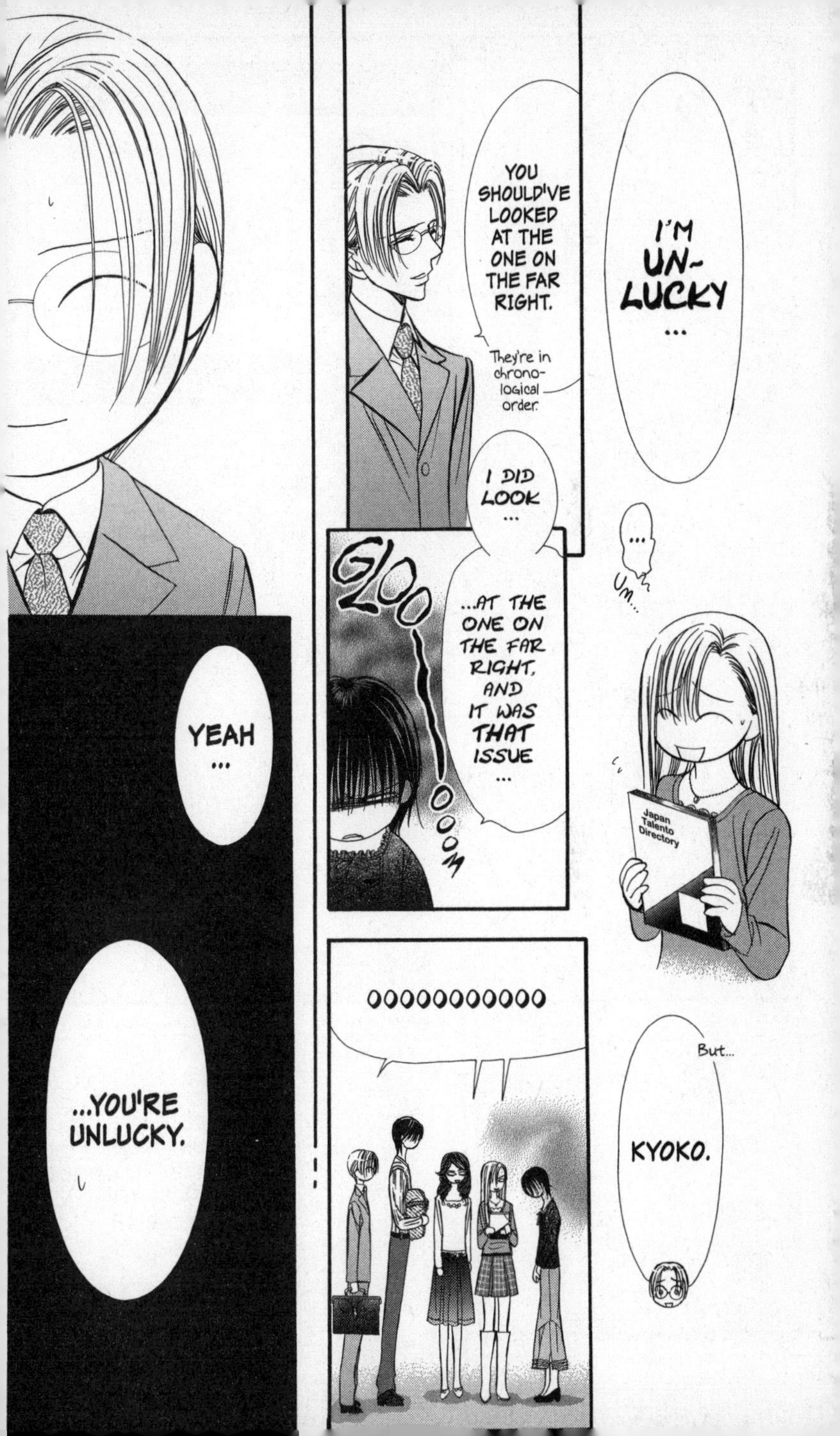

I'M UN-LUCKY...
...
Um...
Japan Talento Directory
But...
KYOKO.
YOU SHOULD'VE LOOKED AT THE ONE ON THE FAR RIGHT.
They're in chrono-logical order.
I DID LOOK...
...AT THE ONE ON THE FAR RIGHT, AND IT WAS THAT ISSUE...
GLOOOOOOM
OOOOOOOOOOO
YEAH...
...YOU'RE UNLUCKY.

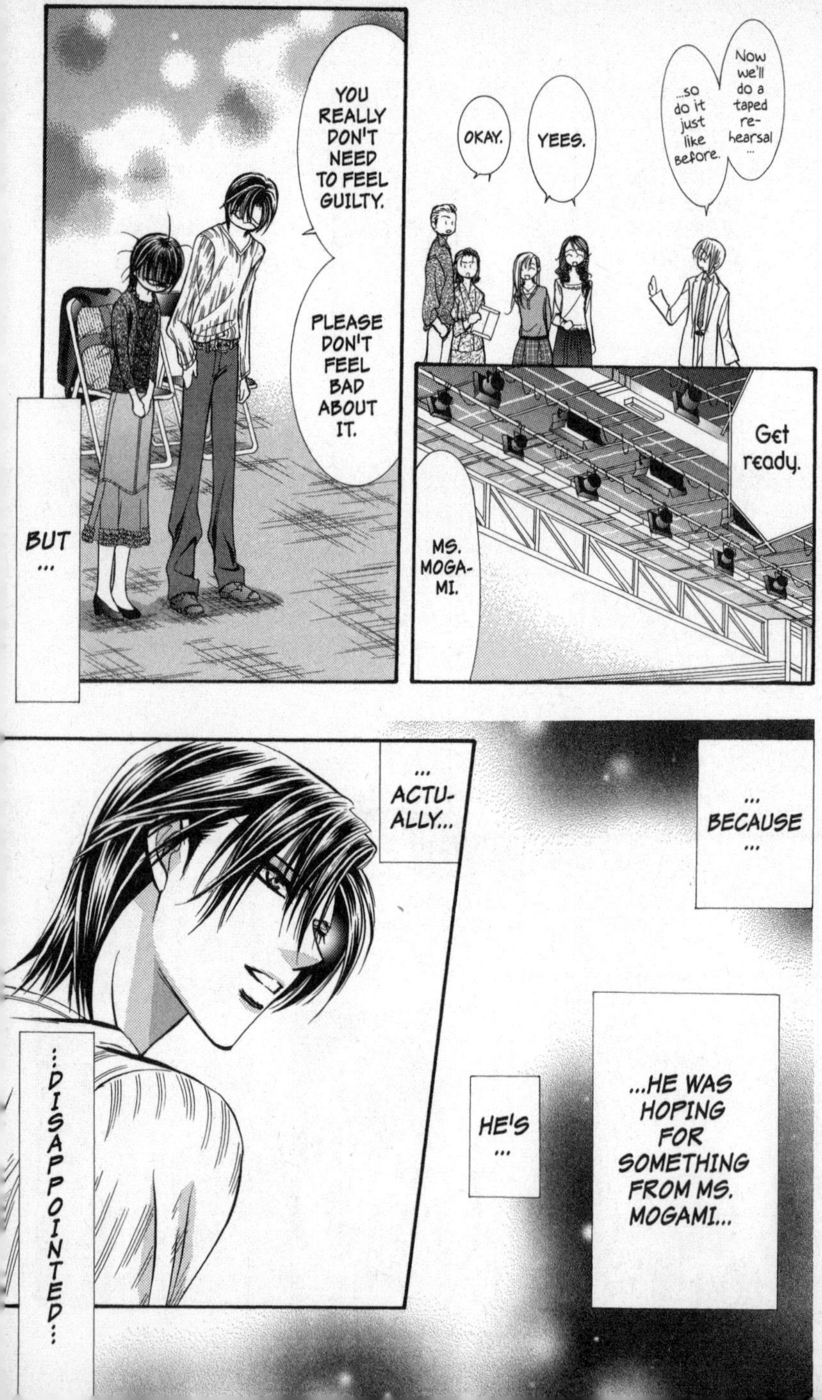
Now we'll do a taped re-hearsal...
...so do it just like before.
YEES.
OKAY.
Get ready.
MS. MOGA-MI.
YOU REALLY DON'T NEED TO FEEL GUILTY.
PLEASE DON'T FEEL BAD ABOUT IT.
BUT...
...BECAUSE...
...HE WAS HOPING FOR SOMETHING FROM MS. MOGAMI...
HE'S...
...ACTU-ALLY...
...DISAPPOINTED...

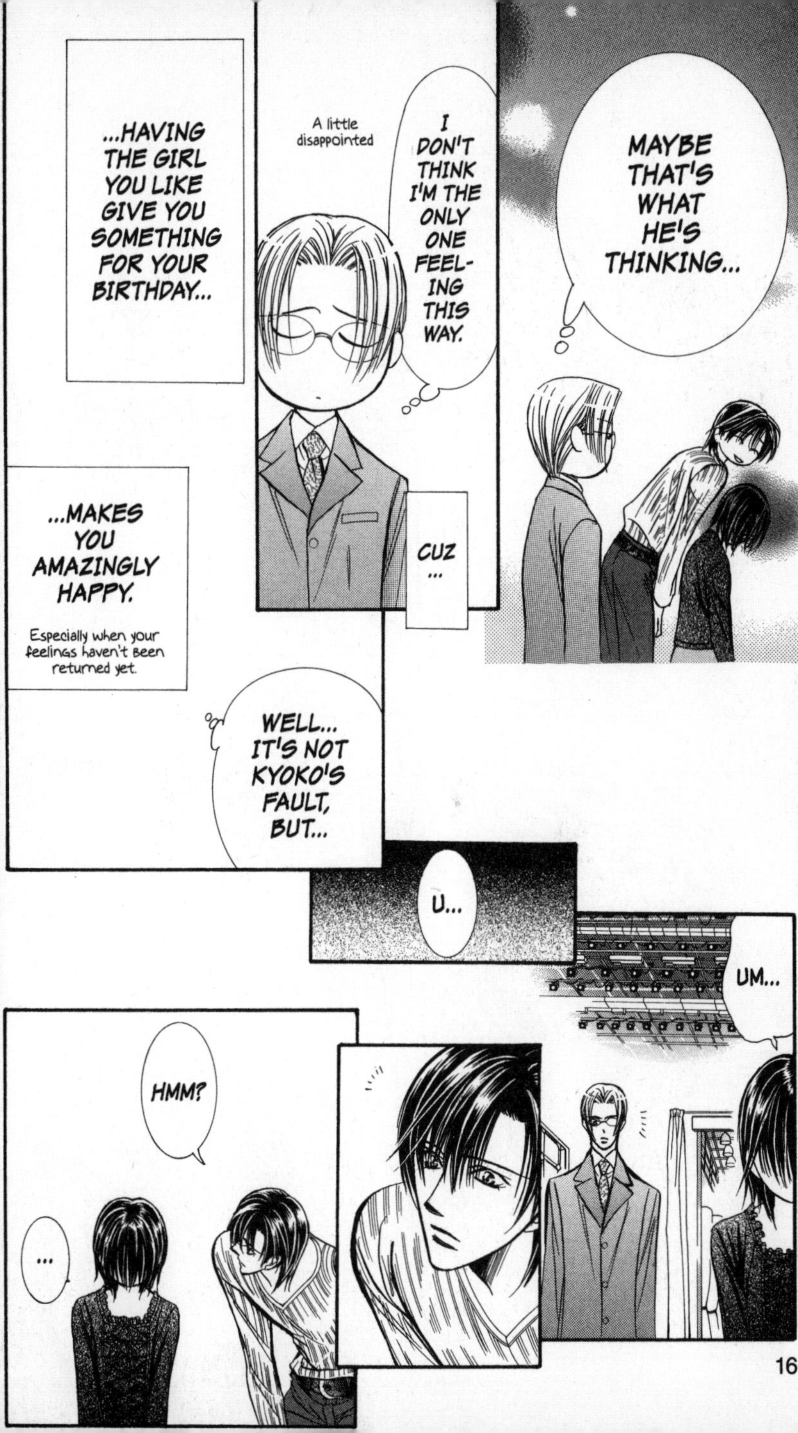

MAYBE THAT'S WHAT HE'S THINKING...
I DON'T THINK I'M THE ONLY ONE FEEL-ING THIS WAY.
A little disappointed
CUZ...
...HAVING THE GIRL YOU LIKE GIVE YOU SOMETHING FOR YOUR BIRTHDAY...
...MAKES YOU AMAZINGLY HAPPY.
Especially when your feelings haven't been returned yet.
WELL... IT'S NOT KYOKO'S FAULT, BUT...
U...
UM...
HMM?
...

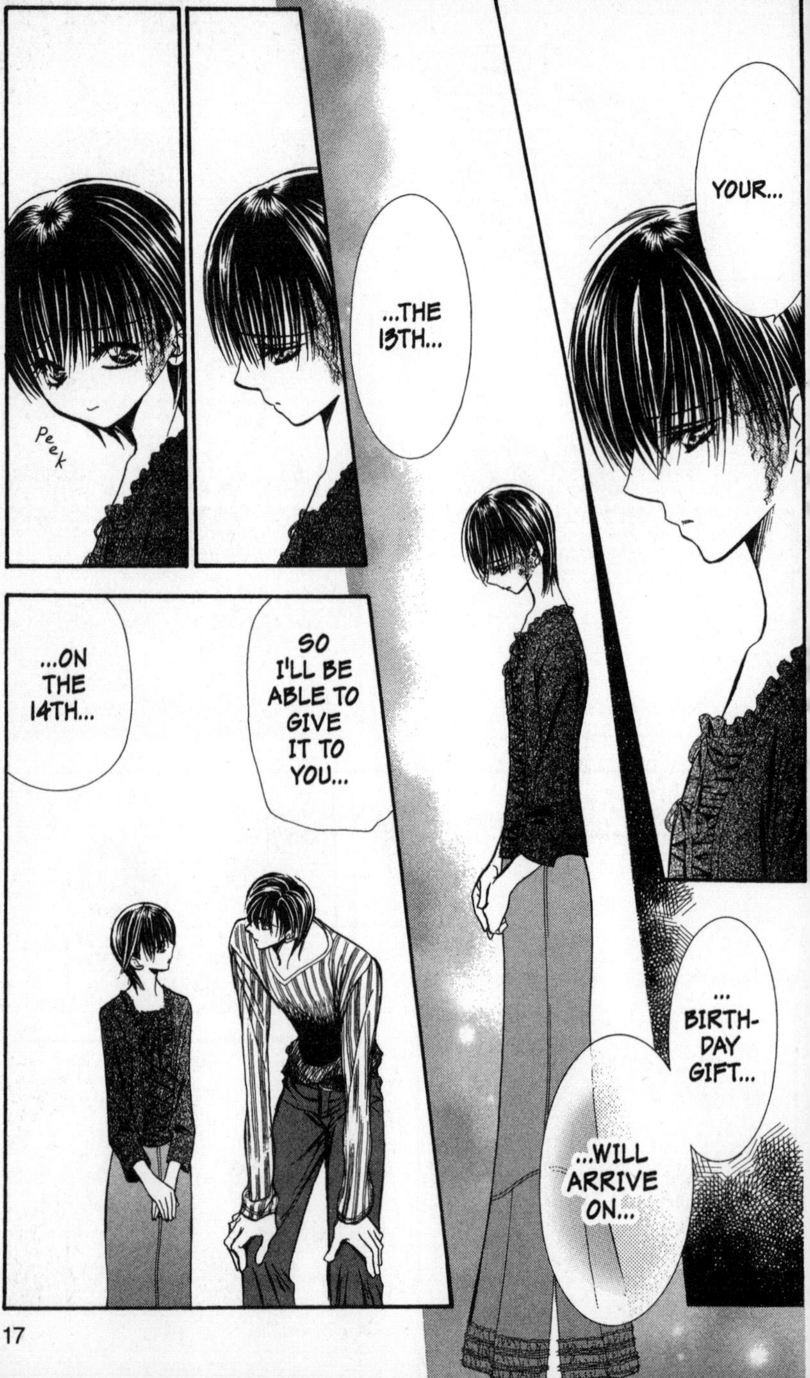
YOUR...
...BIRTH-DAY GIFT...
...WILL ARRIVE ON...
...THE 13TH...
Peek
SO I'LL BE ABLE TO GIVE IT TO YOU...
...ON THE 14TH...

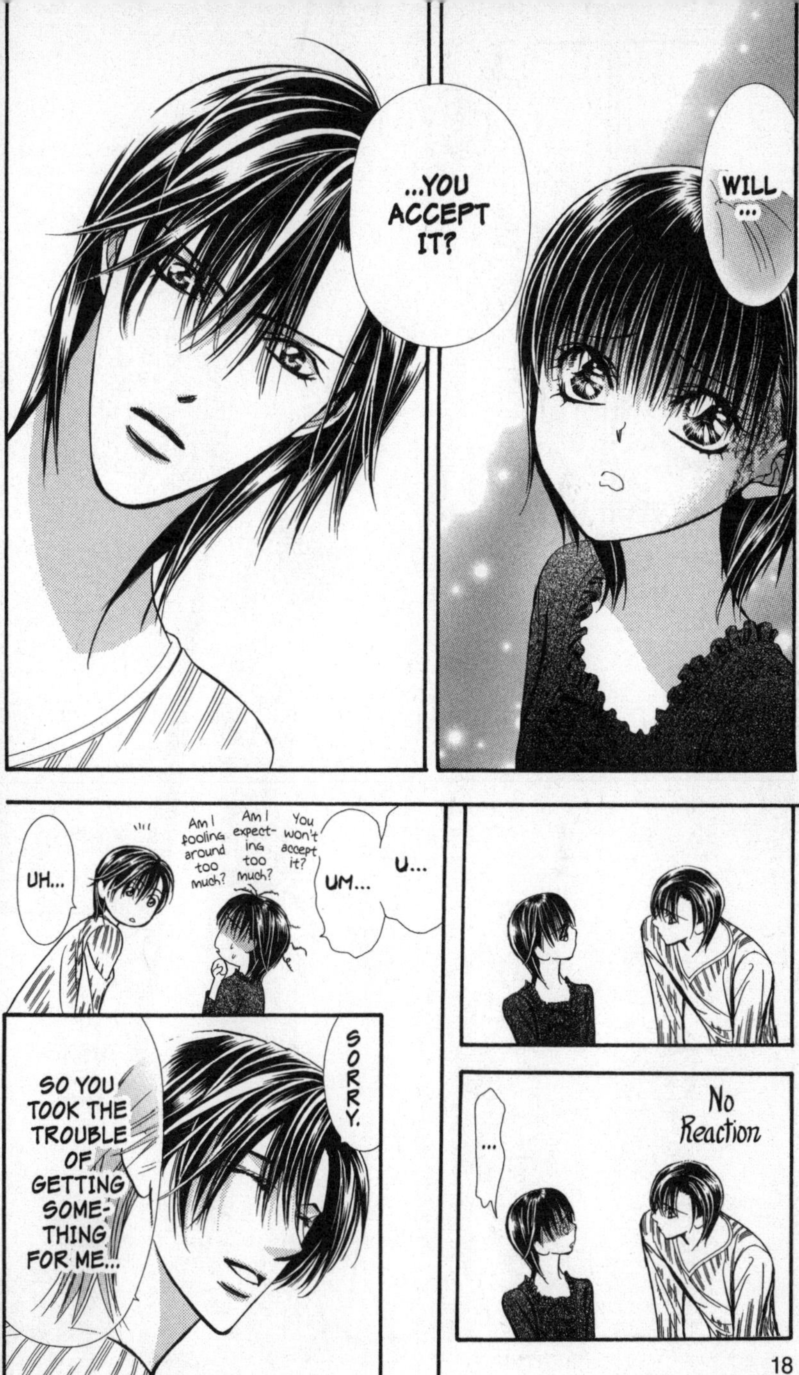
WILL ...
...YOU ACCEPT IT?
No Reaction
...
U...
UM...
You won't accept it?
Am I expecting too much?
Am I fooling around too much?
UH...
SORRY.
SO YOU TOOK THE TROUBLE OF GETTING SOME-THING FOR ME...

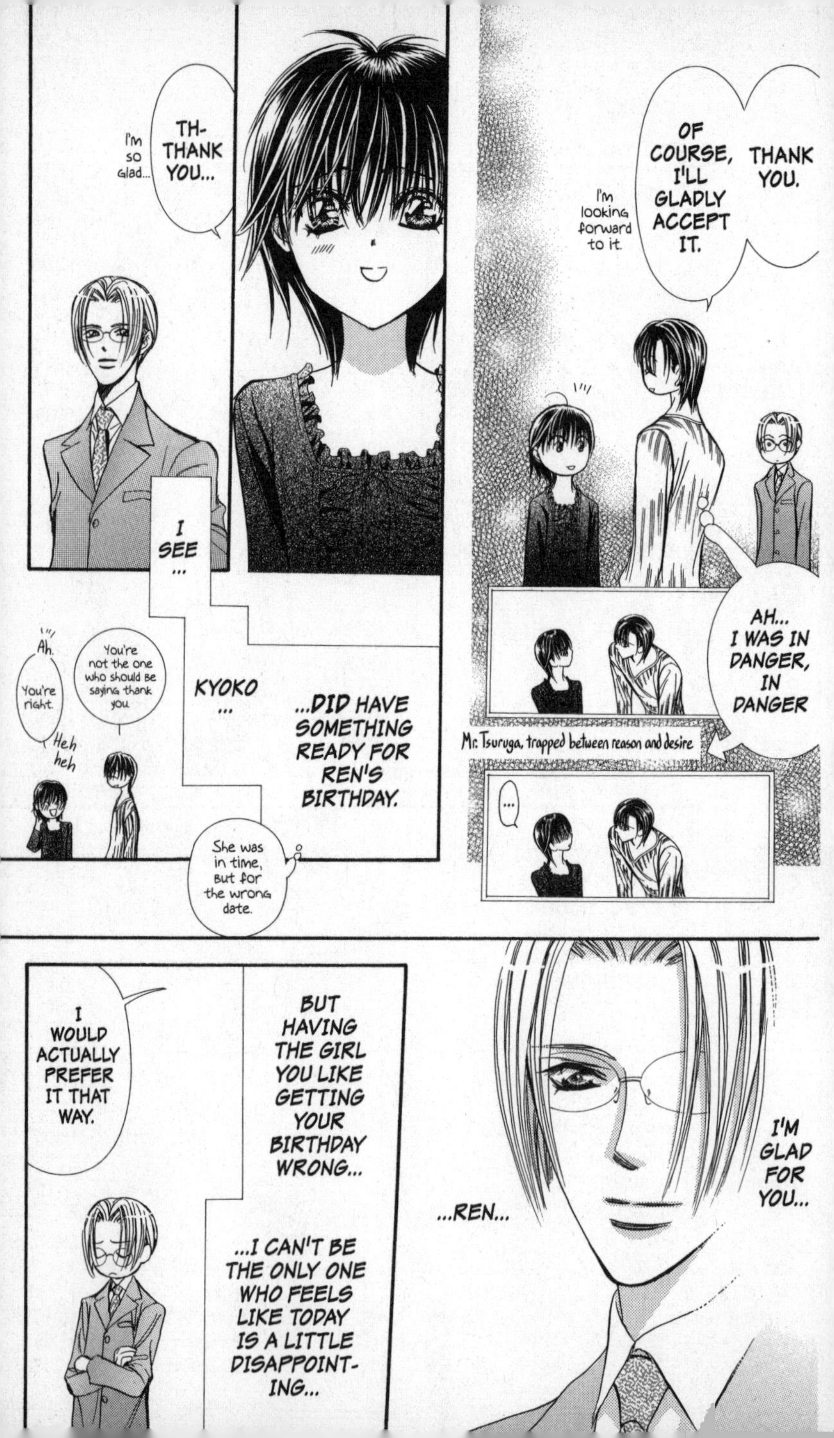
THANK YOU.
OF COURSE, I'LL GLADLY ACCEPT IT.
I'm looking forward to it.
TH-THANK YOU...
I'm so glad...
I SEE...
AH... I WAS IN DANGER, IN DANGER
Mr. Tsuruga, trapped between reason and desire
...
KYOKO...
...DID HAVE SOMETHING READY FOR REN'S BIRTHDAY.
She was in time, but for the wrong date.
You're not the one who should be saying thank you
Ah.
You're right.
Heh heh
I'M GLAD FOR YOU...
...REN...
BUT HAVING THE GIRL YOU LIKE GETTING YOUR BIRTHDAY WRONG...
...I CAN'T BE THE ONLY ONE WHO FEELS LIKE TODAY IS A LITTLE DISAPPOINTING...
I WOULD ACTUALLY PREFER IT THAT WAY.

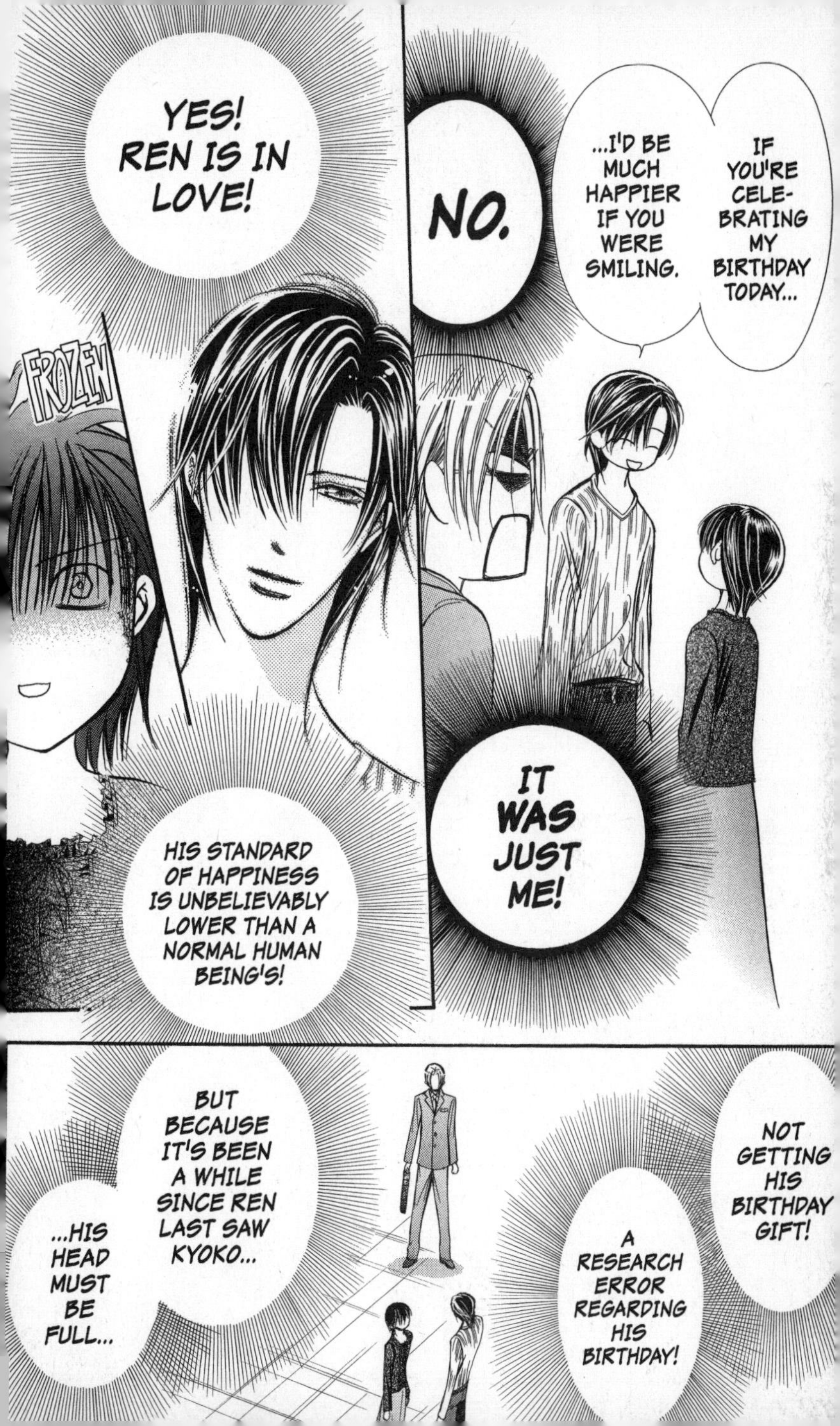
IF YOU'RE CELEBRATING MY BIRTHDAY TODAY...
...I'D BE MUCH HAPPIER IF YOU WERE SMILING.
NO.
IT WAS JUST ME!
YES! REN IS IN LOVE!
FROZEN
HIS STANDARD OF HAPPINESS IS UNBELIEVABLY LOWER THAN A NORMAL HUMAN BEING'S!
NOT GETTING HIS BIRTHDAY GIFT!
A RESEARCH ERROR REGARDING HIS BIRTHDAY!
BUT BECAUSE IT'S BEEN A WHILE SINCE REN LAST SAW KYOKO...
...HIS HEAD MUST BE FULL...

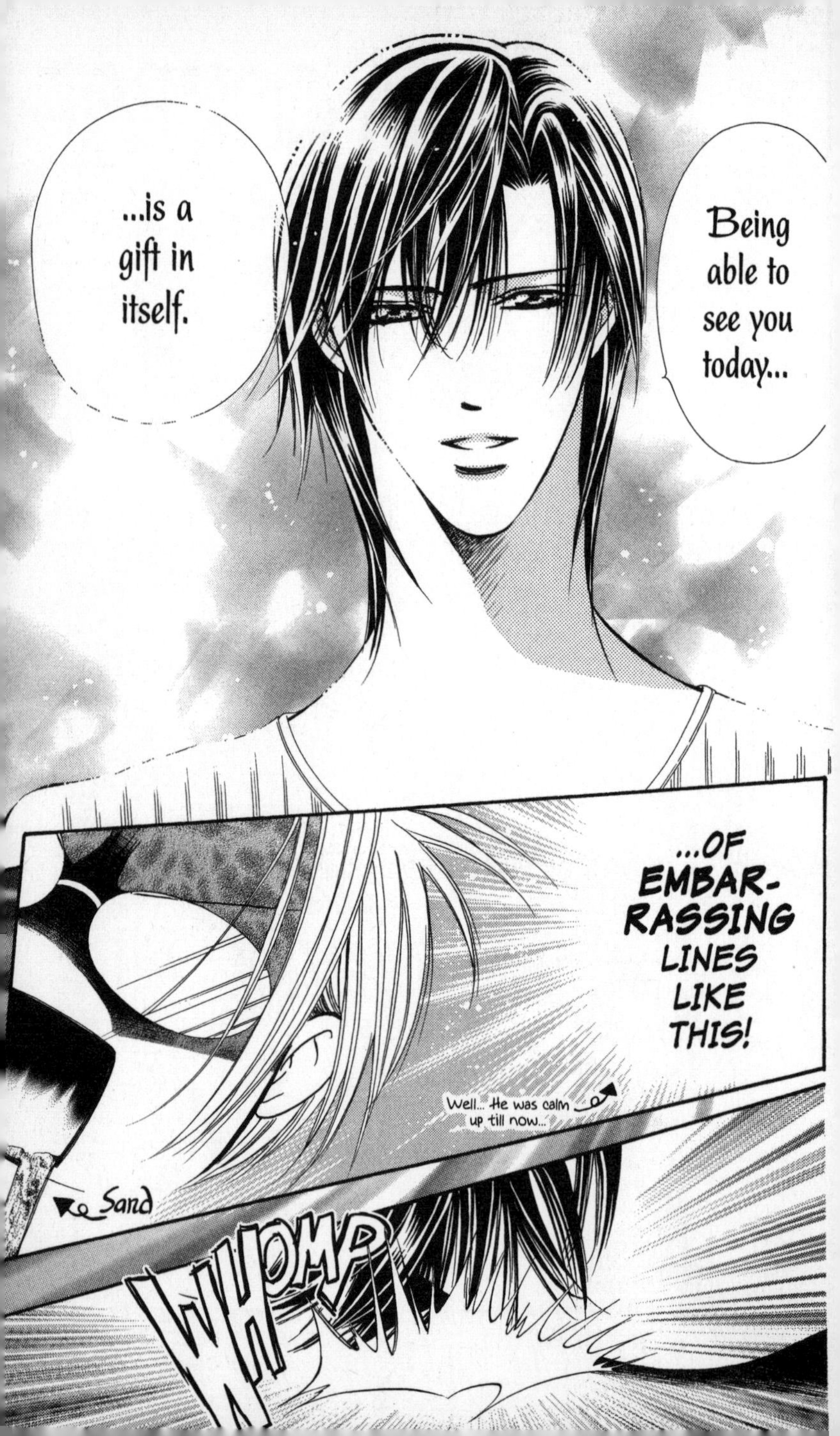
Being able to see you today...
...is a gift in itself.
...OF EMBAR-RASSING LINES LIKE THIS!
Well... He was calm up till now...
Sand
WHOMP

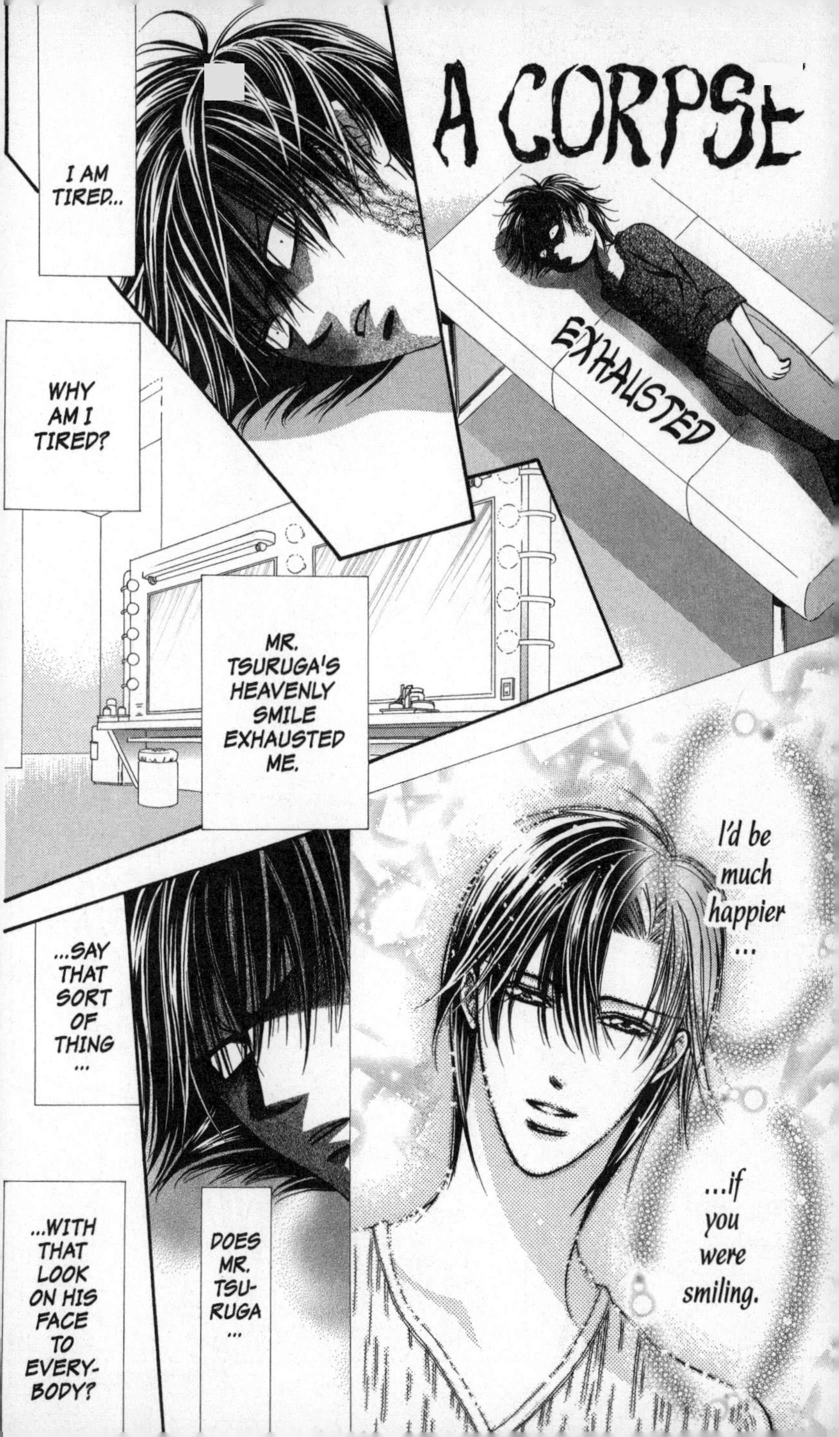
A CORPSE
EXHAUSTED
I AM TIRED...
WHY AM I TIRED?
MR. TSURUGA'S HEAVENLY SMILE EXHAUSTED ME.
I'd be much happier...
...if you were smiling.
DOES MR. TSURUGA...
...SAY THAT SORT OF THING...
...WITH THAT LOOK ON HIS FACE TO EVERYBODY?

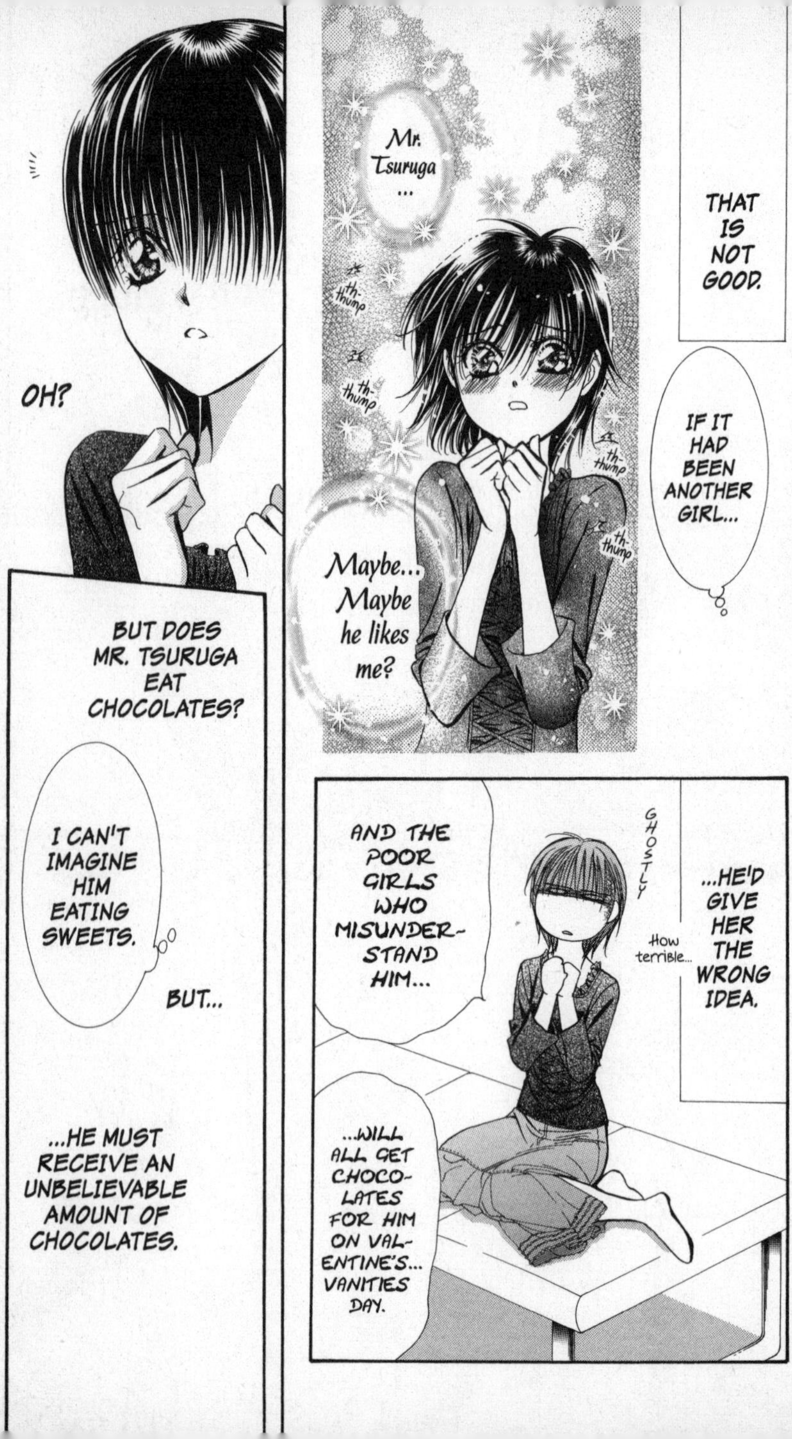
THAT IS NOT GOOD.
IF IT HAD BEEN ANOTHER GIRL...
Mr. Tsuruga...
th-thump th-thump
th-thump th-thump
Maybe... Maybe he likes me?
...HE'D GIVE HER THE WRONG IDEA.
GHOSTLY
How terrible...
AND THE POOR GIRLS WHO MISUNDERSTAND HIM...
...WILL ALL GET CHOCOLATES FOR HIM ON VALENTINE'S... VANITIES DAY.
OH?
BUT DOES MR. TSURUGA EAT CHOCOLATES?
I CAN'T IMAGINE HIM EATING SWEETS.
BUT...
...HE MUST RECEIVE AN UNBELIEVABLE AMOUNT OF CHOCOLATES.

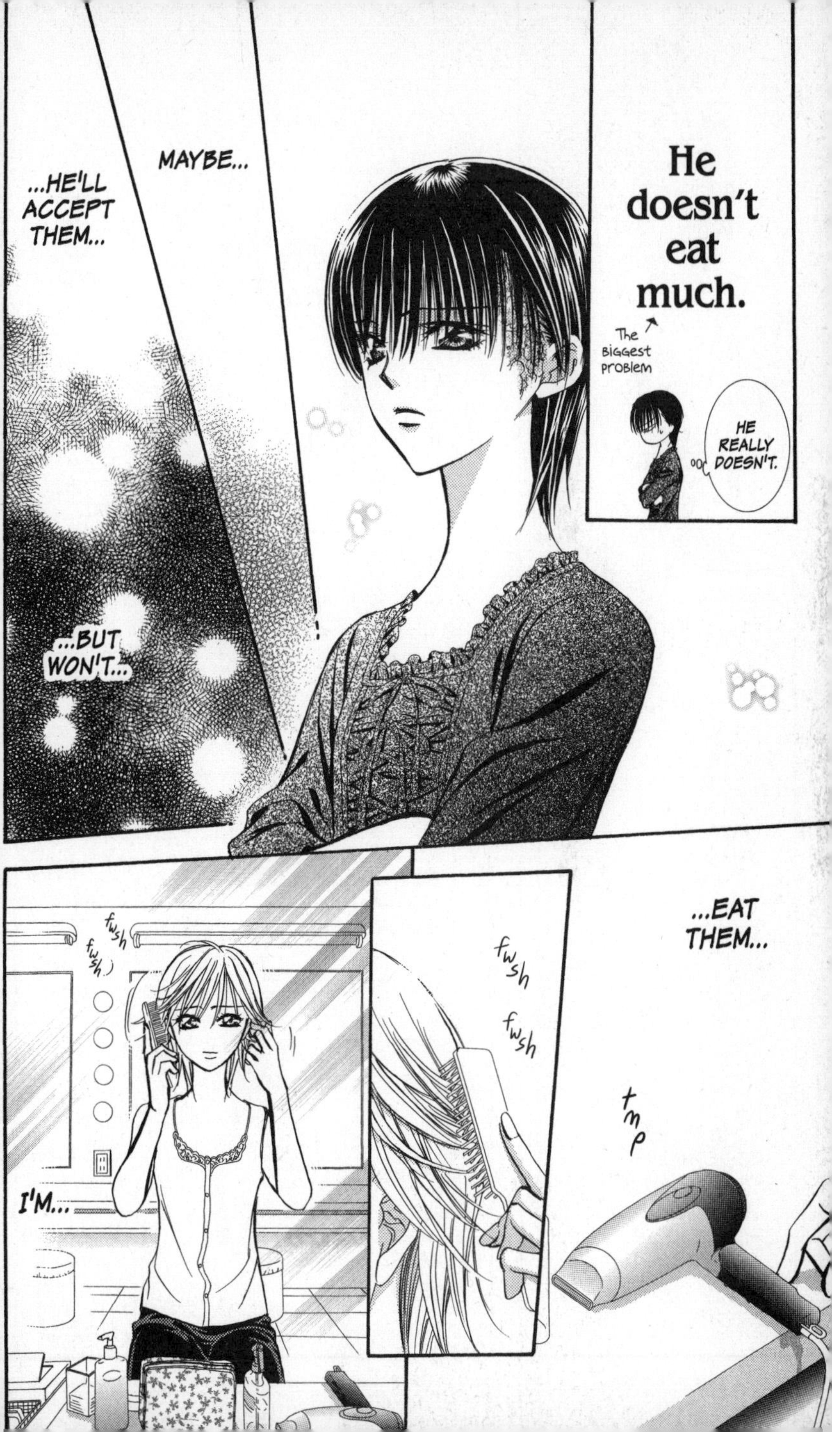
He doesn't eat much.
The Biggest problem
HE REALLY DOESN'T.
MAYBE...
...HE'LL ACCEPT THEM...
...BUT WON'T...
...EAT THEM...
tmp
fwsh
fwsh
fwsh
fwsh
I'M...

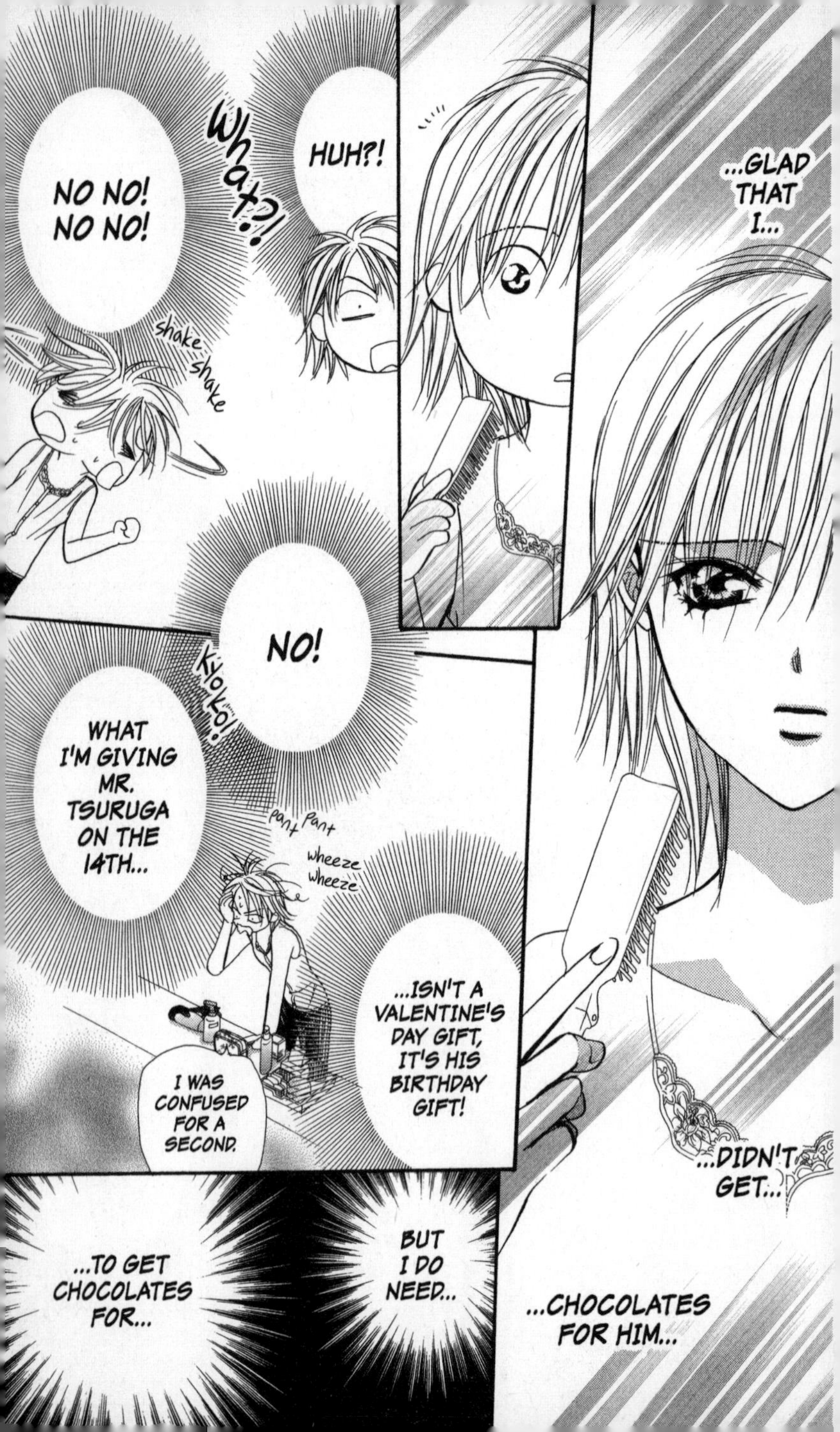
...GLAD THAT I...
...DIDN'T GET...
...CHOCOLATES FOR HIM...
HUH?!
What?!
NO NO! NO NO!
shake shake
NO!
Kyoko!
WHAT I'M GIVING MR. TSURUGA ON THE 14TH...
pant pant
wheeze wheeze
...ISN'T A VALENTINE'S DAY GIFT, IT'S HIS BIRTHDAY GIFT!
I WAS CONFUSED FOR A SECOND.
BUT I DO NEED...
...TO GET CHOCOLATES FOR...

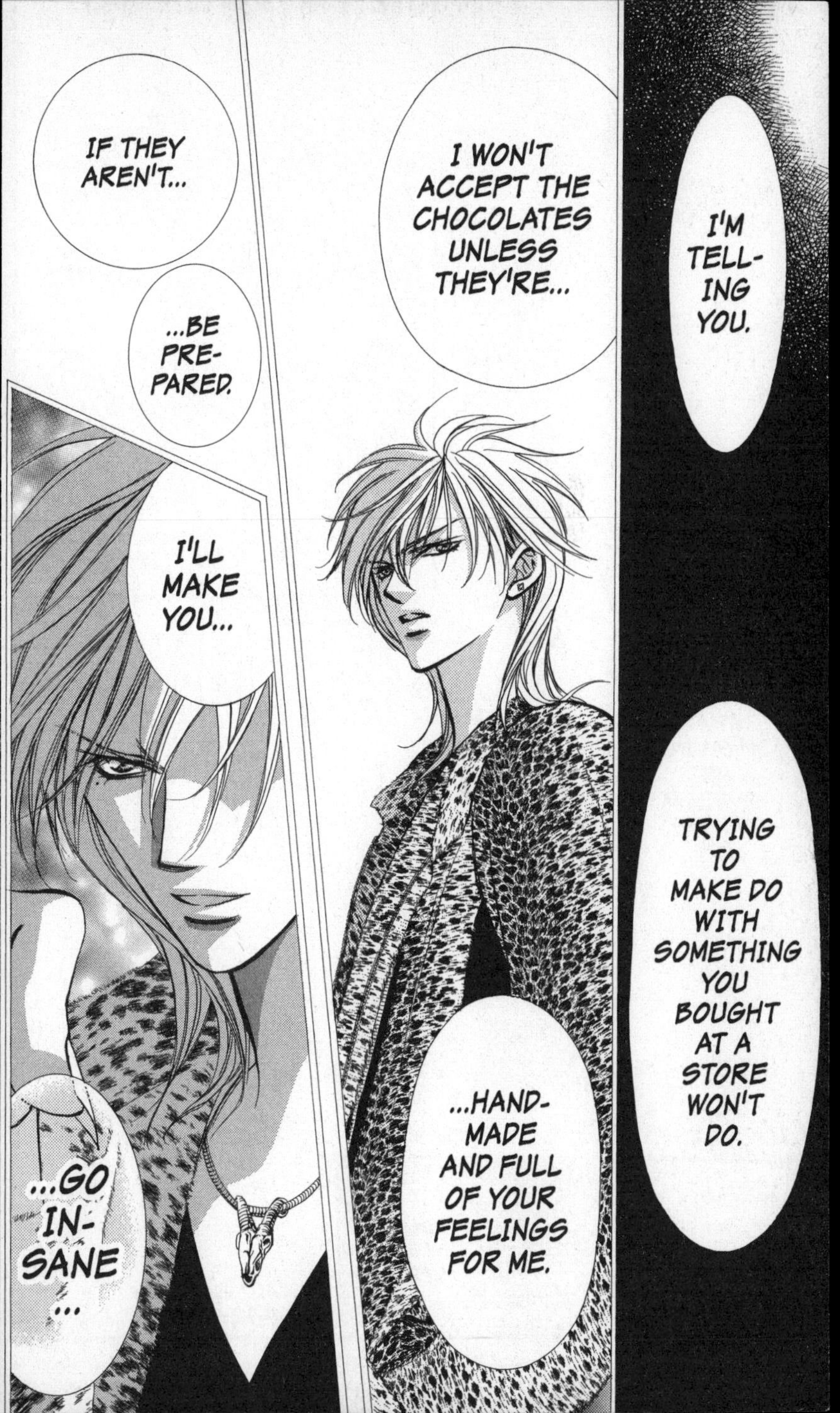
I'M TELL-ING YOU.
TRYING TO MAKE DO WITH SOMETHING YOU BOUGHT AT A STORE WON'T DO.
I WON'T ACCEPT THE CHOCOLATES UNLESS THEY'RE...
...HAND-MADE AND FULL OF YOUR FEELINGS FOR ME.
IF THEY AREN'T...
...BE PRE-PARED.
I'LL MAKE YOU...
...GO IN-SANE...

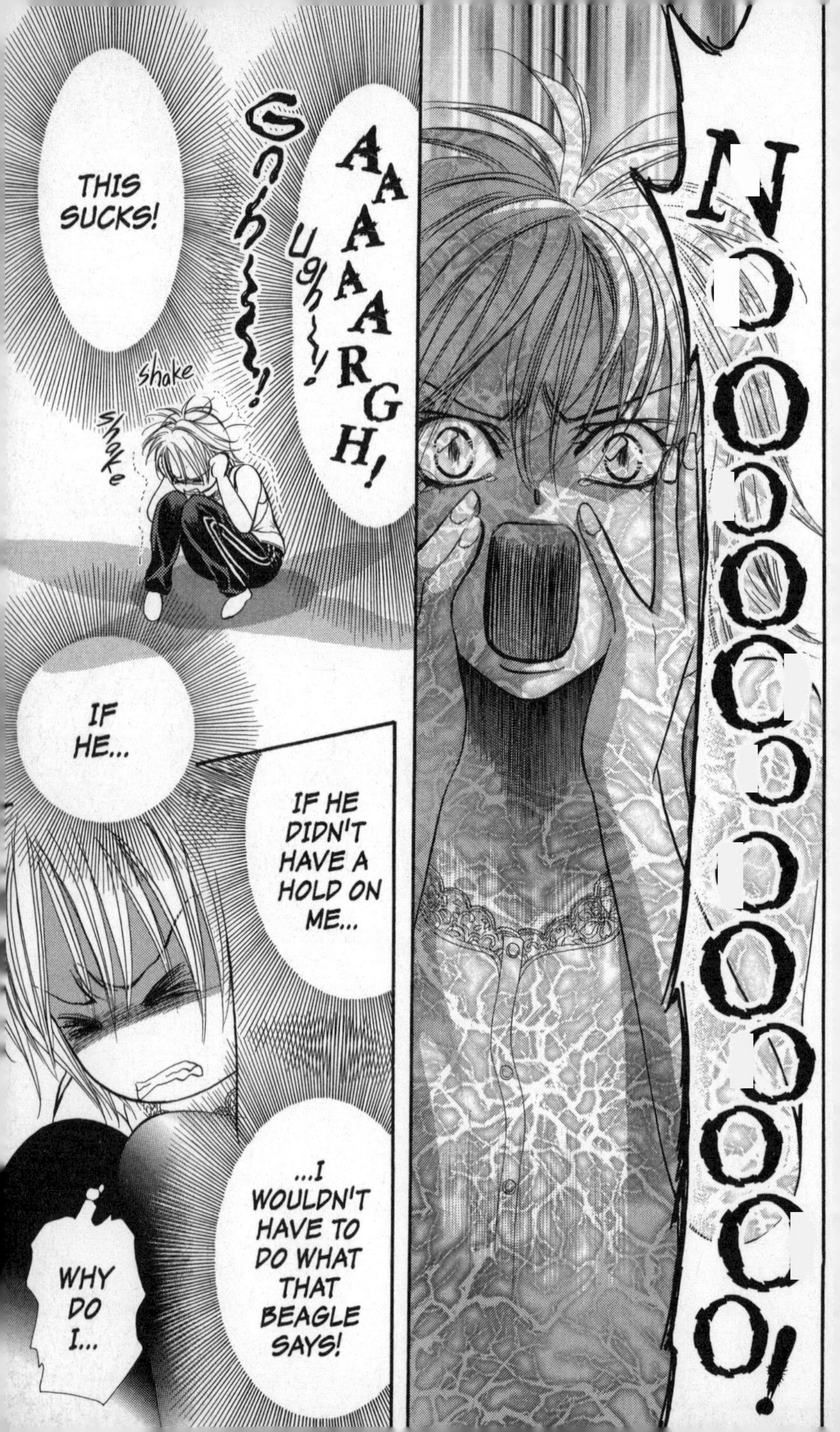
NOOOOOOOOOOOOOOO!
AAAAARGH!
Ugh~!
Gnh~~!
THIS SUCKS!
shake
shake
IF HE...
IF HE DIDN'T HAVE A HOLD ON ME...
...I WOULDN'T HAVE TO DO WHAT THAT BEAGLE SAYS!
WHY DO I...

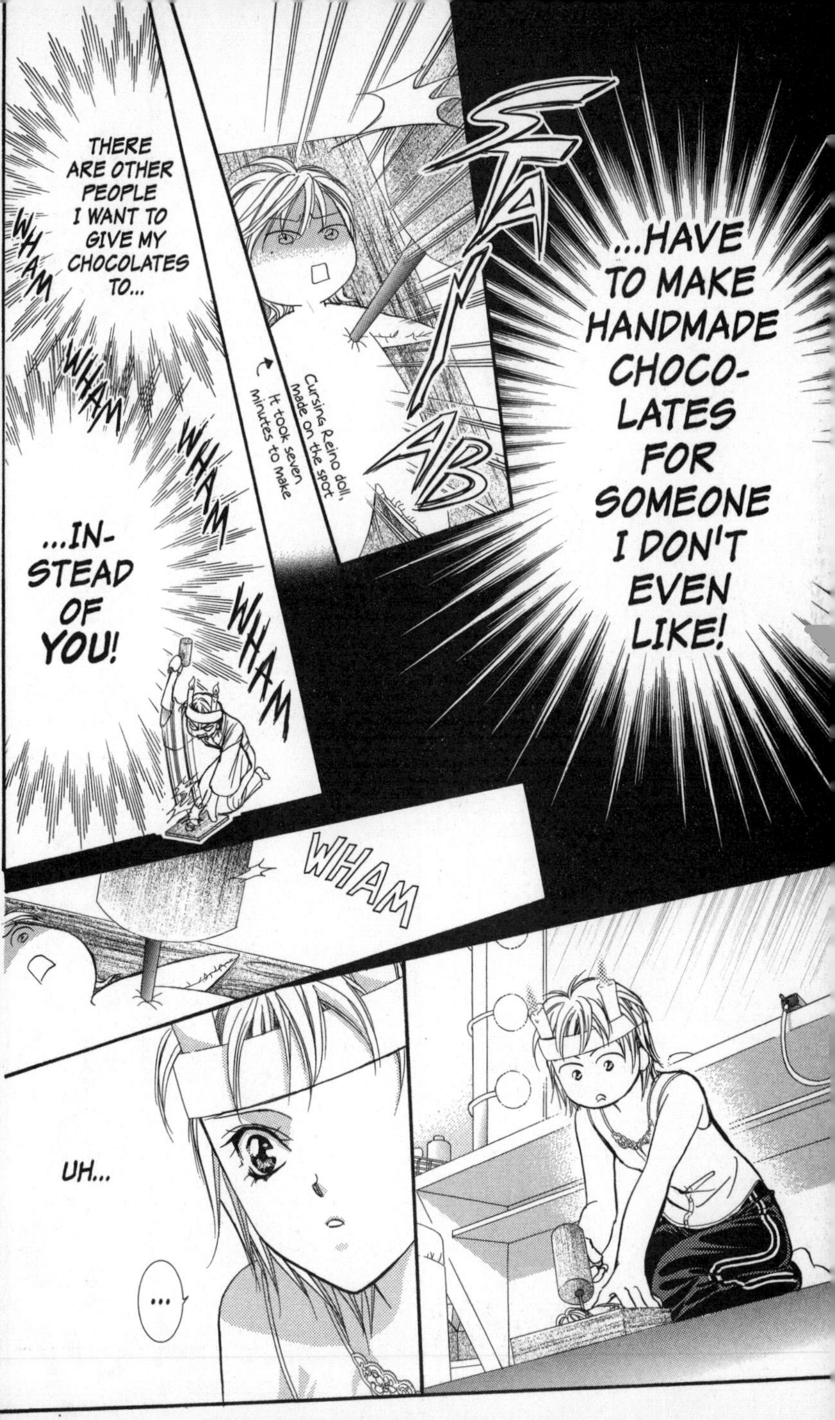
...HAVE TO MAKE HANDMADE CHOCO-LATES FOR SOMEONE I DON'T EVEN LIKE!
STAB
Cursing Reino doll, made on the spot
It took seven minutes to make
THERE ARE OTHER PEOPLE I WANT TO GIVE MY CHOCOLATES TO...
WHAM
WHAM
WHAM
WHAM
...IN-STEAD OF YOU!
WHAM
UH...
...

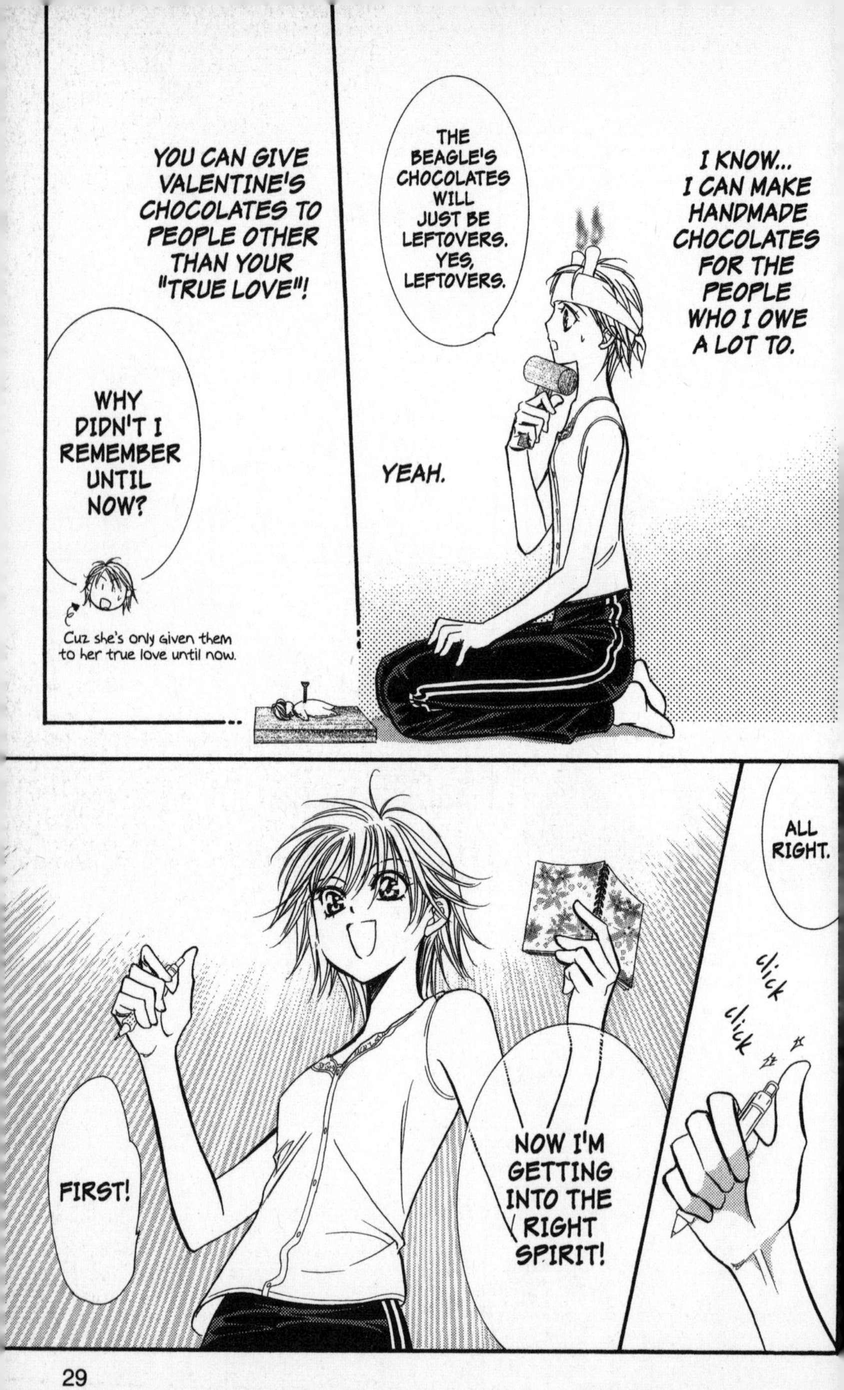
I KNOW... I CAN MAKE HANDMADE CHOCOLATES FOR THE PEOPLE WHO I OWE A LOT TO.
THE BEAGLE'S CHOCOLATES WILL JUST BE LEFTOVERS. YES, LEFTOVERS.
YEAH.
YOU CAN GIVE VALENTINE'S CHOCOLATES TO PEOPLE OTHER THAN YOUR "TRUE LOVE"!
WHY DIDN'T I REMEMBER UNTIL NOW?
Cuz she's only given them to her true love until now.
ALL RIGHT.
click click
NOW I'M GETTING INTO THE RIGHT SPIRIT!
FIRST!

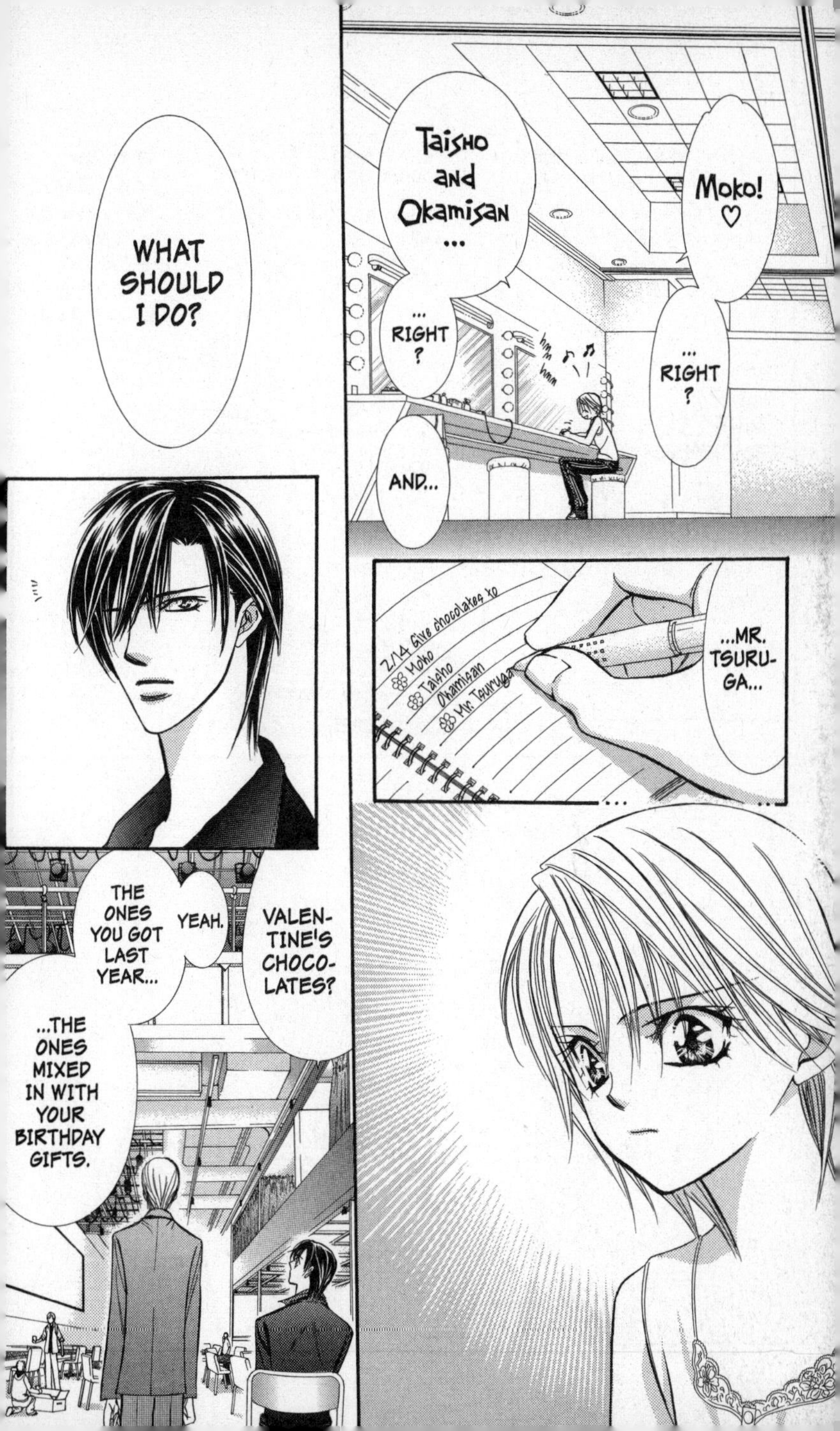
Moko! ♡
... RIGHT?
Taisho and Okamisan ...
... RIGHT?
hm hm hm
AND...
2/14 Give chocolates xo
Moko
Taisho
Okamisan
Mr. Tsuruga
...MR. TSURUGA...
WHAT SHOULD I DO?
VALENTINE'S CHOCOLATES?
YEAH.
THE ONES YOU GOT LAST YEAR...
...THE ONES MIXED IN WITH YOUR BIRTHDAY GIFTS.

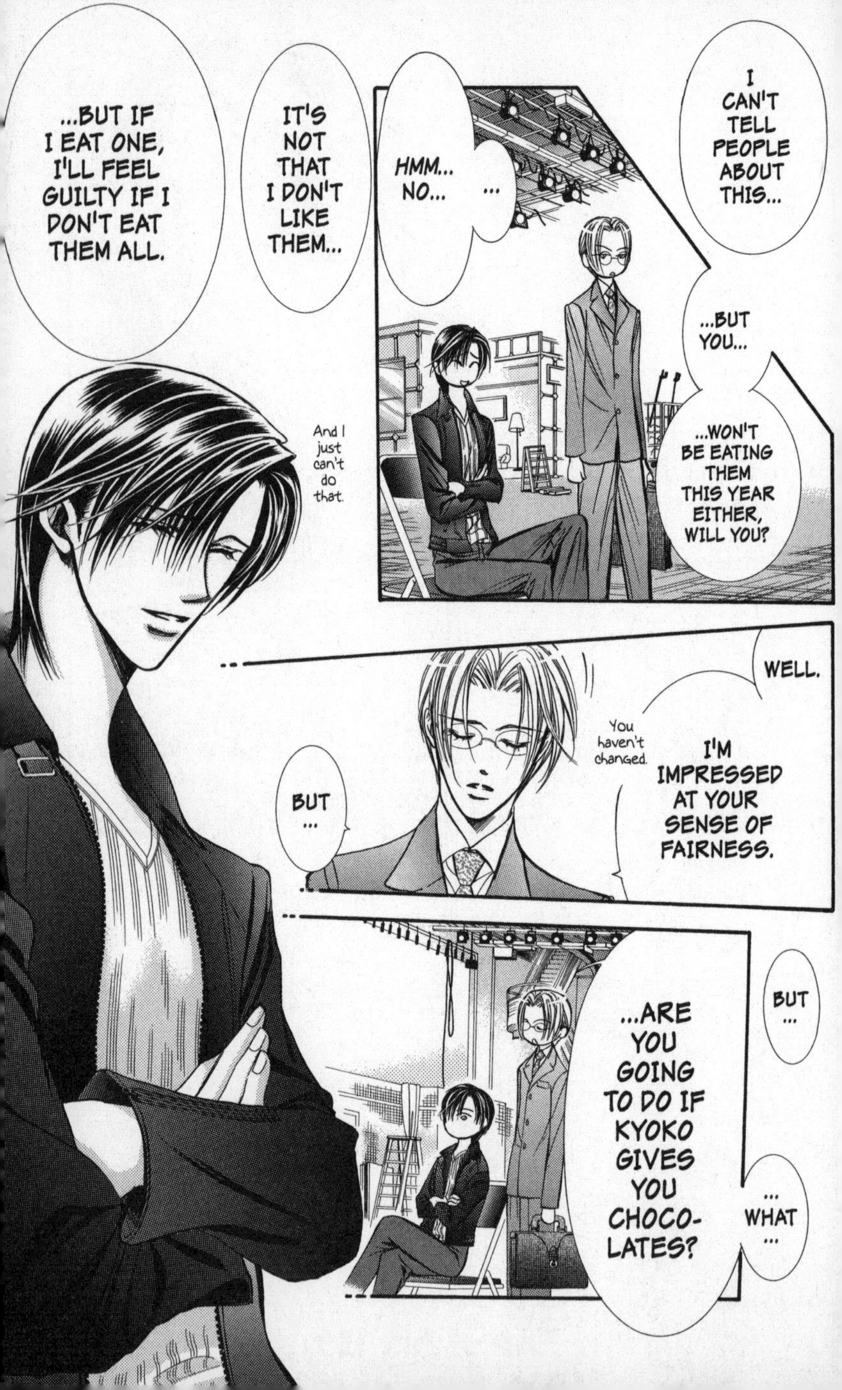
I CAN'T TELL PEOPLE ABOUT THIS...
...BUT YOU...
...WON'T BE EATING THEM THIS YEAR EITHER, WILL YOU?
...
HMM... NO...
IT'S NOT THAT I DON'T LIKE THEM...
...BUT IF I EAT ONE, I'LL FEEL GUILTY IF I DON'T EAT THEM ALL.
And I just can't do that.
WELL.
You haven't changed.
I'M IMPRESSED AT YOUR SENSE OF FAIRNESS.
BUT ...
BUT ...
... WHAT ...
...ARE YOU GOING TO DO IF KYOKO GIVES YOU CHOCO-LATES?

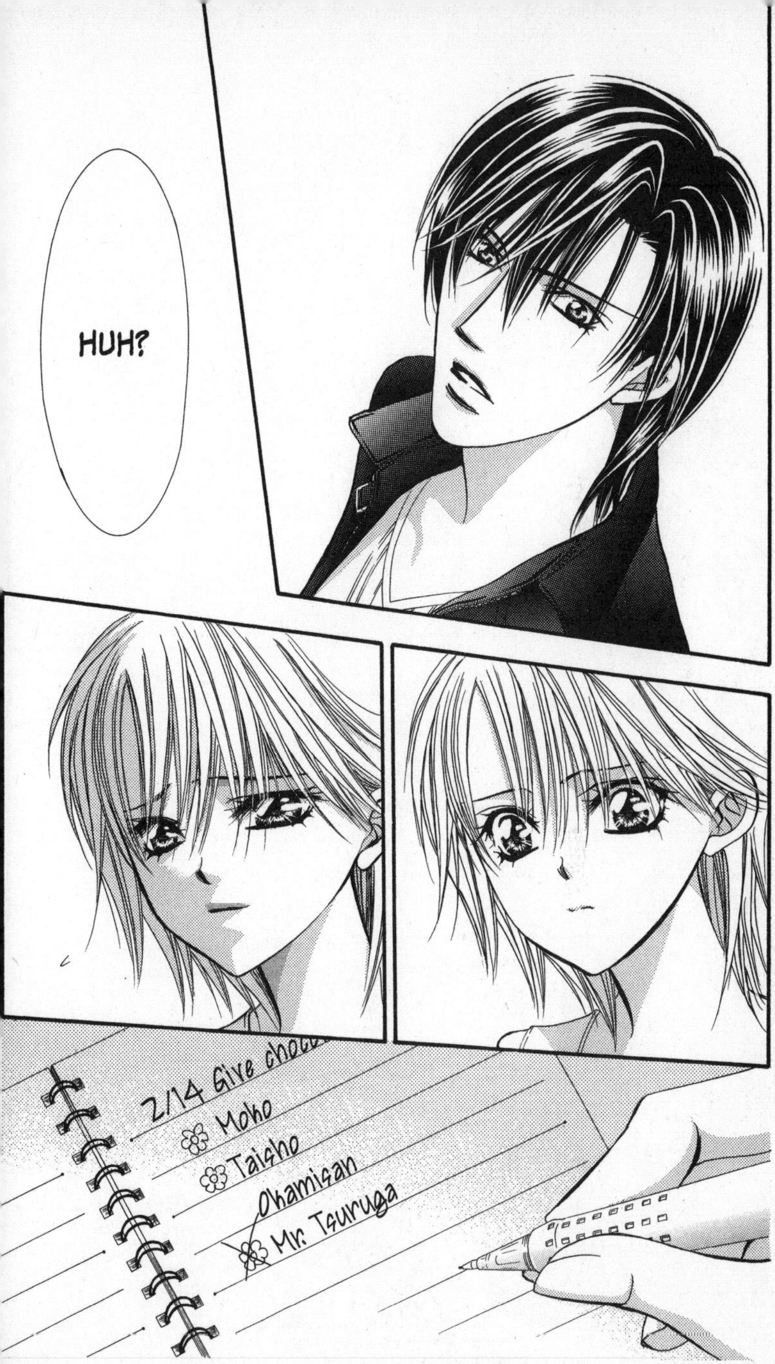
HUH?
2/14 Give choc
Moko
Taisho
Okamisan
Mr. Tsuruga

End of Act 139

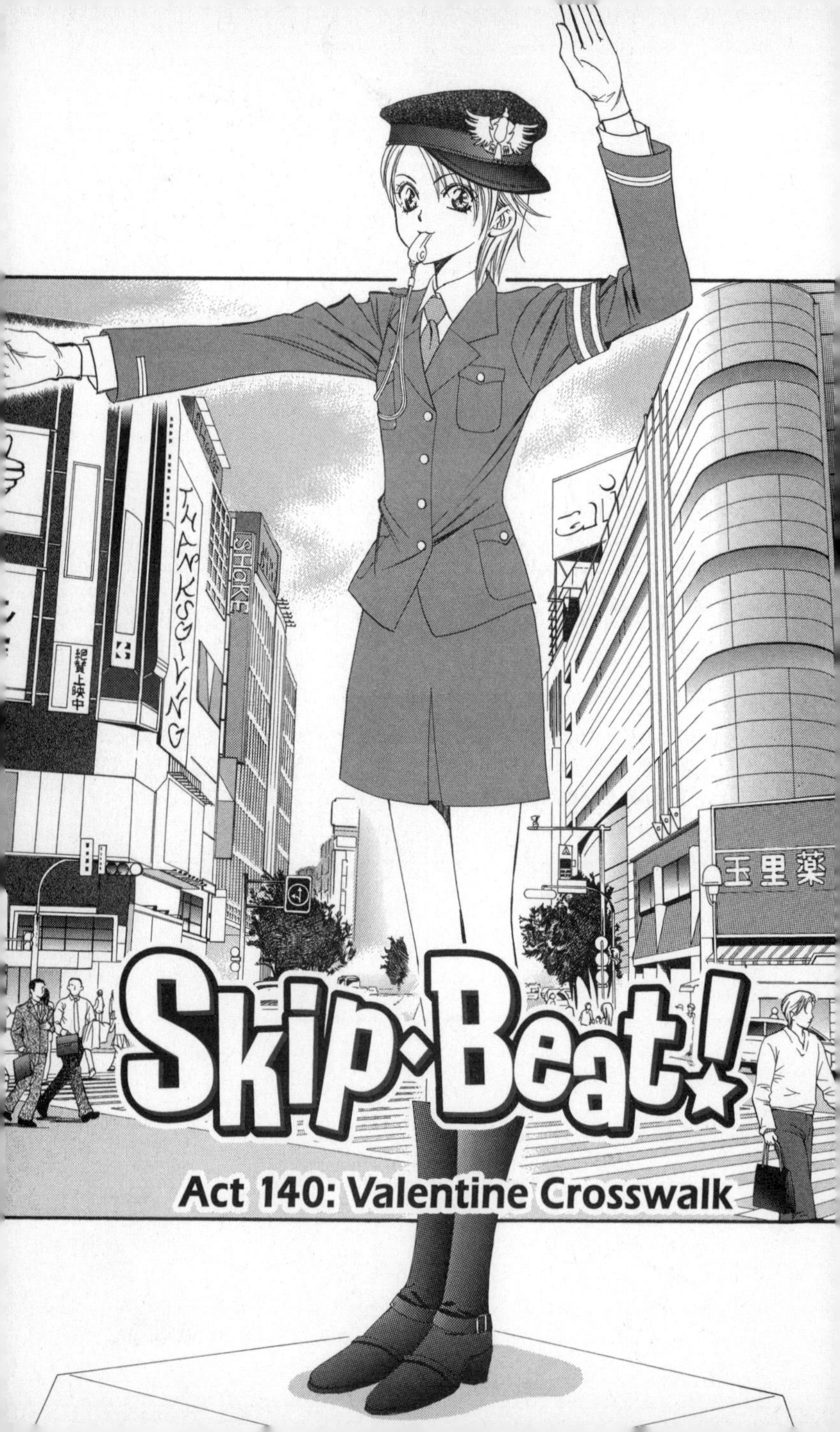
THANKSGIVING
絶賛上映中
玉里薬
Skip·Beat!
Act 140: Valentine Crosswalk

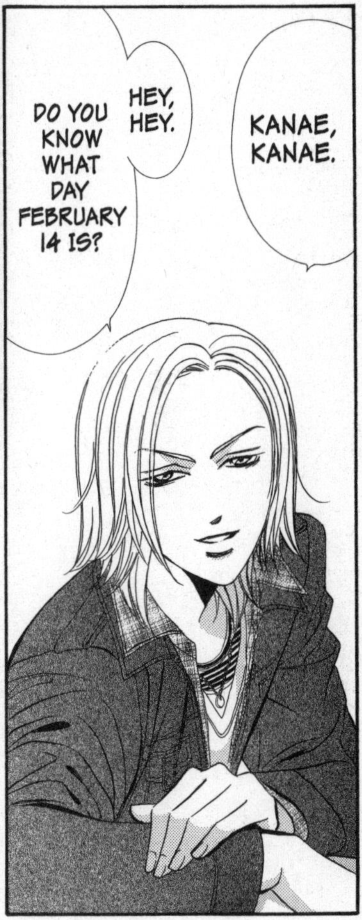
KANAE, KANAE.
HEY, HEY.
DO YOU KNOW WHAT DAY FEBRUARY 14 IS?
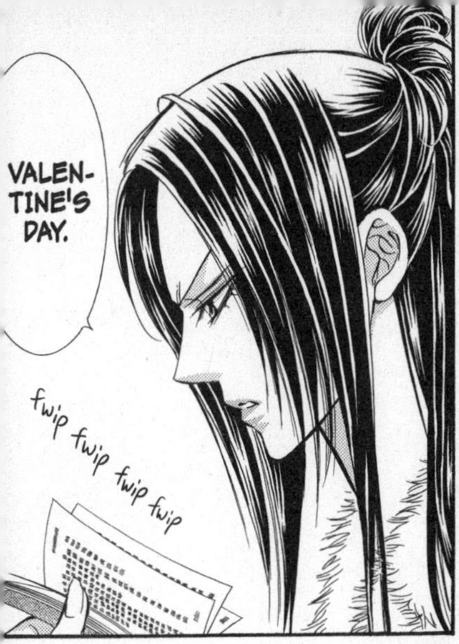
VALEN-TINE'S DAY.
fwip fwip fwip fwip
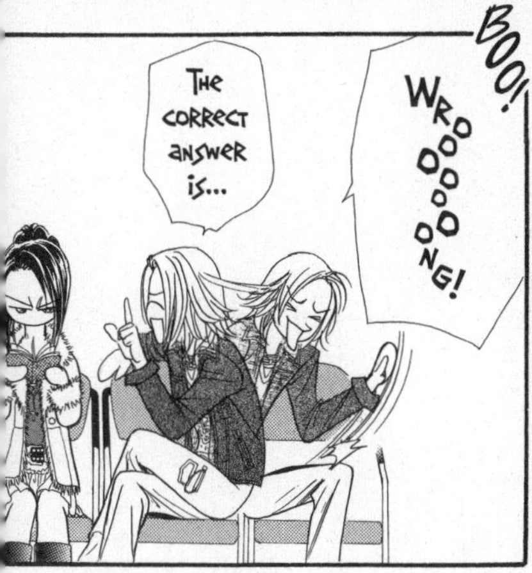
BOO!
WROOOOOOONG!
The correct answer is...
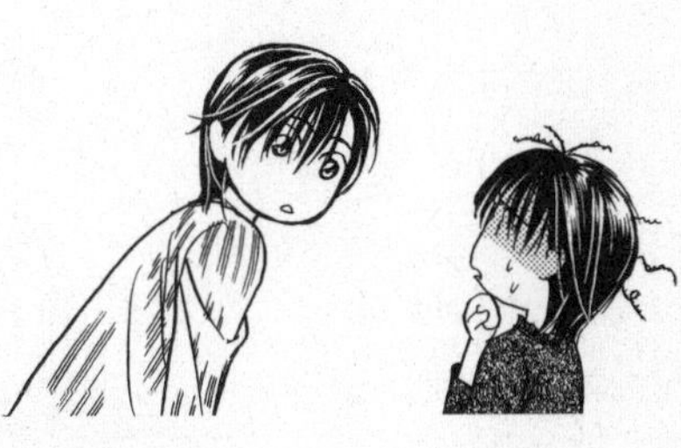

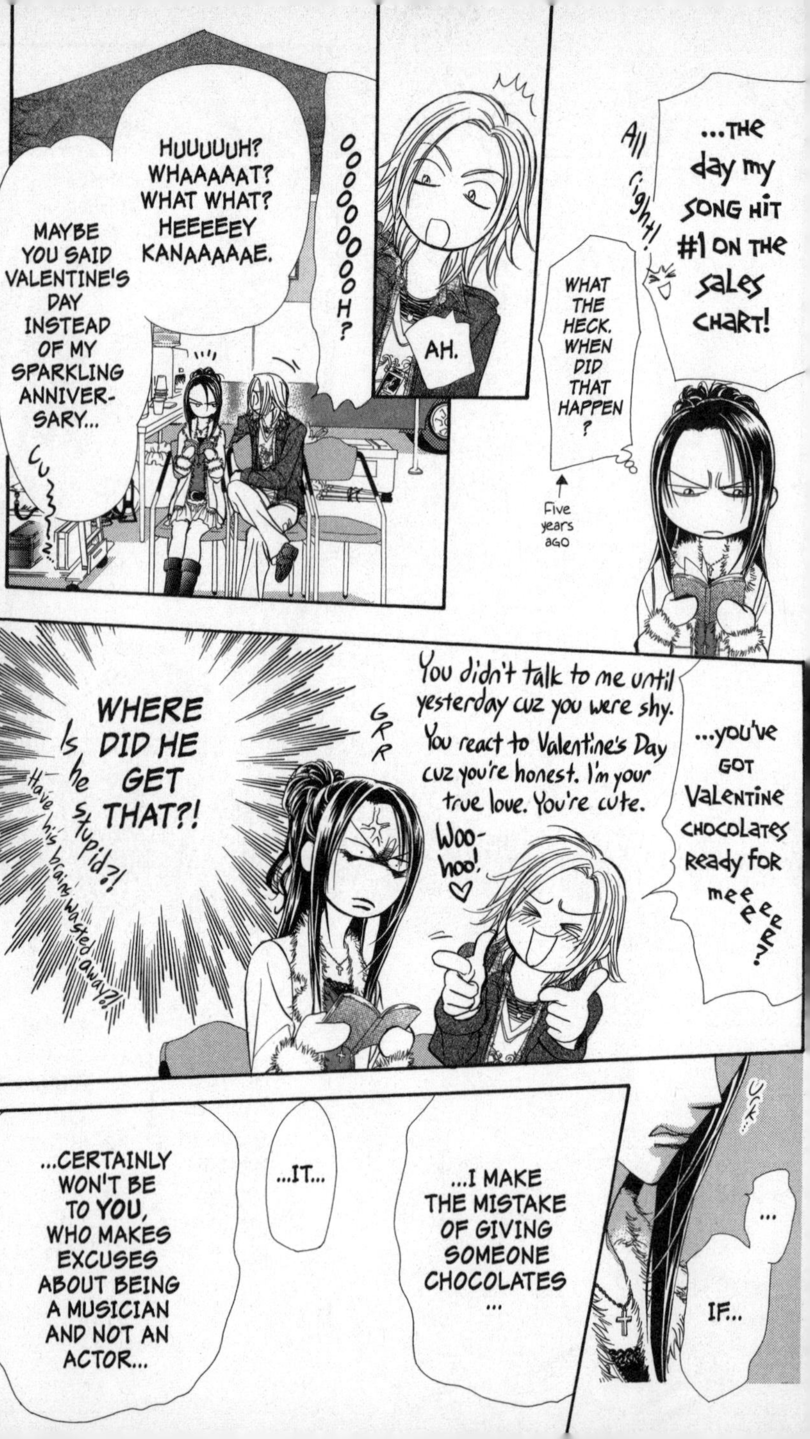
...THE day my SONG HIT #1 ON THE sales CHART!
All right!
WHAT THE HECK. WHEN DID THAT HAPPEN?
Five years ago
AH.
OOOOOOOOOOH?
HUUUUUH? WHAAAAAT? WHAT WHAT? HEEEEEY KANAAAAAE.
MAYBE YOU SAID VALENTINE'S DAY INSTEAD OF MY SPARKLING ANNIVERSARY...
...you've GOT Valentine chocolates ready for meeeee?
You didn't talk to me until yesterday cuz you were shy. You react to Valentine's Day cuz you're honest. I'm your true love. You're cute.
Woo-hoo!
GRR
WHERE DID HE GET THAT?!
Is he stupid?!
Have his brains wasted away?!
Uck...
...
IF...
...I MAKE THE MISTAKE OF GIVING SOMEONE CHOCOLATES...
...IT...
...CERTAINLY WON'T BE TO YOU, WHO MAKES EXCUSES ABOUT BEING A MUSICIAN AND NOT AN ACTOR...

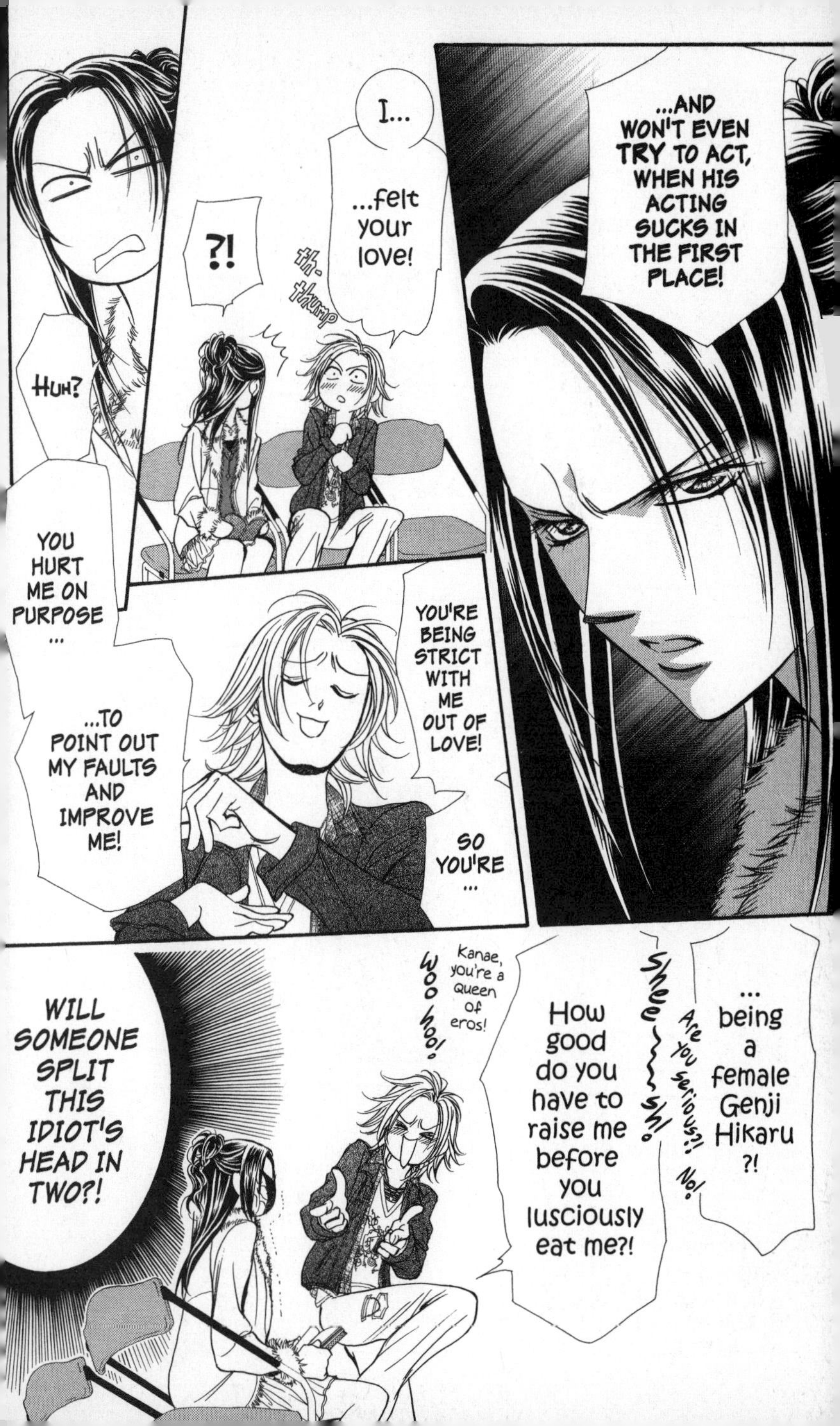

...AND WON'T EVEN TRY TO ACT, WHEN HIS ACTING SUCKS IN THE FIRST PLACE!
I...
...felt your love!
th-thump
?!
Huh?
YOU'RE BEING STRICT WITH ME OUT OF LOVE!
SO YOU'RE...
YOU HURT ME ON PURPOSE...
...TO POINT OUT MY FAULTS AND IMPROVE ME!
... being a female Genji Hikaru?!
Are you serious?! No!
Shee~sh!
How good do you have to raise me before you lusciously eat me?!
Kanae, you're a Queen of eros!
Woo hoo!
WILL SOMEONE SPLIT THIS IDIOT'S HEAD IN TWO?!

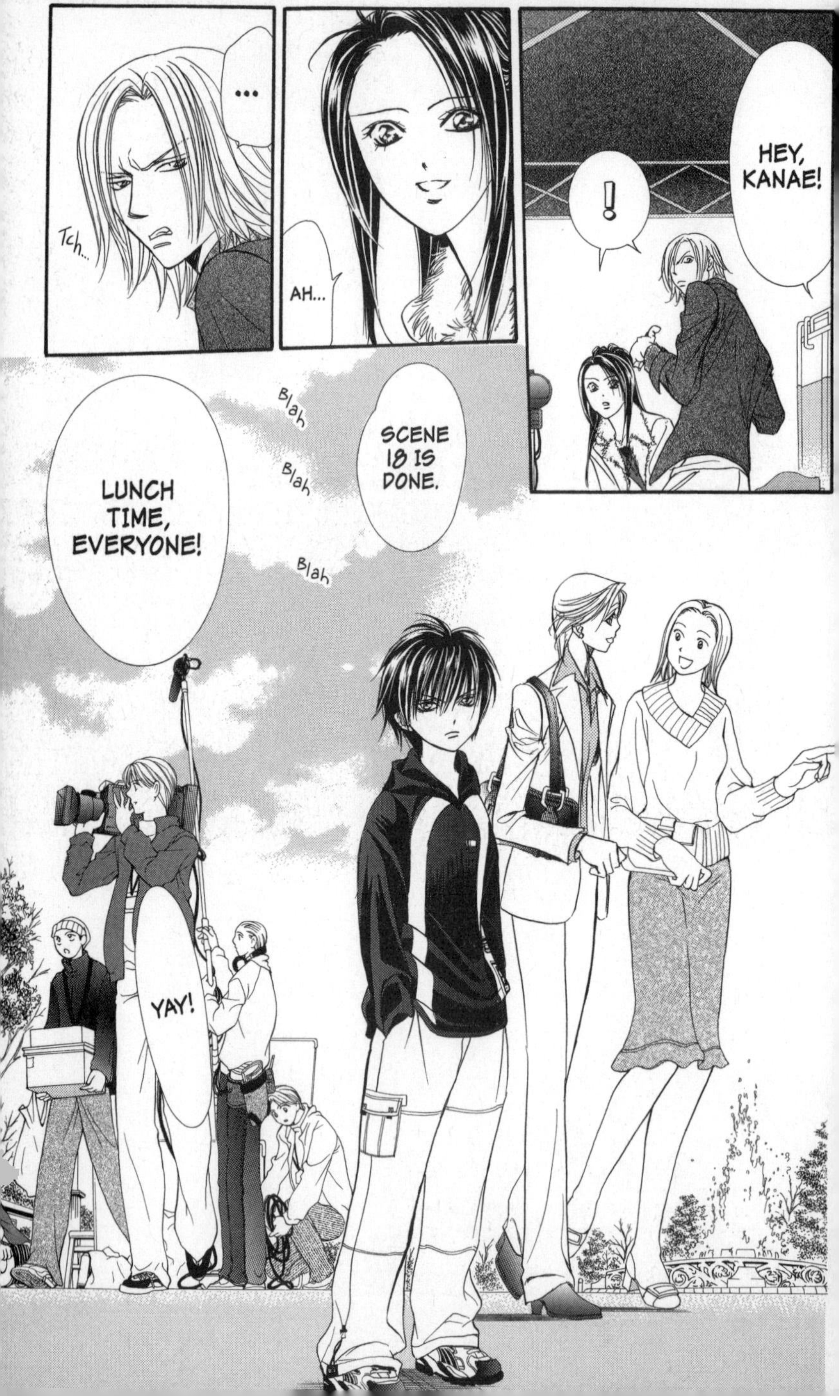
HEY, KANAE!
!
AH...
...
Tch...
SCENE 18 IS DONE.
Blah
Blah
Blah
LUNCH TIME, EVERYONE!
YAY!

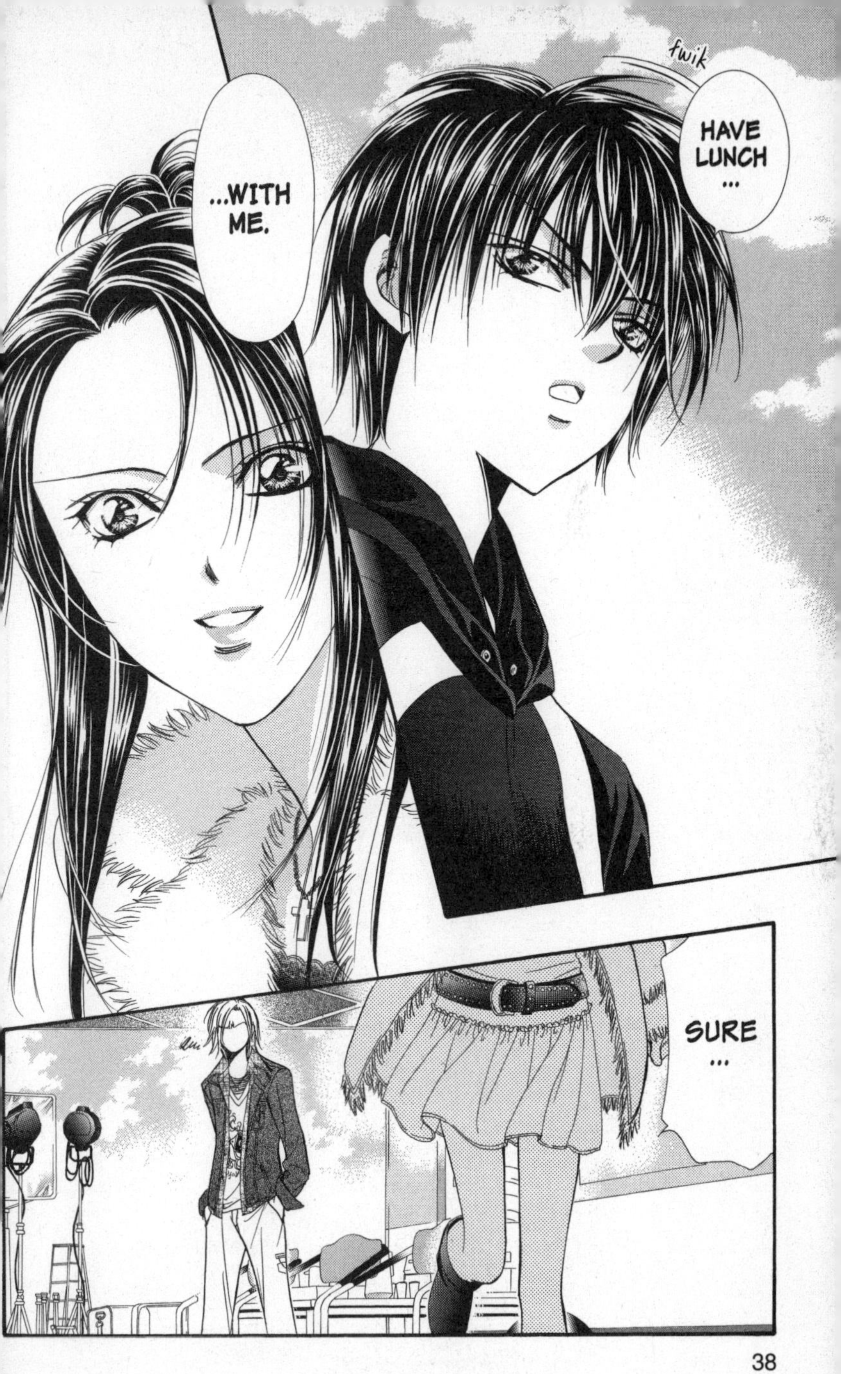
fwik
HAVE LUNCH ...
...WITH ME.
SURE ...

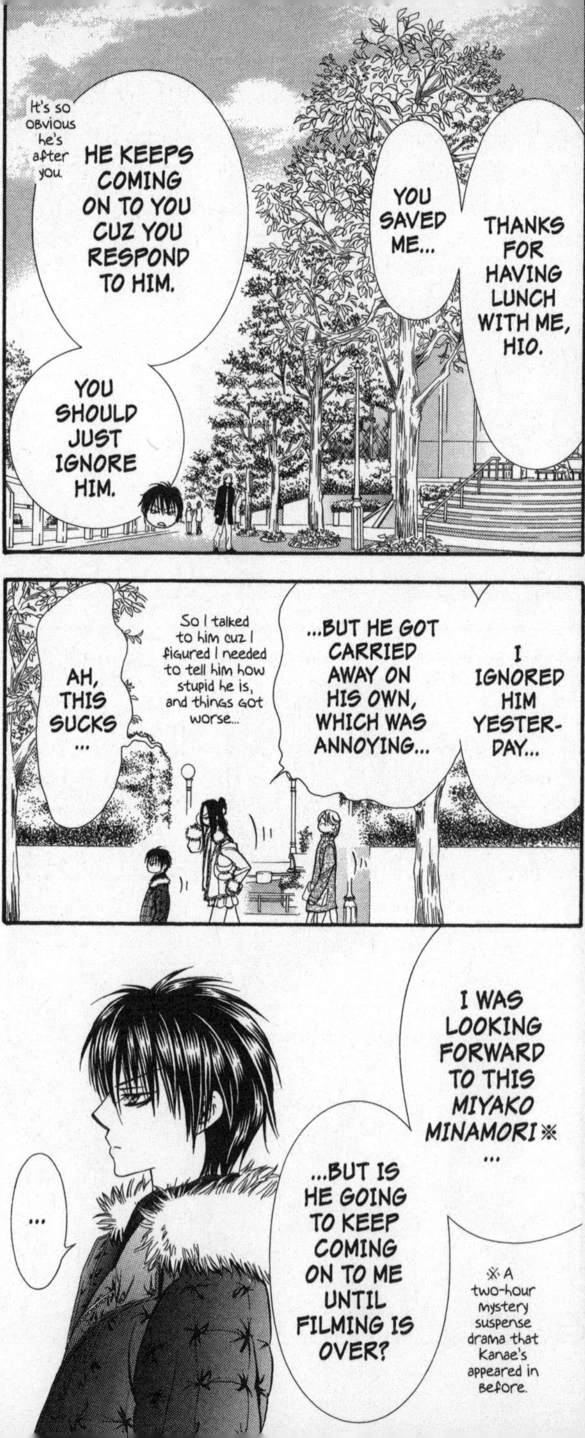
THANKS FOR HAVING LUNCH WITH ME, HIO.
YOU SAVED ME...
HE KEEPS COMING ON TO YOU CUZ YOU RESPOND TO HIM.
It's so obvious he's after you.
YOU SHOULD JUST IGNORE HIM.
I IGNORED HIM YESTERDAY...
...BUT HE GOT CARRIED AWAY ON HIS OWN, WHICH WAS ANNOYING...
So I talked to him cuz I figured I needed to tell him how stupid he is, and things got worse...
AH, THIS SUCKS...
I WAS LOOKING FORWARD TO THIS MIYAKO MINAMORI※...
...BUT IS HE GOING TO KEEP COMING ON TO ME UNTIL FILMING IS OVER?
※A two-hour mystery suspense drama that Kanae's appeared in before.
...

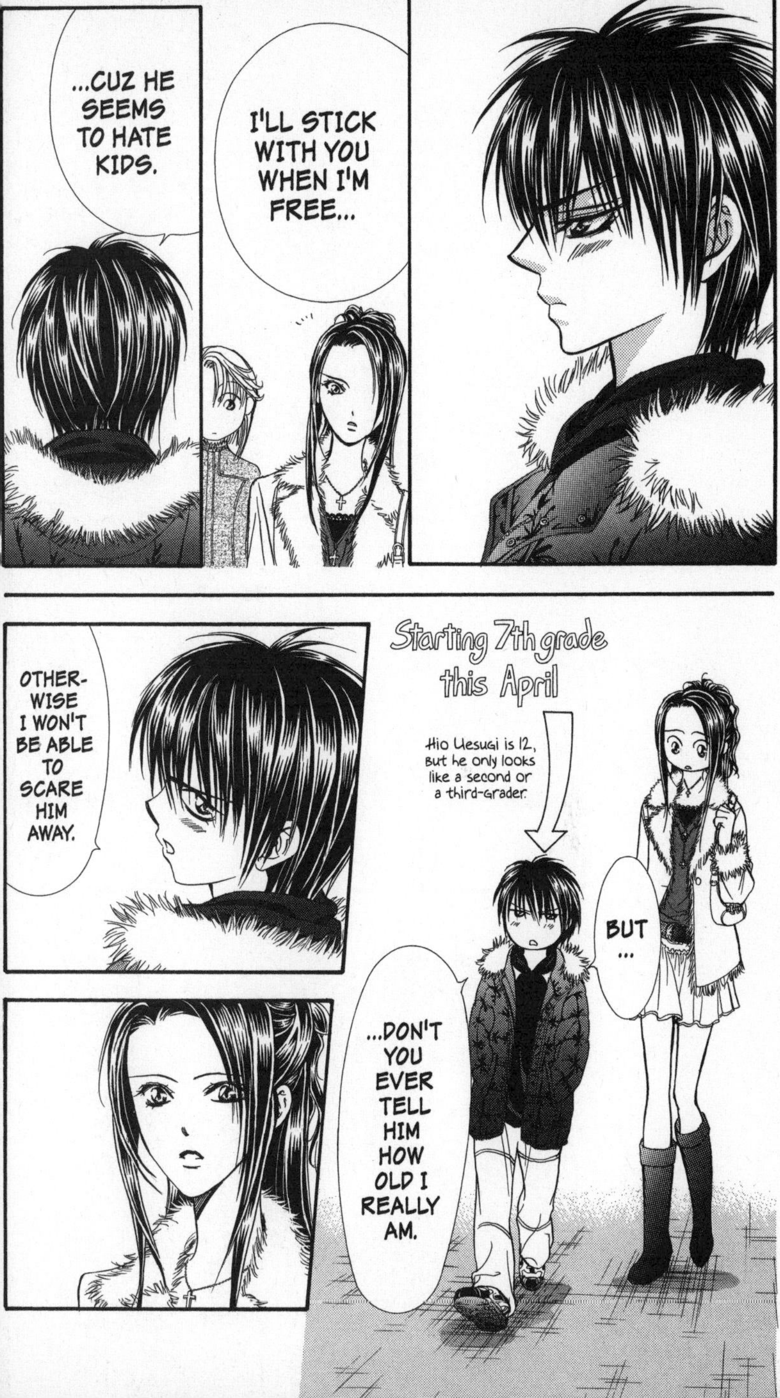

I'LL STICK WITH YOU WHEN I'M FREE...
...CUZ HE SEEMS TO HATE KIDS.
Starting 7th grade this April
Hio Uesugi is 12, but he only looks like a second or a third-grader.
BUT ...
...DON'T YOU EVER TELL HIM HOW OLD I REALLY AM.
OTHER-WISE I WON'T BE ABLE TO SCARE HIM AWAY.

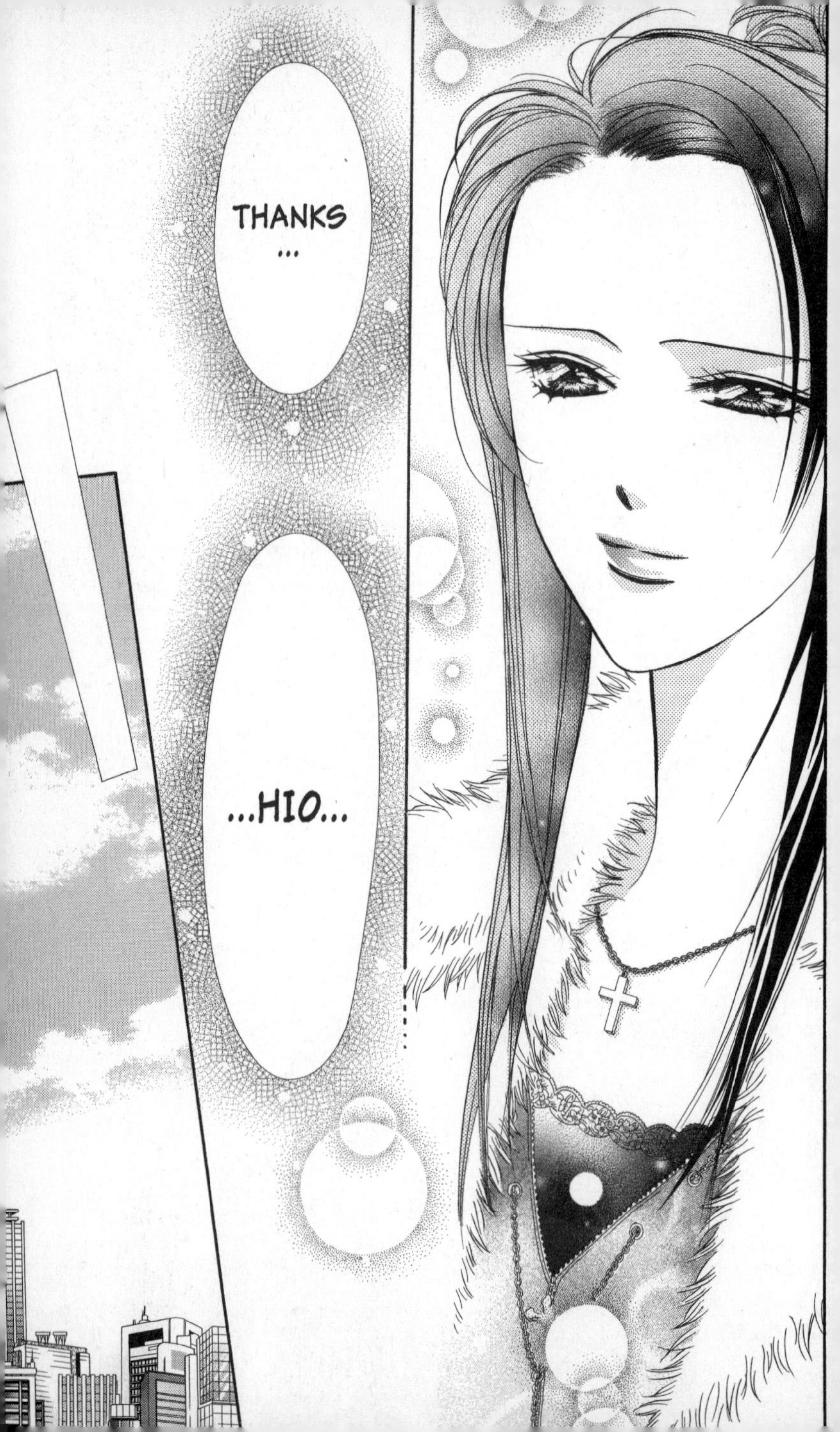
THANKS ...
...HIO...

Recent Calls

2/11	11:15	Mis
	No caller ID	
2/11	10:55	Mis
	No caller ID	
2/11	10:40	Mis
	No caller ID	
2/11	10:32	Mis
	No caller ID	
/11	10:12	Mis

13:34

Recent Calls

2/11	11:15	Missed
	No caller ID	
2/11	10:55	Missed
	No caller ID	
2/11	10:40	Missed
	No caller ID	
2/11	10:32	Missed
	No caller ID	
2/11	10:12	Missed
	No caller ID	

WH...

WHAT'S WITH ALL THESE MISSED CALLS?!

WHAT ?

AND WITH NO CALLER ID!

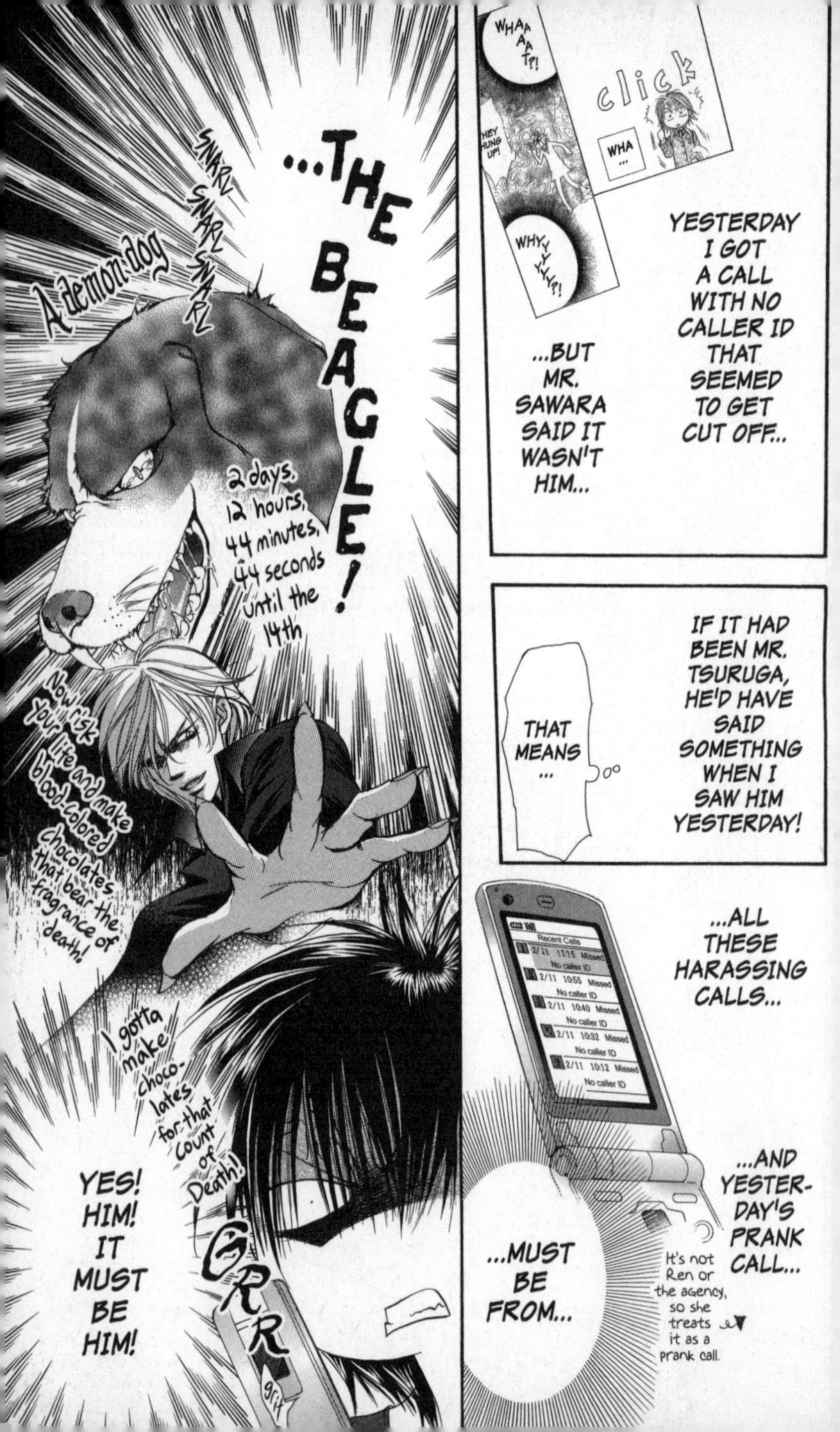
click
WHA...
WHAAAAT?!
HEY HUNG UP!
WHYYYYY?!
YESTERDAY I GOT A CALL WITH NO CALLER ID THAT SEEMED TO GET CUT OFF...
...BUT MR. SAWARA SAID IT WASN'T HIM...
IF IT HAD BEEN MR. TSURUGA, HE'D HAVE SAID SOMETHING WHEN I SAW HIM YESTERDAY!
THAT MEANS...
...ALL THESE HARASSING CALLS...
Recent Calls
2/11 11:15 Missed
No caller ID
2/11 10:55 Missed
No caller ID
2/11 10:40 Missed
No caller ID
2/11 10:32 Missed
No caller ID
2/11 10:12 Missed
No caller ID
...AND YESTERDAY'S PRANK CALL...
It's not Ren or the agency, so she treats it as a prank call.
...MUST BE FROM...
...THE BEAGLE!
SNARL SNARL SNARL
A demon dog
2 days, 12 hours, 44 minutes, 44 seconds until the 14th
Now risk your life and make blood-colored chocolates that bear the fragrance of death!
I gotta make chocolates for that Count of Death!
YES! HIM! IT MUST BE HIM!
GRRR
grit

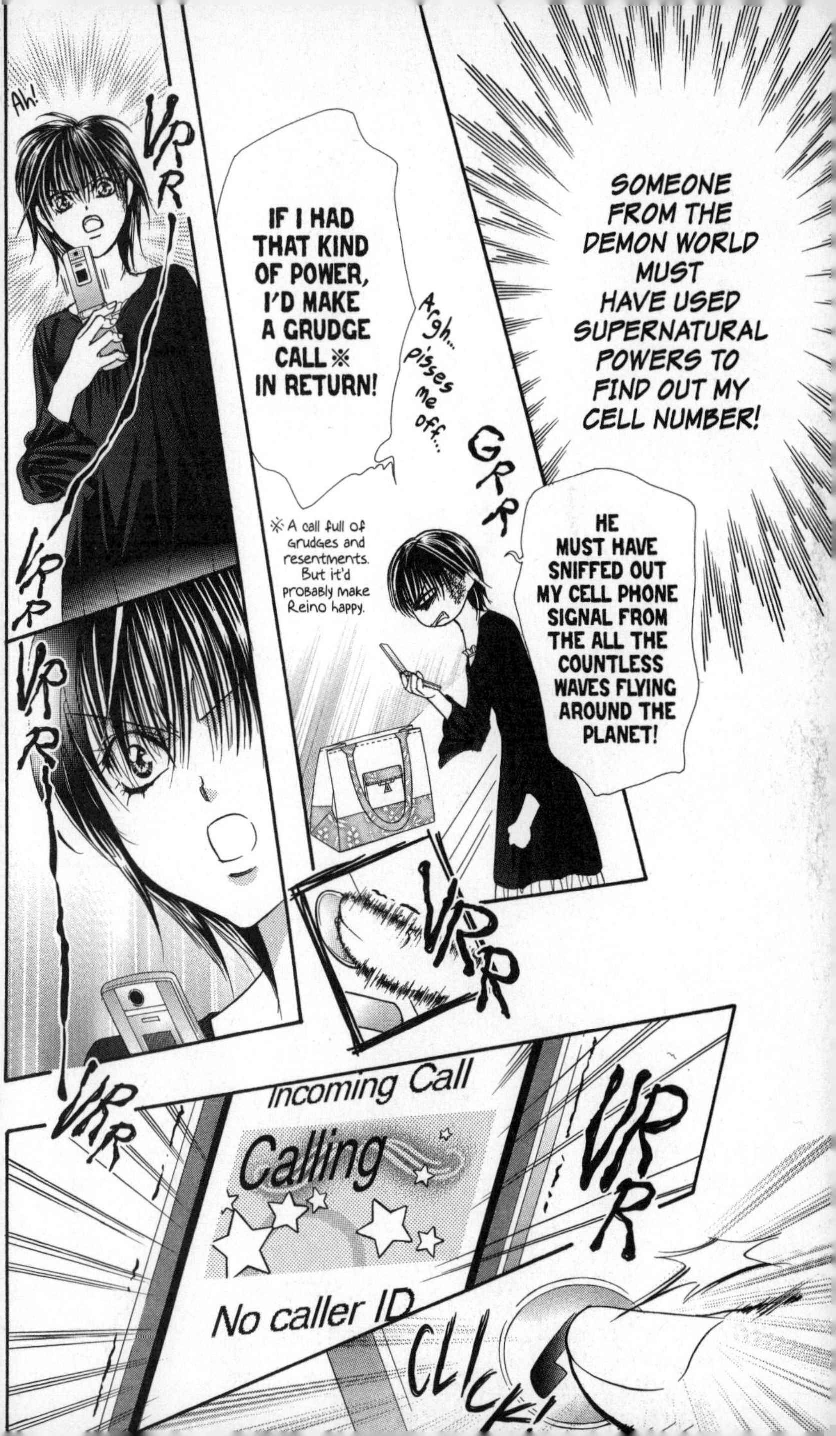
SOMEONE FROM THE DEMON WORLD MUST HAVE USED SUPERNATURAL POWERS TO FIND OUT MY CELL NUMBER!
IF I HAD THAT KIND OF POWER, I'D MAKE A GRUDGE CALL ※ IN RETURN!
Argh... pisses me off...
GRR
HE MUST HAVE SNIFFED OUT MY CELL PHONE SIGNAL FROM THE ALL THE COUNTLESS WAVES FLYING AROUND THE PLANET!
※A call full of grudges and resentments. But it'd probably make Reino happy.
Ah!
VRR
VRR
VRR
VRR
VRR
Incoming Call
Calling
No caller ID
VRR
CLICK!

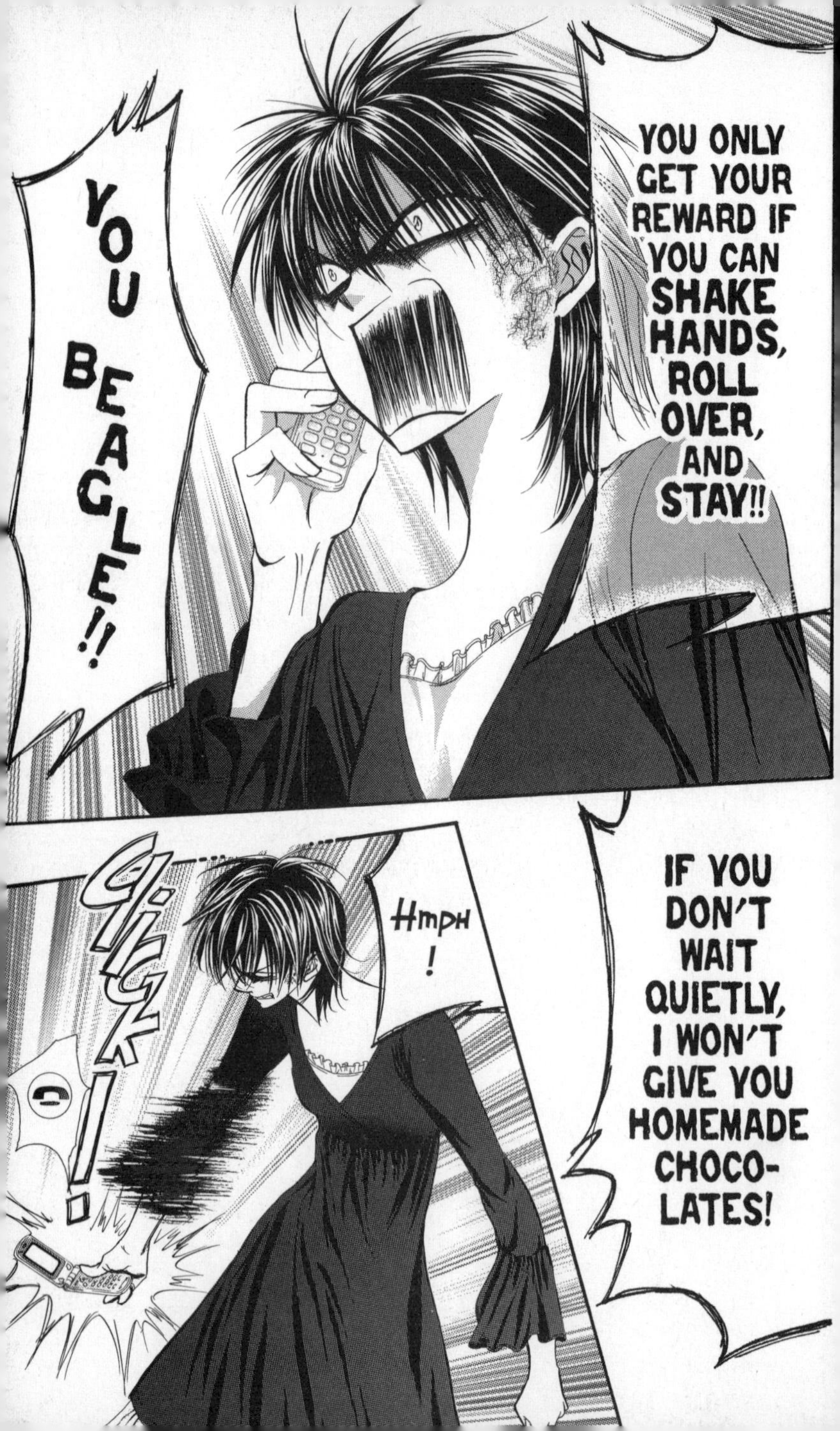
YOU ONLY GET YOUR REWARD IF YOU CAN SHAKE HANDS, ROLL OVER, AND STAY!!
YOU BEAGLE!!
IF YOU DON'T WAIT QUIETLY, I WON'T GIVE YOU HOMEMADE CHOCO-LATES!
Hmph!
CLICK!

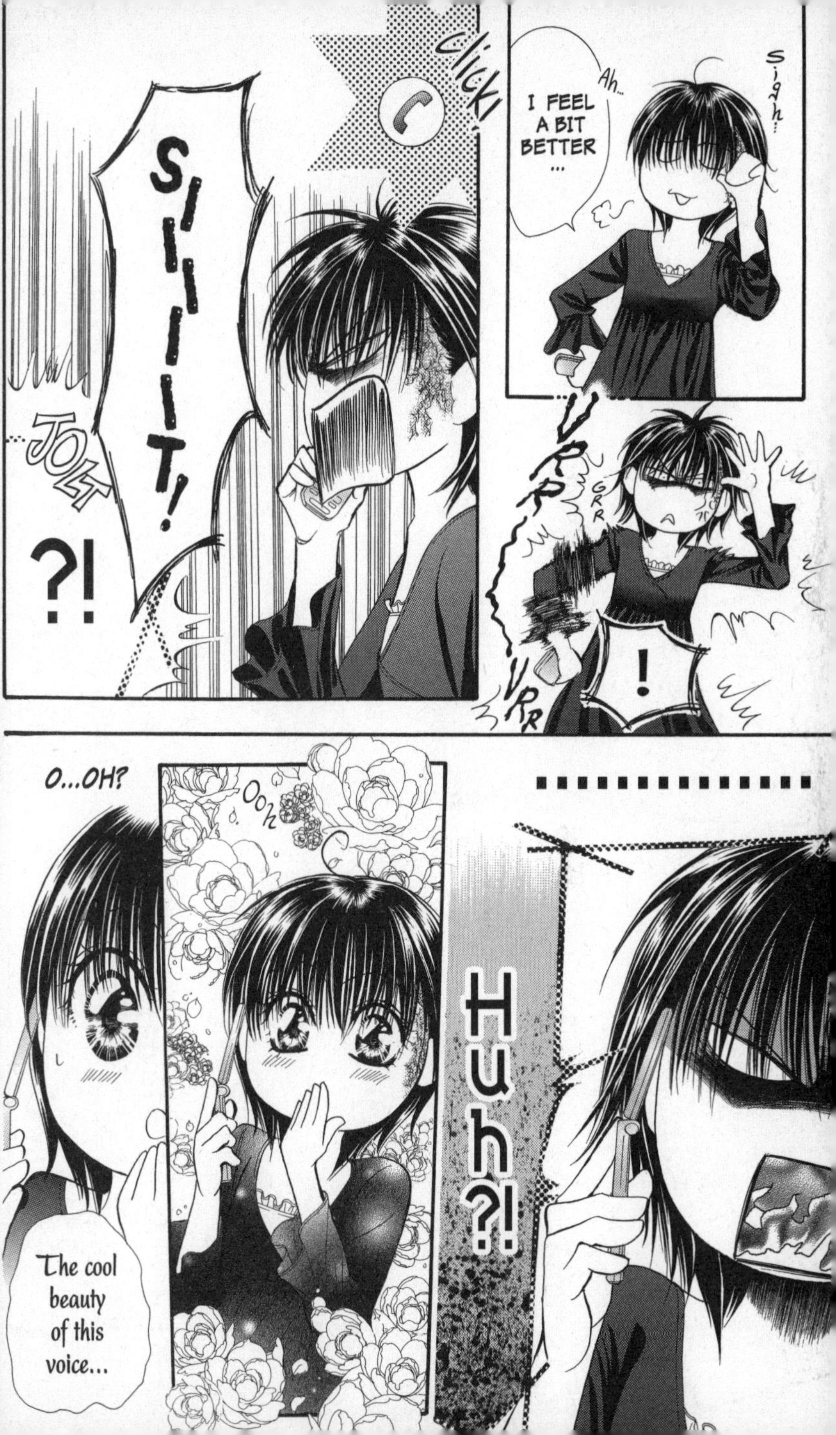
Sigh...
Ah...
I FEEL A BIT BETTER ...
VRR VRR
GRR
!
CLICK!
SIIIIT!
JOLT
?!
....
Huh?!
Ooh
O...OH?
The cool beauty of this voice...

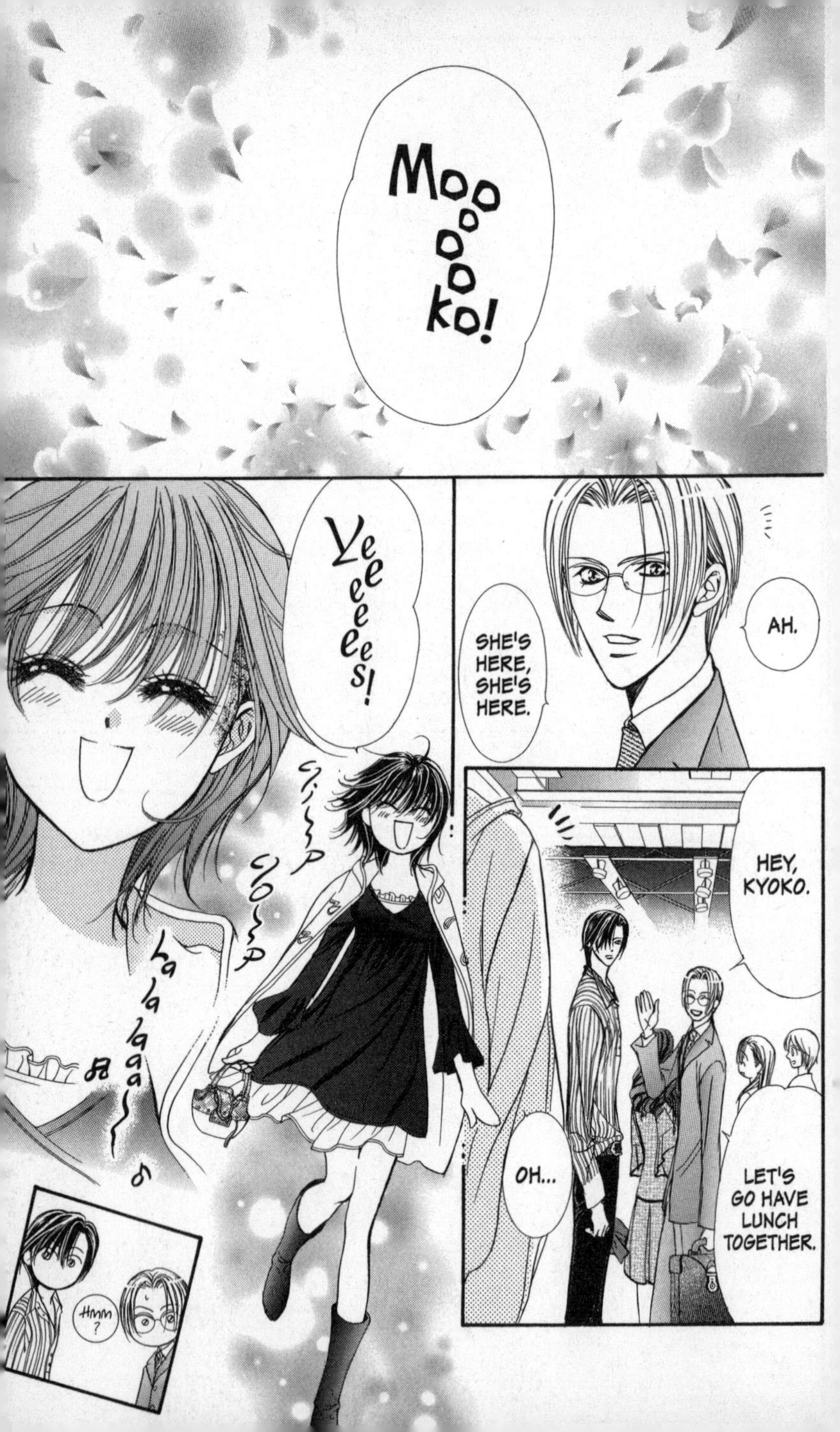
Moooooko!
AH.
SHE'S HERE, SHE'S HERE.
HEY, KYOKO.
LET'S GO HAVE LUNCH TOGETHER.
OH...
Yeeeeeees!
La la laaa~~ ♫
Hmm?

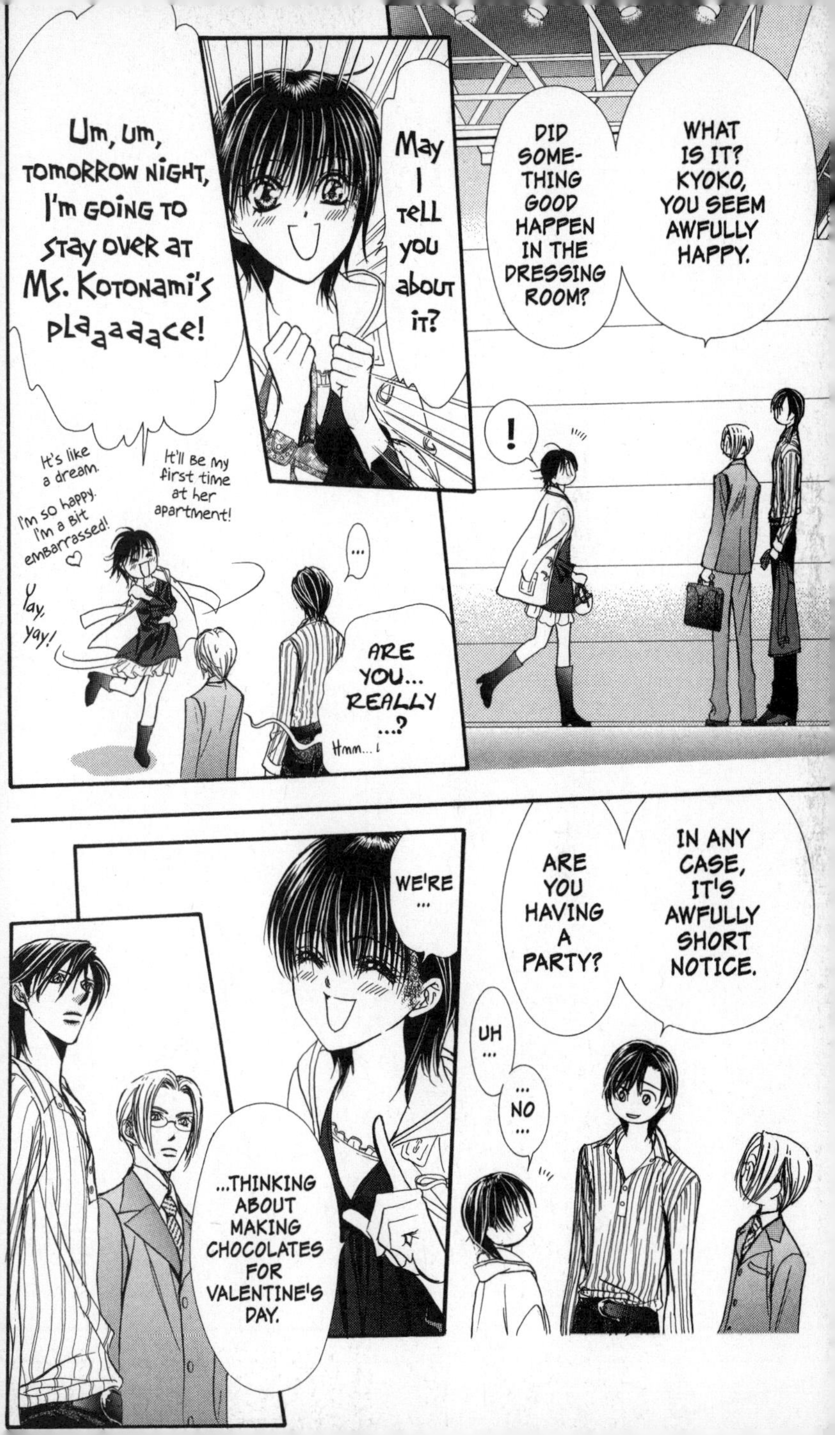
WHAT IS IT? KYOKO, YOU SEEM AWFULLY HAPPY.
DID SOMETHING GOOD HAPPEN IN THE DRESSING ROOM?
!
May I tell you about it?
Um, um, tomorrow night, I'm going to stay over at Ms. Kotonami's plaaaaace!
It'll be my first time at her apartment!
It's like a dream.
I'm so happy. I'm a bit embarrassed!
Yay, yay!
...
ARE YOU... REALLY ...?
Hmm...
IN ANY CASE, IT'S AWFULLY SHORT NOTICE.
ARE YOU HAVING A PARTY?
UH ...
... NO ...
WE'RE ...
...THINKING ABOUT MAKING CHOCOLATES FOR VALENTINE'S DAY.

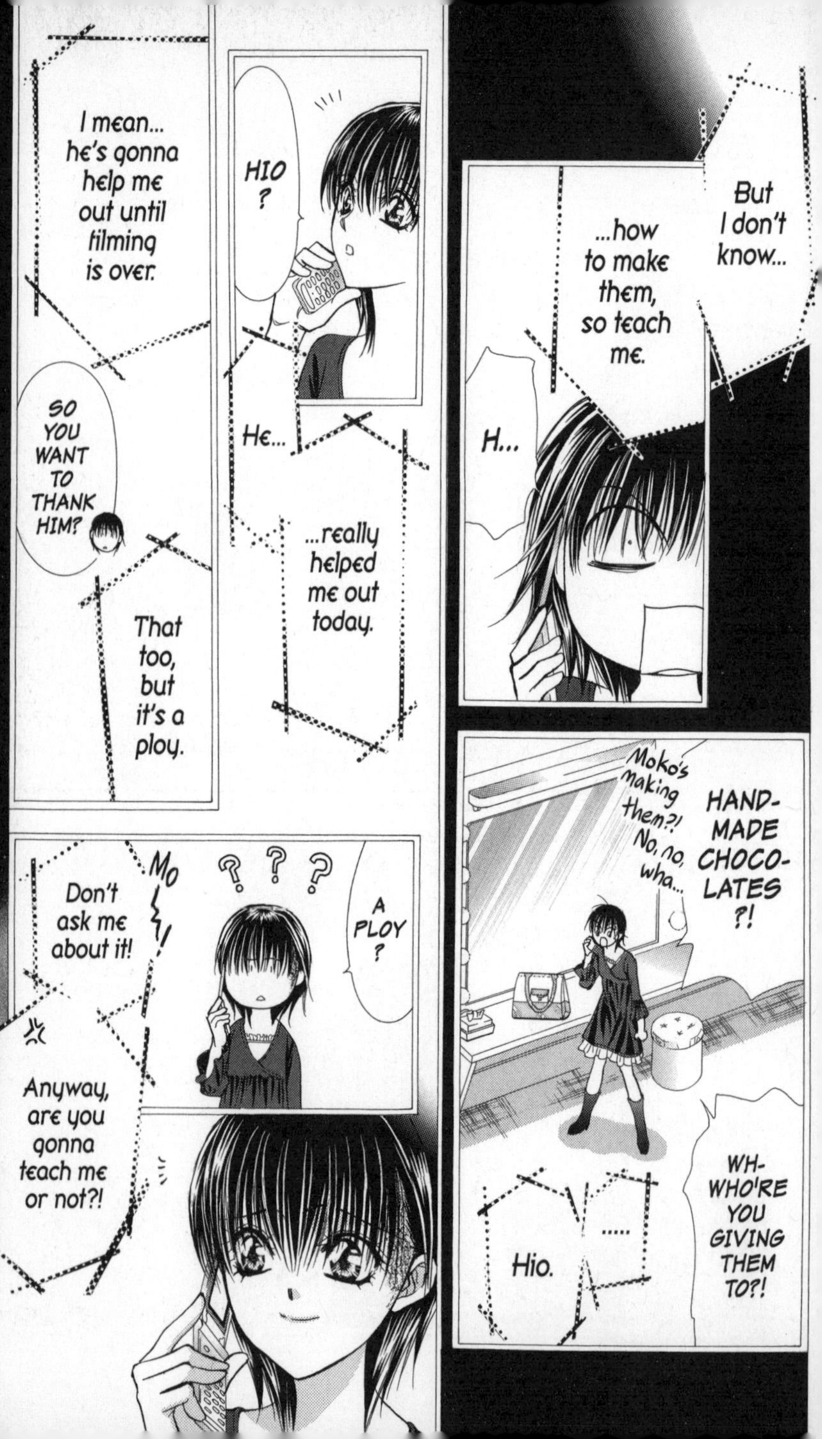

But I don't know...
...how to make them, so teach me.
H...
HAND-MADE CHOCOLATES?!
Moko's making them?! No, no, wha...
WH-WHO'RE YOU GIVING THEM TO?!
....
Hio.
HIO?
He...
...really helped me out today.
I mean... he's gonna help me out until filming is over.
SO YOU WANT TO THANK HIM?
That too, but it's a ploy.
A PLOY?
MO
Don't ask me about it!
Anyway, are you gonna teach me or not?!

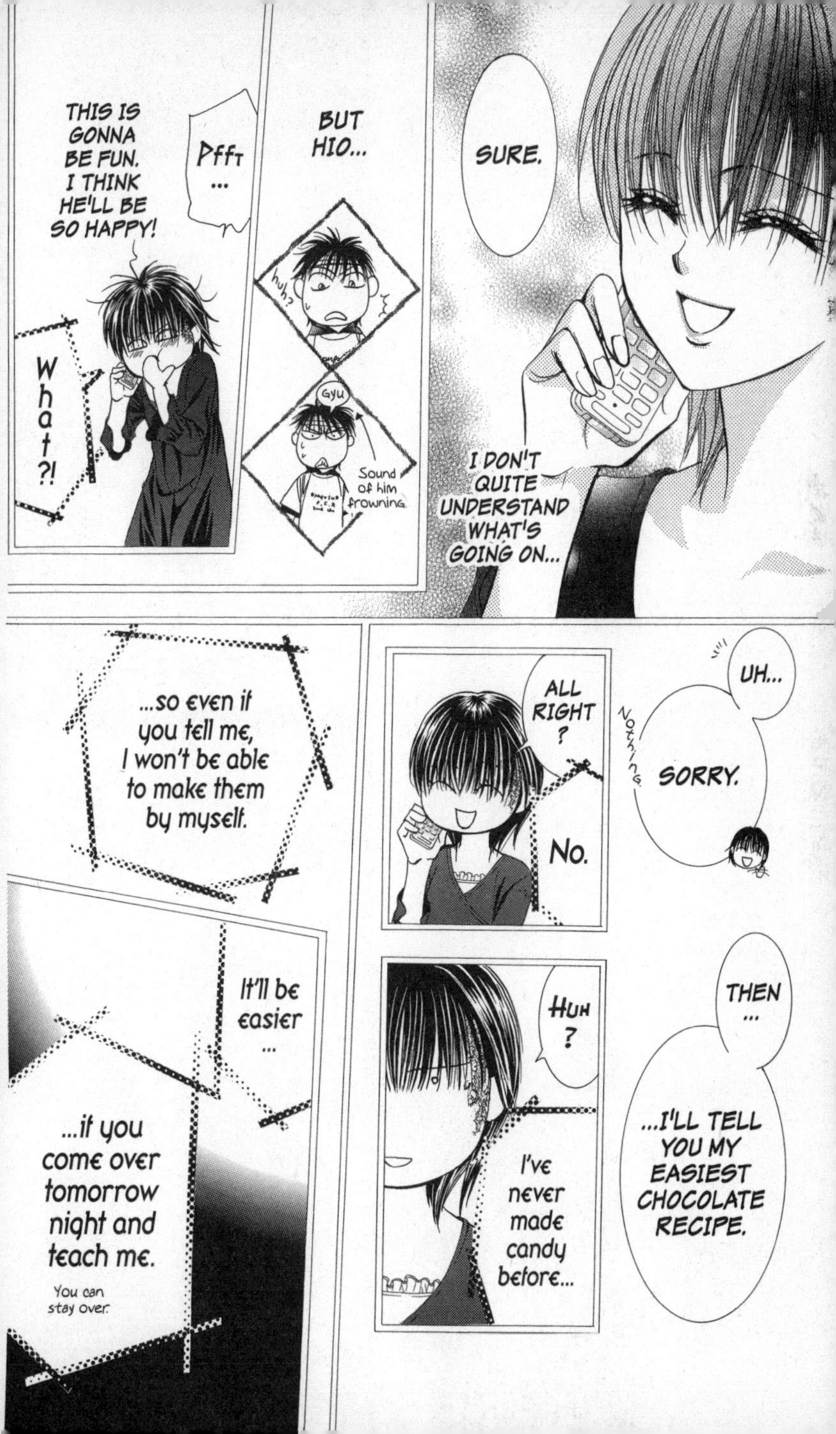
SURE.
I DON'T QUITE UNDERSTAND WHAT'S GOING ON...
BUT HIO...
huh?
Gyu
Sound of him frowning.
THIS IS GONNA BE FUN. I THINK HE'LL BE SO HAPPY!
Pfft...
What?!
UH...
SORRY.
Nothing.
ALL RIGHT?
No.
THEN...
...I'LL TELL YOU MY EASIEST CHOCOLATE RECIPE.
Huh?
I've never made candy before...
...so even if you tell me, I won't be able to make them by myself.
It'll be easier...
...if you come over tomorrow night and teach me.
You can stay over.

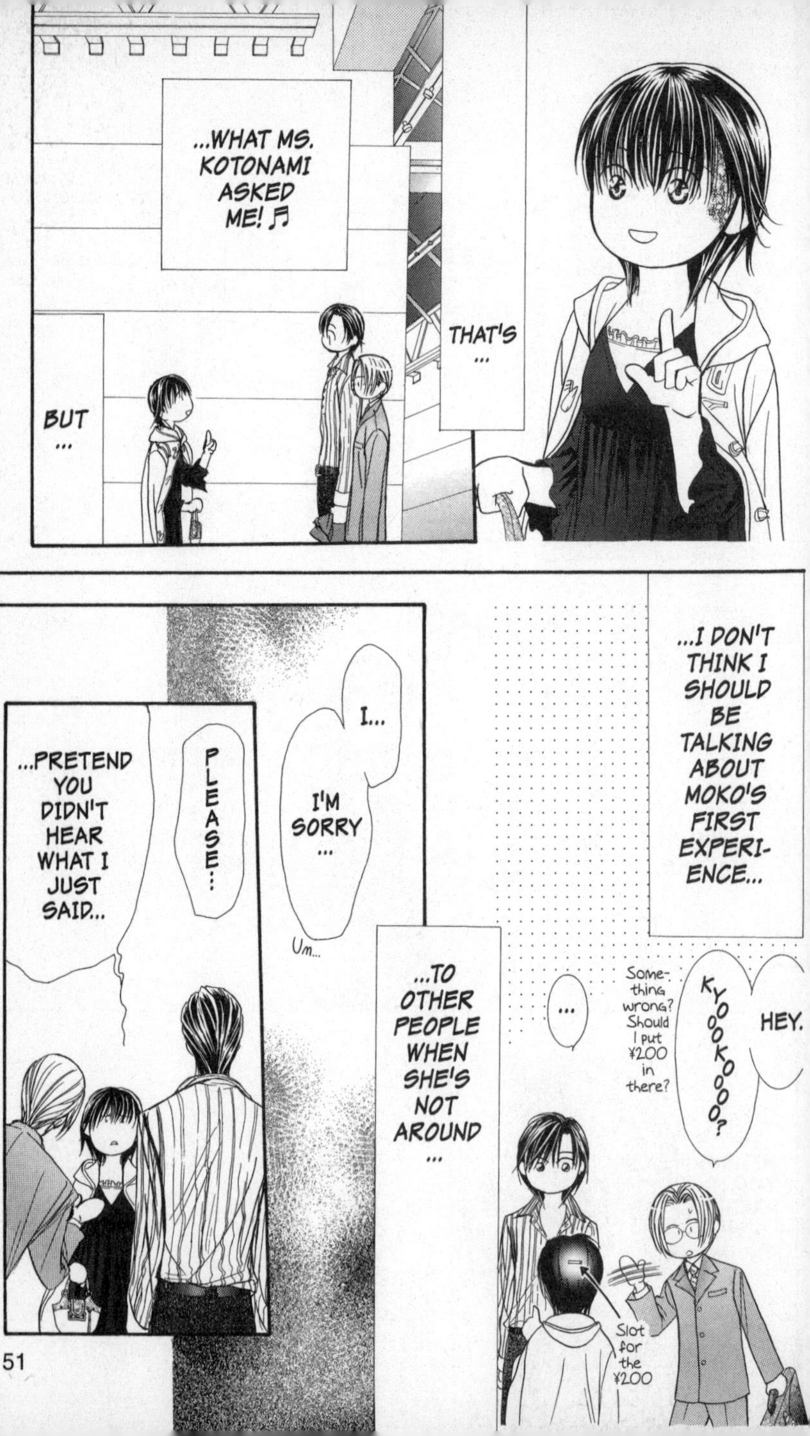
THAT'S ...
...WHAT MS. KOTONAMI ASKED ME! ♬
BUT ...
...I DON'T THINK I SHOULD BE TALKING ABOUT MOKO'S FIRST EXPERIENCE...
...TO OTHER PEOPLE WHEN SHE'S NOT AROUND ...
HEY.
KYOOOKOOOOO?
Something wrong? Should I put ¥200 in there?
...
Slot for the ¥200
I...
I'M SORRY ...
Um...
PLEASE...
...PRETEND YOU DIDN'T HEAR WHAT I JUST SAID...

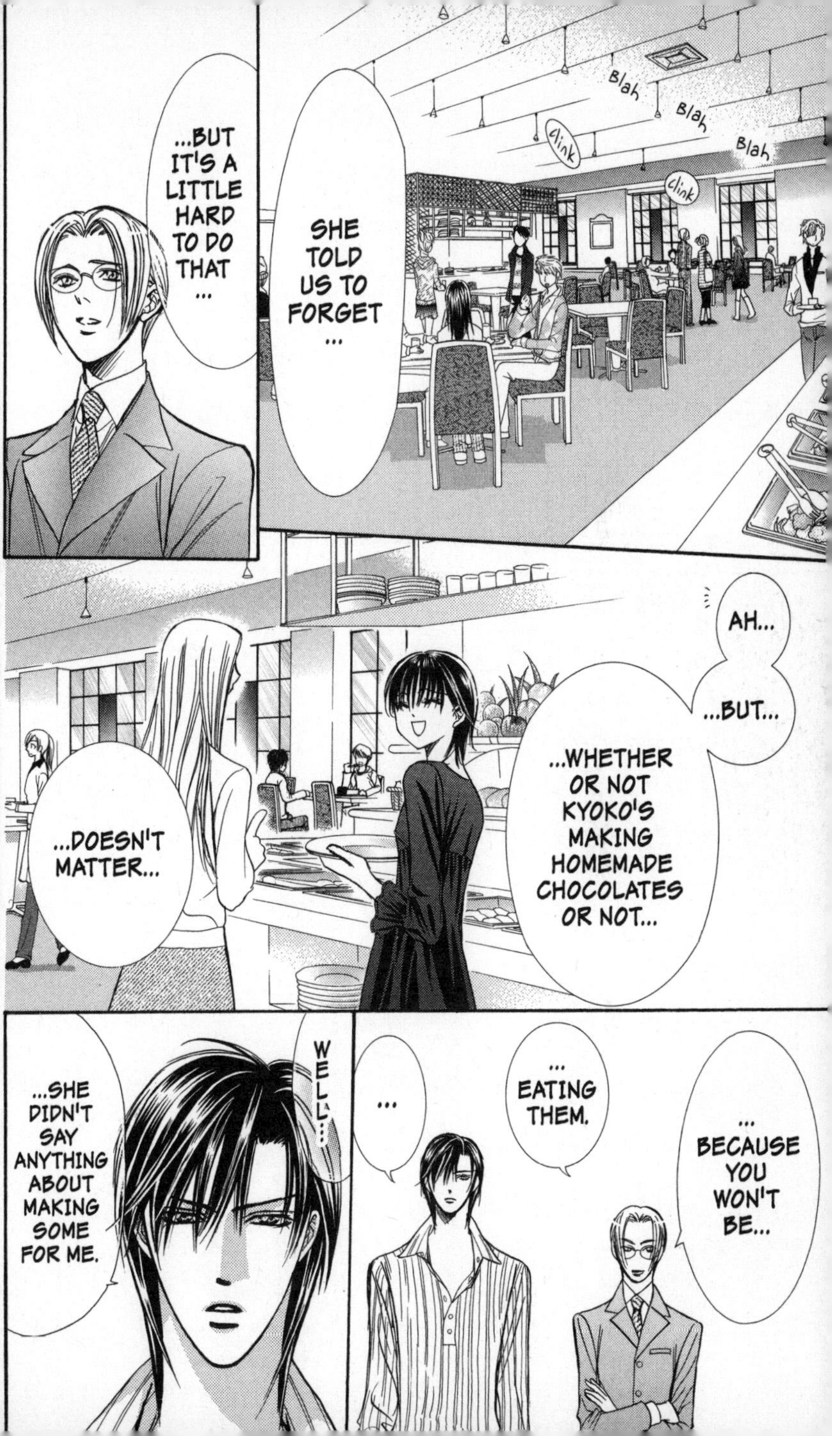
Blah
Blah
Blah
clink
clink
SHE TOLD US TO FORGET...
...BUT IT'S A LITTLE HARD TO DO THAT...
AH...
...BUT...
...WHETHER OR NOT KYOKO'S MAKING HOMEMADE CHOCOLATES OR NOT...
...DOESN'T MATTER...
...BECAUSE YOU WON'T BE...
...EATING THEM.
...
WELL...
...SHE DIDN'T SAY ANYTHING ABOUT MAKING SOME FOR ME.

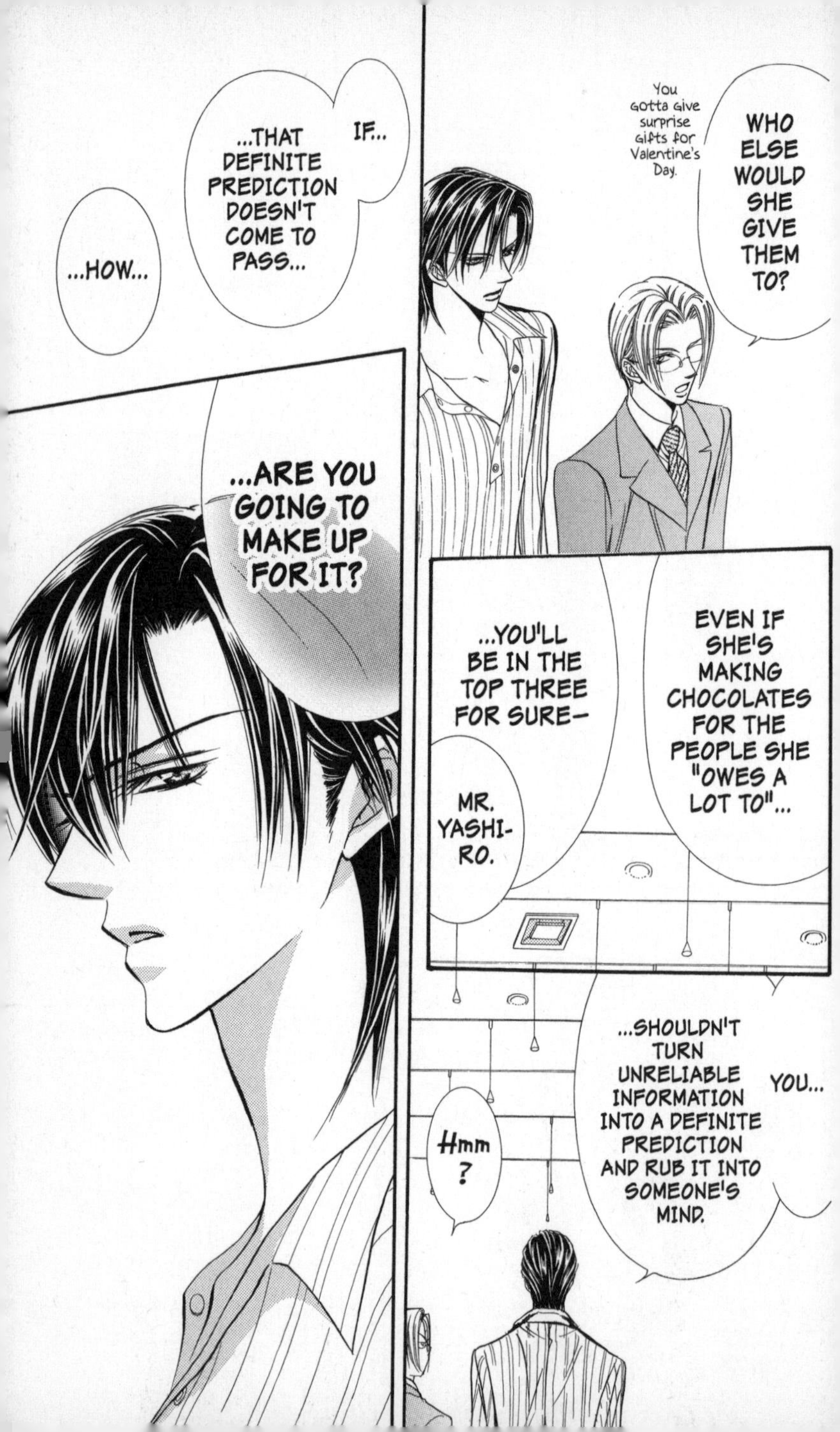
WHO ELSE WOULD SHE GIVE THEM TO?
You Gotta Give surprise Gifts for Valentine's Day.
EVEN IF SHE'S MAKING CHOCOLATES FOR THE PEOPLE SHE "OWES A LOT TO"...
...YOU'LL BE IN THE TOP THREE FOR SURE–
MR. YASHIRO.
YOU...
...SHOULDN'T TURN UNRELIABLE INFORMATION INTO A DEFINITE PREDICTION AND RUB IT INTO SOMEONE'S MIND.
Hmm?
IF...
...THAT DEFINITE PREDICTION DOESN'T COME TO PASS...
...HOW...
...ARE YOU GOING TO MAKE UP FOR IT?

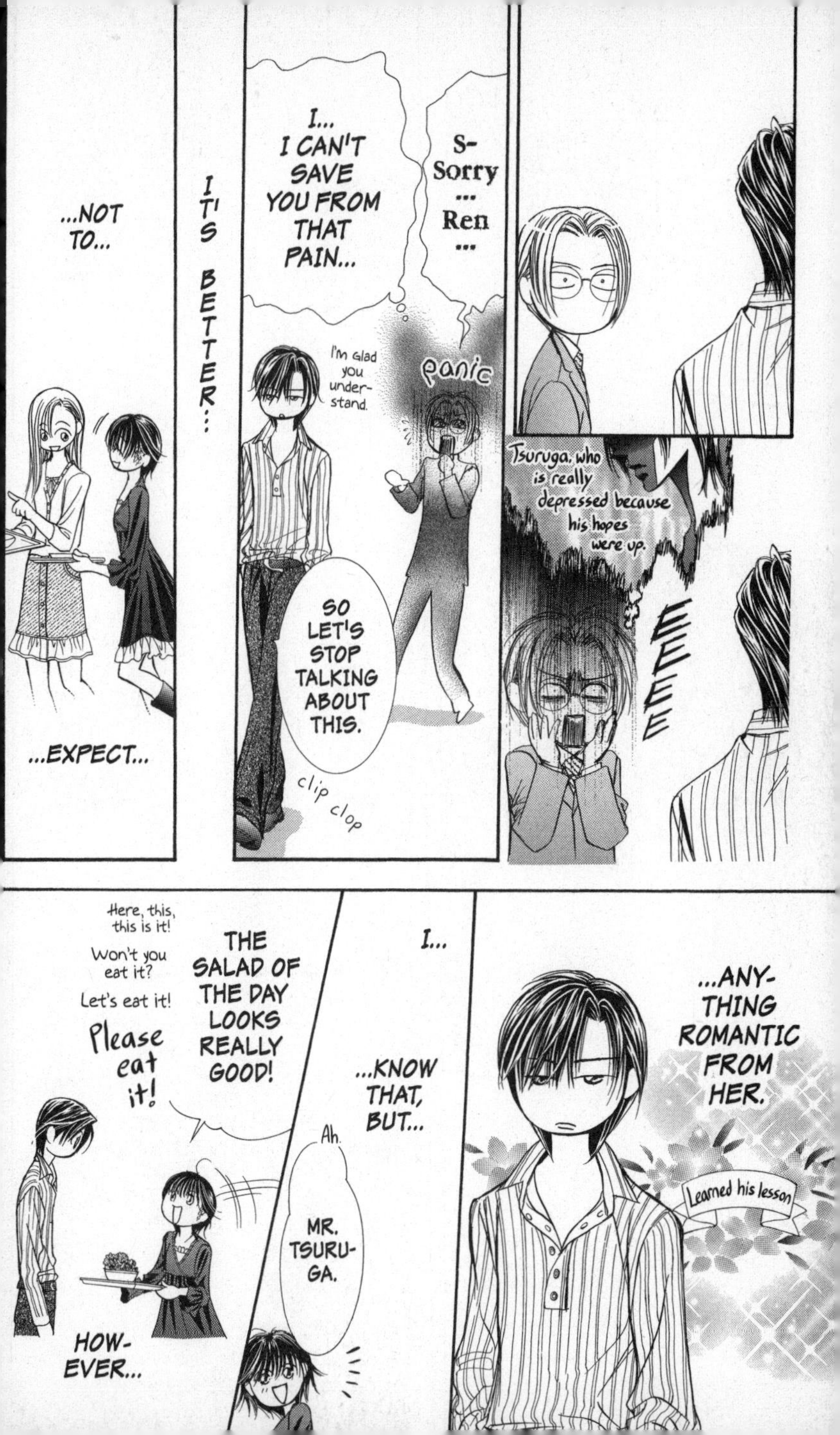
Tsuruga, who is really depressed because his hopes were up.
EEEEE
S- Sorry ... Ren ...
I... I CAN'T SAVE YOU FROM THAT PAIN...
panic
I'm glad you understand.
SO LET'S STOP TALKING ABOUT THIS.
clip clop
IT'S BETTER...
...NOT TO...
...EXPECT...
...ANY-THING ROMANTIC FROM HER.
Learned his lesson
I...
...KNOW THAT, BUT...
Ah.
MR. TSURU-GA.
THE SALAD OF THE DAY LOOKS REALLY GOOD!
Here, this, this is it!
Won't you eat it?
Let's eat it!
Please eat it!
HOW-EVER...

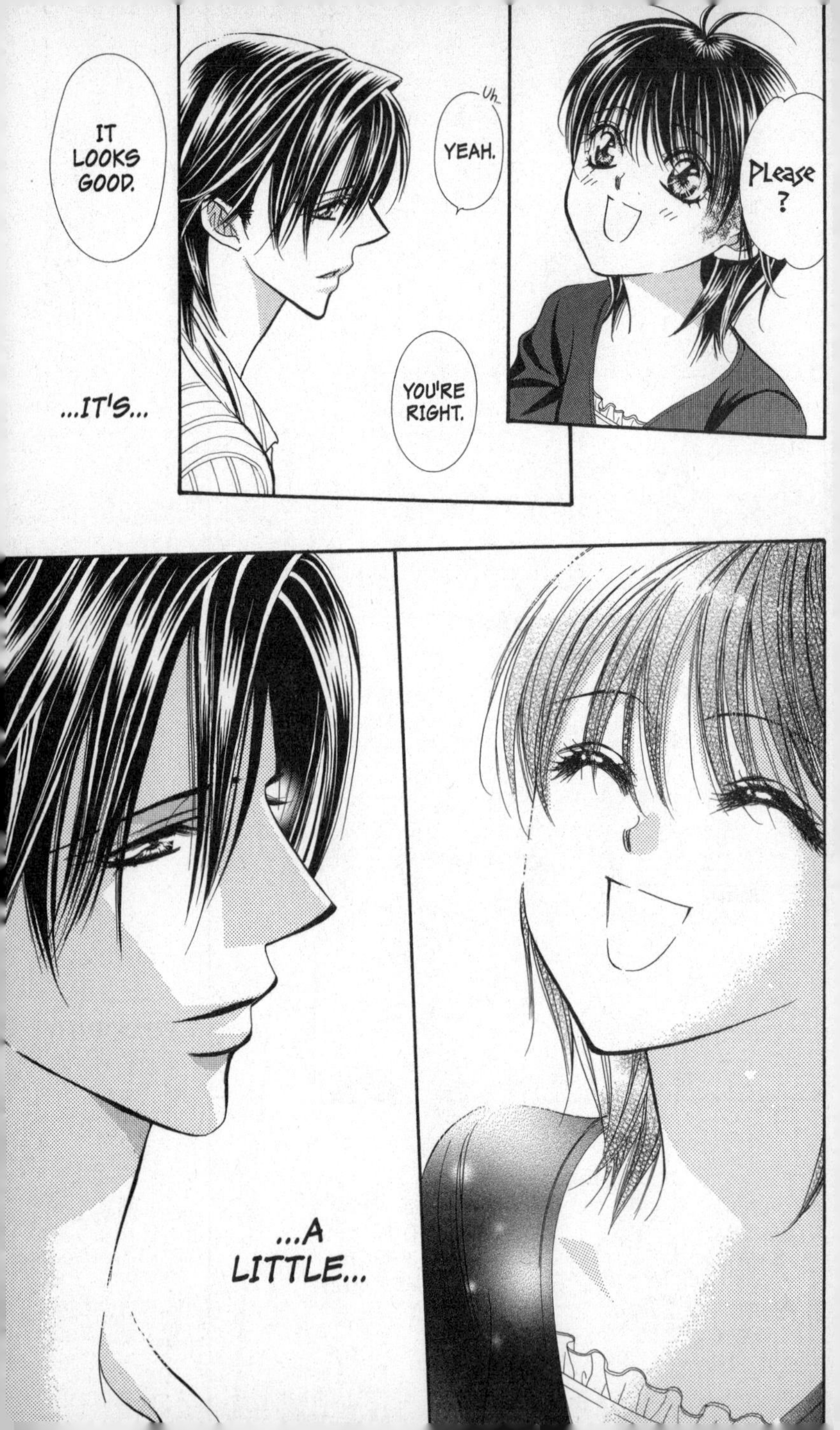
Please?
Uh...
YEAH.
YOU'RE RIGHT.
IT LOOKS GOOD.
...IT'S...
...A LITTLE...

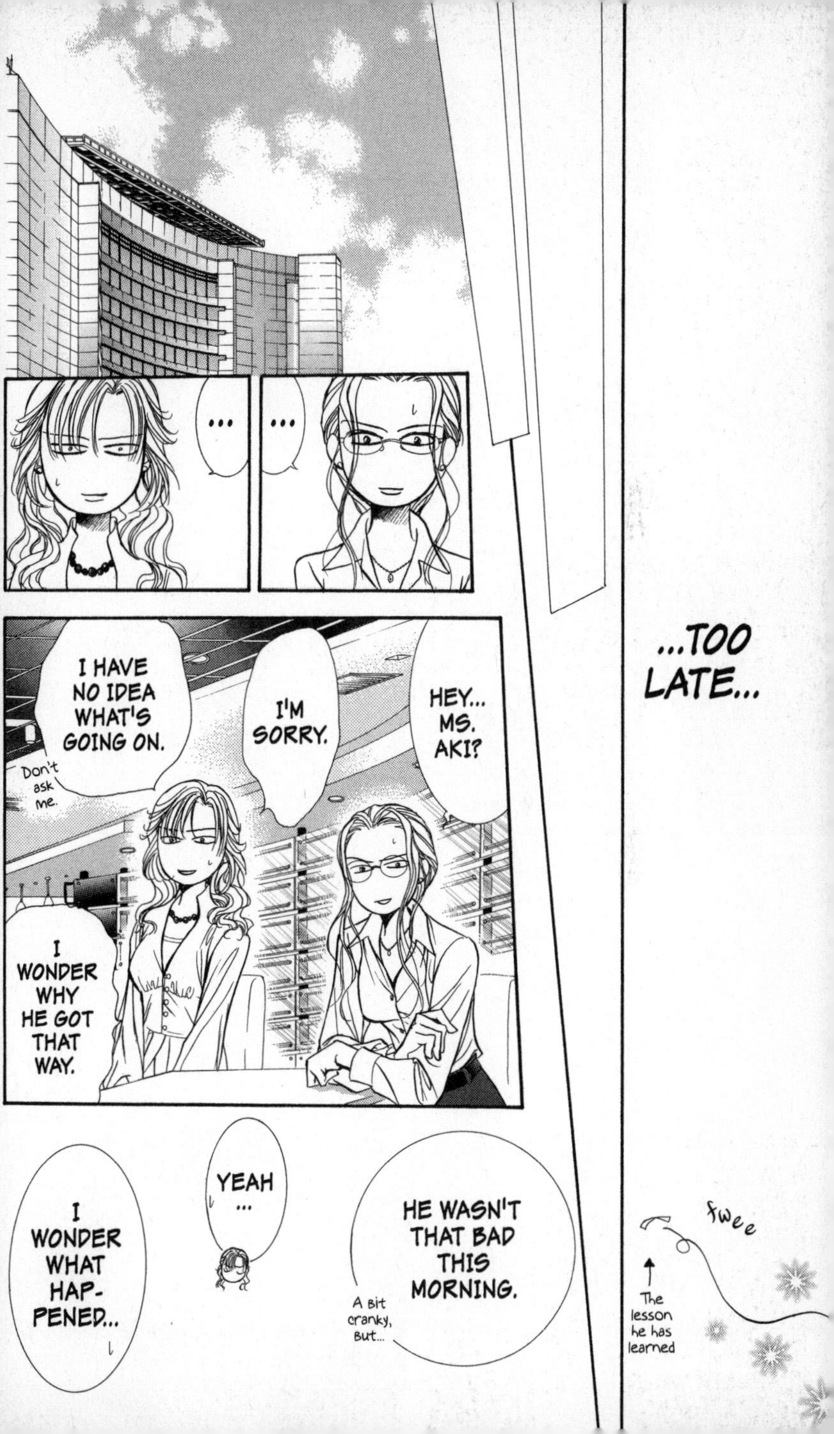
...TOO LATE...
The lesson he has learned
fwee
...
...
HEY... MS. AKI?
I'M SORRY.
I HAVE NO IDEA WHAT'S GOING ON.
Don't ask me.
I WONDER WHY HE GOT THAT WAY.
HE WASN'T THAT BAD THIS MORNING.
A bit cranky, but...
YEAH ...
I WONDER WHAT HAP-PENED...

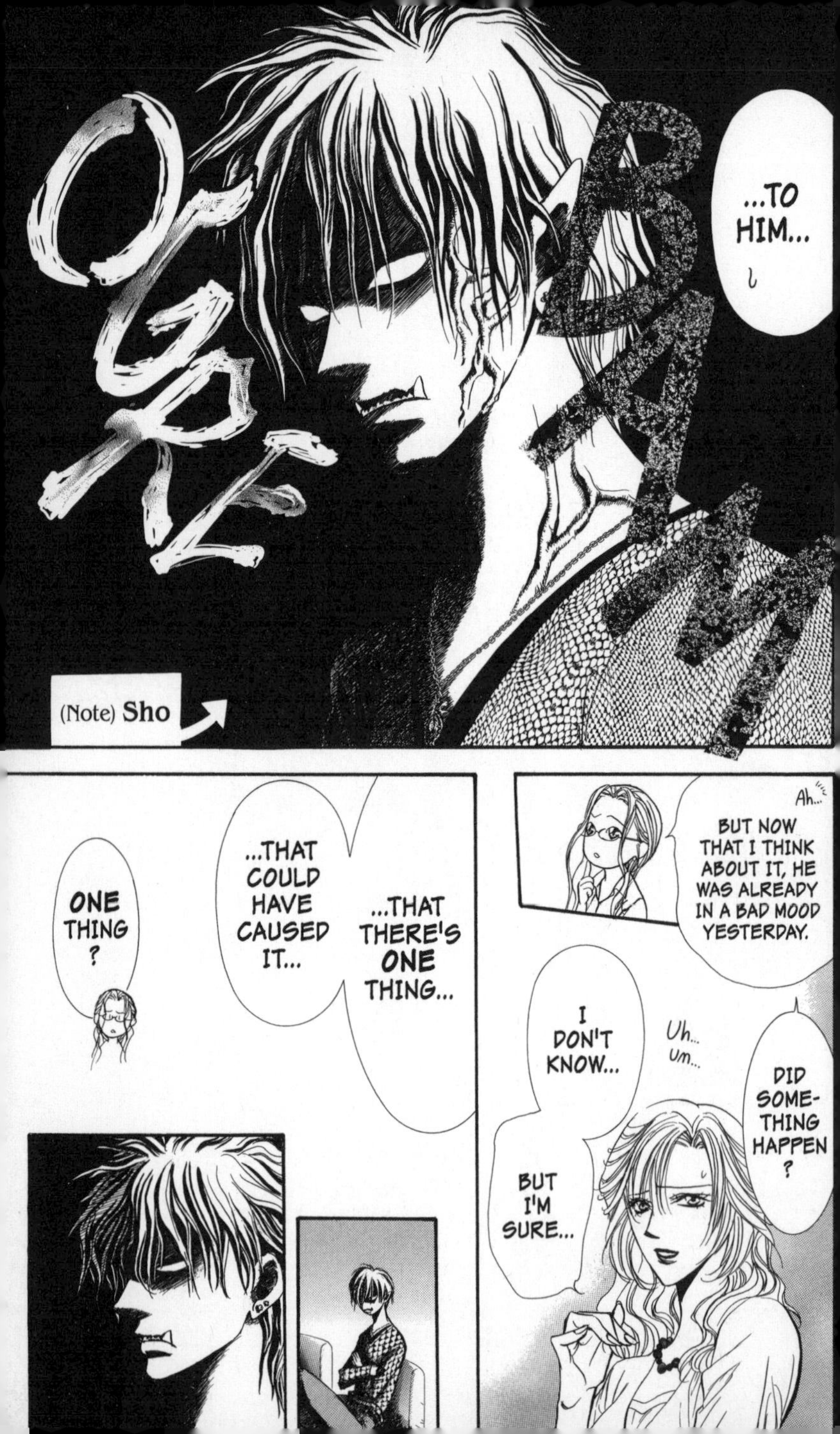
...TO HIM...
BAM
(Note) Sho
Ah...
BUT NOW THAT I THINK ABOUT IT, HE WAS ALREADY IN A BAD MOOD YESTERDAY.
DID SOMETHING HAPPEN?
Uh... Um...
I DON'T KNOW...
BUT I'M SURE...
...THAT THERE'S ONE THING...
...THAT COULD HAVE CAUSED IT...
ONE THING?

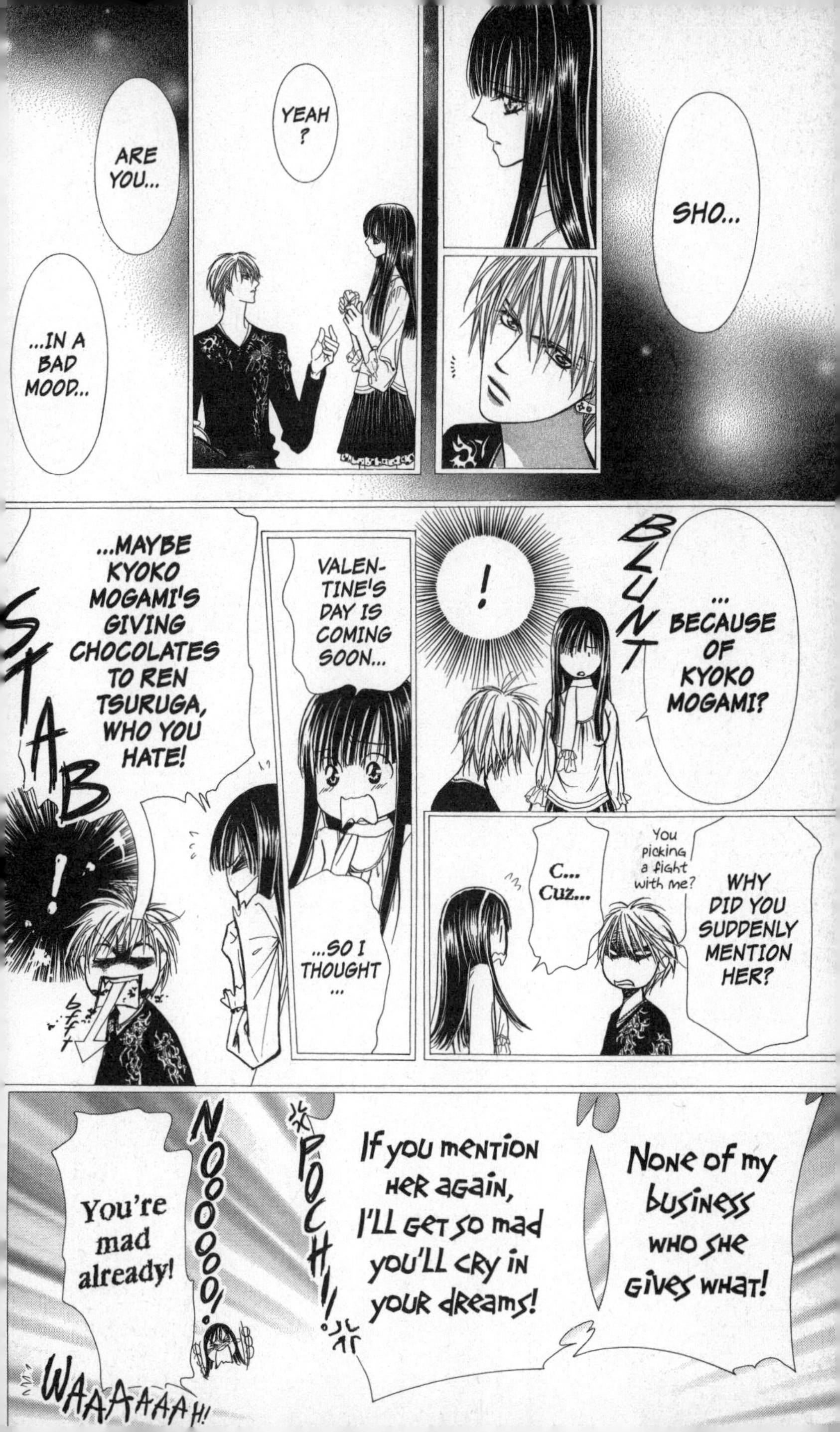
SHO...
YEAH?
ARE YOU...
...IN A BAD MOOD...
BLUNT
...BECAUSE OF KYOKO MOGAMI?
!
WHY DID YOU SUDDENLY MENTION HER?
You picking a fight with me?
C... Cuz...
VALEN-TINE'S DAY IS COMING SOON...
...SO I THOUGHT...
...MAYBE KYOKO MOGAMI'S GIVING CHOCOLATES TO REN TSURUGA, WHO YOU HATE!
STAB
!
None of my business who she gives what!
If you mention her again, I'LL get so mad you'LL cry in your dreams!
POCHI!!
NOOOOOO!
You're mad already!
WAAAAAAH!

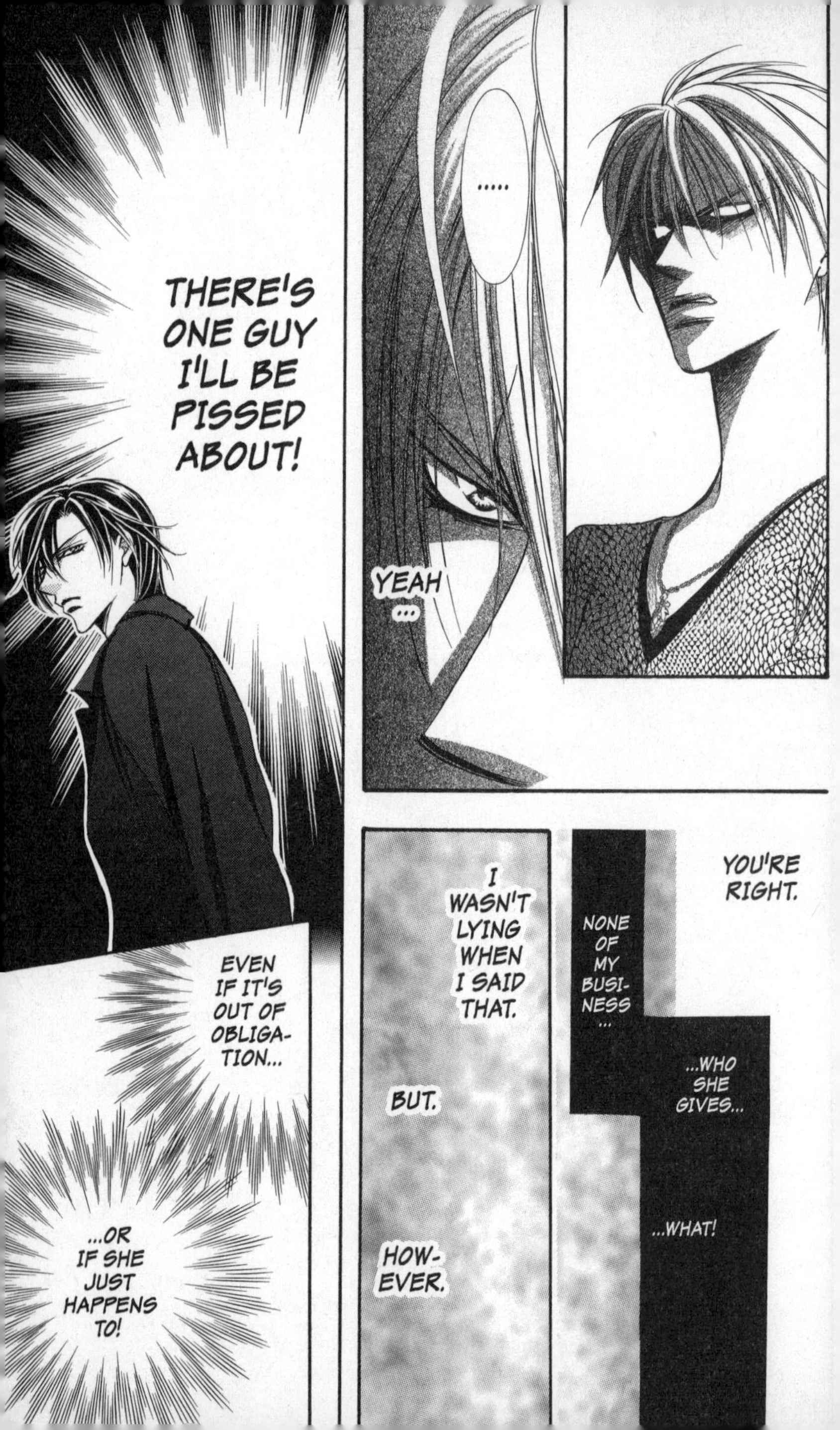
.....
YEAH...
YOU'RE RIGHT.
NONE OF MY BUSINESS...
...WHO SHE GIVES...
...WHAT!
I WASN'T LYING WHEN I SAID THAT.
BUT.
HOWEVER.
THERE'S ONE GUY I'LL BE PISSED ABOUT!
EVEN IF IT'S OUT OF OBLIGATION...
...OR IF SHE JUST HAPPENS TO!

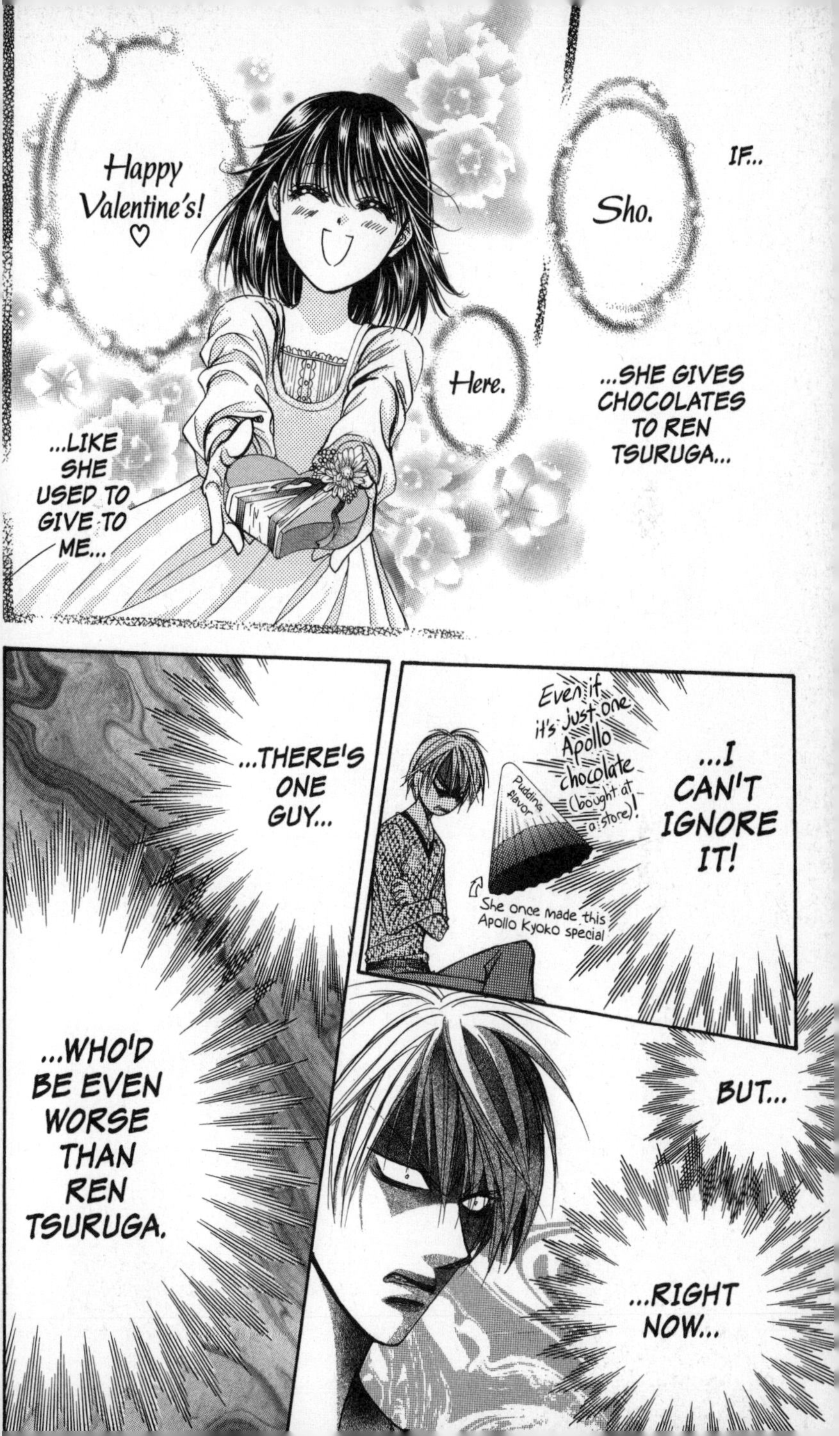
IF...
Sho.
...SHE GIVES CHOCOLATES TO REN TSURUGA...
Here.
Happy Valentine's! ♡
...LIKE SHE USED TO GIVE TO ME...
...I CAN'T IGNORE IT!
Even if it's just one Apollo chocolate (bought at a store)!
Pudding flavor
She once made this Apollo Kyoko special
BUT...
...RIGHT NOW...
...THERE'S ONE GUY...
...WHO'D BE EVEN WORSE THAN REN TSURUGA.

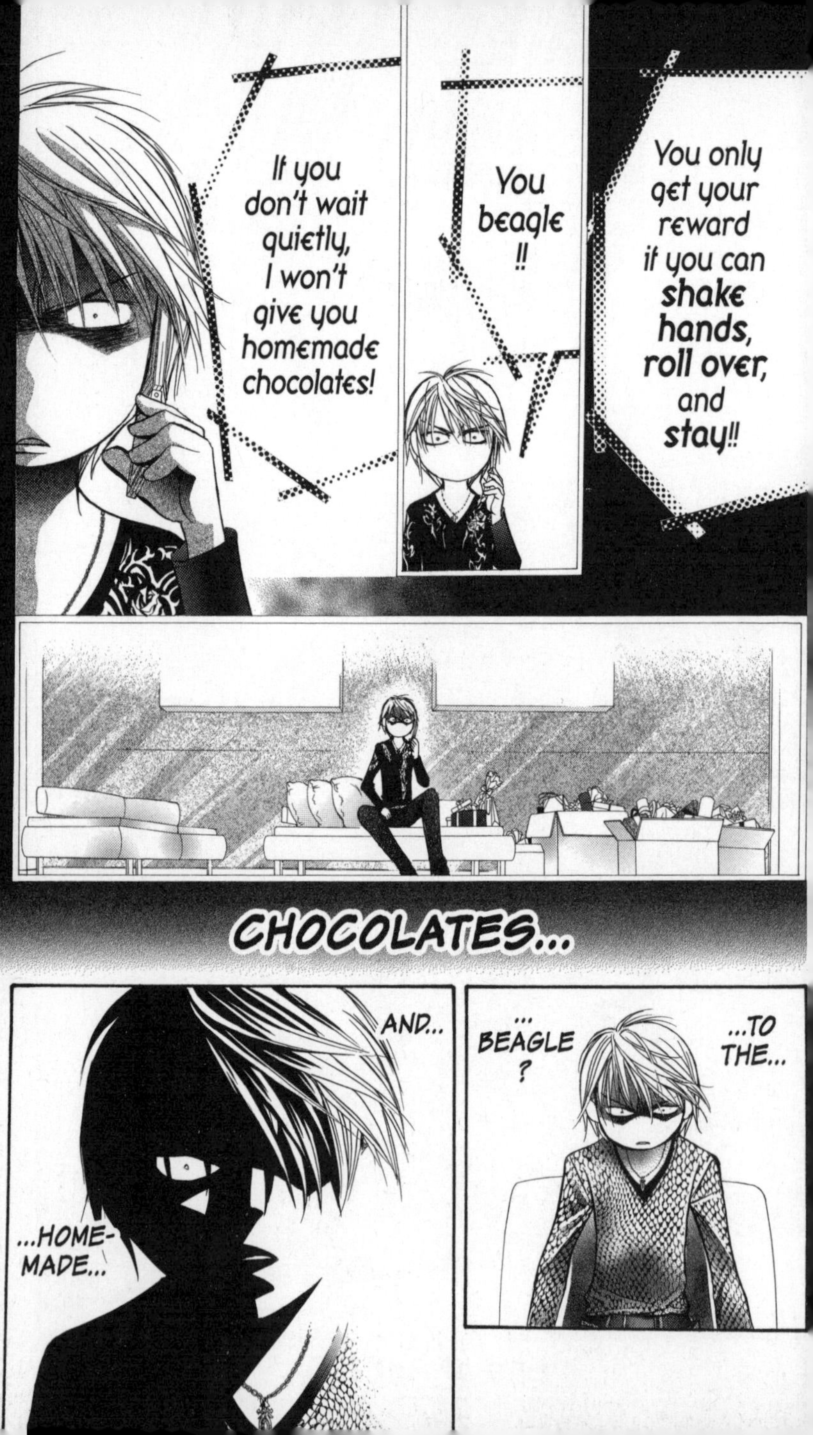
You only get your reward if you can shake hands, roll over, and stay!!
You beagle!!
If you don't wait quietly, I won't give you homemade chocolates!
CHOCOLATES...
...TO THE...
...BEAGLE?
AND...
...HOME-MADE...

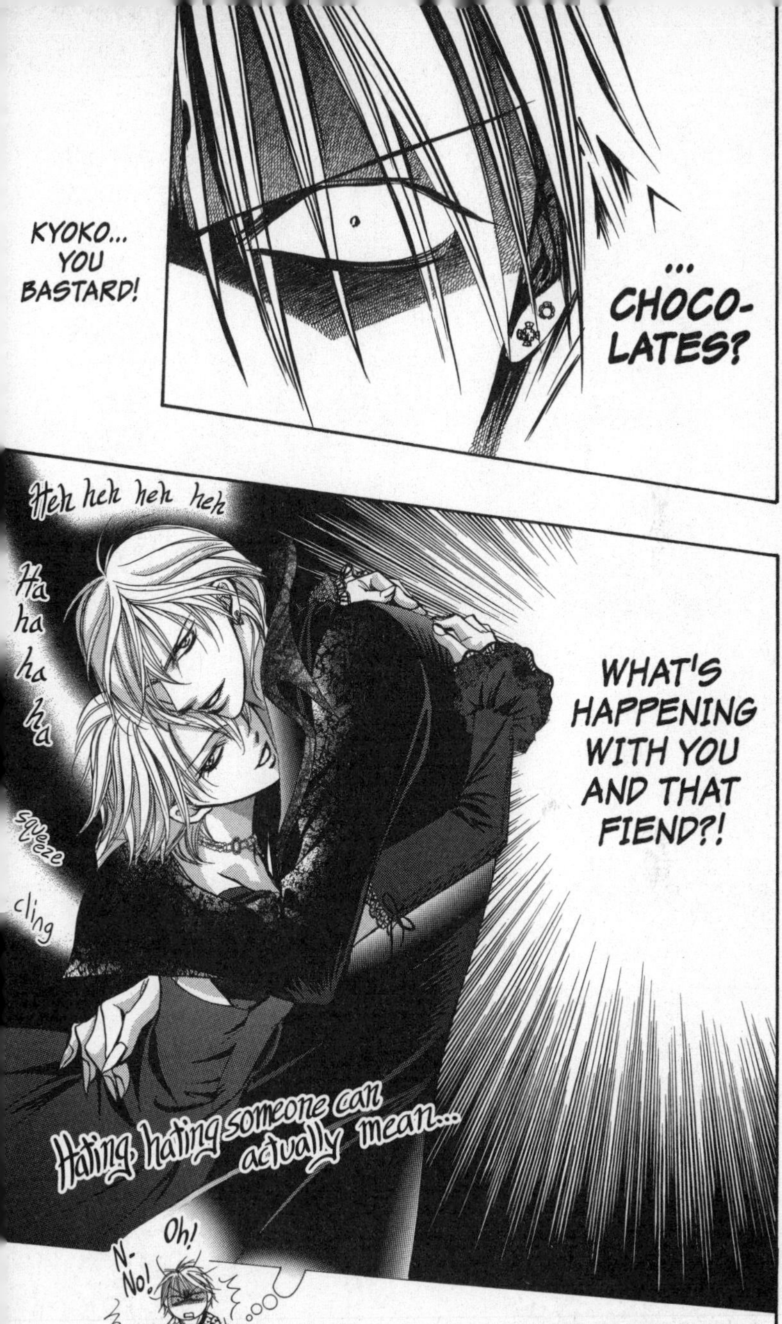
...CHOCOLATES?
KYOKO... YOU BASTARD!
WHAT'S HAPPENING WITH YOU AND THAT FIEND?!
Heh heh heh heh
Ha ha ha ha
squeeze
cling
Hating, hating someone can actually mean...
Oh!
N-No!

End of Act 140

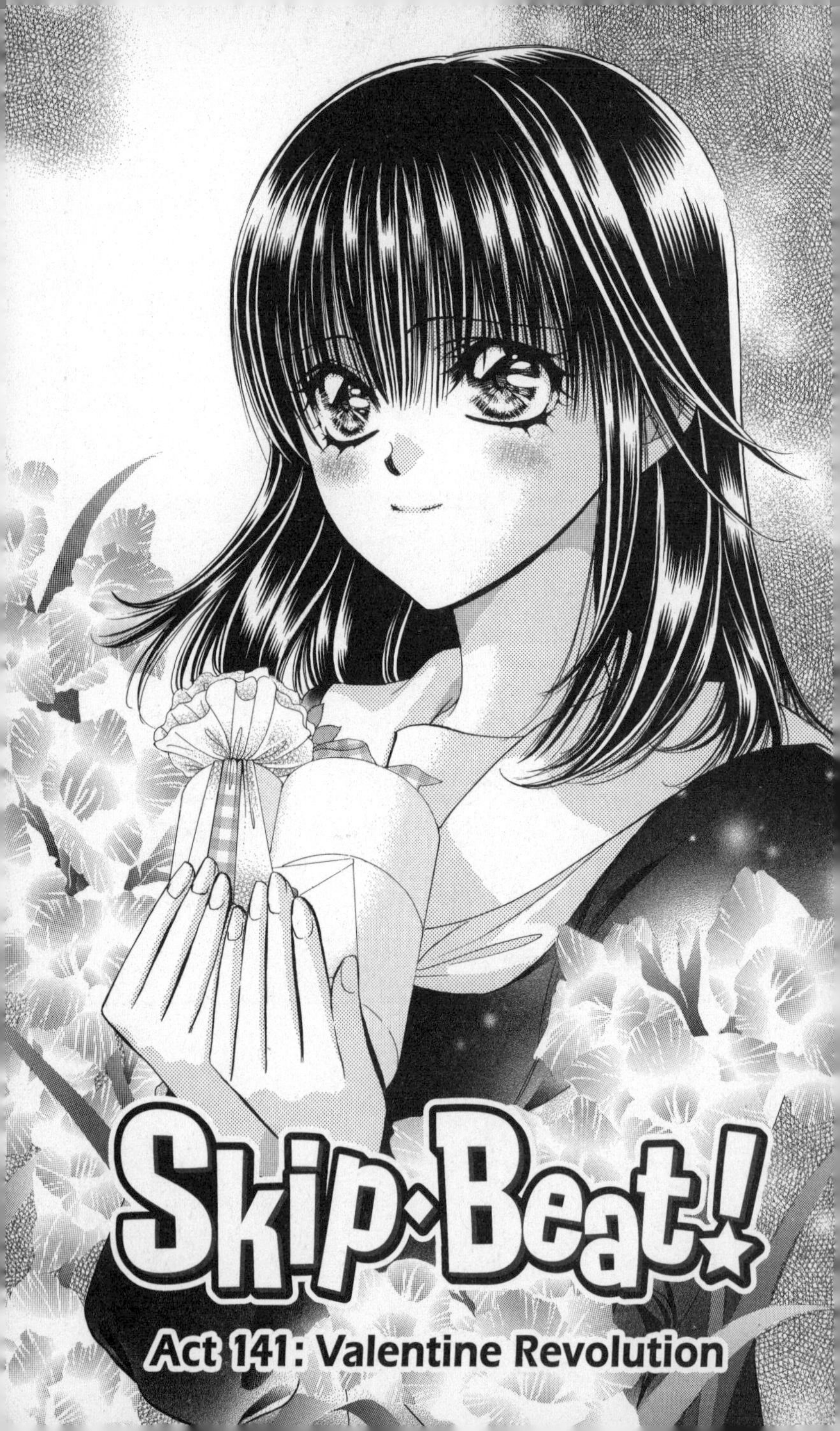
Skip·Beat!
Act 141: Valentine Revolution

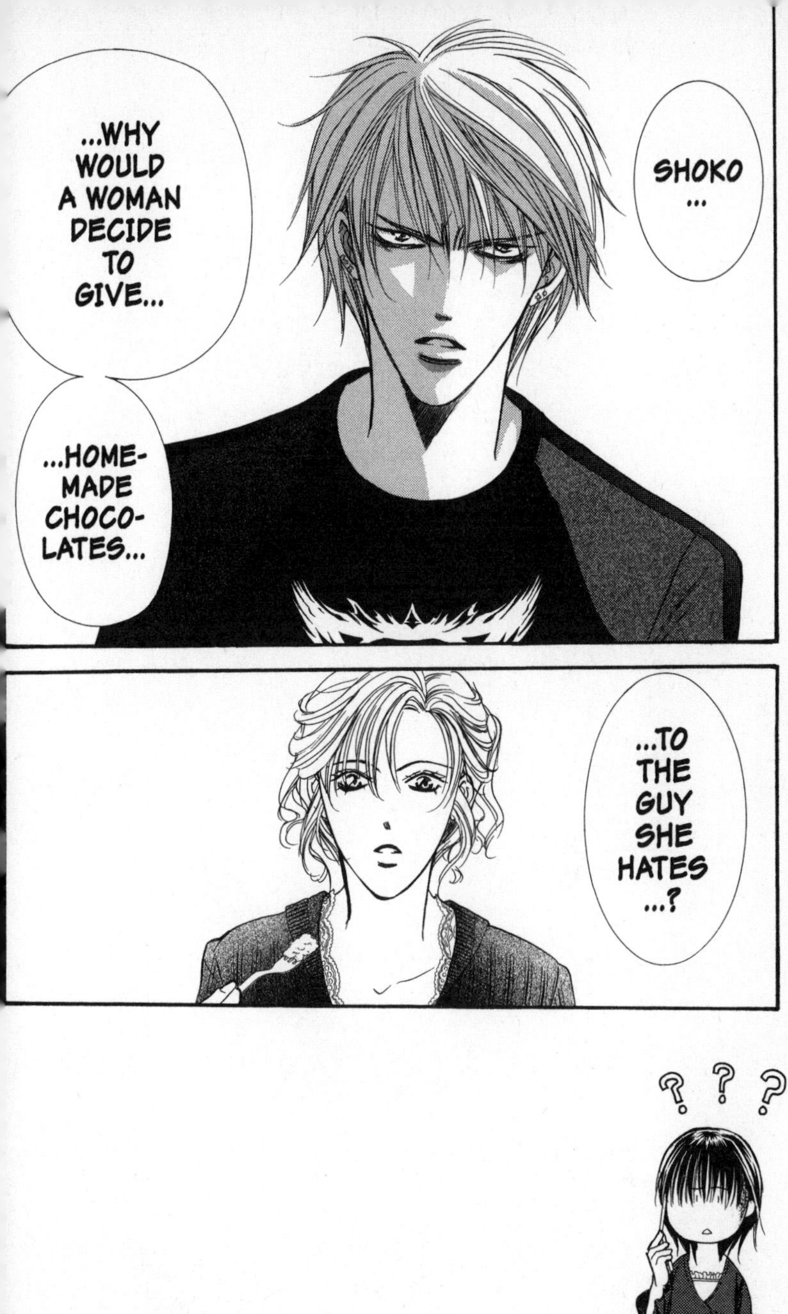
SHOKO ...
...WHY WOULD A WOMAN DECIDE TO GIVE...
...HOME-MADE CHOCO-LATES...
...TO THE GUY SHE HATES ...?
? ? ?

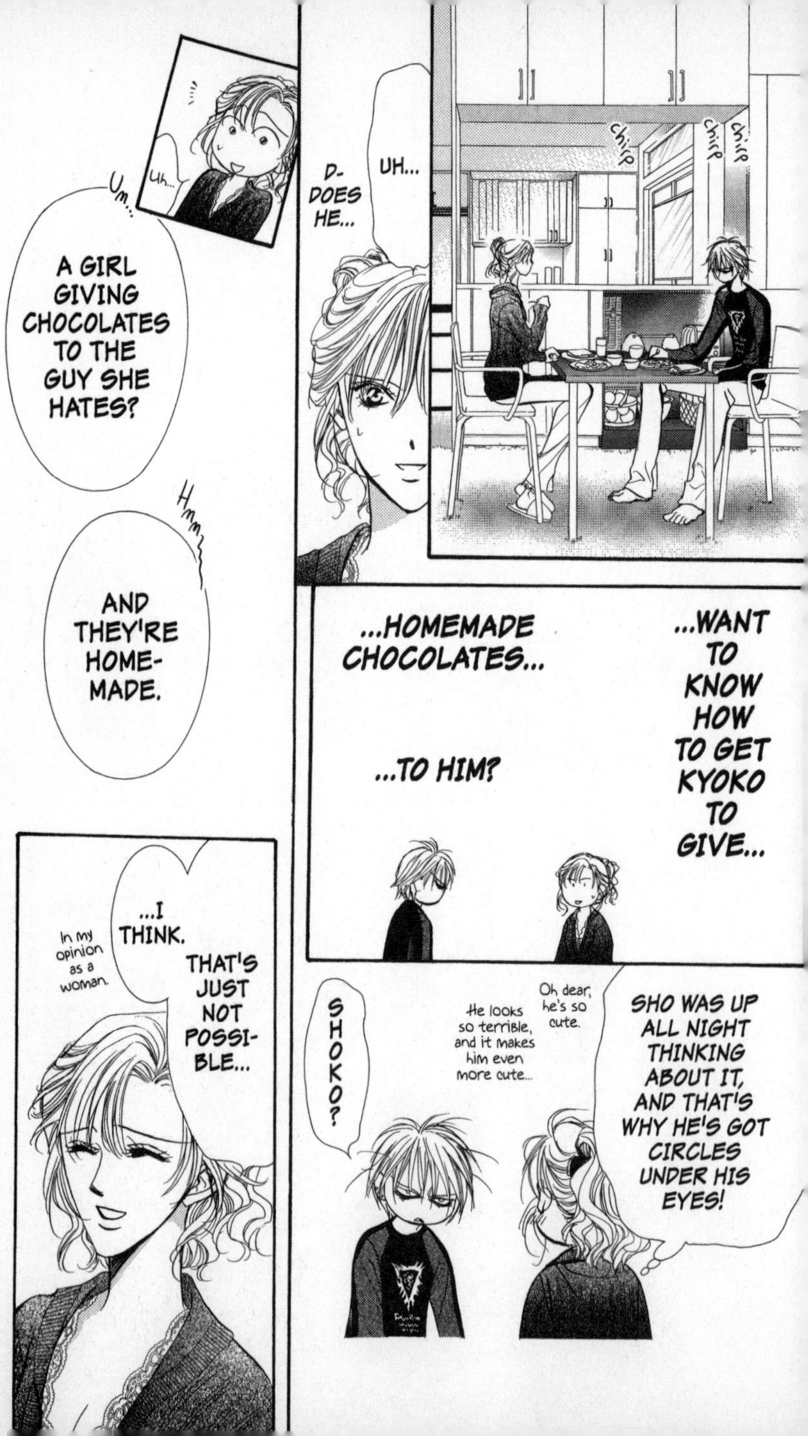
chirp
chirp
chirp
UH...
D-DOES HE...
...WANT TO KNOW HOW TO GET KYOKO TO GIVE...
...HOMEMADE CHOCOLATES...
...TO HIM?
SHO WAS UP ALL NIGHT THINKING ABOUT IT, AND THAT'S WHY HE'S GOT CIRCLES UNDER HIS EYES!
Oh dear, he's so cute.
He looks so terrible, and it makes him even more cute...
SHOKO?
Uh...
Um...
A GIRL GIVING CHOCOLATES TO THE GUY SHE HATES?
Hmm
AND THEY'RE HOME-MADE.
THAT'S JUST NOT POSSI-BLE...
...I THINK.
In my opinion as a woman.

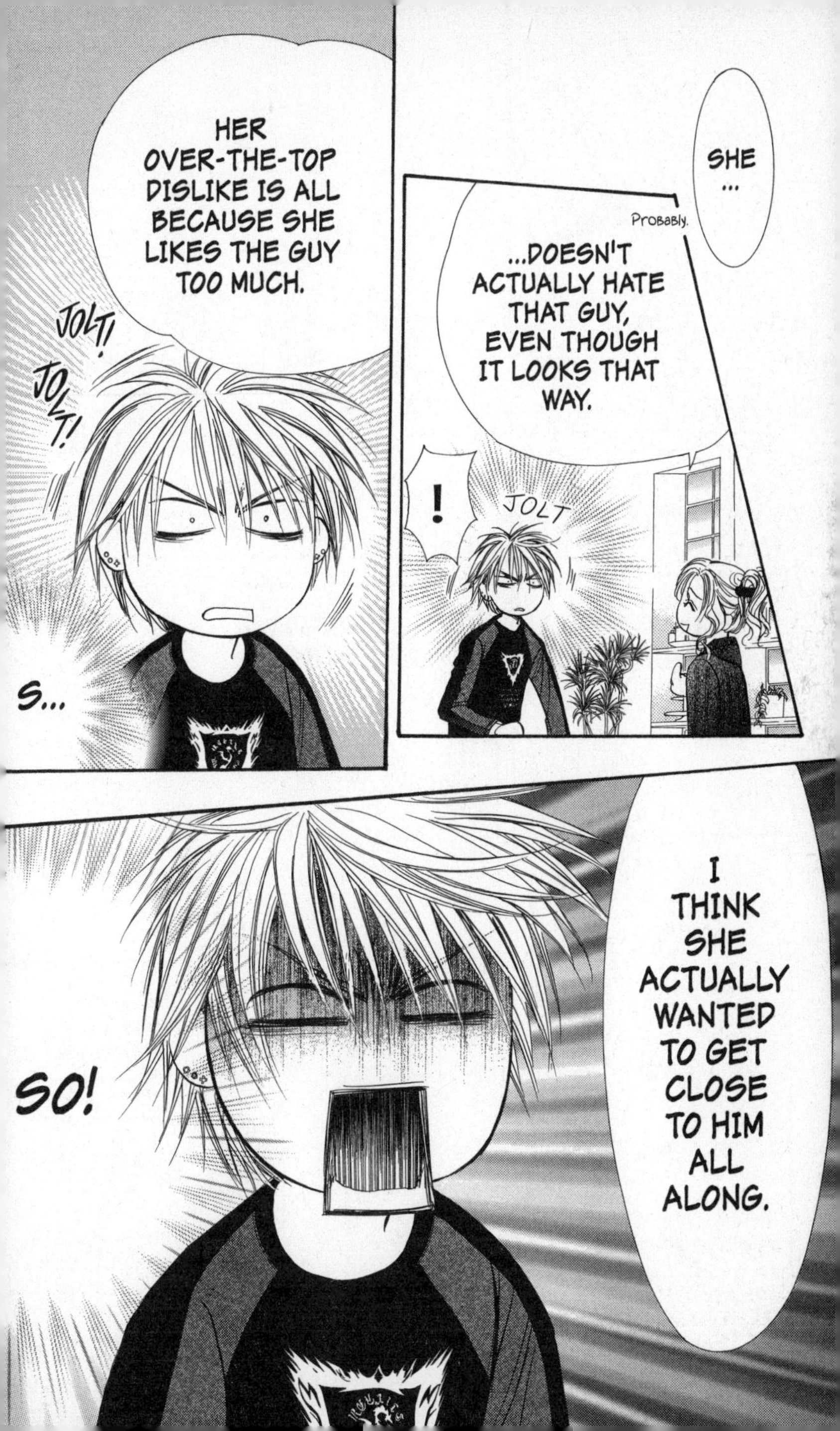
SHE ...
Probably.
...DOESN'T ACTUALLY HATE THAT GUY, EVEN THOUGH IT LOOKS THAT WAY.
!
JOLT
HER OVER-THE-TOP DISLIKE IS ALL BECAUSE SHE LIKES THE GUY TOO MUCH.
JOLT!
JOLT!
S...
I THINK SHE ACTUALLY WANTED TO GET CLOSE TO HIM ALL ALONG.
SO!

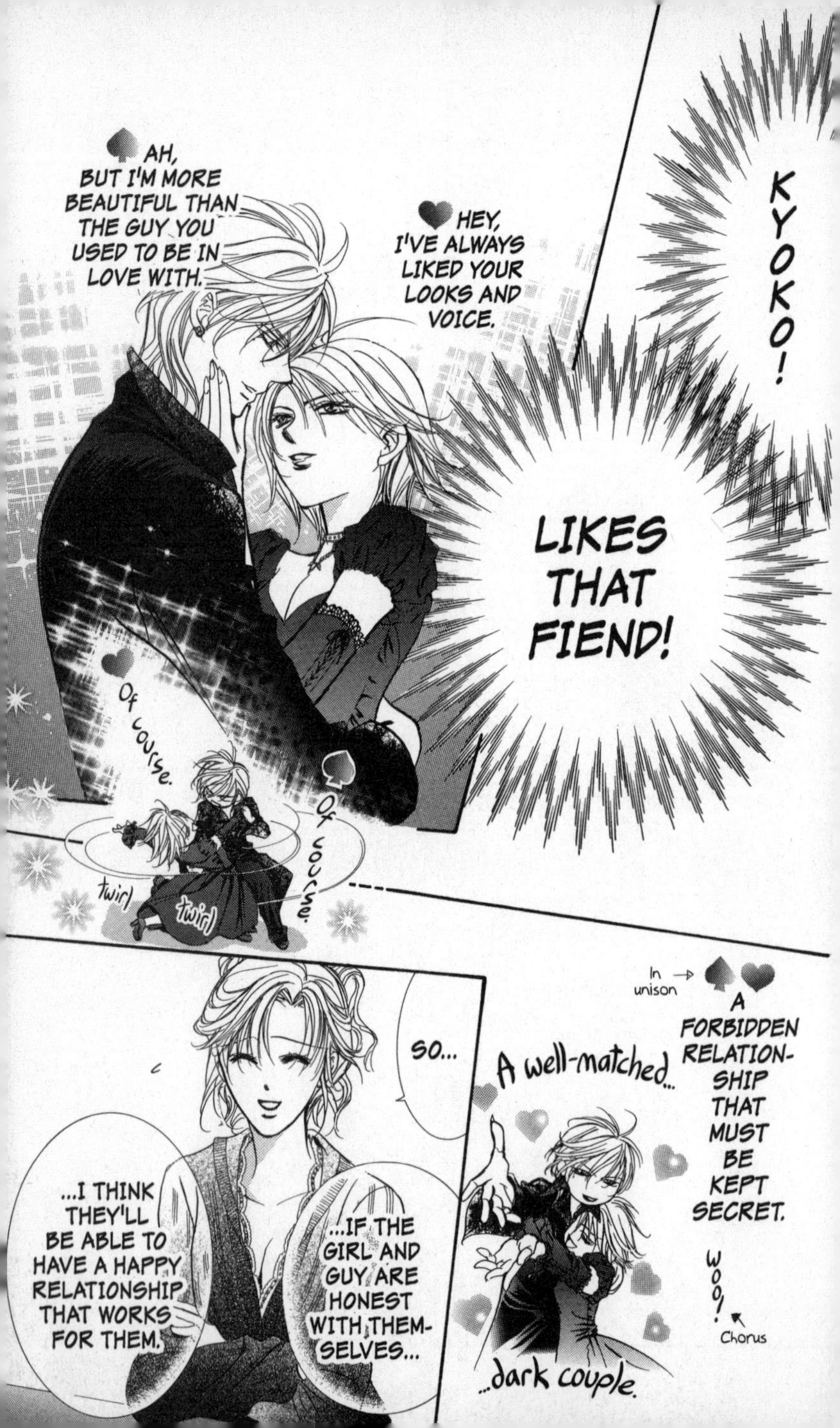
KYOKO!
LIKES THAT FIEND!
HEY, I'VE ALWAYS LIKED YOUR LOOKS AND VOICE.
AH, BUT I'M MORE BEAUTIFUL THAN THE GUY YOU USED TO BE IN LOVE WITH.
Of course.
Of course.
twirl
twirl
In unison
A FORBIDDEN RELATION-SHIP THAT MUST BE KEPT SECRET.
A well-matched...
...dark couple.
WOO!
Chorus
SO...
...IF THE GIRL AND GUY ARE HONEST WITH THEM-SELVES...
...I THINK THEY'LL BE ABLE TO HAVE A HAPPY RELATIONSHIP THAT WORKS FOR THEM.

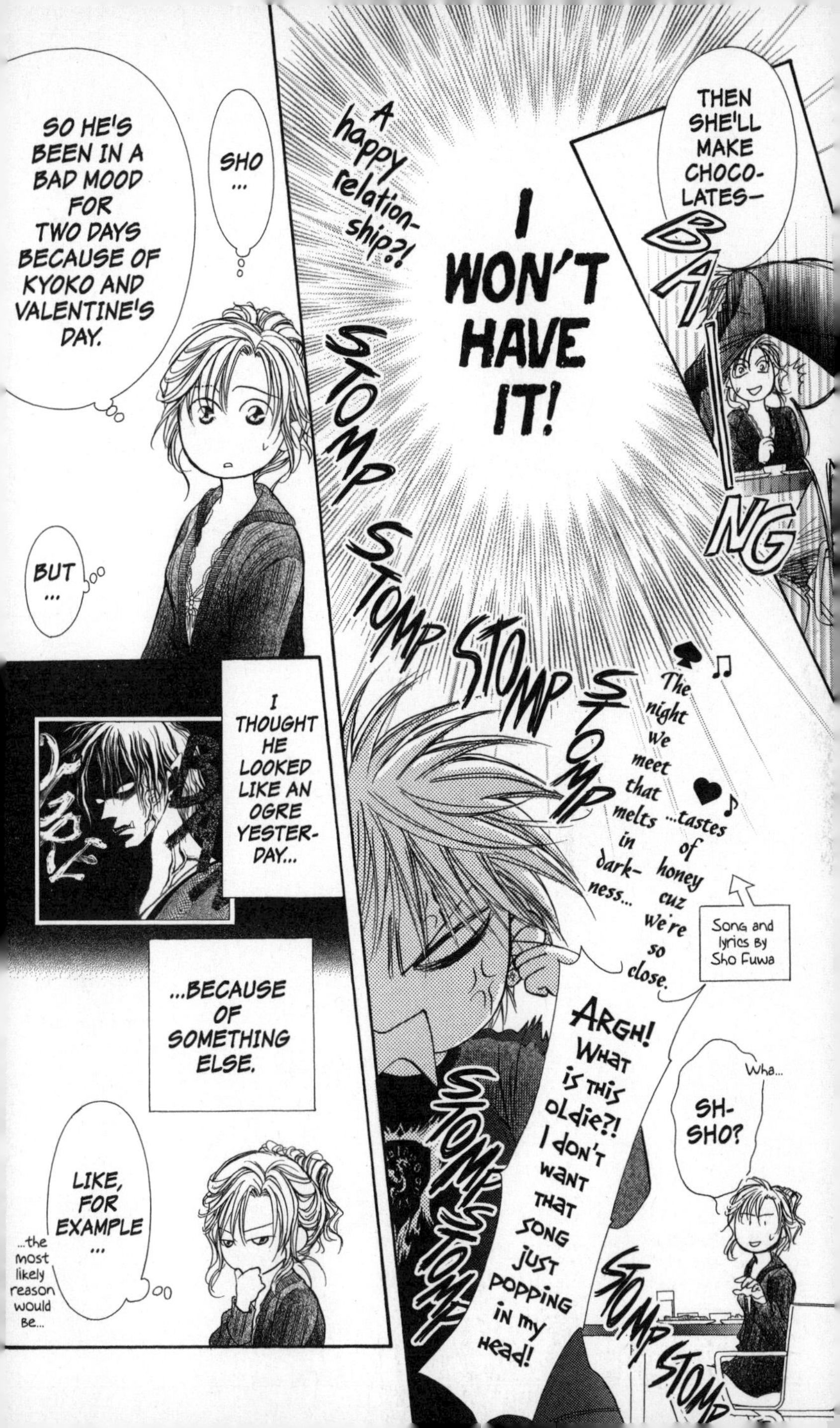
THEN SHE'LL MAKE CHOCO-LATES—
BANG
I WON'T HAVE IT!
A happy relation-ship?!
STOMP STOMP STOMP STOMP
The night we meet that melts in darkness...
...tastes of honey cuz we're so close.
Song and lyrics by Sho Fuwa
Wha...
SH-SHO?
ARGH! WHAT IS THIS OLDIE?! I DON'T WANT THAT SONG JUST POPPING IN MY HEAD!
STOMP STOMP STOMP STOMP
SHO...
SO HE'S BEEN IN A BAD MOOD FOR TWO DAYS BECAUSE OF KYOKO AND VALENTINE'S DAY.
BUT...
I THOUGHT HE LOOKED LIKE AN OGRE YESTER-DAY...
...BECAUSE OF SOMETHING ELSE.
LIKE, FOR EXAMPLE...
...the most likely reason would be...

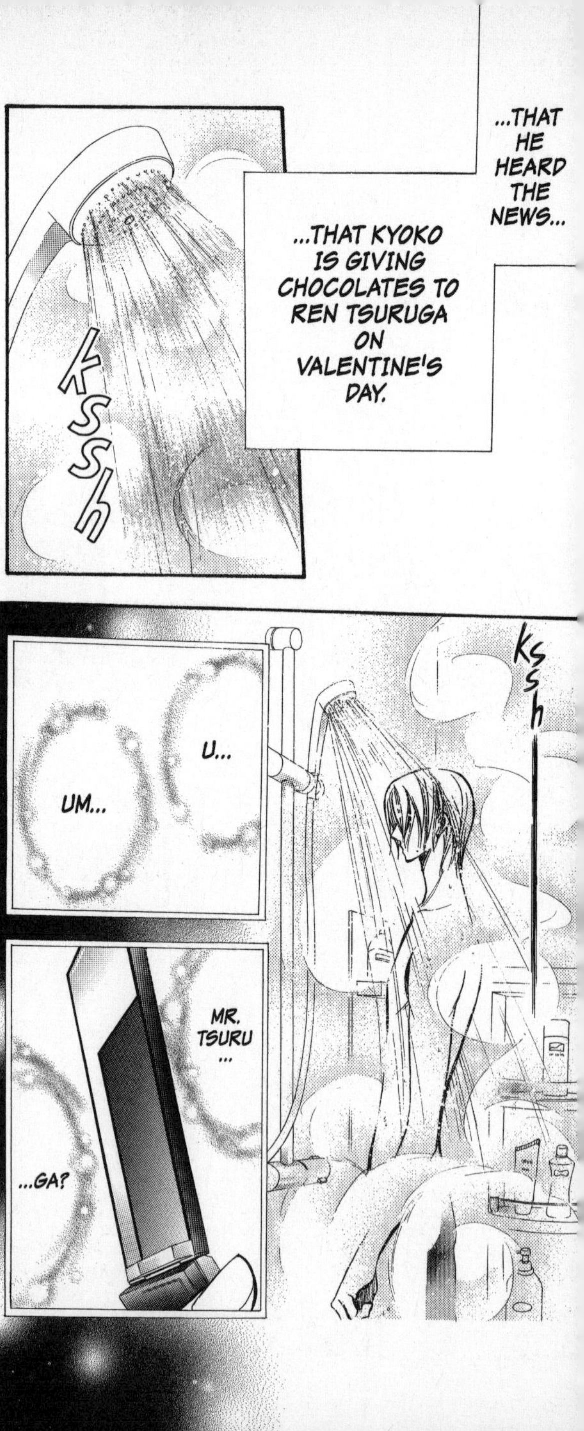
...THAT HE HEARD THE NEWS...
...THAT KYOKO IS GIVING CHOCOLATES TO REN TSURUGA ON VALENTINE'S DAY.
kssh
Kssh
U...
UM...
MR. TSURU...
...GA?
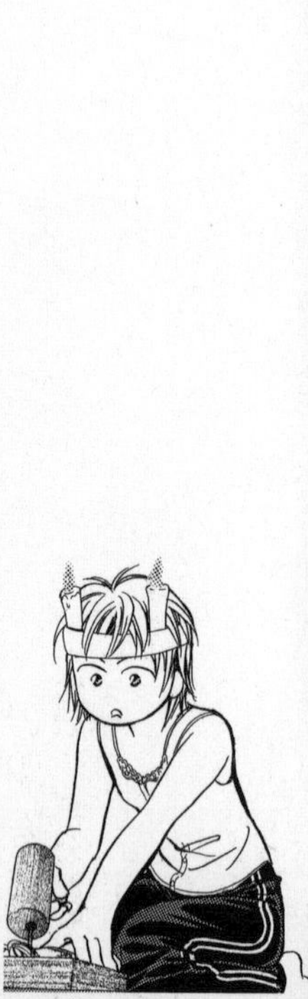

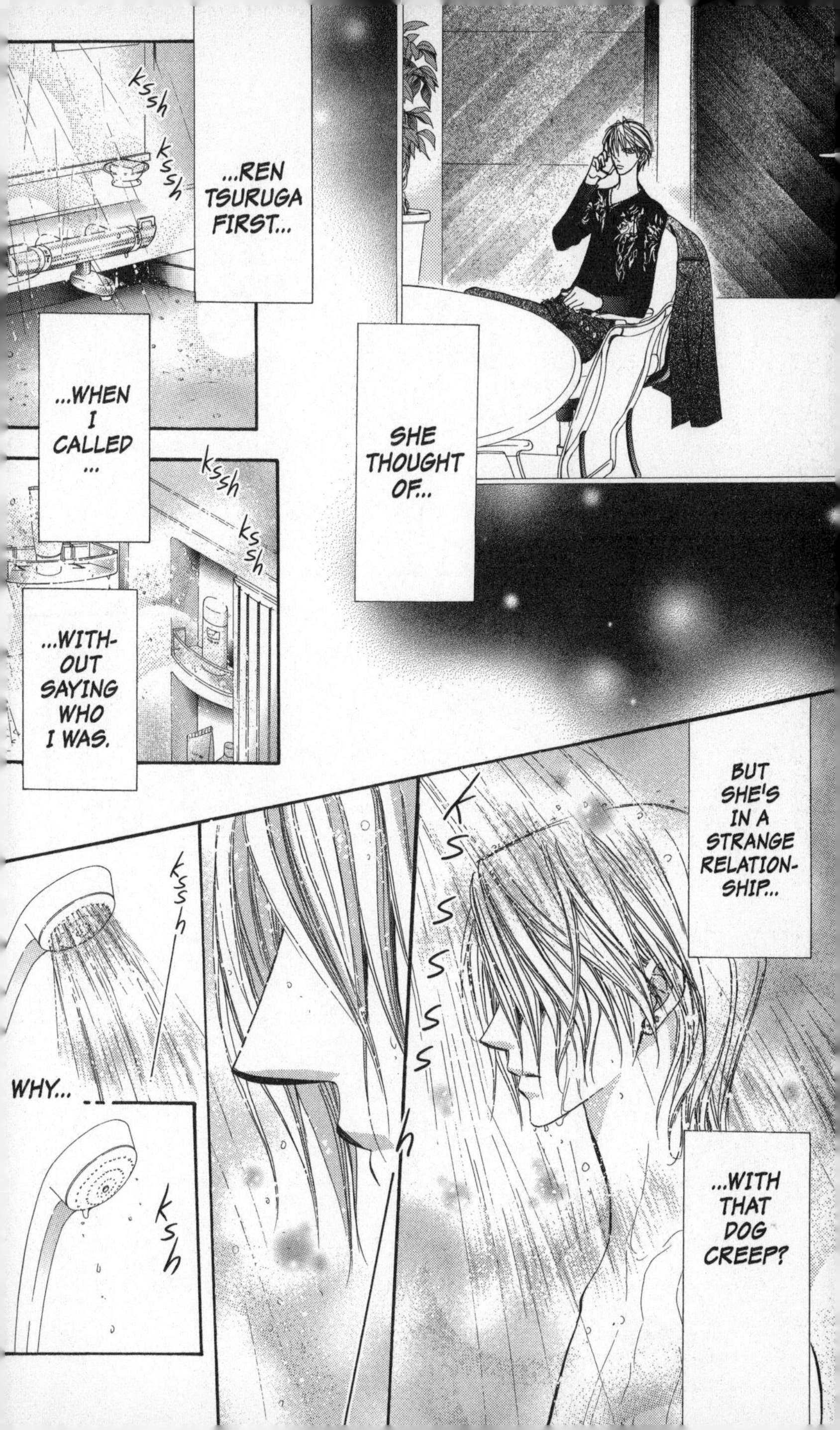
SHE THOUGHT OF...
kssh
kssh
...REN TSURUGA FIRST...
...WHEN I CALLED...
kssh
kssh
...WITHOUT SAYING WHO I WAS.
BUT SHE'S IN A STRANGE RELATIONSHIP...
...WITH THAT DOG CREEP?
ksssssh
kssh
WHY...
ksh

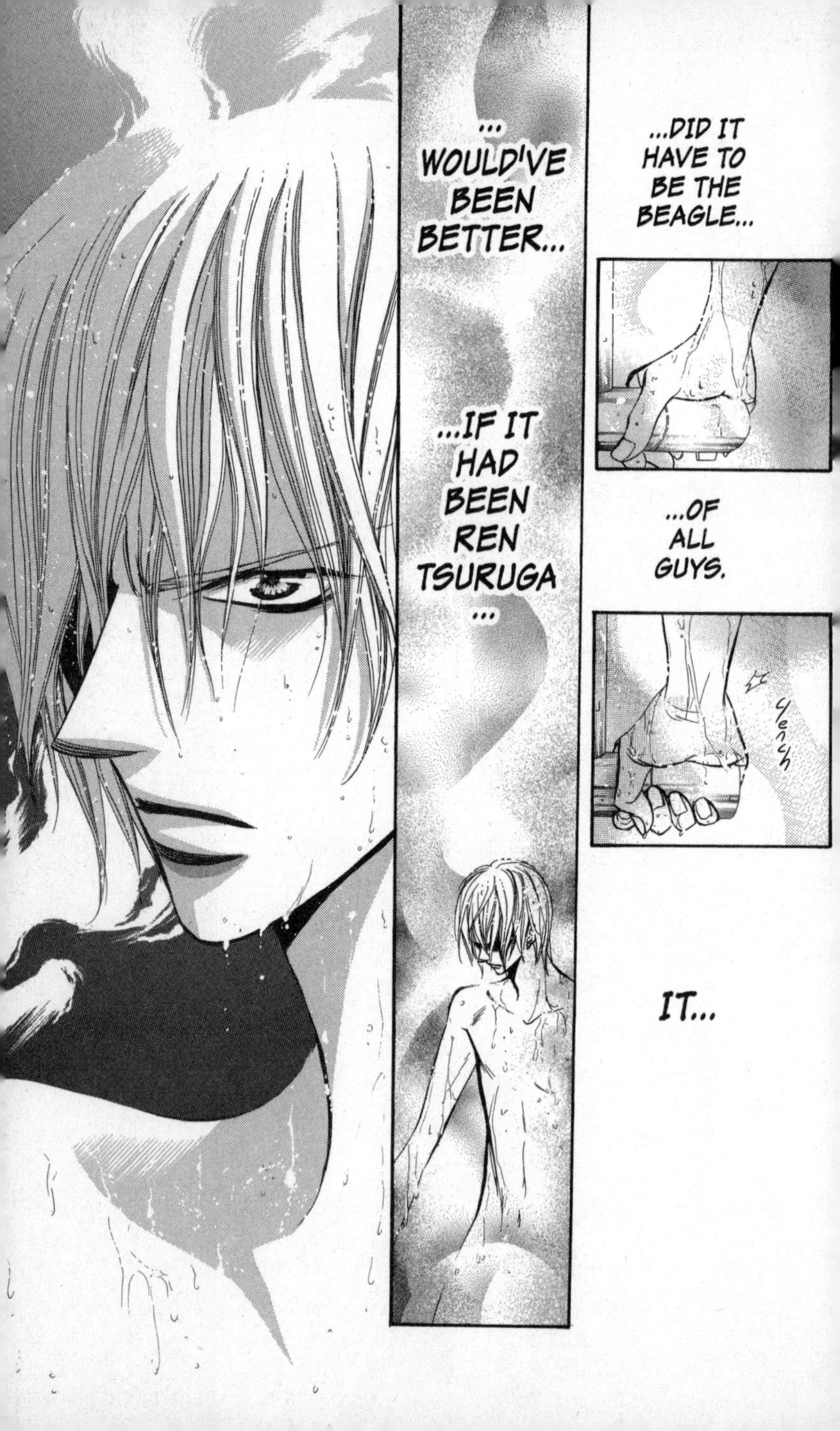

...DID IT HAVE TO BE THE BEAGLE...
...OF ALL GUYS.
clench
IT...
... WOULD'VE BEEN BETTER...
...IF IT HAD BEEN REN TSURUGA ...

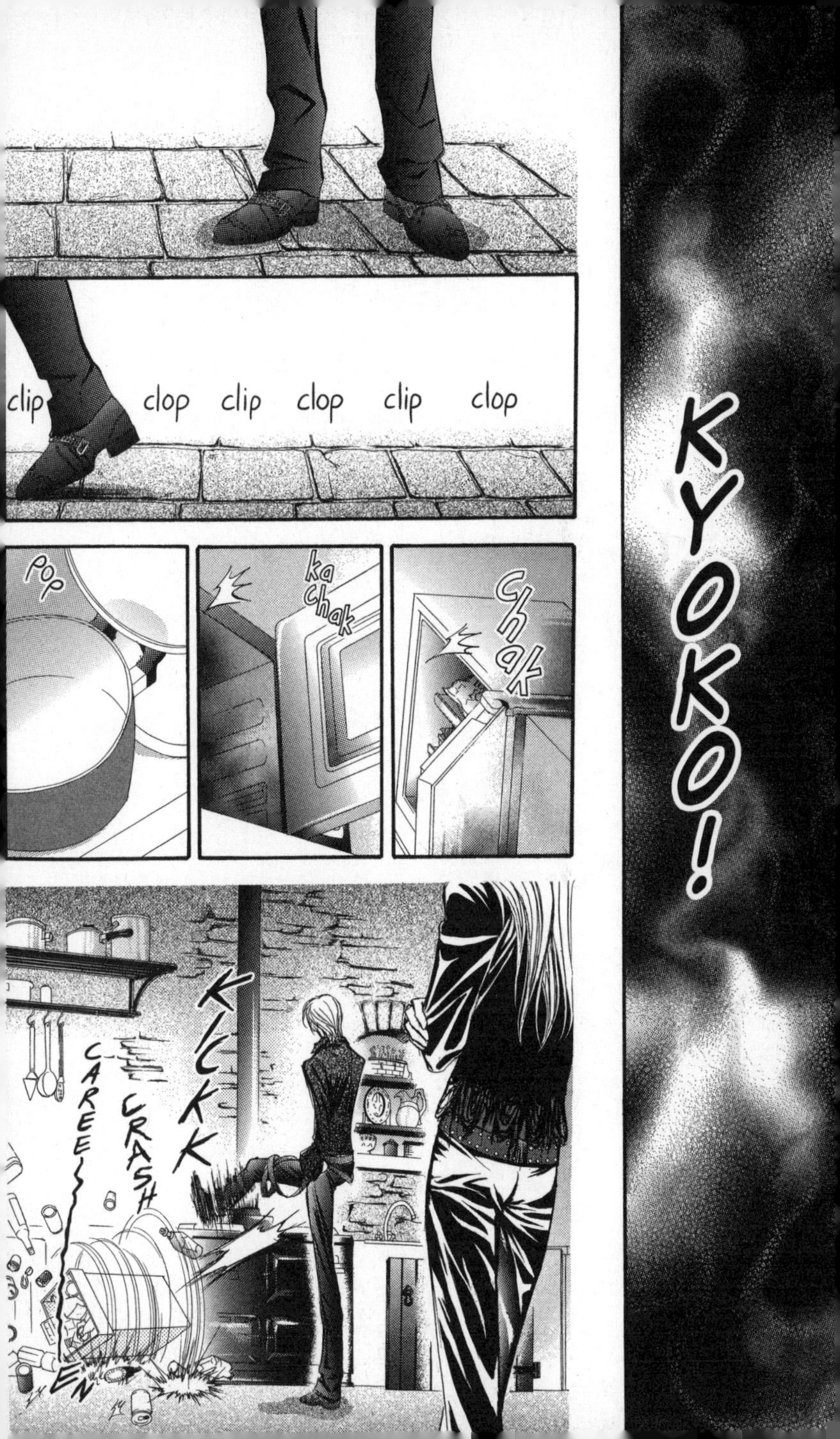
KYOKO!
clip clop clip clop clip clop
chak
ka chak
pop
KICKK
CRASH
CAREEEN

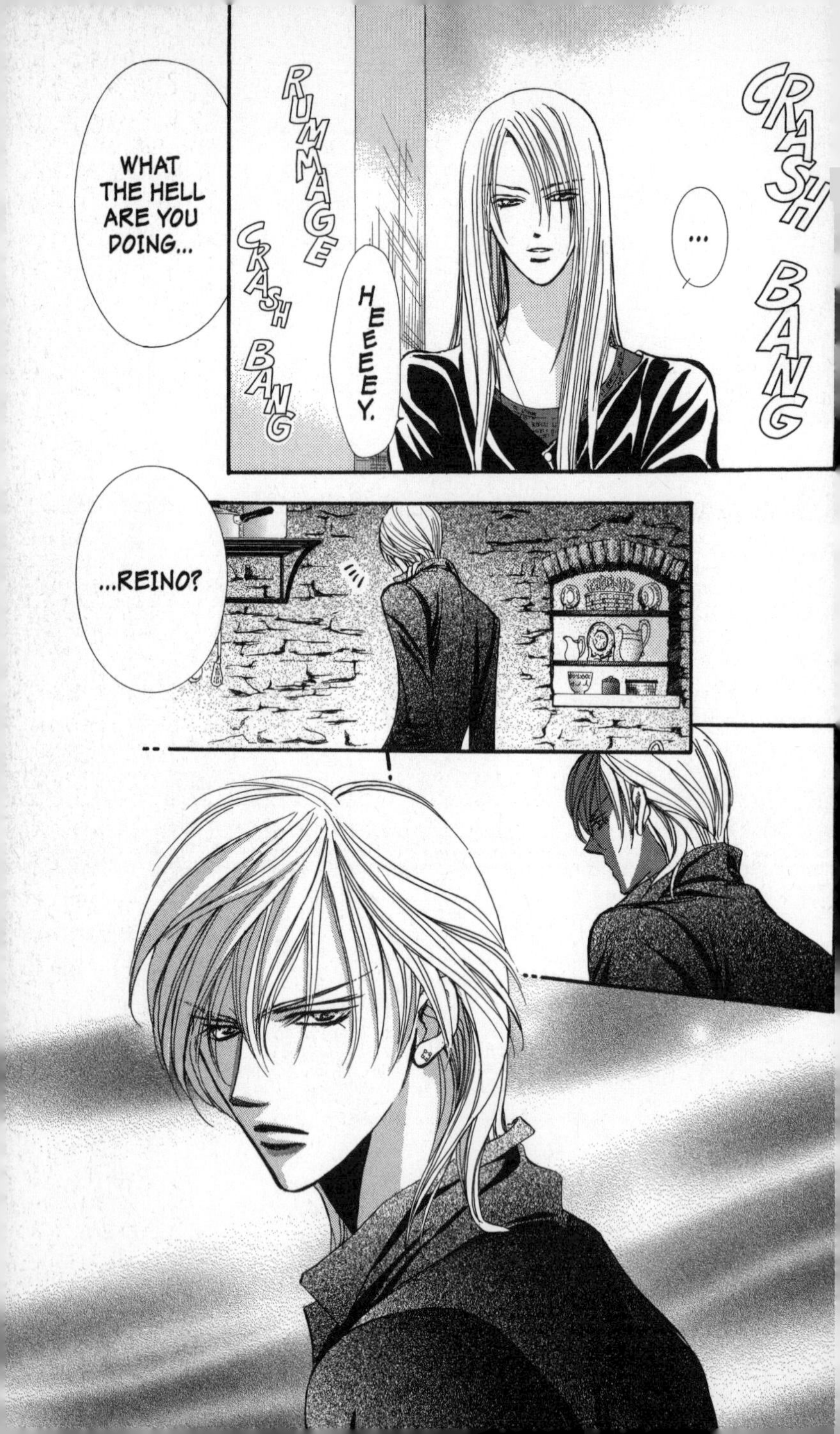
CRASH BANG
...
HEEEEY.
RUMMAGE
CRASH BANG
WHAT THE HELL ARE YOU DOING...
...REINO?

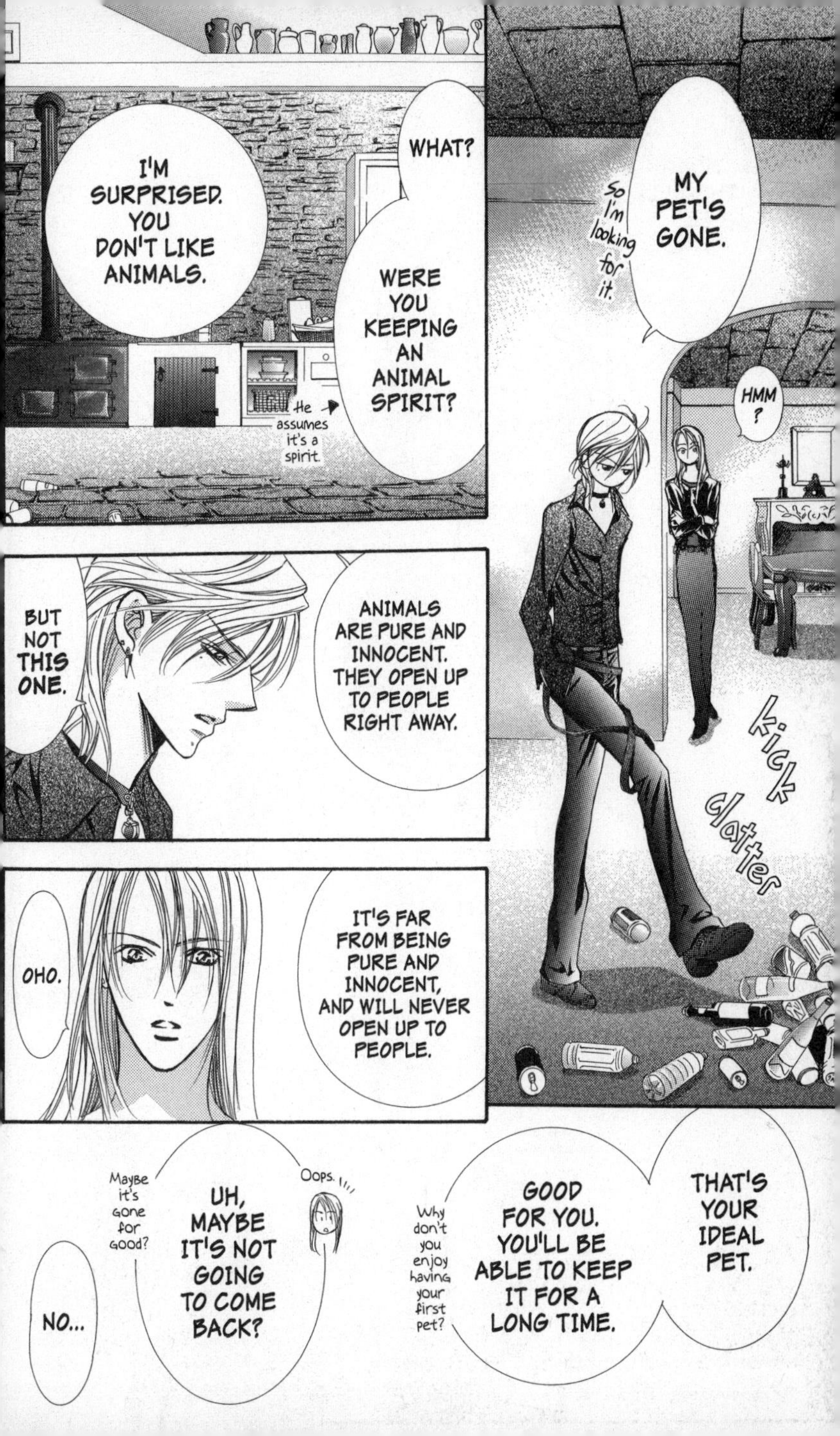

MY PET'S GONE.
So I'm looking for it.
HMM?
kick
clatter
WHAT?
WERE YOU KEEPING AN ANIMAL SPIRIT?
He assumes it's a spirit.
I'M SURPRISED. YOU DON'T LIKE ANIMALS.
ANIMALS ARE PURE AND INNOCENT. THEY OPEN UP TO PEOPLE RIGHT AWAY.
BUT NOT THIS ONE.
IT'S FAR FROM BEING PURE AND INNOCENT, AND WILL NEVER OPEN UP TO PEOPLE.
OHO.
THAT'S YOUR IDEAL PET.
GOOD FOR YOU. YOU'LL BE ABLE TO KEEP IT FOR A LONG TIME.
Why don't you enjoy having your first pet?
Oops.
UH, MAYBE IT'S NOT GOING TO COME BACK?
Maybe it's gone for good?
NO...

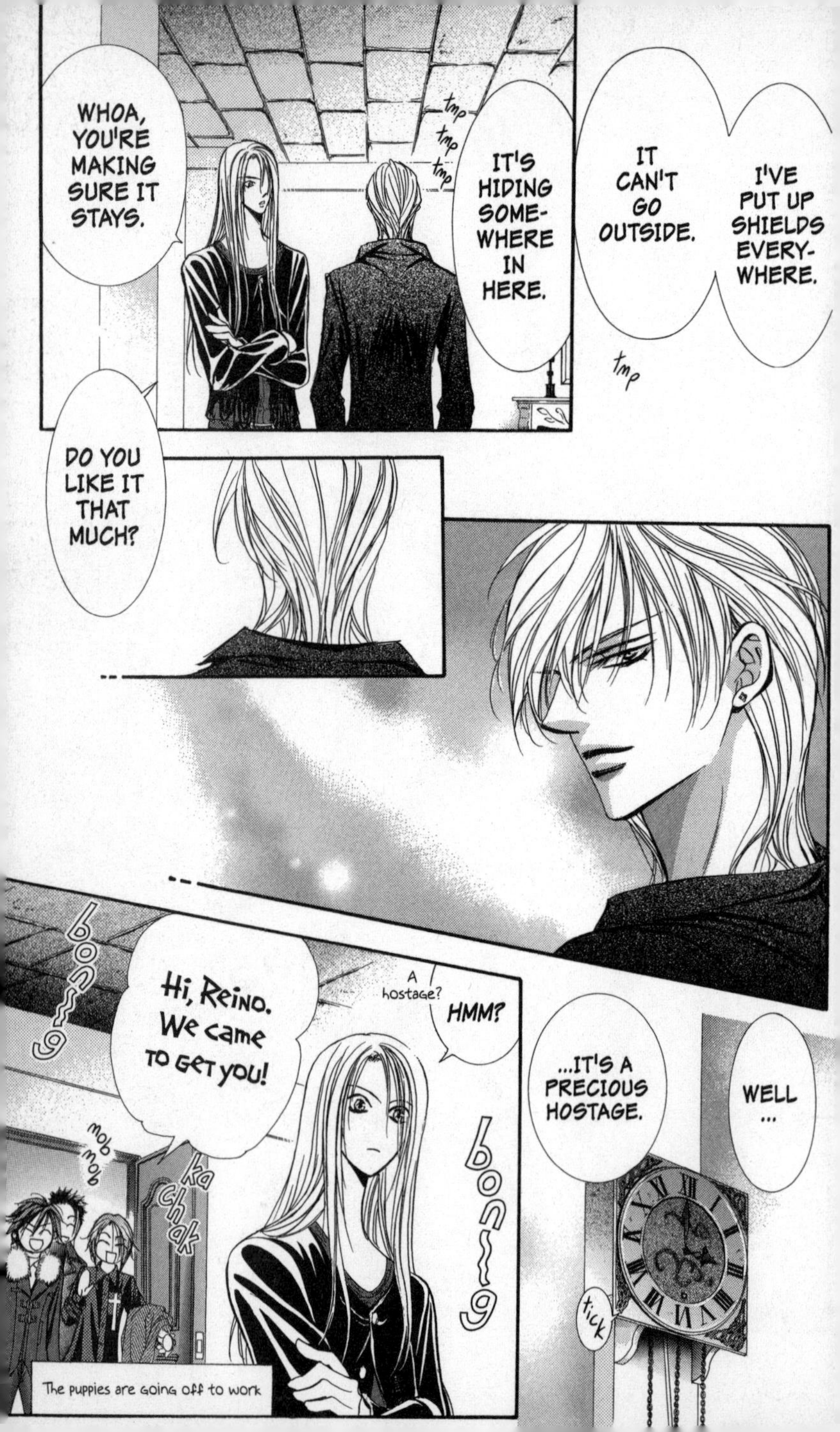
I'VE PUT UP SHIELDS EVERY-WHERE.
IT CAN'T GO OUTSIDE.
tmp
IT'S HIDING SOME-WHERE IN HERE.
tmp tmp tmp
WHOA, YOU'RE MAKING SURE IT STAYS.
DO YOU LIKE IT THAT MUCH?
--
--
WELL ...
...IT'S A PRECIOUS HOSTAGE.
tick
HMM?
A hostage?
bon~g
Hi, Reino. We came to get you!
bon~g
ka chak
mob mob
The puppies are going off to work

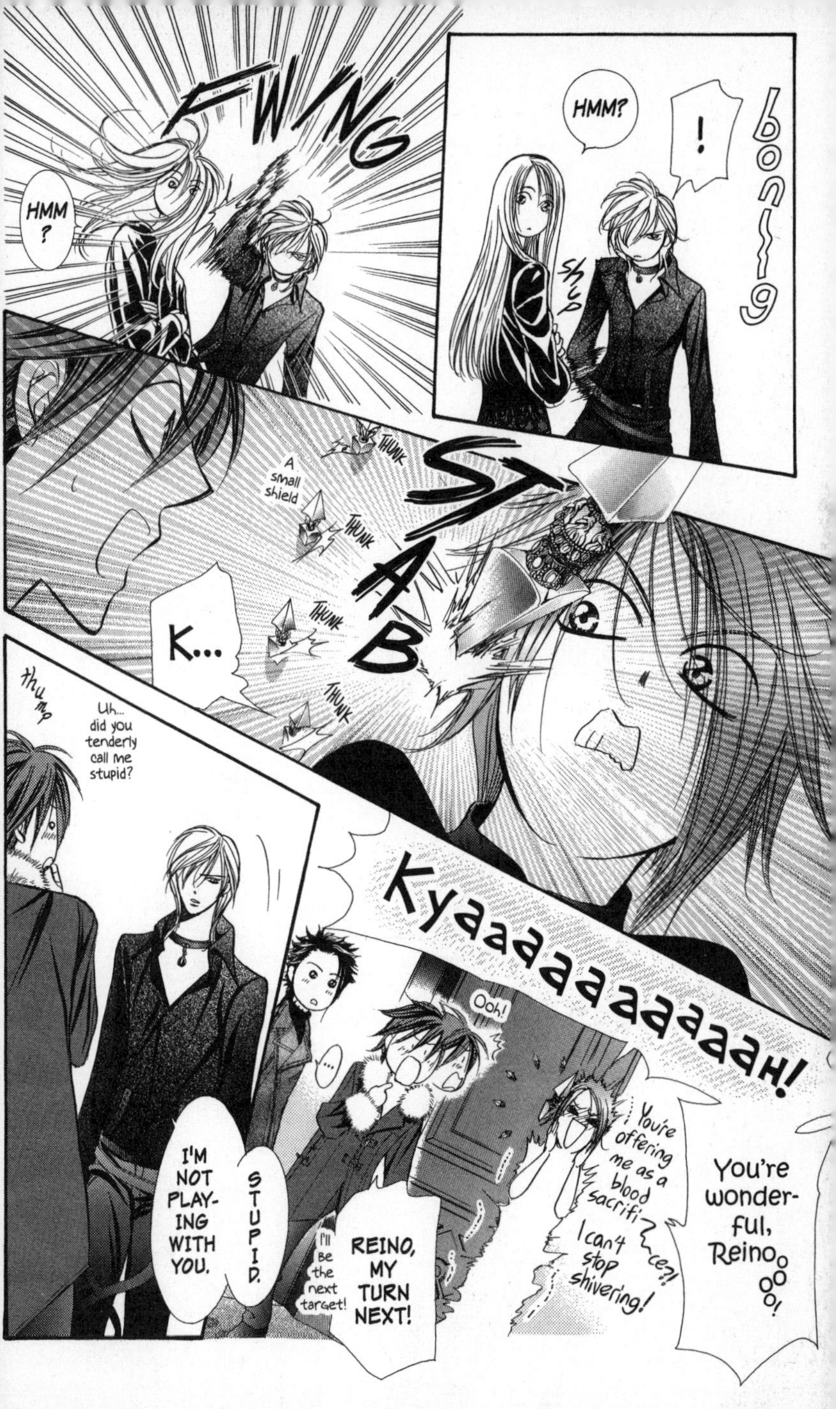
HMM?
!
bong~g
SKRP
FWING
HMM?
STAB
THUNK
A small shield
THUNK
THUNK
THUNK
K...
Kyaaaaaaaaaaaaah!
You're wonderful, Reinooooo!
You're offering me as a blood sacrifice?!
I can't stop shivering!
Ooh!
REINO, MY TURN NEXT!
I'll be the next target!
...
STUPID.
I'M NOT PLAYING WITH YOU.
Uh... did you tenderly call me stupid?
thump

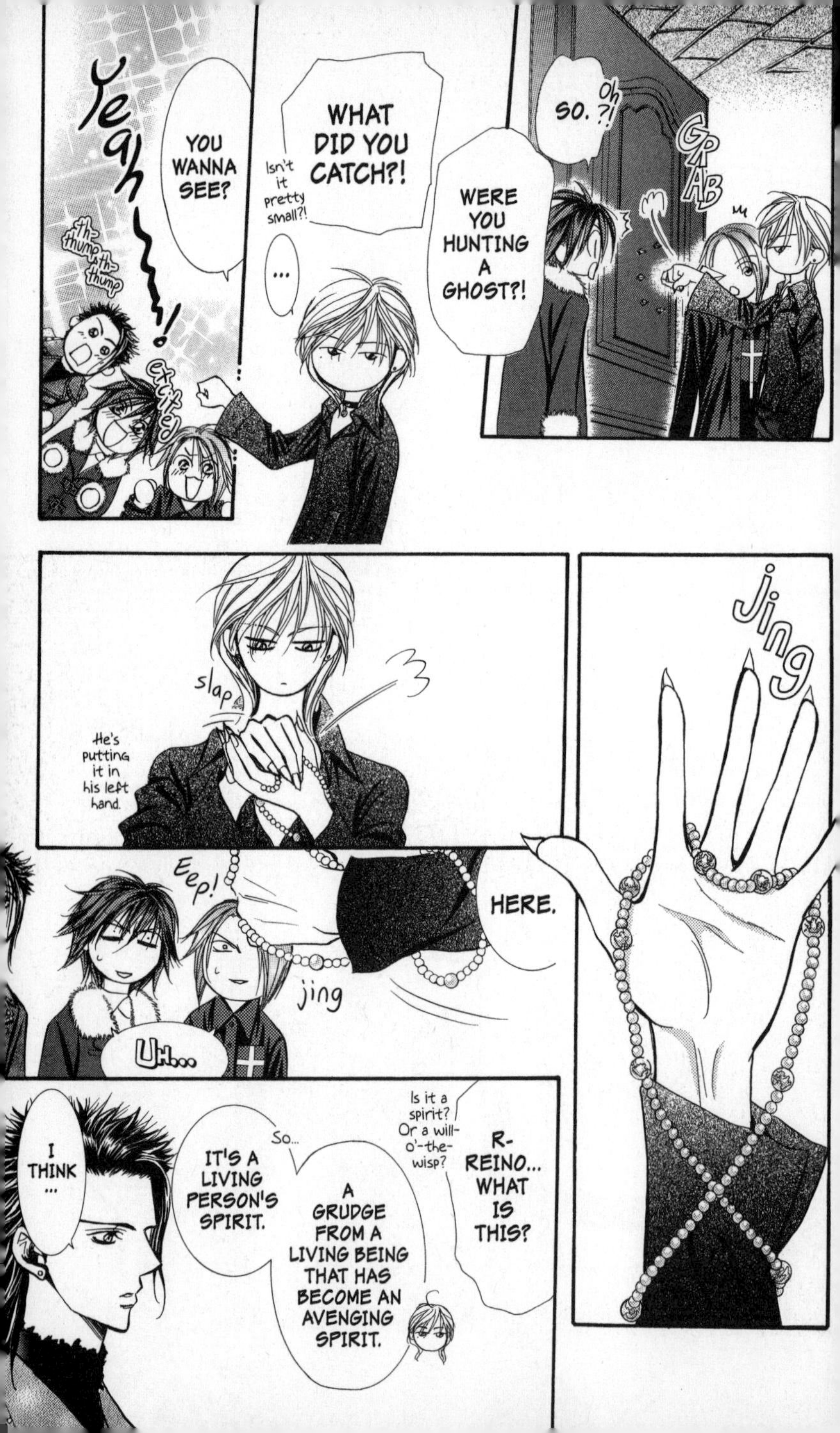
Oh SO. ?!
GRAB
WERE YOU HUNTING A GHOST?!
WHAT DID YOU CATCH?!
Isn't it pretty small?!
...
YOU WANNA SEE?
Yeah~!
th-thump th-thump
excited
jing
slap
He's putting it in his left hand.
HERE.
jing
Eep!
Uh...
R-REINO... WHAT IS THIS?
Is it a spirit? Or a will-o'-the-wisp?
I THINK...
IT'S A LIVING PERSON'S SPIRIT.
So...
A GRUDGE FROM A LIVING BEING THAT HAS BECOME AN AVENGING SPIRIT.

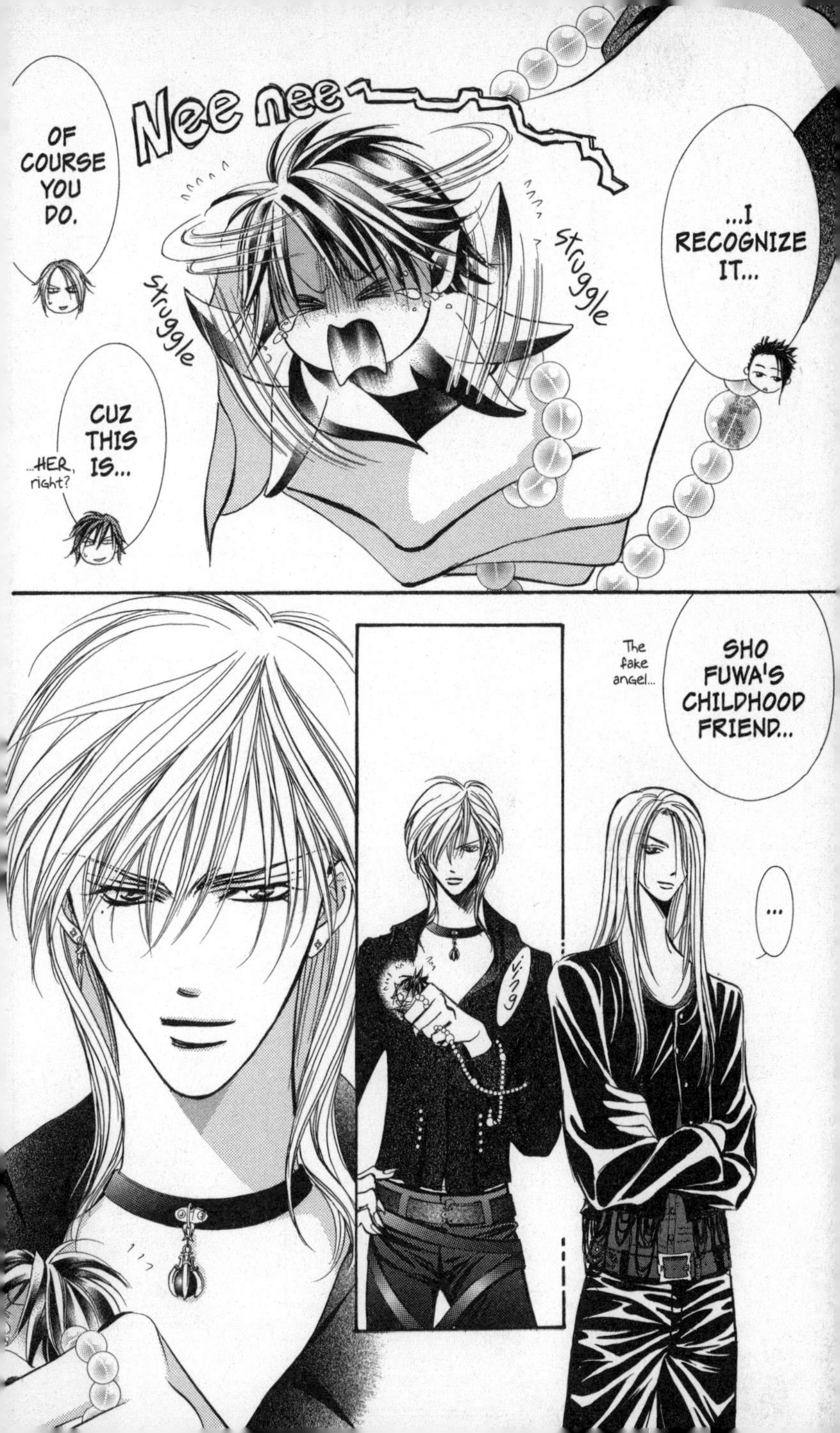

...I RECOGNIZE IT...
Nee nee
struggle
struggle
OF COURSE YOU DO.
CUZ THIS IS...
...HER, right?
SHO FUWA'S CHILDHOOD FRIEND...
The fake angel...
...

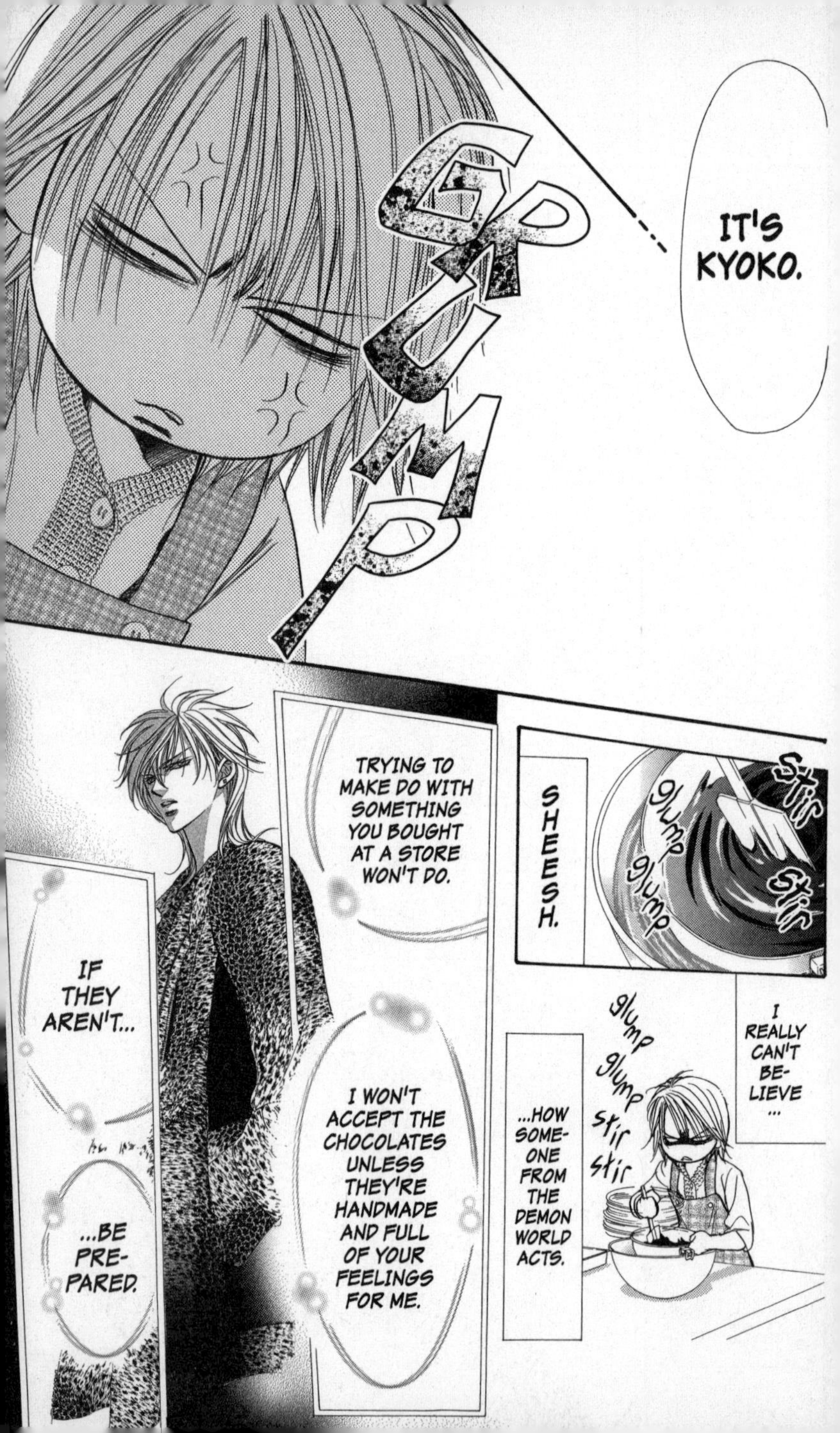
IT'S KYOKO.
GRUMP
stir
glump glump
stir
SHEESH.
I REALLY CAN'T BE-LIEVE...
glump glump stir stir
...HOW SOME-ONE FROM THE DEMON WORLD ACTS.
TRYING TO MAKE DO WITH SOMETHING YOU BOUGHT AT A STORE WON'T DO.
I WON'T ACCEPT THE CHOCOLATES UNLESS THEY'RE HANDMADE AND FULL OF YOUR FEELINGS FOR ME.
IF THEY AREN'T...
...BE PRE-PARED.

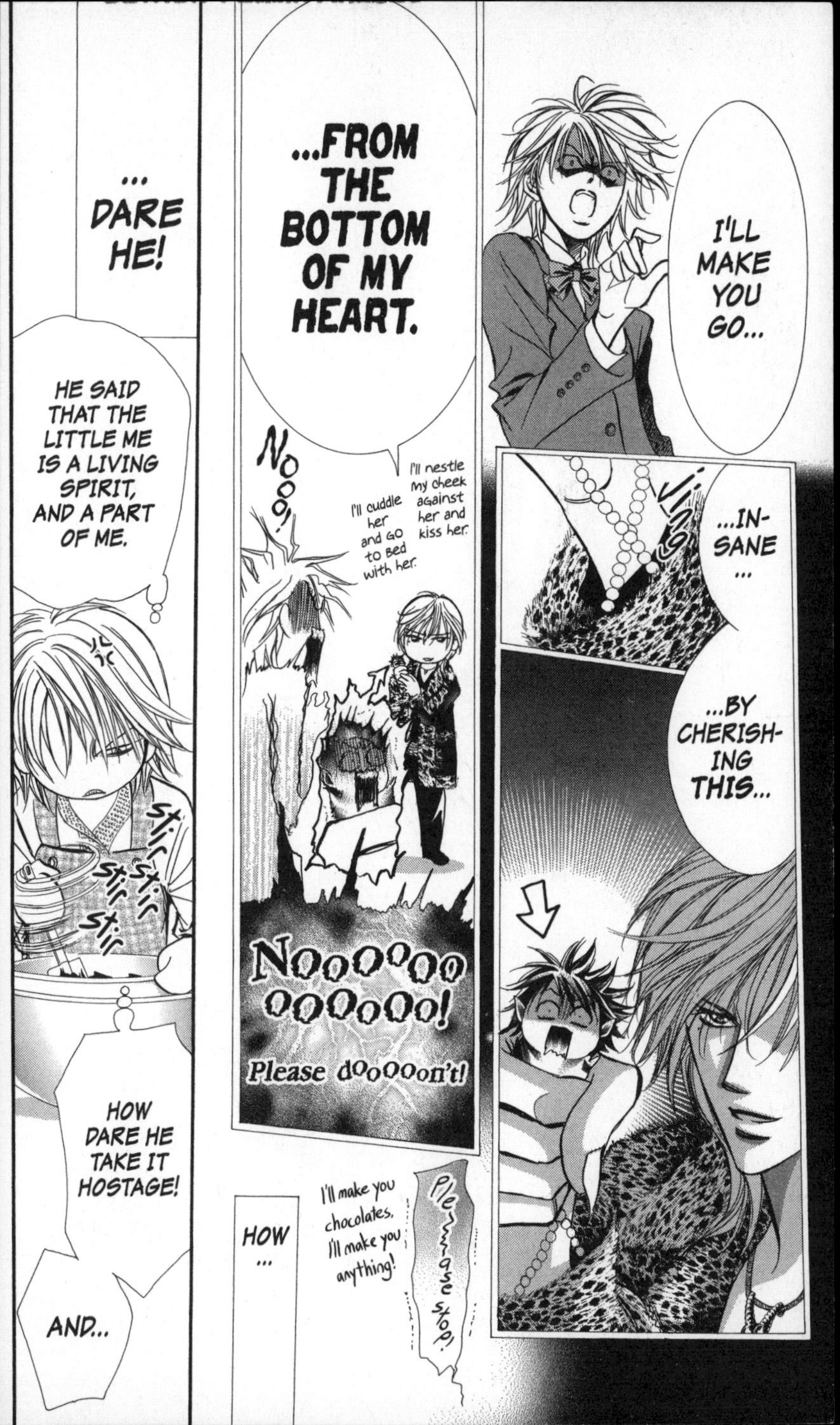
I'LL MAKE YOU GO...
...IN-SANE...
jing
...BY CHERISH-ING THIS...
...FROM THE BOTTOM OF MY HEART.
I'll nestle my cheek against her and kiss her.
I'll cuddle her and GO to Bed with her.
Noooo!
Nooooooo oooooo!
Please dooooon't!
Pleeease stop!
I'll make you chocolates, I'll make you anything!
HOW...
... DARE HE!
HE SAID THAT THE LITTLE ME IS A LIVING SPIRIT, AND A PART OF ME.
stir stir stir stir
HOW DARE HE TAKE IT HOSTAGE!
AND...

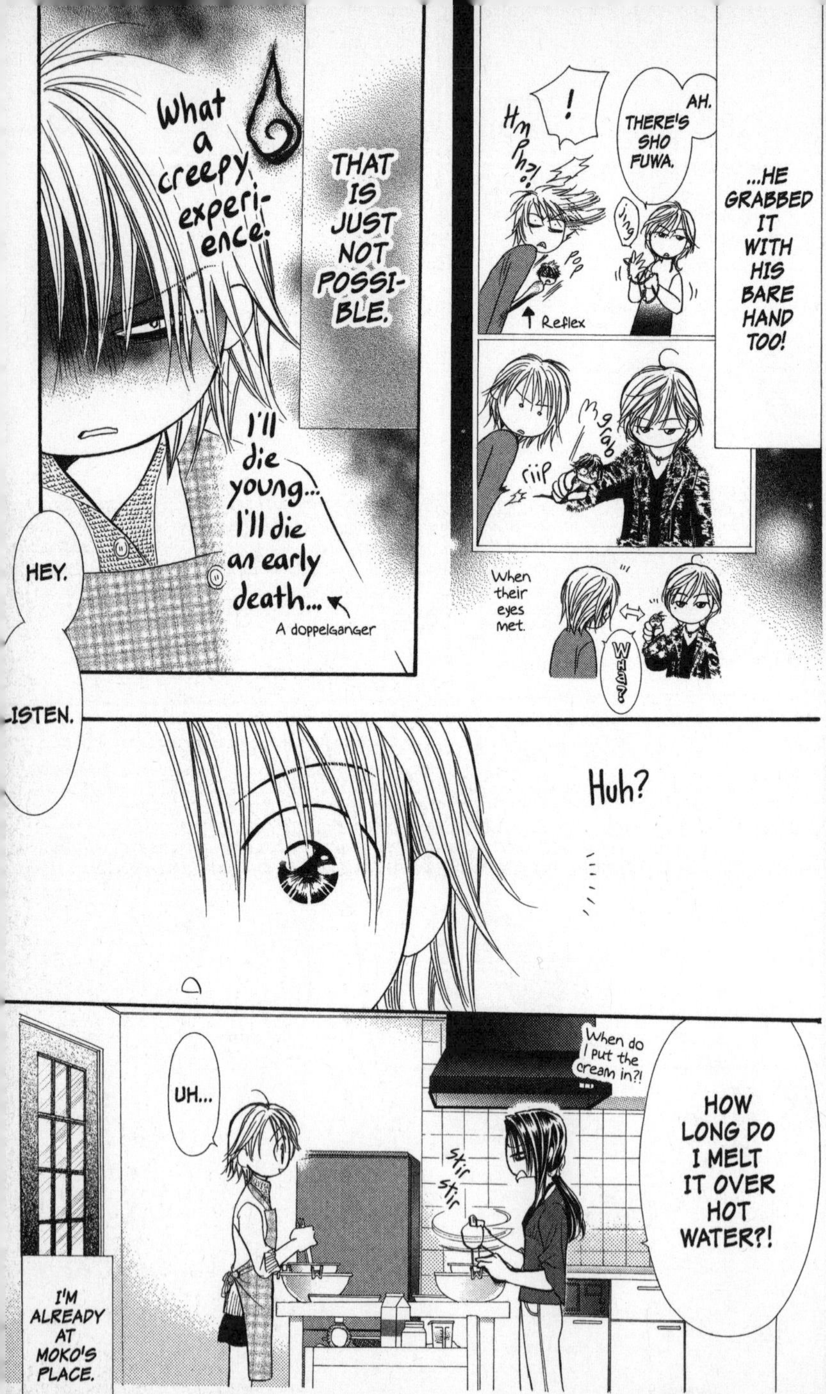
...HE GRABBED IT WITH HIS BARE HAND TOO!
AH. THERE'S SHO FUWA.
!
Hmph?!
jing
pop
Reflex
grab
riip
When their eyes met.
What?
THAT IS JUST NOT POSSIBLE.
What a creepy experience.
I'll die young... I'll die an early death...
A doppelganger
HEY.
LISTEN.
Huh?
HOW LONG DO I MELT IT OVER HOT WATER?!
When do I put the cream in?!
stir stir
UH...
I'M ALREADY AT MOKO'S PLACE.

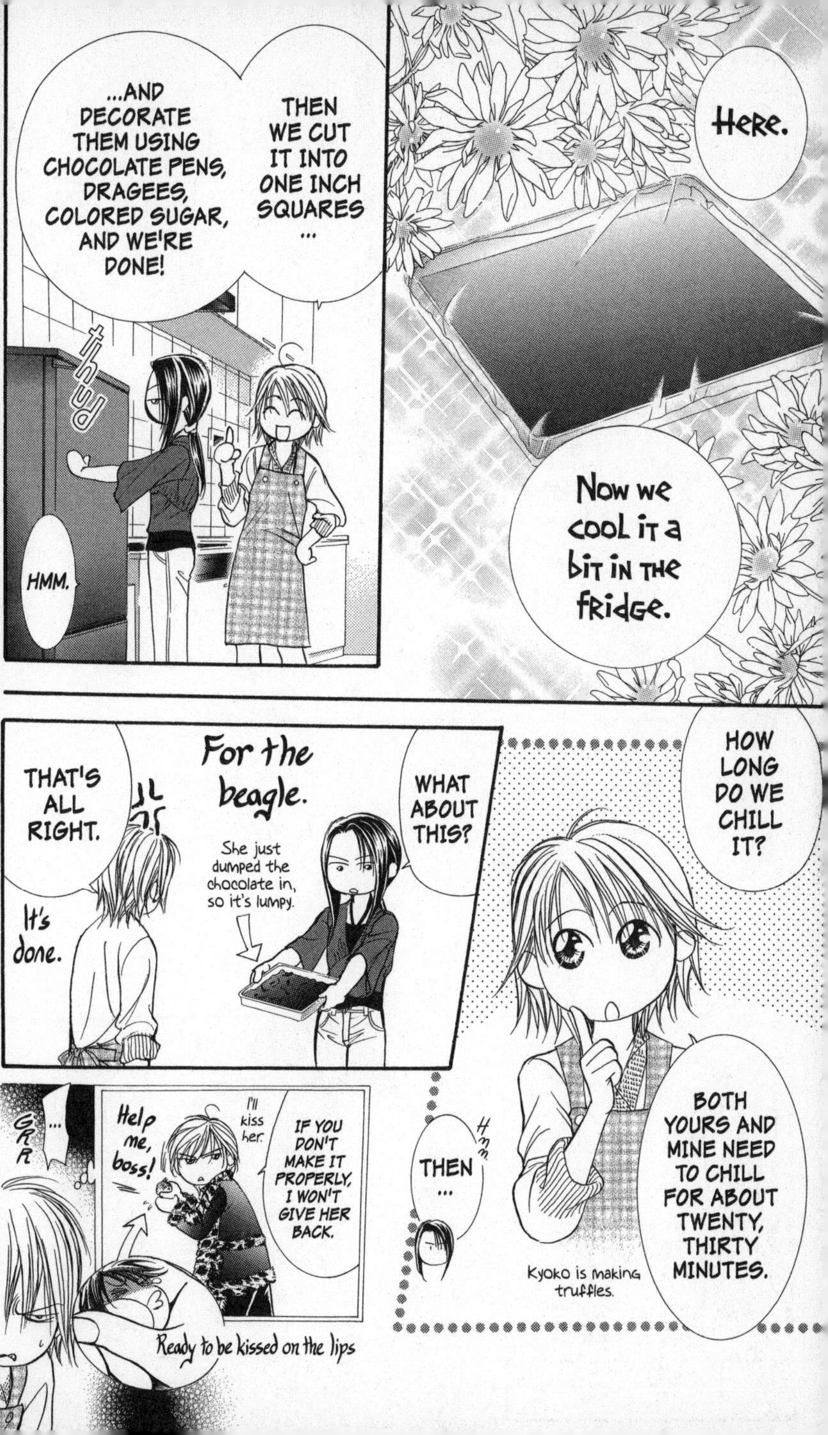
Here.
Now we cool it a bit in the fridge.
THEN WE CUT IT INTO ONE INCH SQUARES ...
...AND DECORATE THEM USING CHOCOLATE PENS, DRAGEES, COLORED SUGAR, AND WE'RE DONE!
thud
HMM.
HOW LONG DO WE CHILL IT?
BOTH YOURS AND MINE NEED TO CHILL FOR ABOUT TWENTY, THIRTY MINUTES.
Kyoko is making truffles.
Hmm
THEN ...
WHAT ABOUT THIS?
For the beagle.
She just dumped the chocolate in, so it's lumpy.
THAT'S ALL RIGHT.
It's done.
IF YOU DON'T MAKE IT PROPERLY, I WON'T GIVE HER BACK.
I'll kiss her.
Help me, boss!
...
GRR
Ready to be kissed on the lips

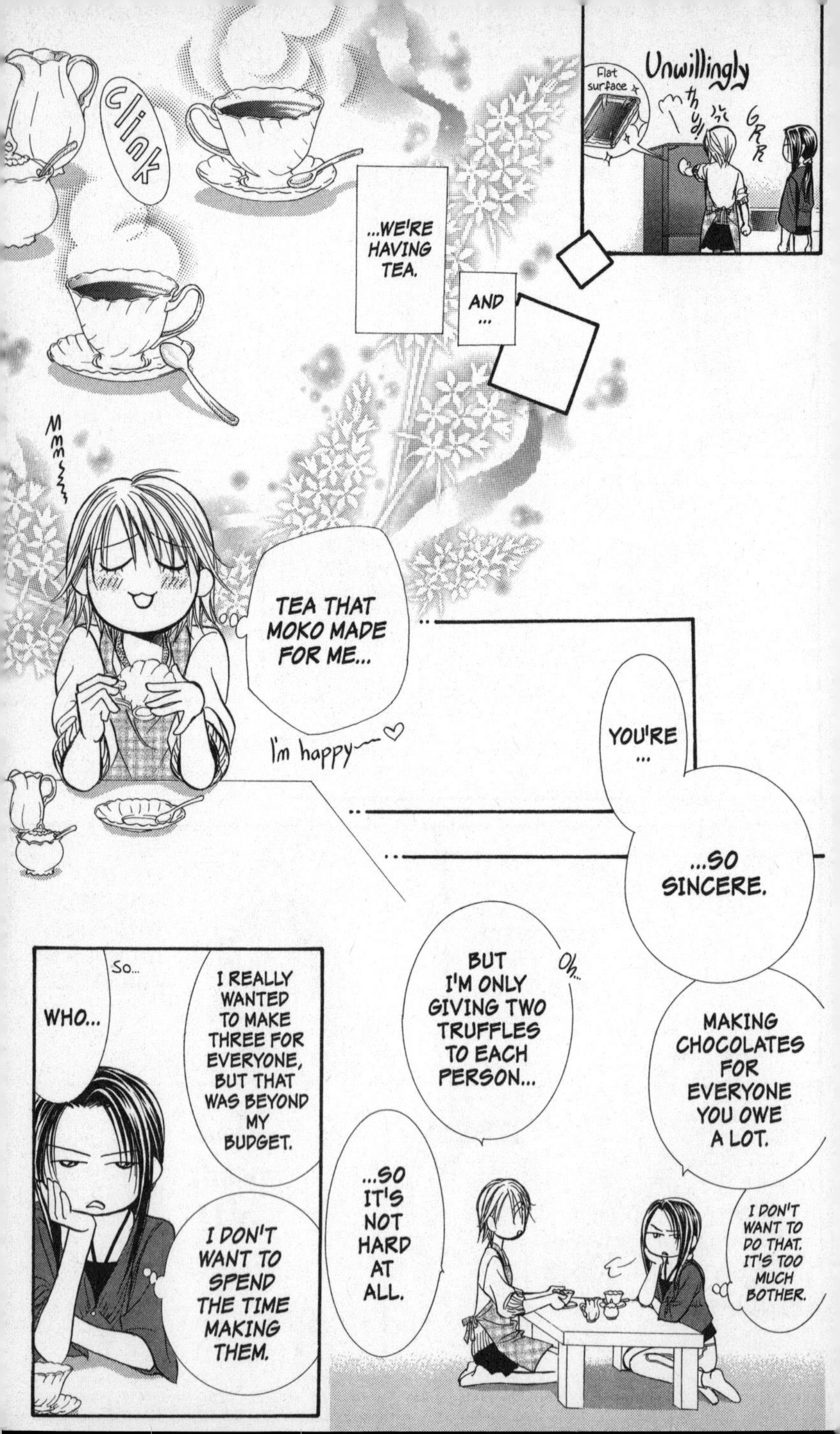
Unwillingly
Flat surface
thud!
GRR
click
...WE'RE HAVING TEA.
AND ...
Mmm~
TEA THAT MOKO MADE FOR ME...
I'm happy~♡
YOU'RE ...
...SO SINCERE.
MAKING CHOCOLATES FOR EVERYONE YOU OWE A LOT.
I DON'T WANT TO DO THAT. IT'S TOO MUCH BOTHER.
Oh...
BUT I'M ONLY GIVING TWO TRUFFLES TO EACH PERSON...
...SO IT'S NOT HARD AT ALL.
I REALLY WANTED TO MAKE THREE FOR EVERYONE, BUT THAT WAS BEYOND MY BUDGET.
So...
WHO...
I DON'T WANT TO SPEND THE TIME MAKING THEM.

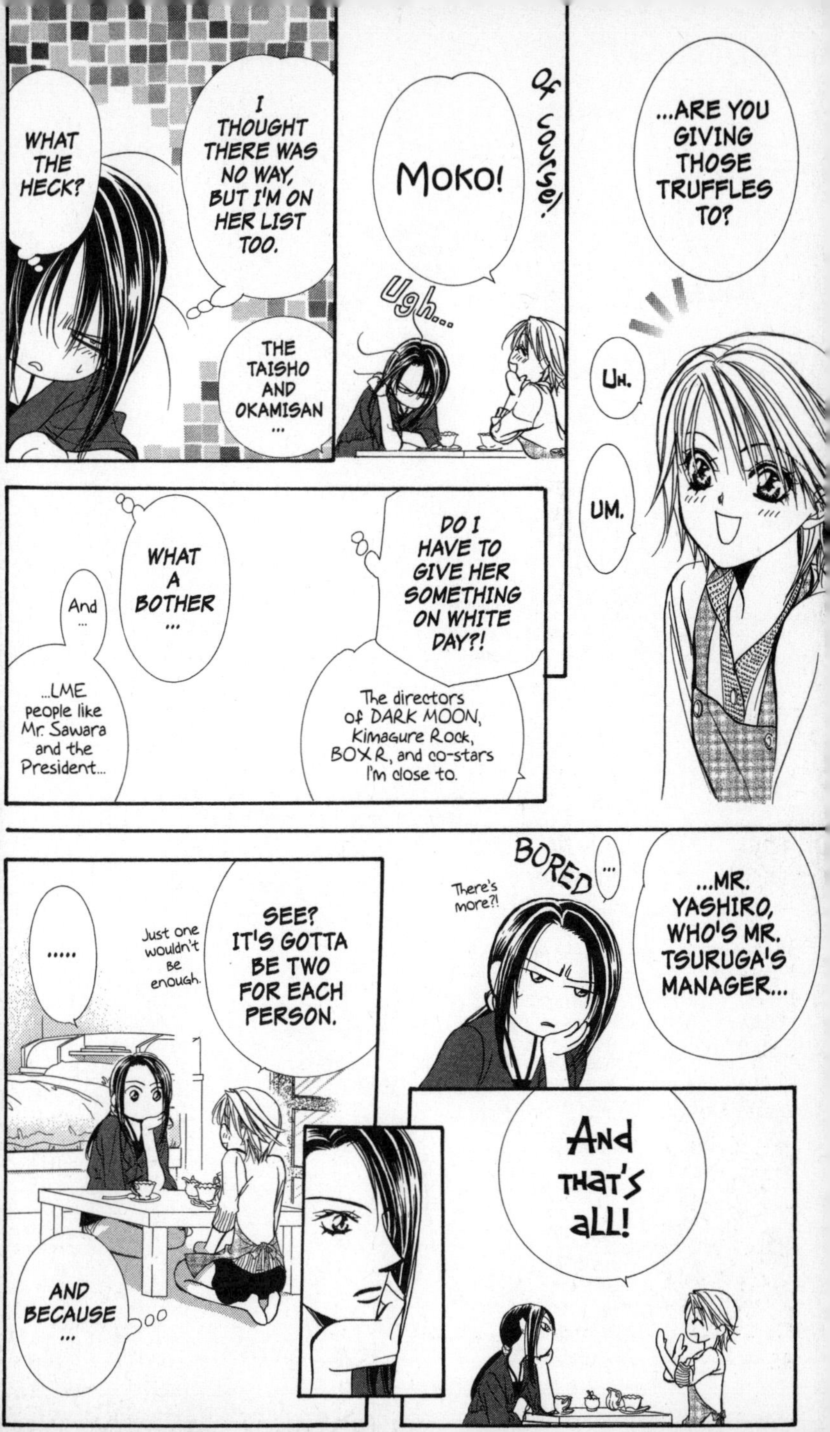
...ARE YOU GIVING THOSE TRUFFLES TO?
UH.
UM.
Of course!
MOKO!
Ugh...
I THOUGHT THERE WAS NO WAY, BUT I'M ON HER LIST TOO.
WHAT THE HECK?
THE TAISHO AND OKAMISAN ...
DO I HAVE TO GIVE HER SOMETHING ON WHITE DAY?!
The directors of DARK MOON, Kimagure Rock, BOX R, and co-stars I'm close to.
WHAT A BOTHER ...
And ...
...LME people like Mr. Sawara and the President...
...MR. YASHIRO, WHO'S MR. TSURUGA'S MANAGER...
...
BORED
There's more?!
And that's all!
SEE? IT'S GOTTA BE TWO FOR EACH PERSON.
Just one wouldn't be enough.
.....
AND BECAUSE ...

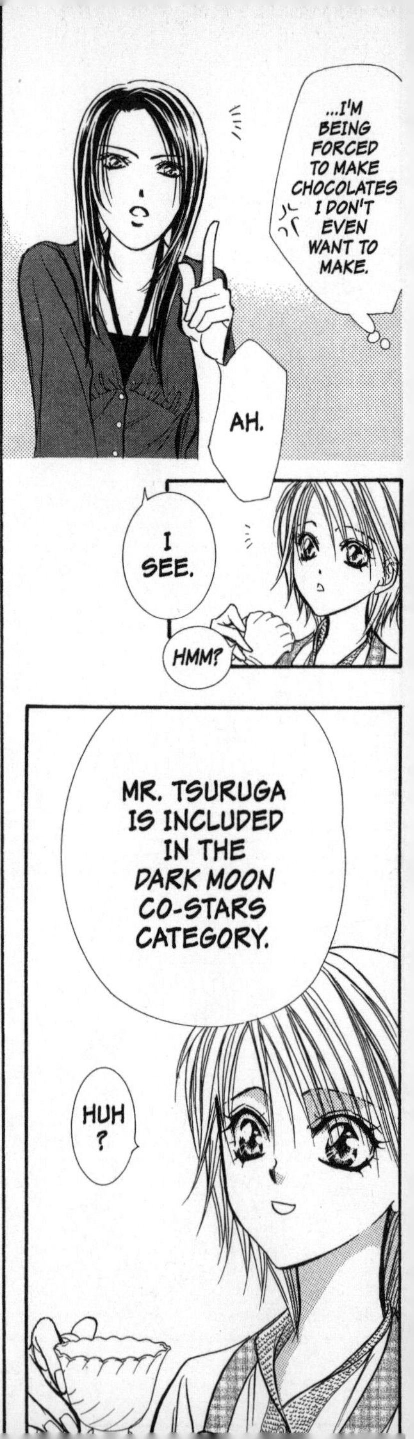
...I'M BEING FORCED TO MAKE CHOCOLATES I DON'T EVEN WANT TO MAKE.
AH.
I SEE.
HMM?
MR. TSURUGA IS INCLUDED IN THE *DARK MOON* CO-STARS CATEGORY.
HUH?
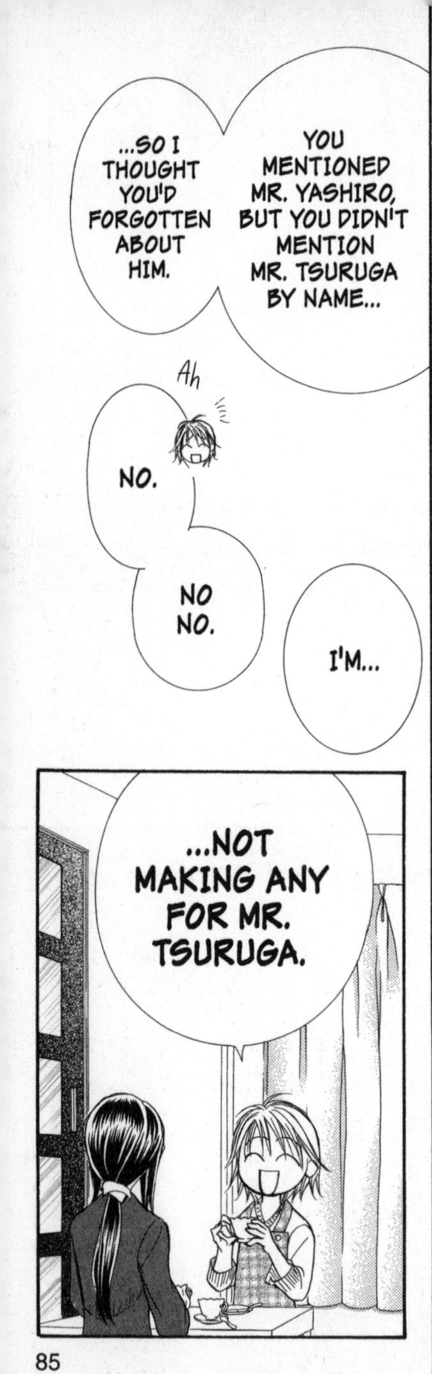
YOU MENTIONED MR. YASHIRO, BUT YOU DIDN'T MENTION MR. TSURUGA BY NAME...
...SO I THOUGHT YOU'D FORGOTTEN ABOUT HIM.
Ah
NO.
NO NO.
I'M...
...NOT MAKING ANY FOR MR. TSURUGA.

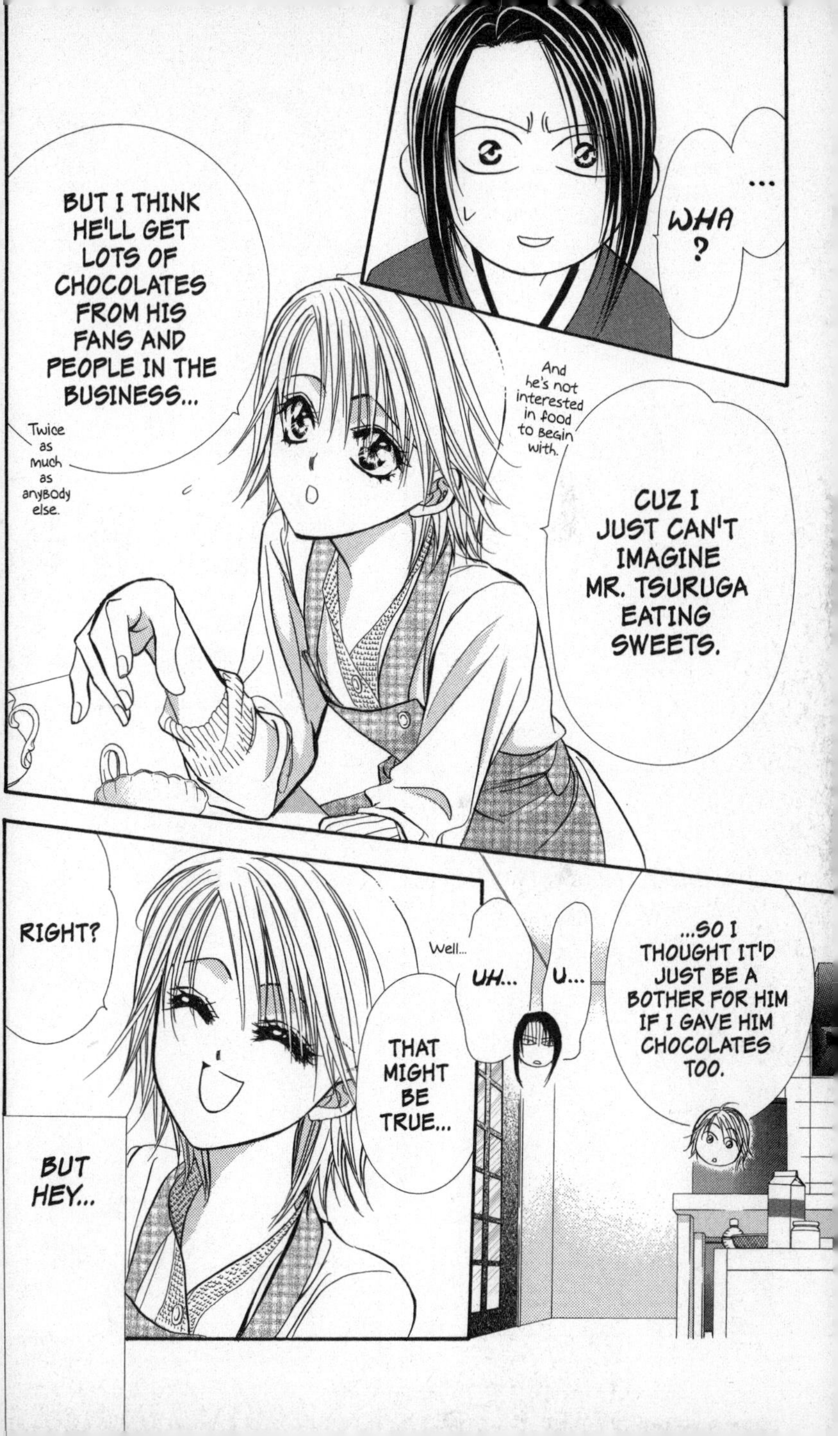

... WHA?
CUZ I JUST CAN'T IMAGINE MR. TSURUGA EATING SWEETS.
And he's not interested in food to begin with.
BUT I THINK HE'LL GET LOTS OF CHOCOLATES FROM HIS FANS AND PEOPLE IN THE BUSINESS...
Twice as much as anybody else.
...SO I THOUGHT IT'D JUST BE A BOTHER FOR HIM IF I GAVE HIM CHOCOLATES TOO.
U...
UH...
Well...
THAT MIGHT BE TRUE...
RIGHT?
BUT HEY...

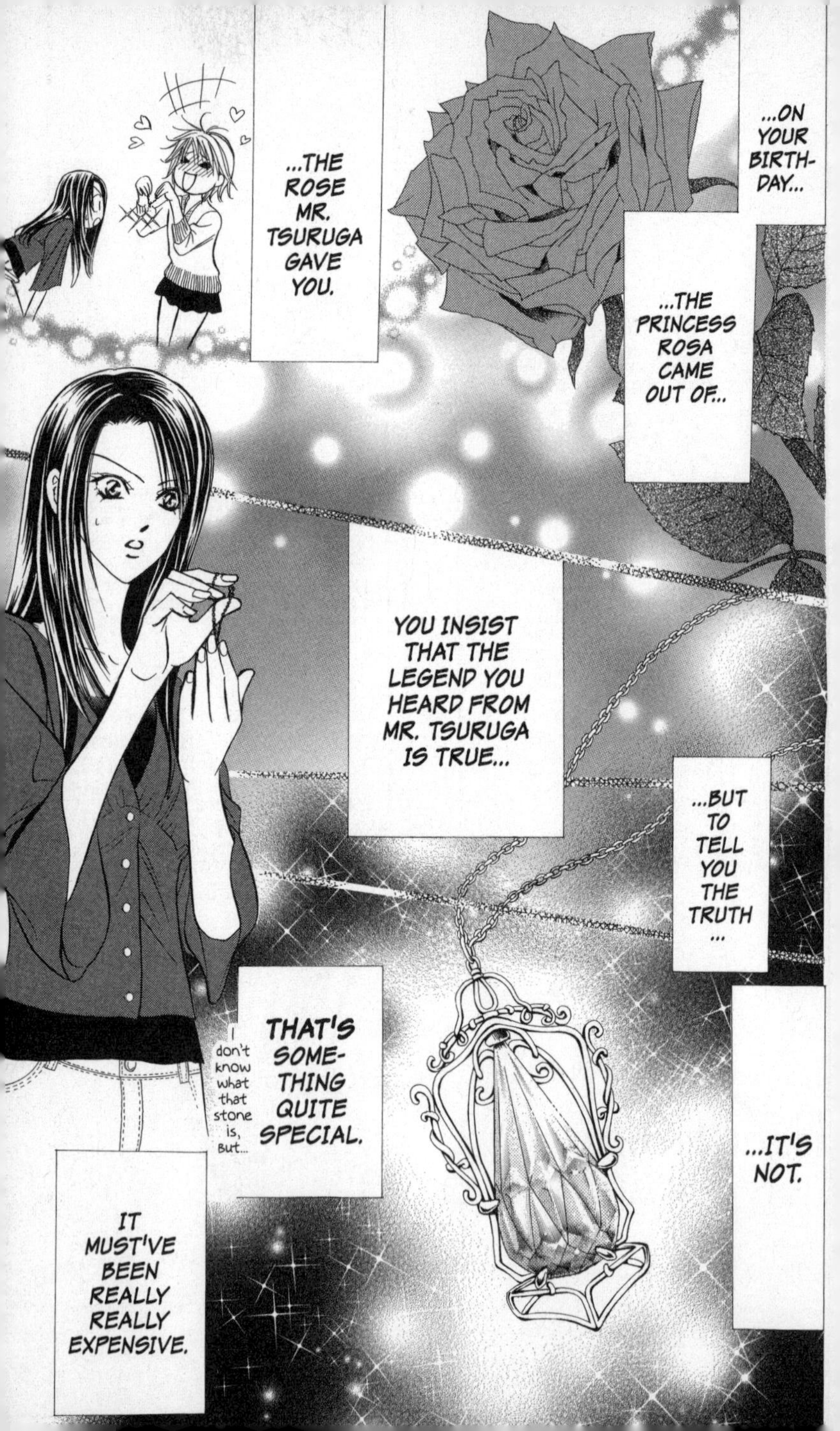
...ON YOUR BIRTH-DAY...
...THE PRINCESS ROSA CAME OUT OF...
...THE ROSE MR. TSURUGA GAVE YOU.
YOU INSIST THAT THE LEGEND YOU HEARD FROM MR. TSURUGA IS TRUE...
...BUT TO TELL YOU THE TRUTH...
...IT'S NOT.
THAT'S SOME-THING QUITE SPECIAL.
I don't know what that stone is, but...
IT MUST'VE BEEN REALLY REALLY EXPENSIVE.

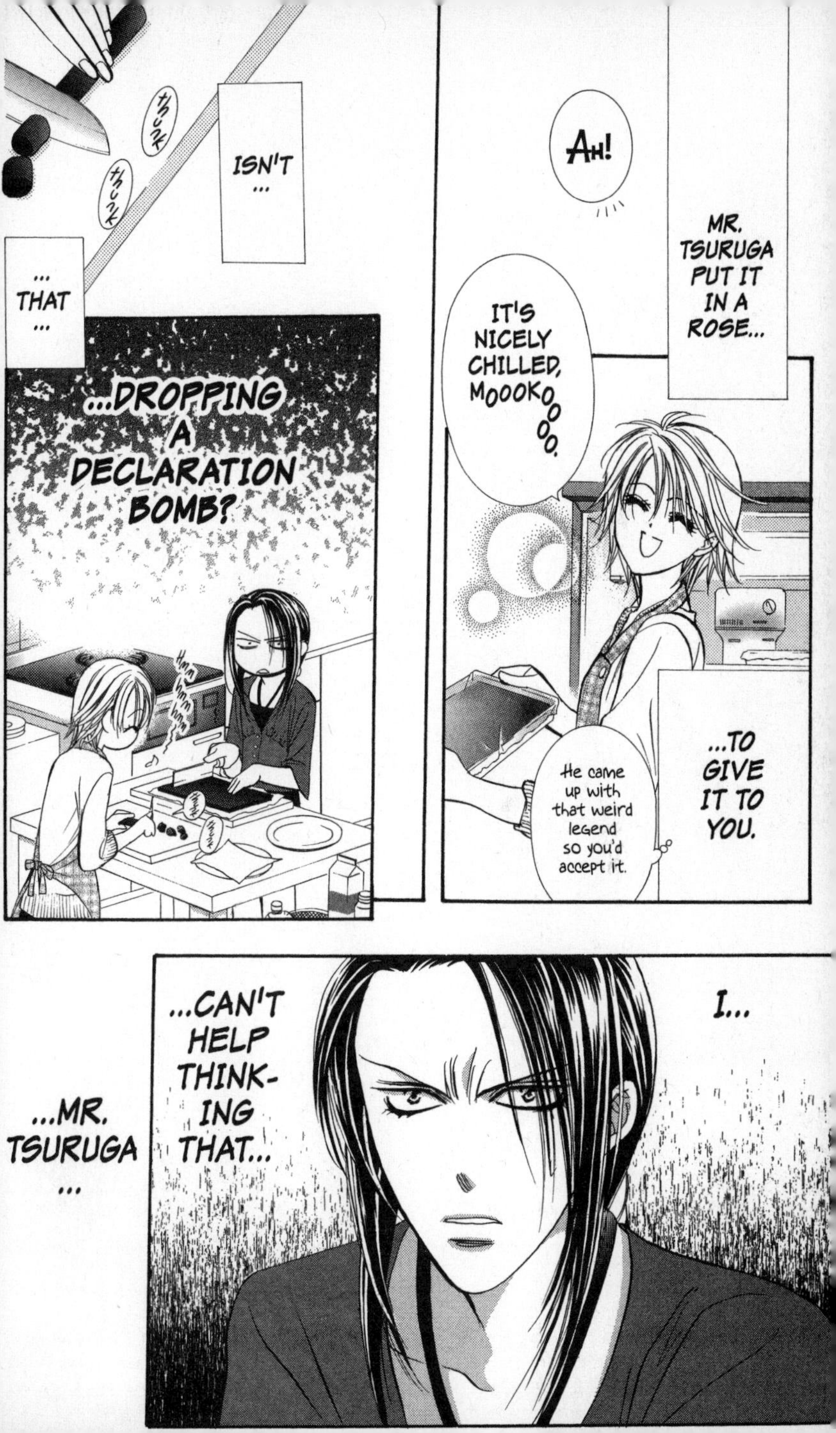
MR. TSURUGA PUT IT IN A ROSE...
AH!
IT'S NICELY CHILLED, MOOOKOOOOO.
...TO GIVE IT TO YOU.
He came up with that weird legend so you'd accept it.
ISN'T ...
thunk
thunk
... THAT ...
...DROPPING A DECLARATION BOMB?
Hmm hmm hmm
I...
...CAN'T HELP THINKING THAT...
...MR. TSURUGA ...

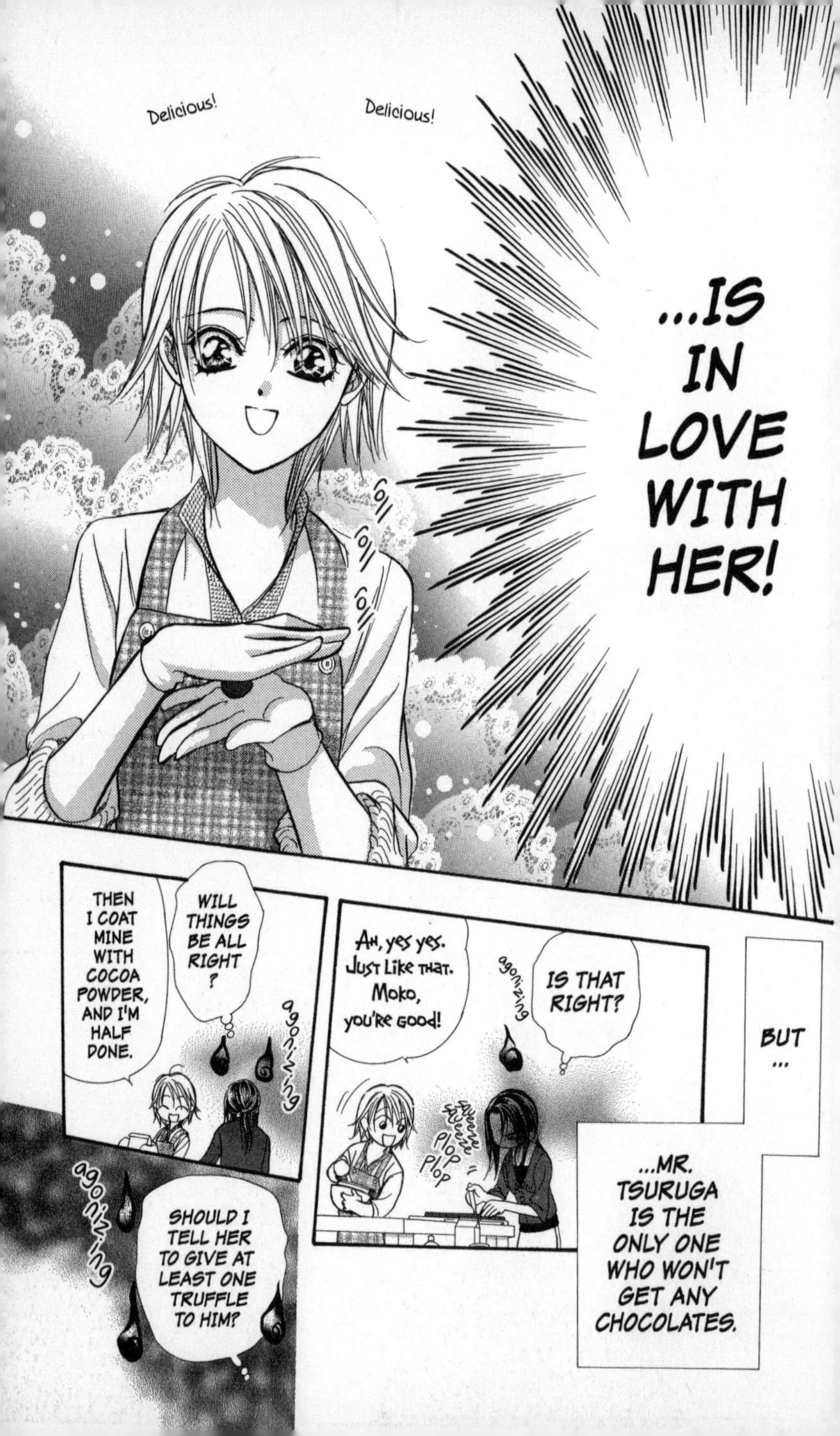
...IS IN LOVE WITH HER!
Delicious!
Delicious!
coll coll coll
BUT...
IS THAT RIGHT?
agonizing
Ah, yes yes. Just like that. Moko, you're good!
squeeze squeeze
plop plop
WILL THINGS BE ALL RIGHT?
THEN I COAT MINE WITH COCOA POWDER, AND I'M HALF DONE.
agonizing
...MR. TSURUGA IS THE ONLY ONE WHO WON'T GET ANY CHOCOLATES.
SHOULD I TELL HER TO GIVE AT LEAST ONE TRUFFLE TO HIM?
agonizing

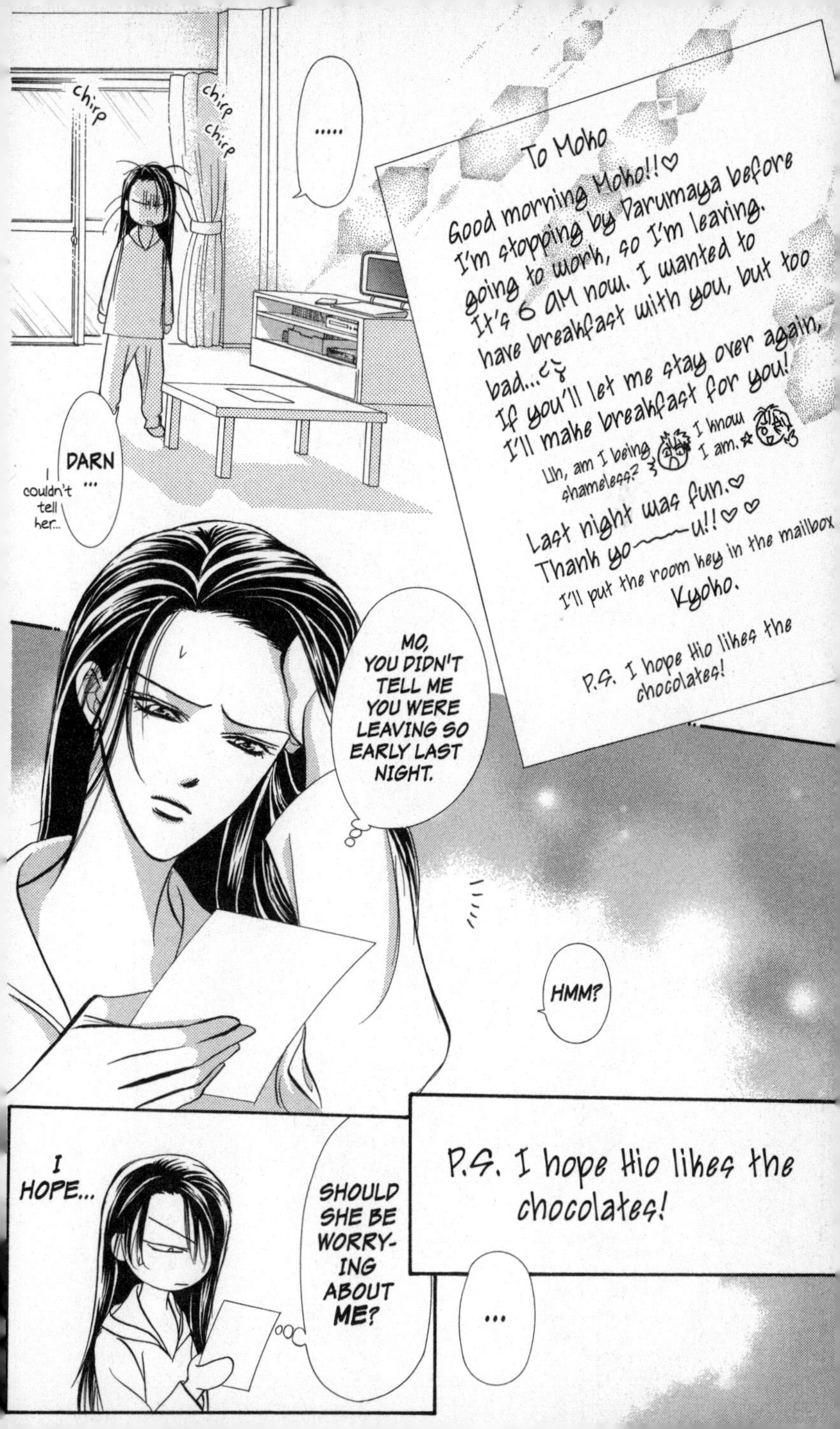
To Moko
Good morning Moko!!♡
I'm stopping by Darumaya before going to work, so I'm leaving. It's 6 AM now. I wanted to have breakfast with you, but too bad...
If you'll let me stay over again, I'll make breakfast for you!
Uh, am I being shameless?
I know I am.☆
Last night was fun.♡
Thank yo——u!!♡♡
I'll put the room key in the mailbox
Kyoko.
P.S. I hope Hio likes the chocolates!
.....
chirp chirp
chirp
DARN ...
I couldn't tell her...
MO, YOU DIDN'T TELL ME YOU WERE LEAVING SO EARLY LAST NIGHT.
HMM?
P.S. I hope Hio likes the chocolates!
...
SHOULD SHE BE WORRYING ABOUT ME?
I HOPE...

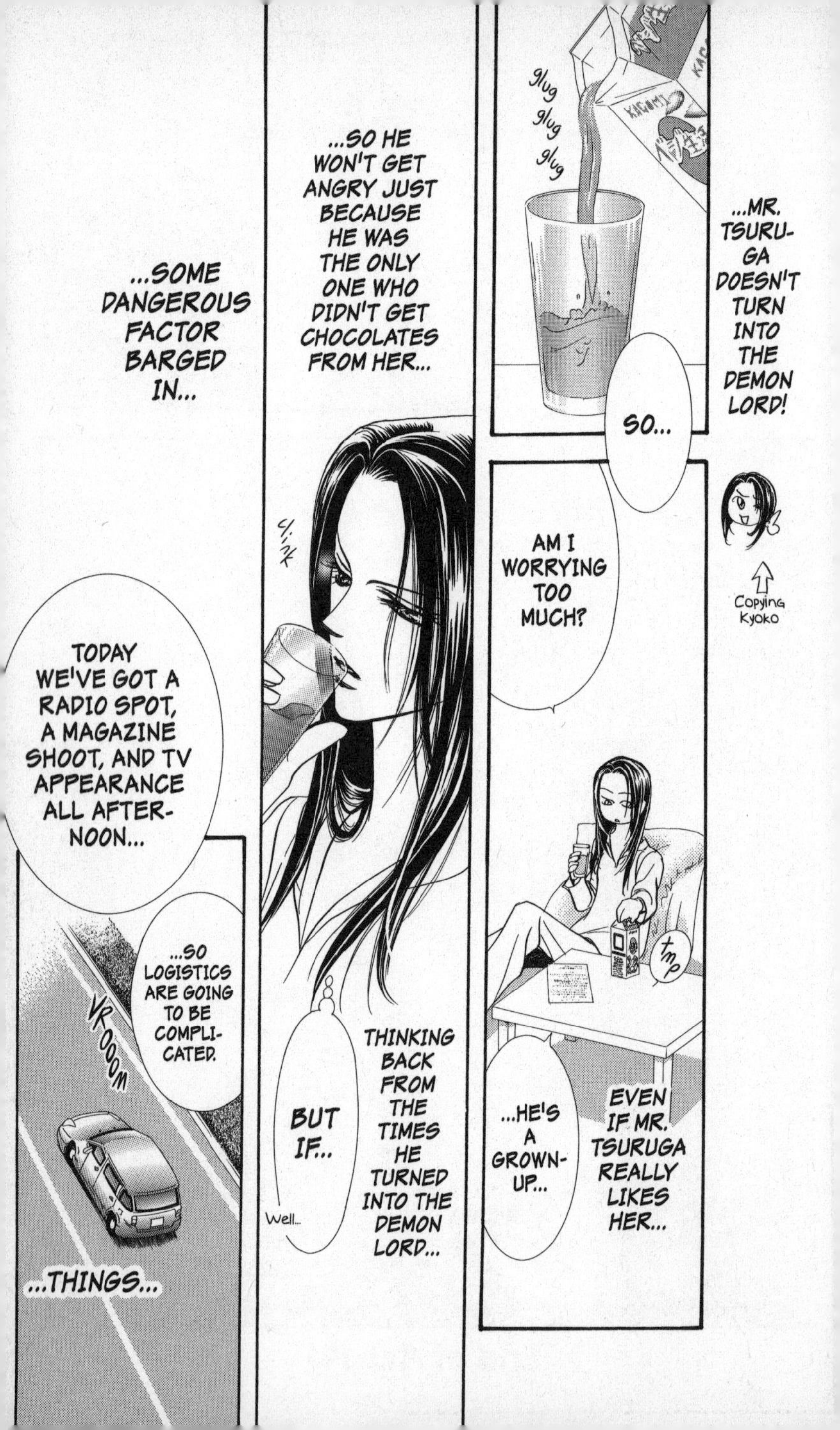
glug glug glug
KAGOMI
...MR. TSURUGA DOESN'T TURN INTO THE DEMON LORD!
Copying Kyoko
SO...
AM I WORRYING TOO MUCH?
tmp
EVEN IF MR. TSURUGA REALLY LIKES HER...
...HE'S A GROWN-UP...
...SO HE WON'T GET ANGRY JUST BECAUSE HE WAS THE ONLY ONE WHO DIDN'T GET CHOCOLATES FROM HER...
clink
THINKING BACK FROM THE TIMES HE TURNED INTO THE DEMON LORD...
BUT IF...
Well...
...SOME DANGEROUS FACTOR BARGED IN...
TODAY WE'VE GOT A RADIO SPOT, A MAGAZINE SHOOT, AND TV APPEARANCE ALL AFTER-NOON...
...SO LOGISTICS ARE GOING TO BE COMPLI-CATED.
VROOOM
...THINGS...

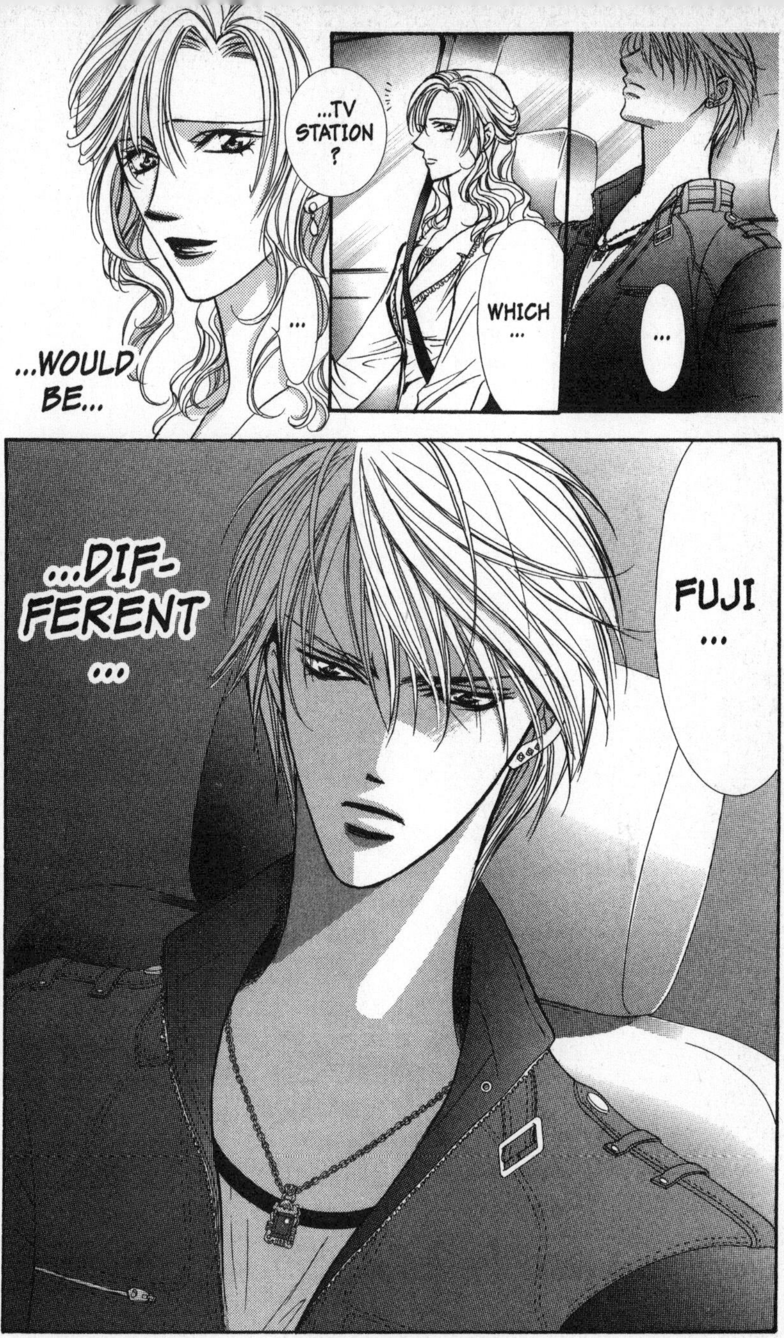
...
WHICH ...
...TV STATION ?
...
...WOULD BE...
FUJI ...
...DIF-FERENT ...

End of Act 141

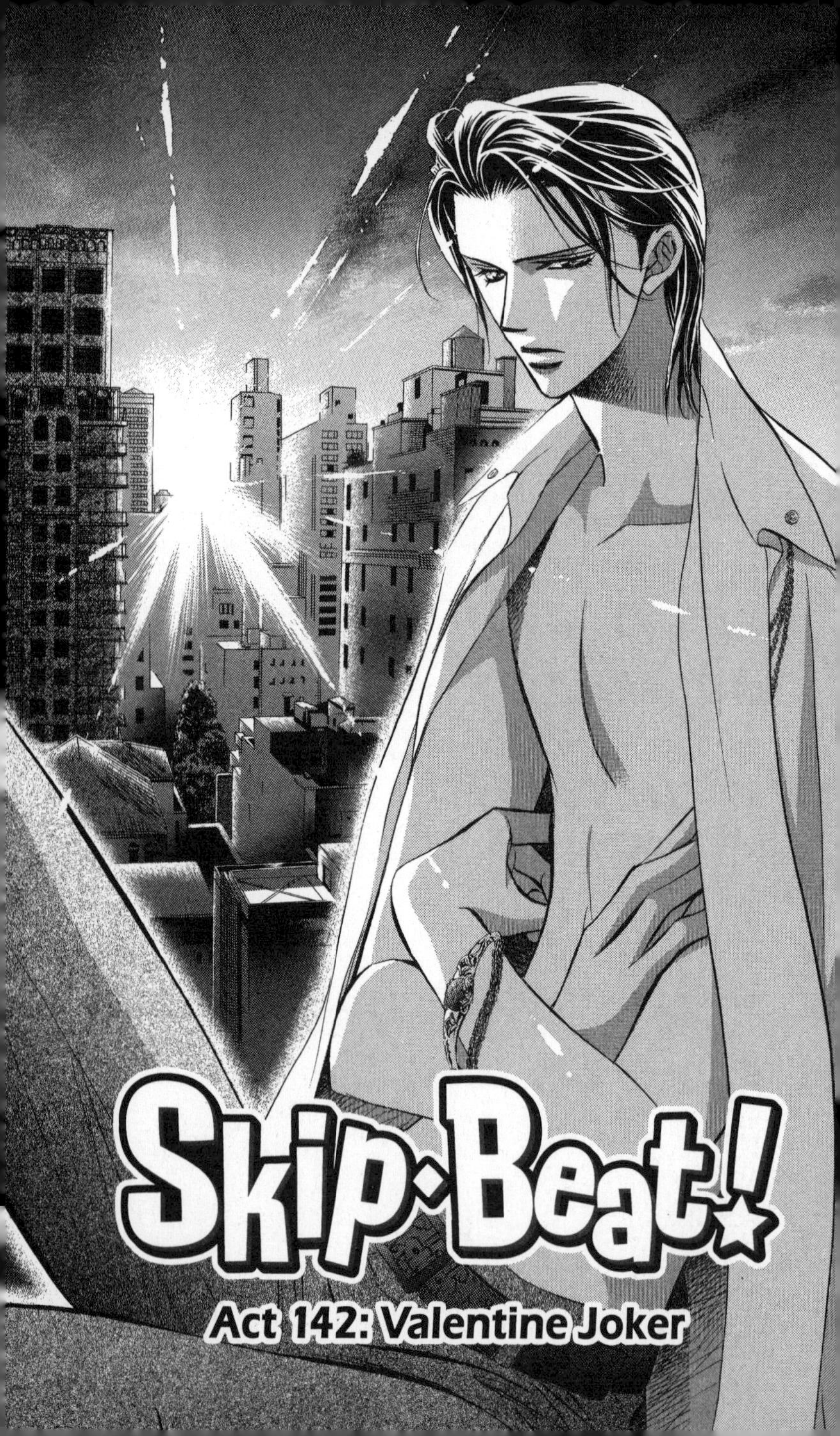
Skip·Beat!
Act 142: Valentine Joker

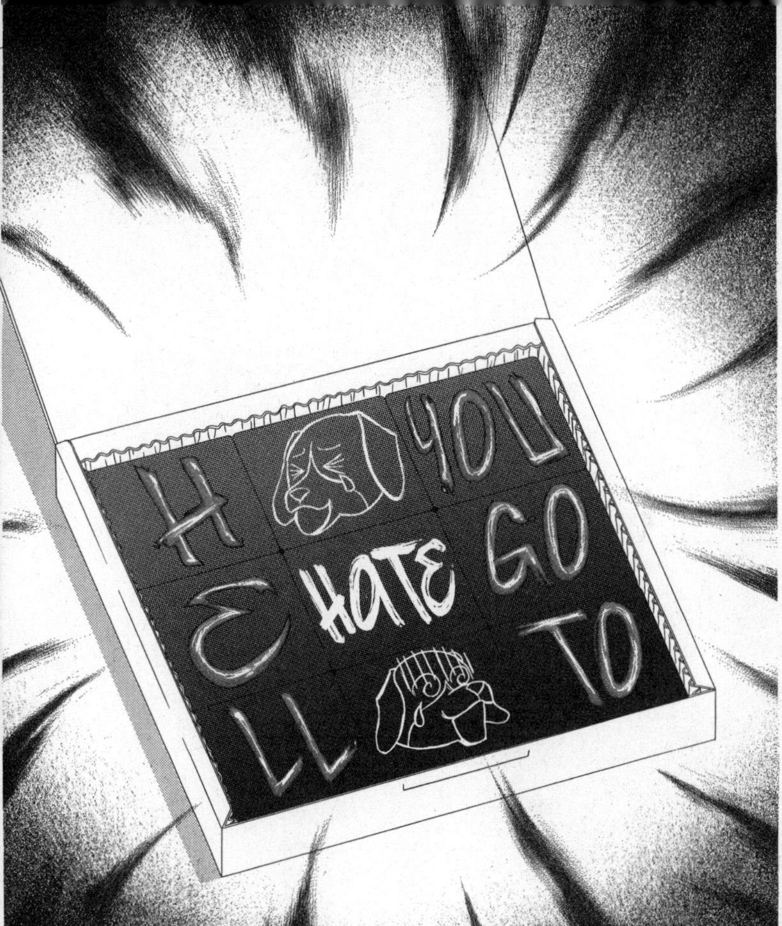
H
YOU
E
HATE
GO
LL
TO
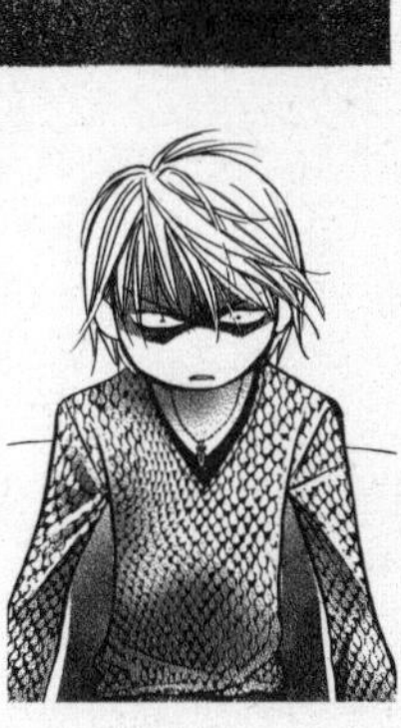

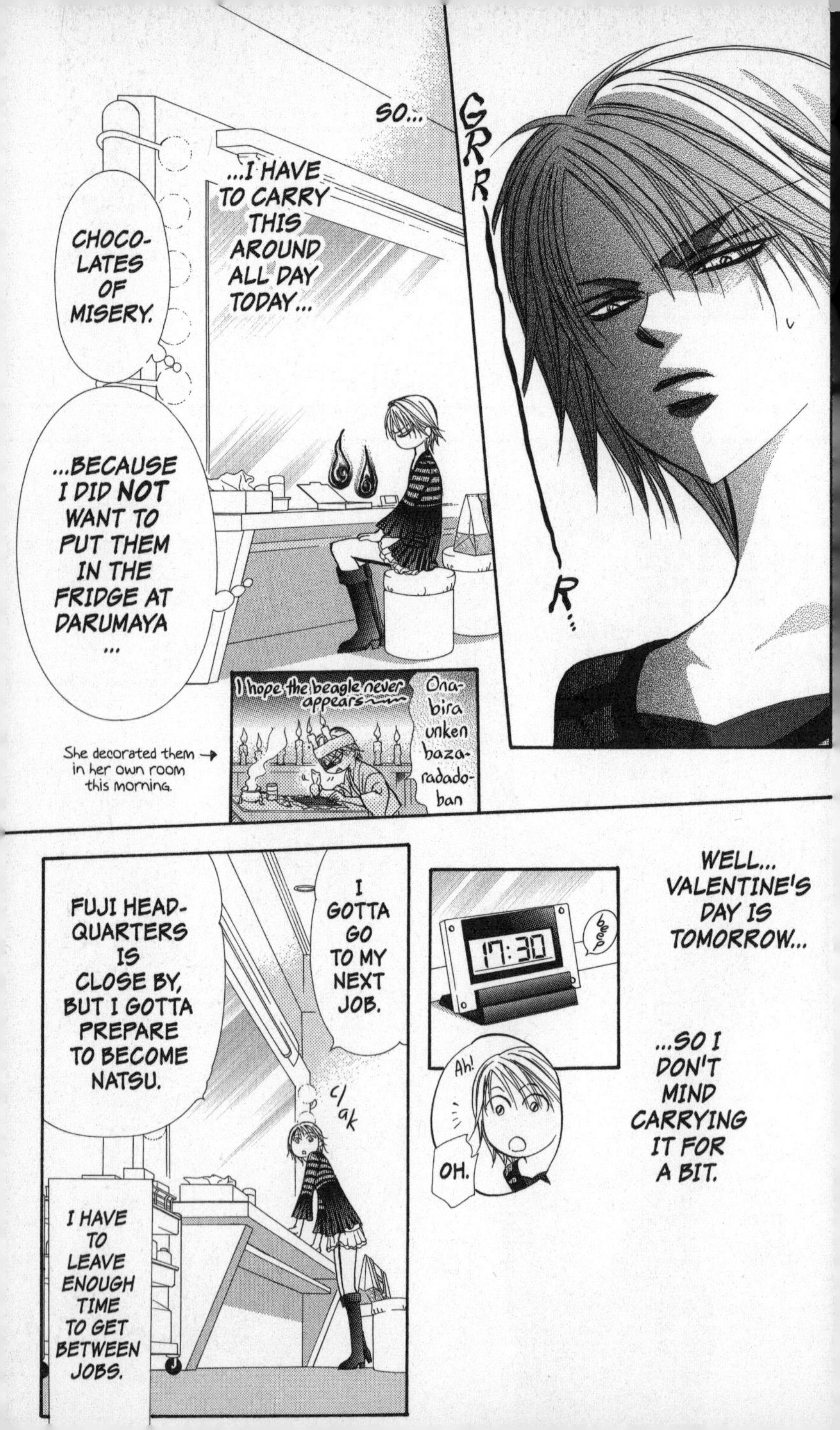
GRRR...
R...
SO...
...I HAVE TO CARRY THIS AROUND ALL DAY TODAY...
CHOCO-LATES OF MISERY.
...BECAUSE I DID NOT WANT TO PUT THEM IN THE FRIDGE AT DARUMAYA...
Ona-bira unken baza-radado-ban
I hope the beagle never appears
She decorated them in her own room this morning.
WELL... VALENTINE'S DAY IS TOMORROW...
...SO I DON'T MIND CARRYING IT FOR A BIT.
beep
17:30
Ah!
OH.
I GOTTA GO TO MY NEXT JOB.
clak
FUJI HEAD-QUARTERS IS CLOSE BY, BUT I GOTTA PREPARE TO BECOME NATSU.
I HAVE TO LEAVE ENOUGH TIME TO GET BETWEEN JOBS.

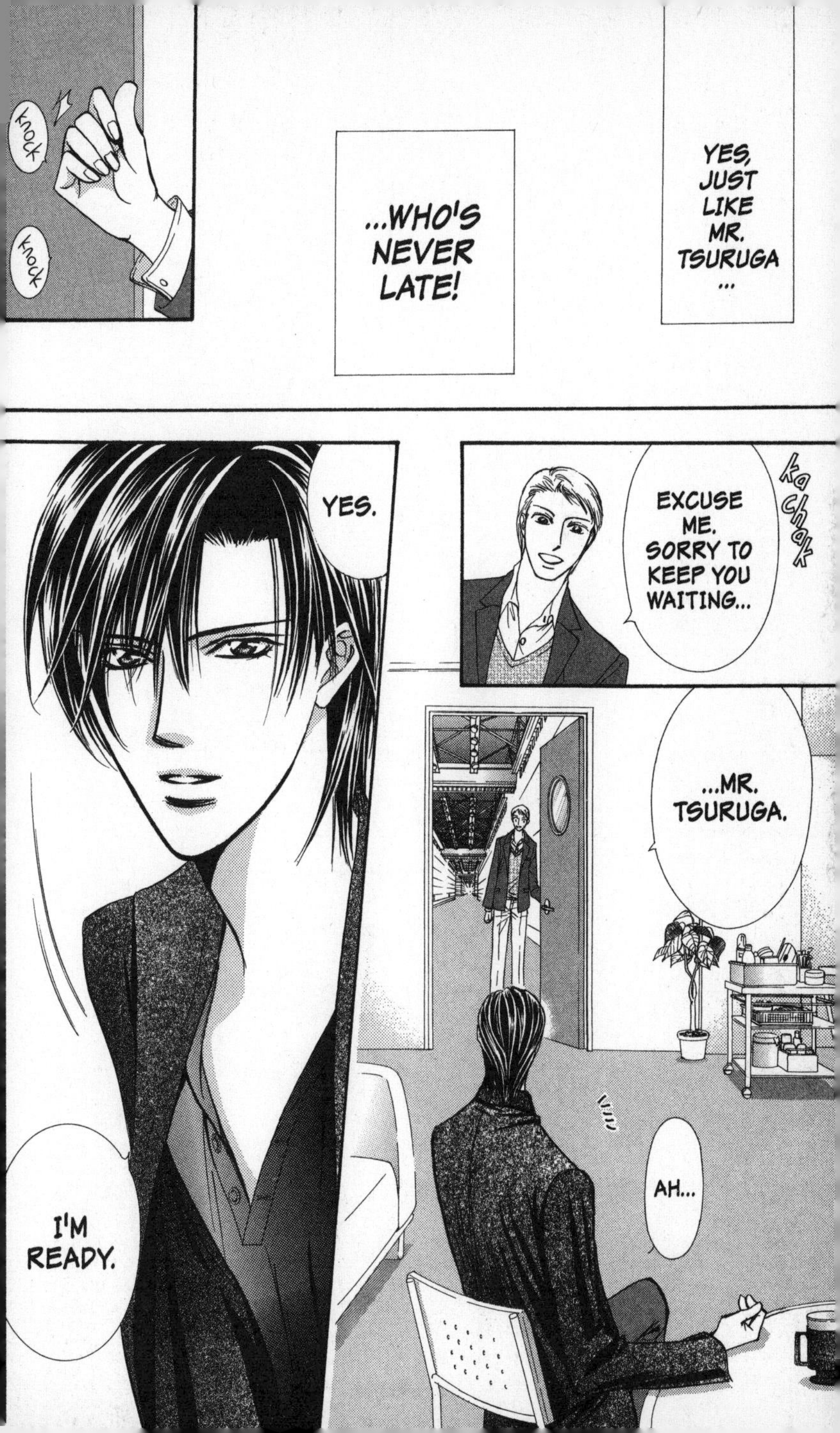
YES, JUST LIKE MR. TSURUGA ...
...WHO'S NEVER LATE!
knock
knock
ka chak
EXCUSE ME. SORRY TO KEEP YOU WAITING...
...MR. TSURUGA.
AH...
YES.
I'M READY.

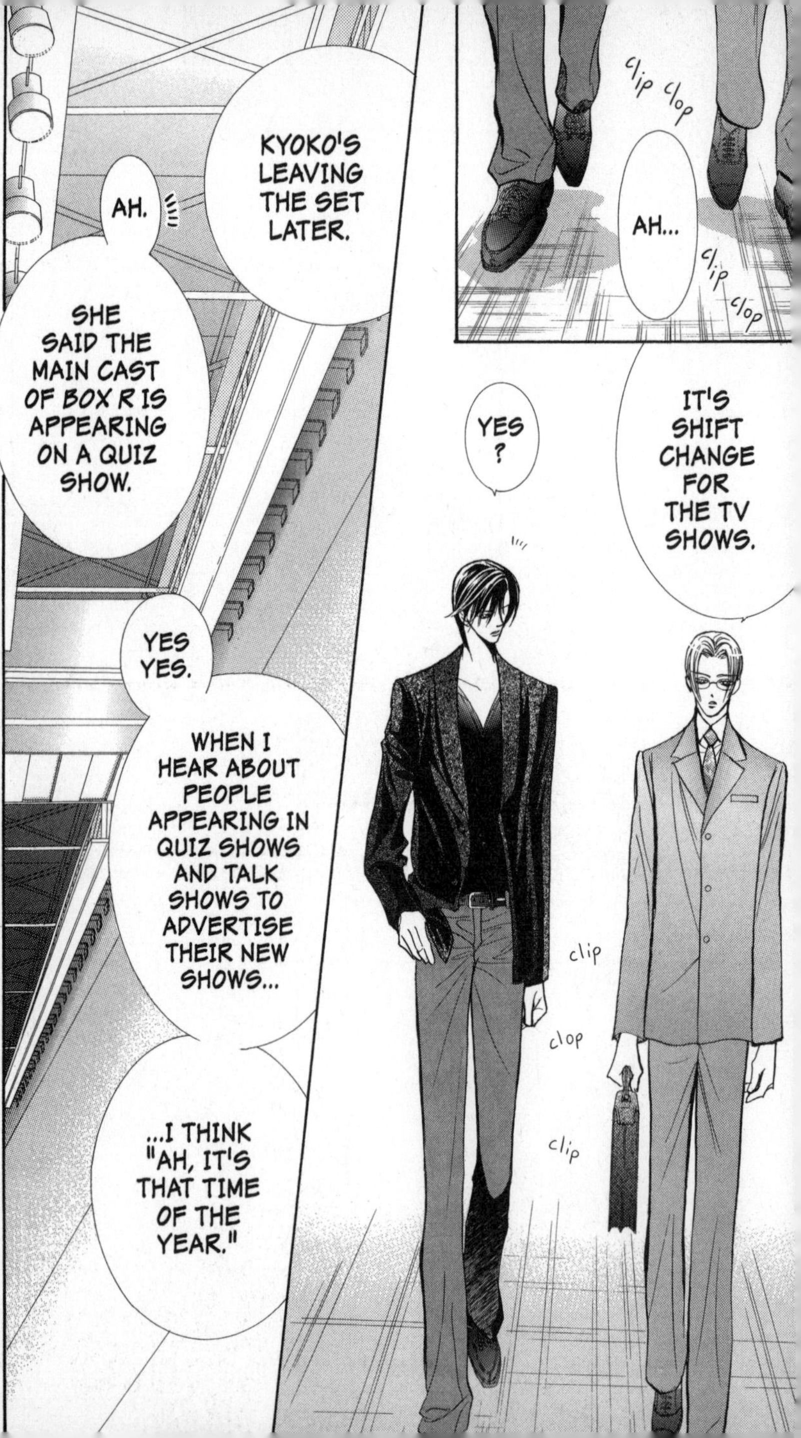
clip clop
AH...
clip clop
IT'S SHIFT CHANGE FOR THE TV SHOWS.
YES?
clip
clop
clip
KYOKO'S LEAVING THE SET LATER.
AH.
SHE SAID THE MAIN CAST OF BOX R IS APPEARING ON A QUIZ SHOW.
YES YES.
WHEN I HEAR ABOUT PEOPLE APPEARING IN QUIZ SHOWS AND TALK SHOWS TO ADVERTISE THEIR NEW SHOWS...
...I THINK "AH, IT'S THAT TIME OF THE YEAR."

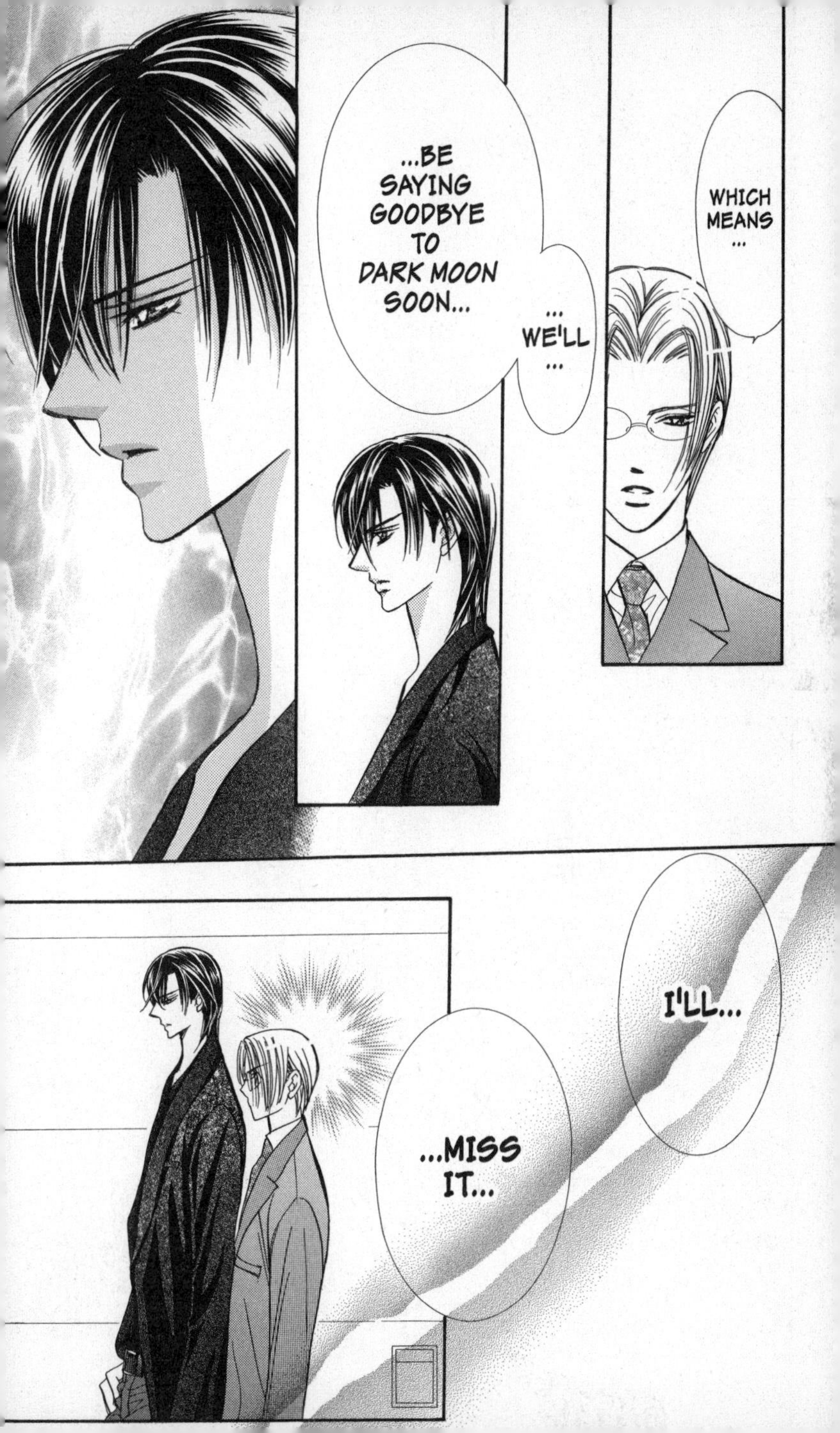
WHICH MEANS ...
... WE'LL ...
...BE SAYING GOODBYE TO DARK MOON SOON...
I'LL...
...MISS IT...

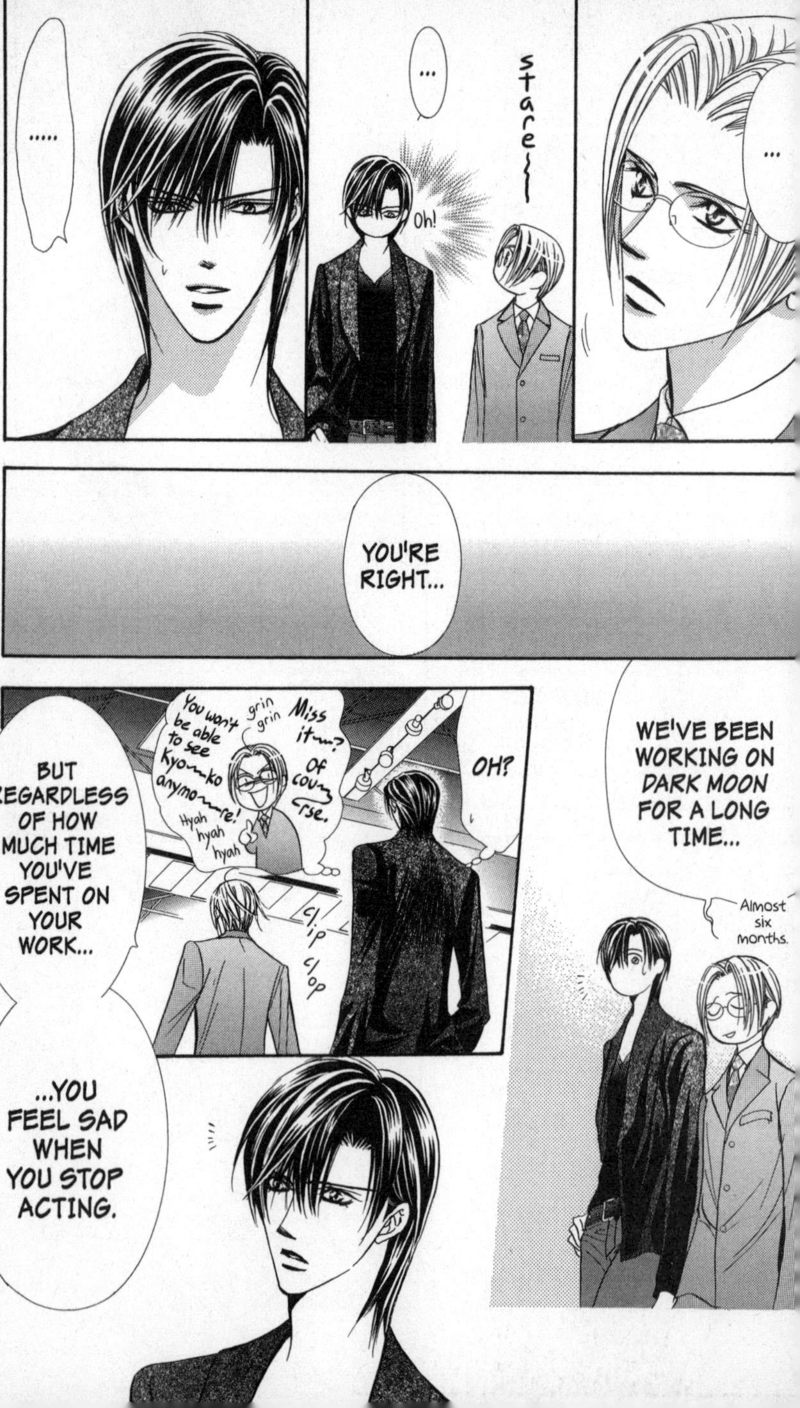
...
stare~~
...
Oh!
......
YOU'RE RIGHT...
WE'VE BEEN WORKING ON DARK MOON FOR A LONG TIME...
Almost six months.
OH?
Miss it~~? Of cou~rse.
grin grin
You won't be able to see Kyo~ko anymo~re!
Hyah hyah hyah
clip clop
BUT REGARDLESS OF HOW MUCH TIME YOU'VE SPENT ON YOUR WORK...
...YOU FEEL SAD WHEN YOU STOP ACTING.

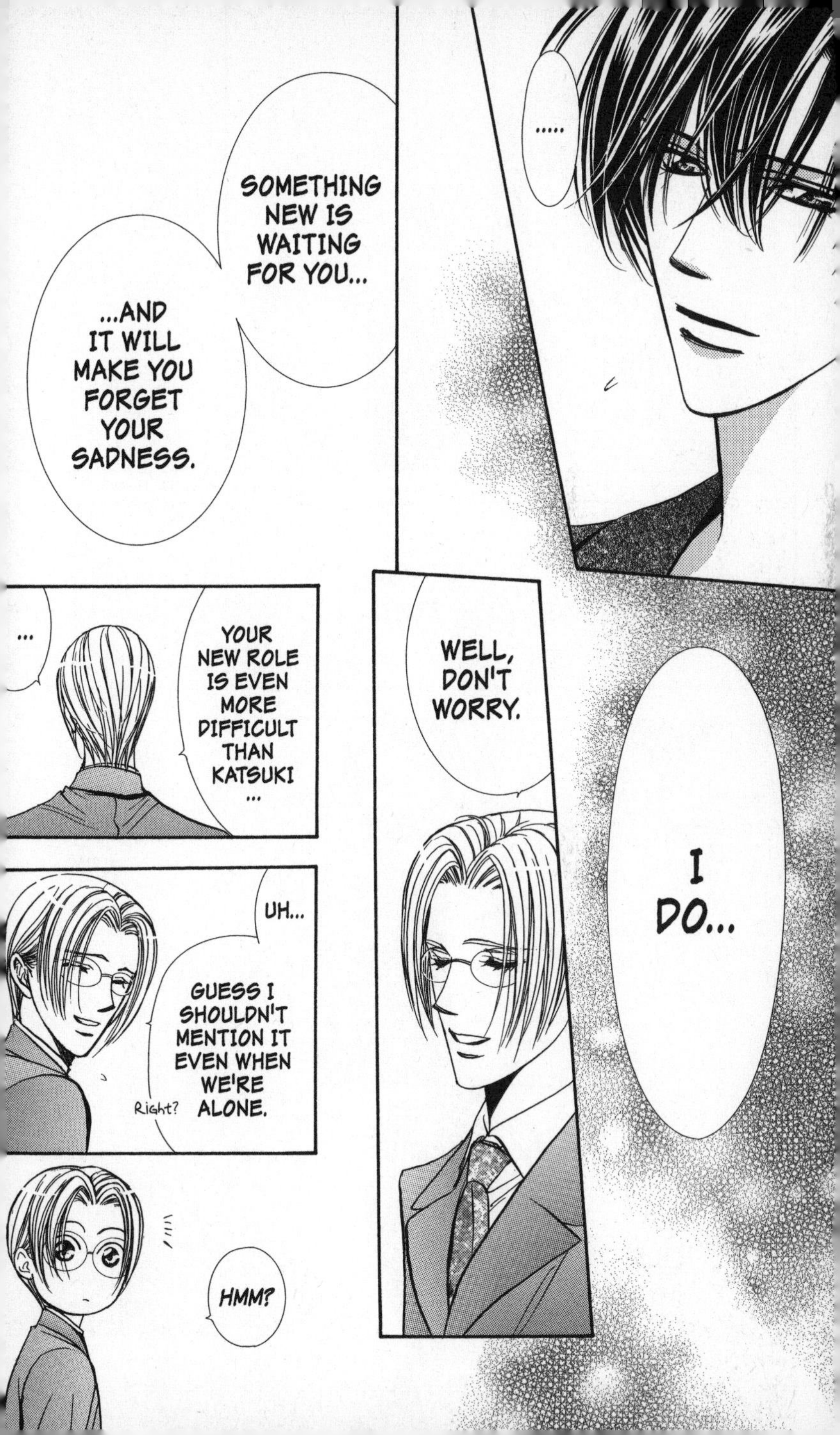

.....
SOMETHING NEW IS WAITING FOR YOU...
...AND IT WILL MAKE YOU FORGET YOUR SADNESS.
I DO...
WELL, DON'T WORRY.
YOUR NEW ROLE IS EVEN MORE DIFFICULT THAN KATSUKI ...
...
UH...
GUESS I SHOULDN'T MENTION IT EVEN WHEN WE'RE ALONE.
Right?
HMM?

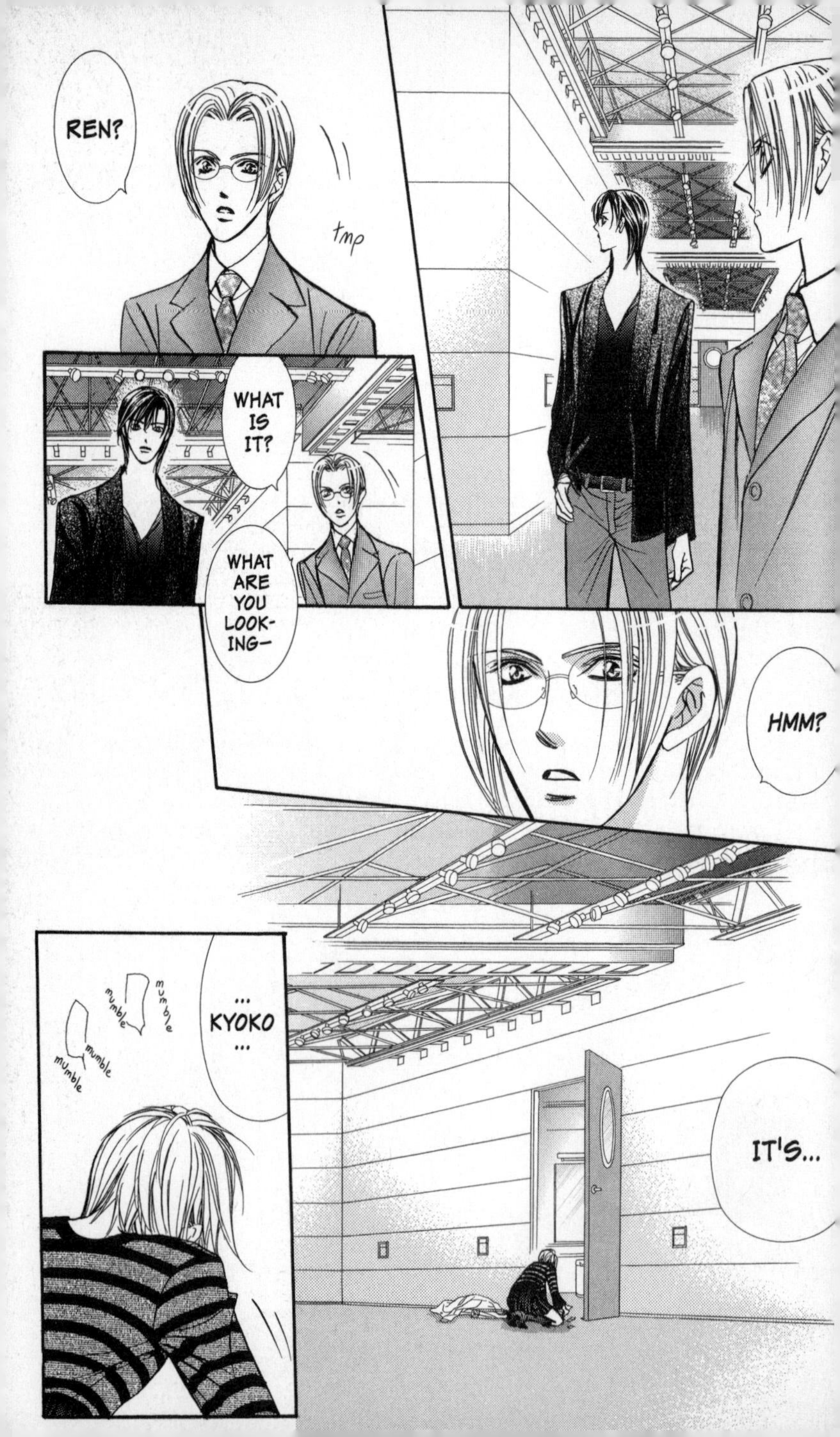
REN?
tmp
WHAT IS IT?
WHAT ARE YOU LOOKING-ING—
HMM?
IT'S...
...KYOKO...
mumble mumble
mumble mumble

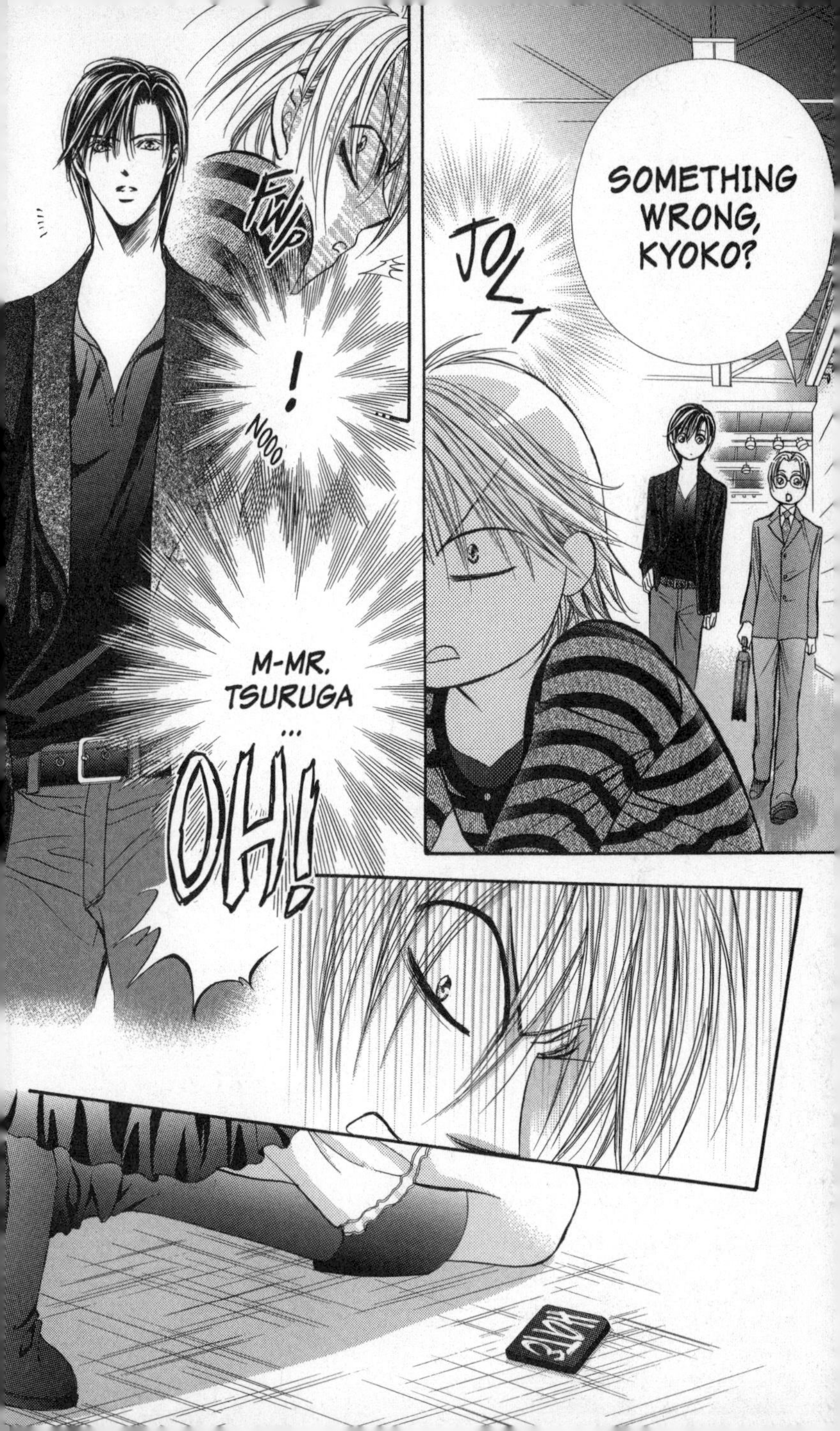
SOMETHING WRONG, KYOKO?
JOLT
FWIP
!
NOOO
M-MR. TSURUGA ...
OH!

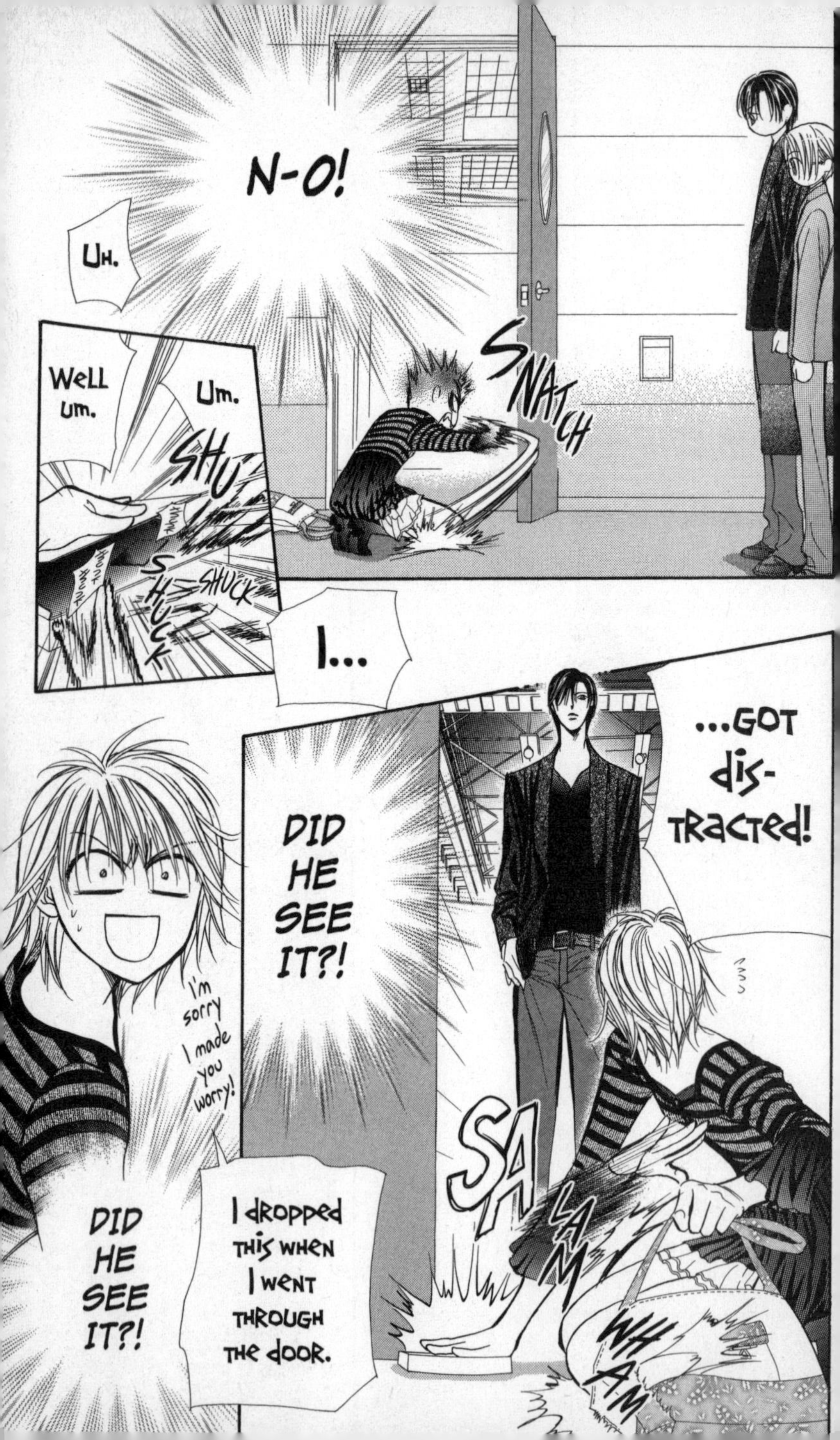
N-O!
Uh.
SNATCH
Um.
Well um.
SHU
SHUCK
SHUCK
I...
...GOT dis-tracted!
SA LAM
WHAM
DID HE SEE IT?!
I'm sorry I made you worry!
I dropped this when I went through the door.
DID HE SEE IT?!

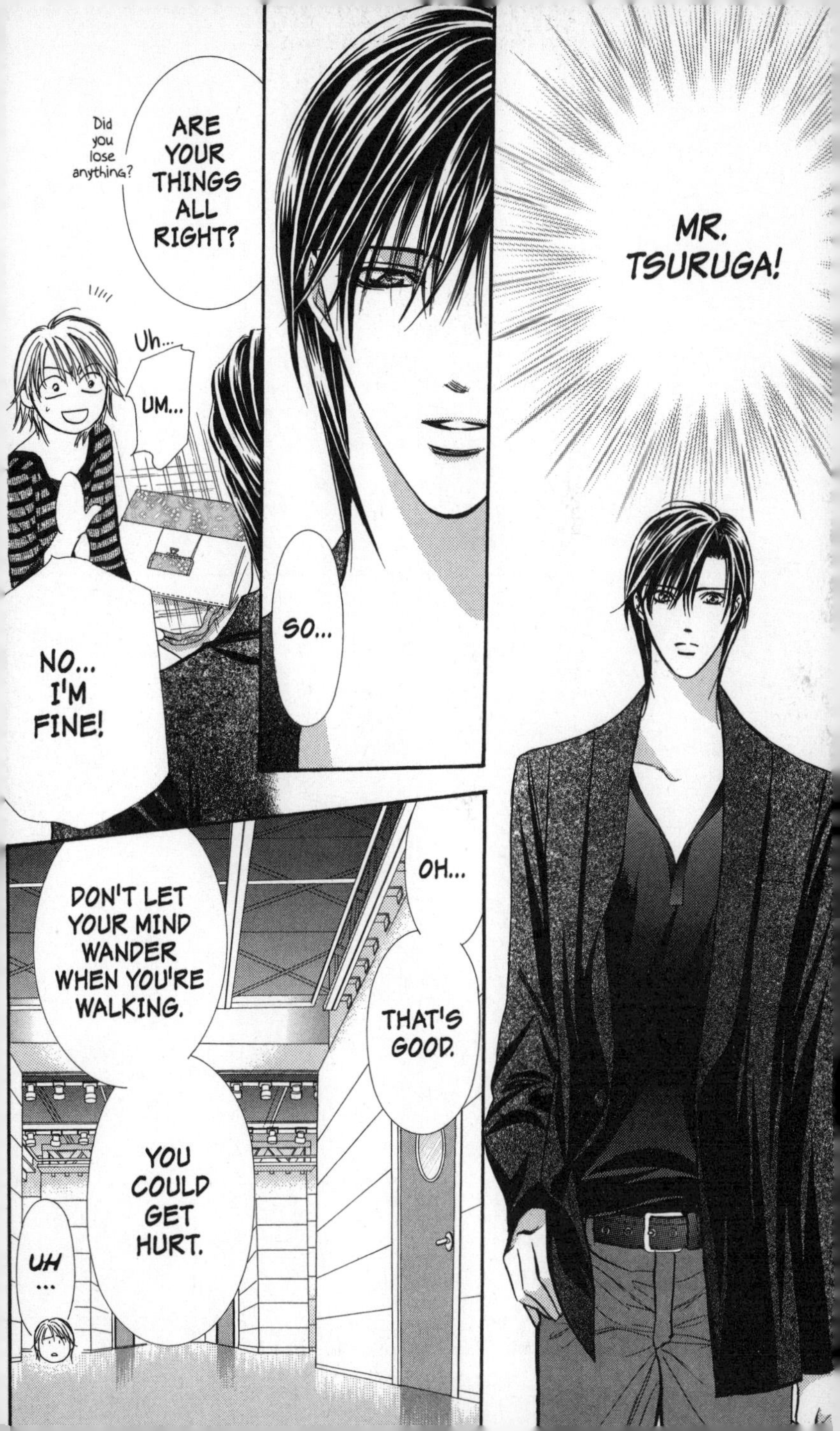
MR. TSURUGA!
ARE YOUR THINGS ALL RIGHT?
Did you lose anything?
Uh...
UM...
NO... I'M FINE!
SO...
OH...
THAT'S GOOD.
DON'T LET YOUR MIND WANDER WHEN YOU'RE WALKING.
YOU COULD GET HURT.
UH ...

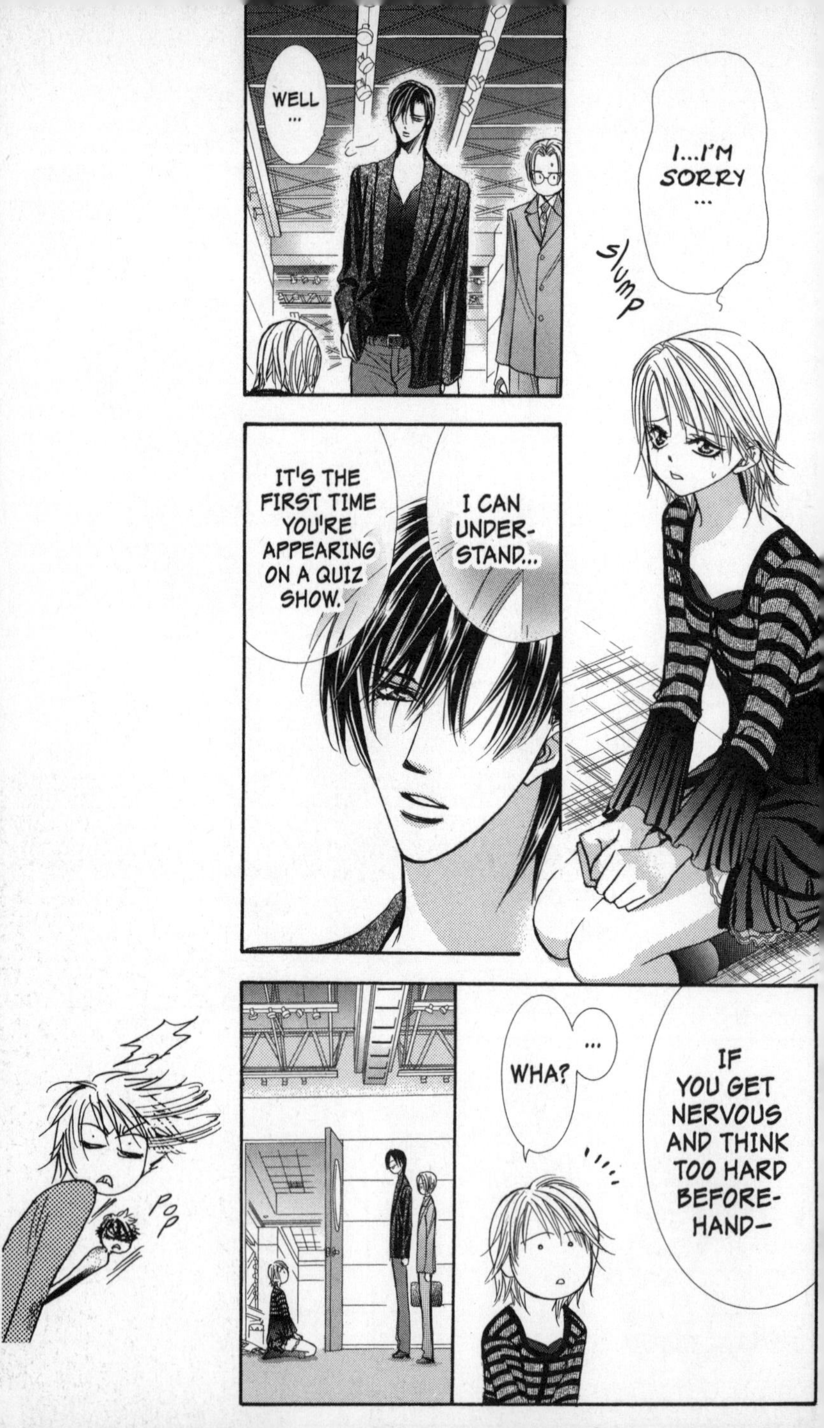

I...I'M SORRY ...
slump
WELL ...
I CAN UNDER-STAND...
IT'S THE FIRST TIME YOU'RE APPEARING ON A QUIZ SHOW.
IF YOU GET NERVOUS AND THINK TOO HARD BEFORE-HAND—
...
WHA?
POP

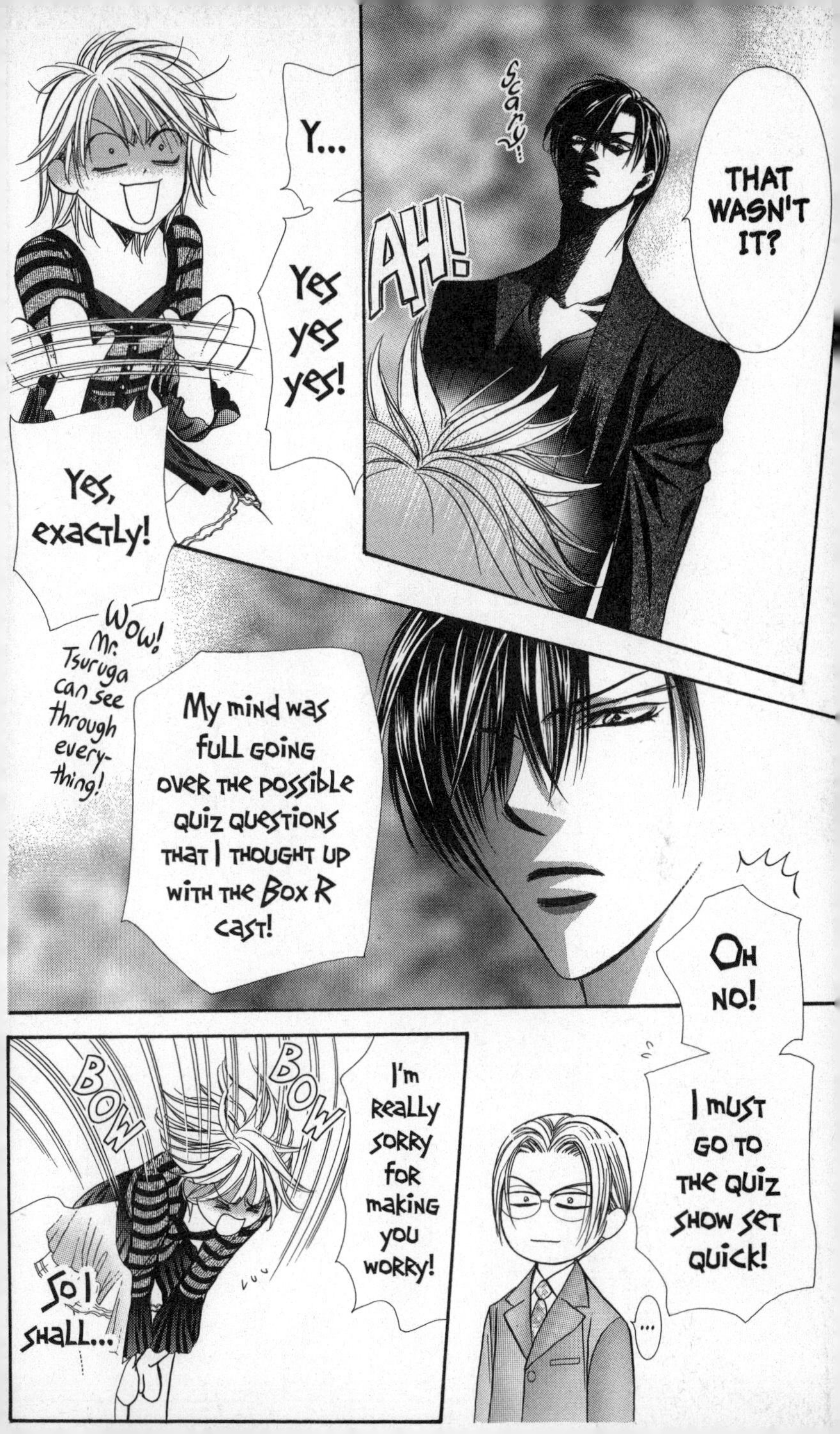

THAT WASN'T IT?
Scary...
AH!
Y...
Yes yes yes!
Yes, exactly!
Oh no!
My mind was full going over the possible quiz questions that I thought up with the Box R cast!
Wow! Mr. Tsuruga can see through everything!
I must go to the quiz show set quick!
...
I'm really sorry for making you worry!
BOW
BOW
So I shall...

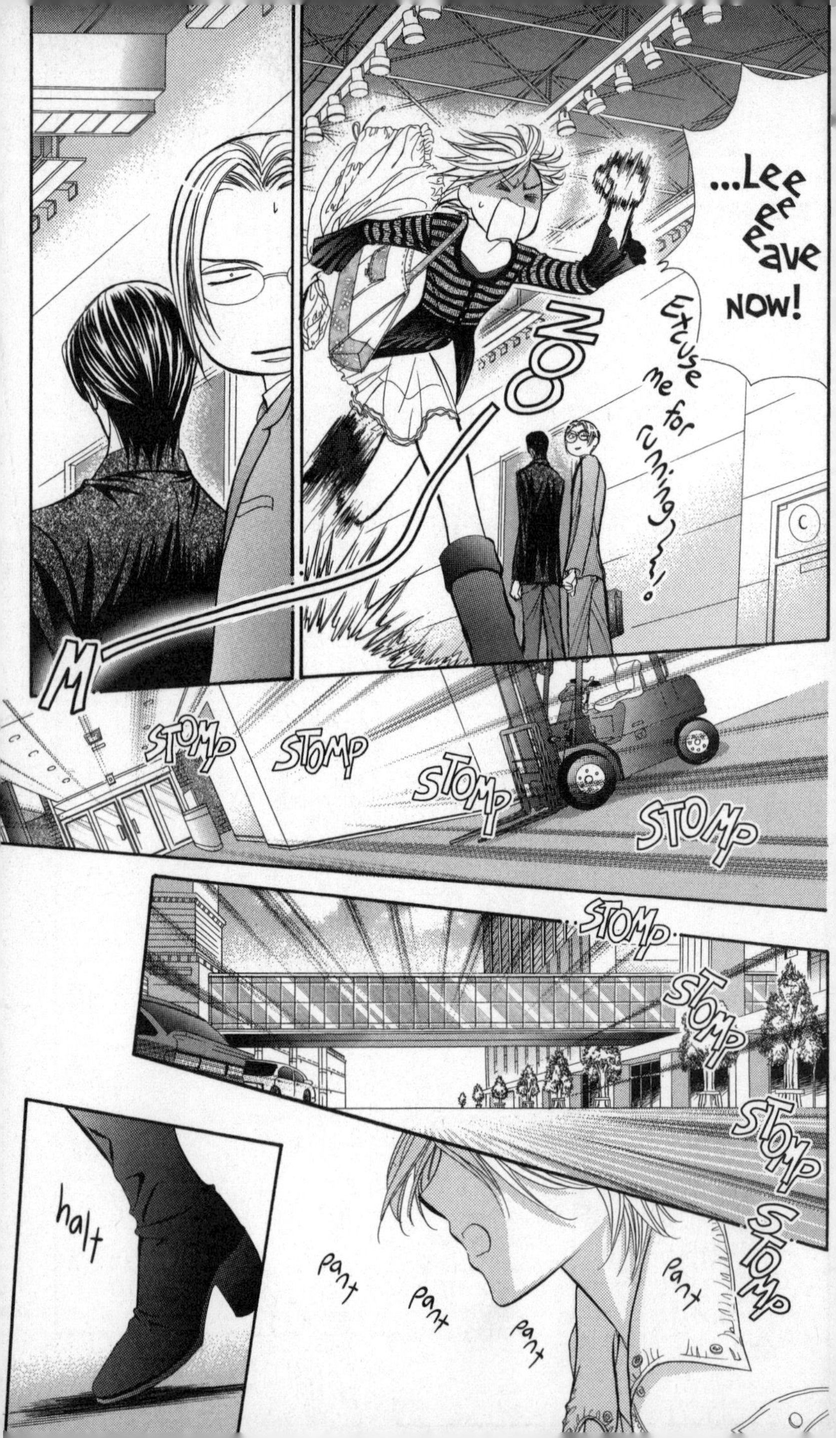
...Leeeeeave NOW!
Excuse me for running~~!
ZOOM
STOMP
STOMP
STOMP
STOMP
STOMP
STOMP
STOMP
STOMP
pant
pant
pant
pant
halt

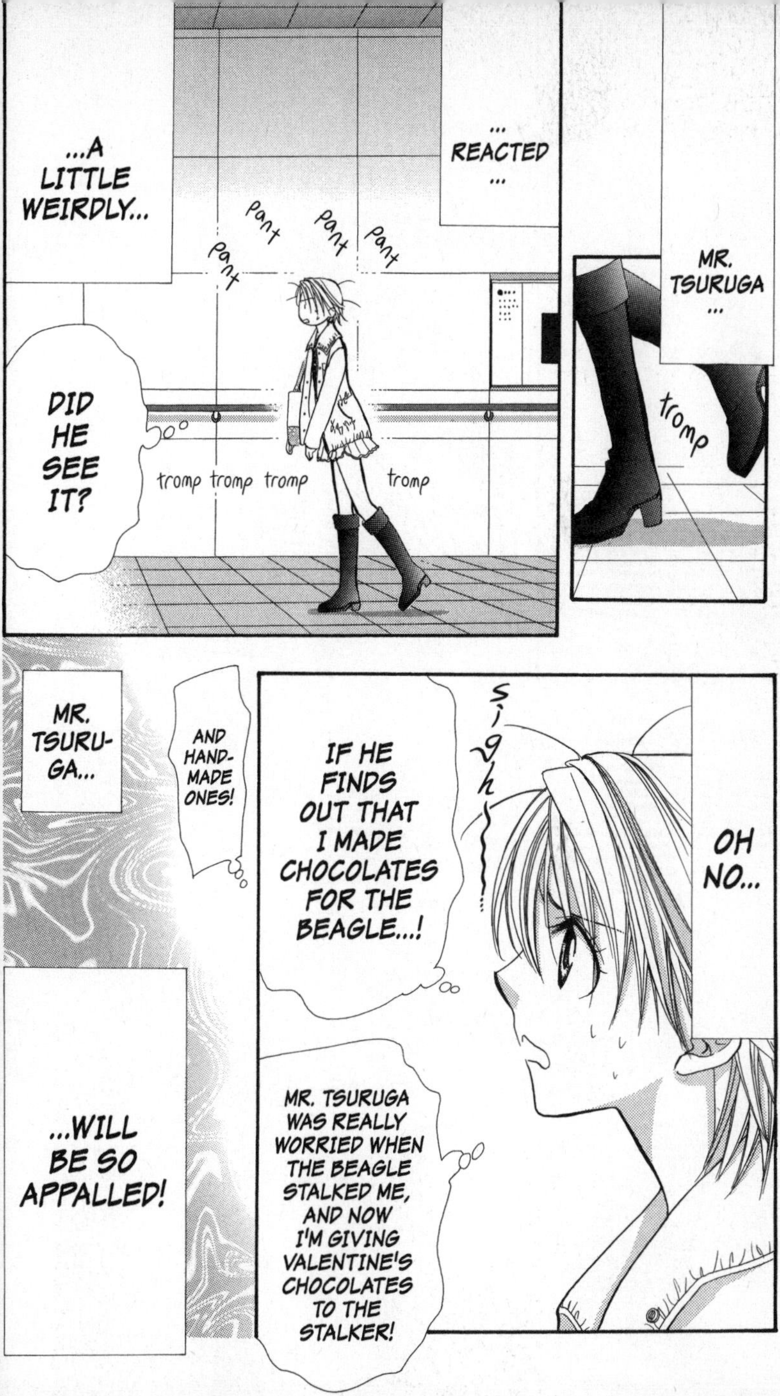

MR. TSURUGA ...
tromp
... REACTED ...
...A LITTLE WEIRDLY...
pant pant pant pant
DID HE SEE IT?
tromp tromp tromp
tromp
OH NO...
sigh
IF HE FINDS OUT THAT I MADE CHOCOLATES FOR THE BEAGLE...!
MR. TSURUGA WAS REALLY WORRIED WHEN THE BEAGLE STALKED ME, AND NOW I'M GIVING VALENTINE'S CHOCOLATES TO THE STALKER!
AND HAND-MADE ONES!
MR. TSURU-GA...
...WILL BE SO APPALLED!

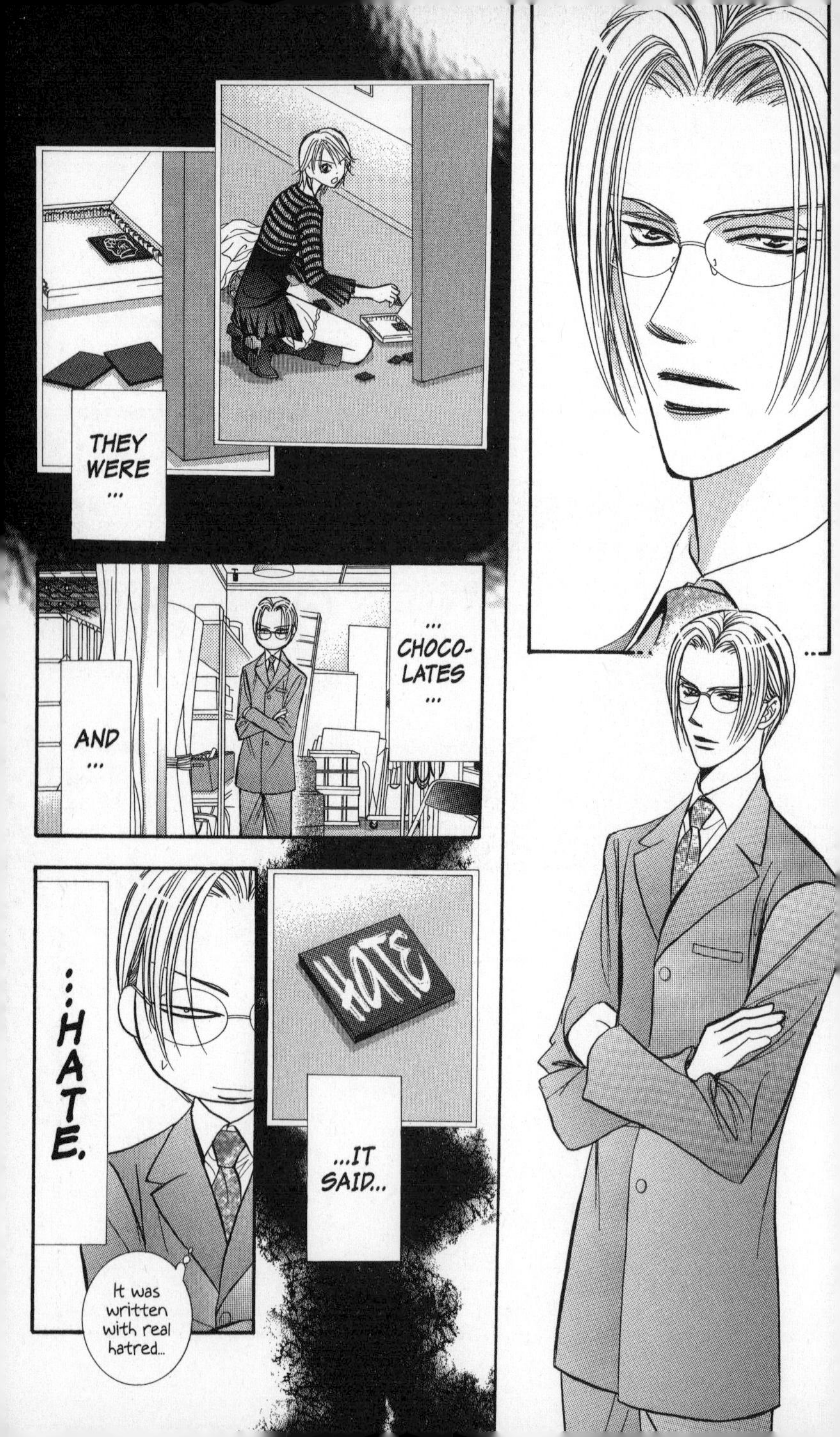

...
...
THEY WERE ...
... CHOCOLATES ...
AND ...
...IT SAID...
...HATE.
It was written with real hatred...

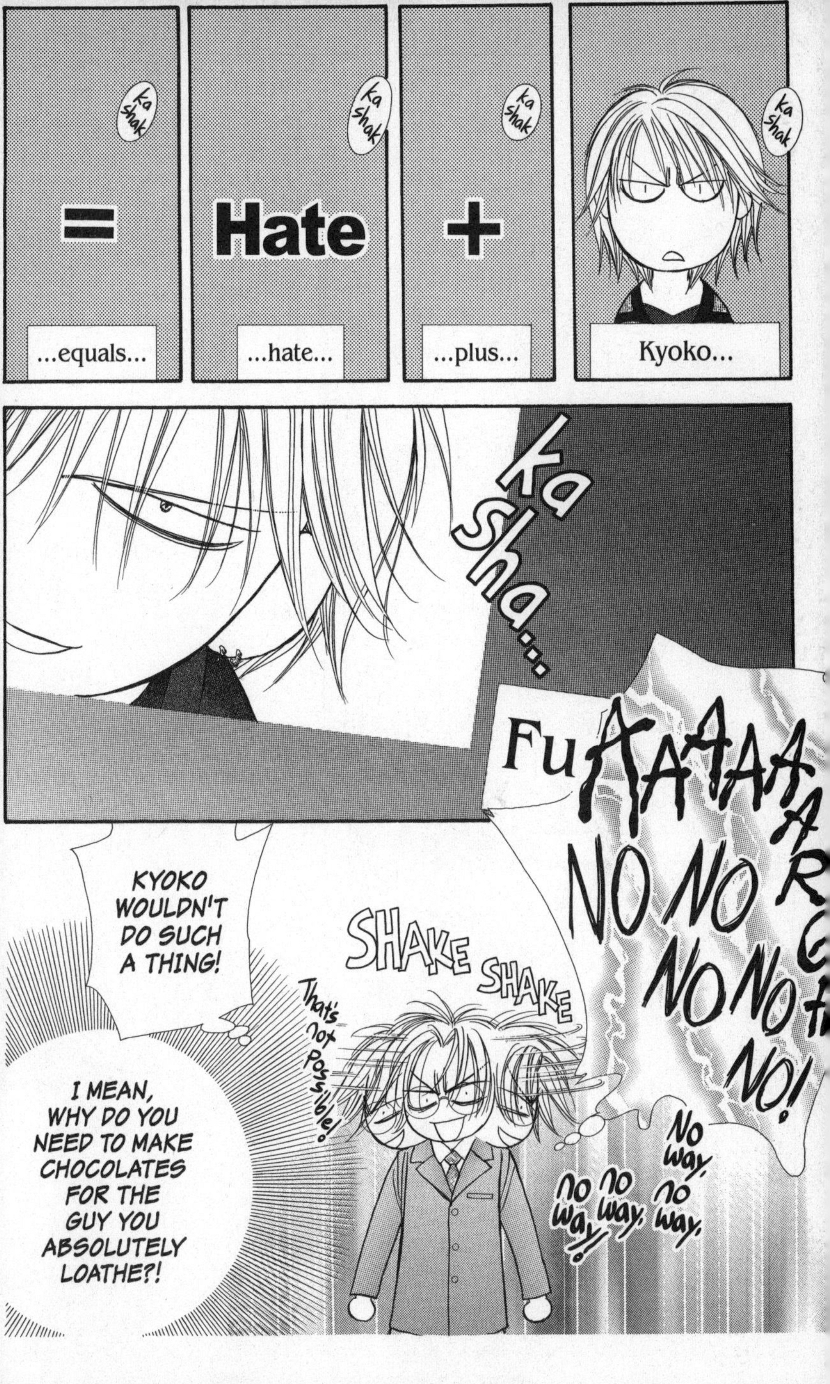
ka shak
Kyoko...
ka shak
+
...plus...
ka shak
Hate
...hate...
ka shak
=
...equals...
ka sha...
FuAAAAARG
NO NO NO NO NO!
KYOKO WOULDN'T DO SUCH A THING!
SHAKE SHAKE
That's not possible!
No way, no way, no way, no way!!
I MEAN, WHY DO YOU NEED TO MAKE CHOCOLATES FOR THE GUY YOU ABSOLUTELY LOATHE?!

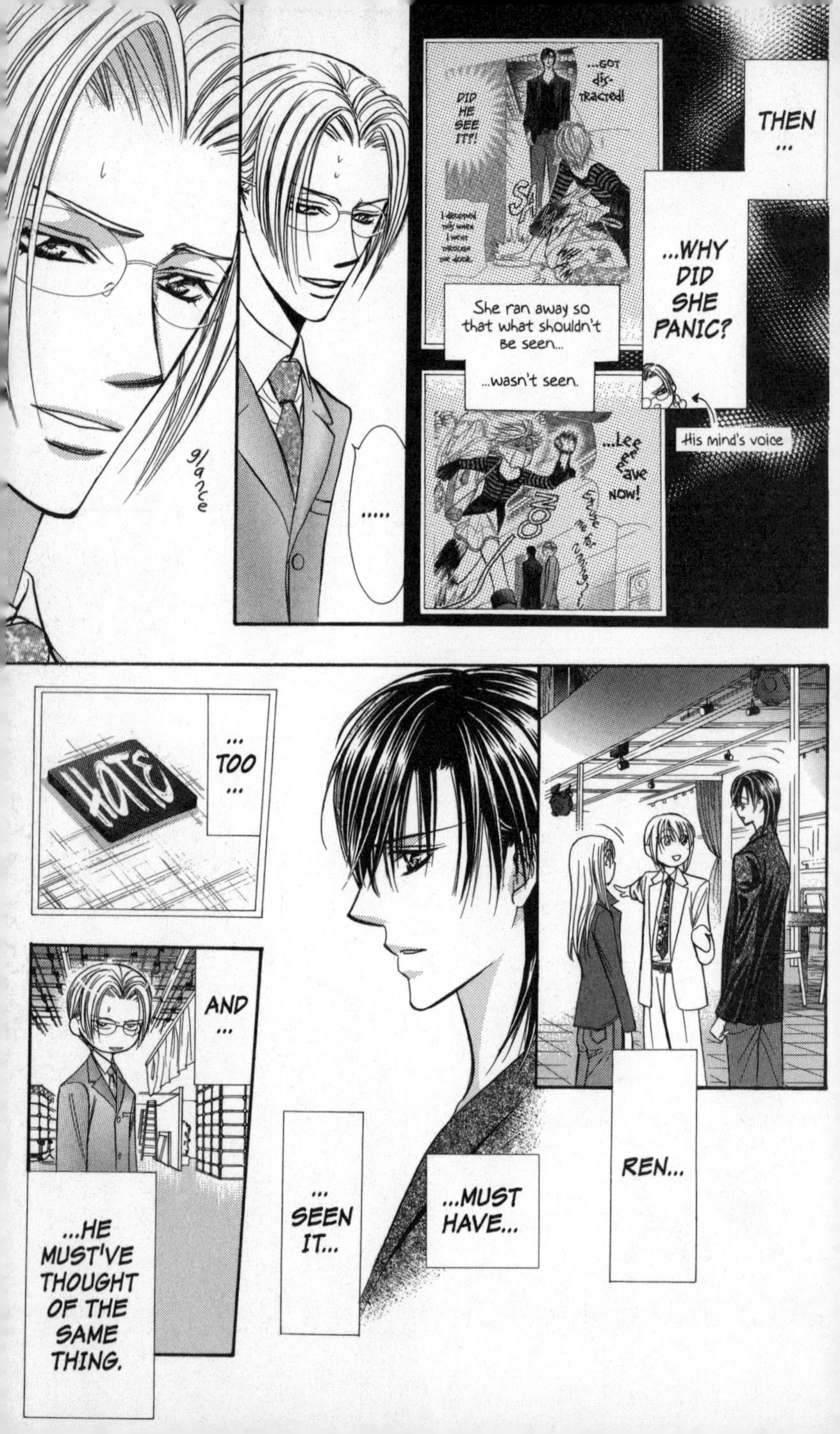
THEN...
...WHY DID SHE PANIC?
His mind's voice
DID HE SEE IT!
...GOT dis-tracted!
She ran away so that what shouldn't be seen...
...wasn't seen.
.....
glance
REN...
...MUST HAVE...
...SEEN IT...
...TOO...
AND...
...HE MUST'VE THOUGHT OF THE SAME THING.

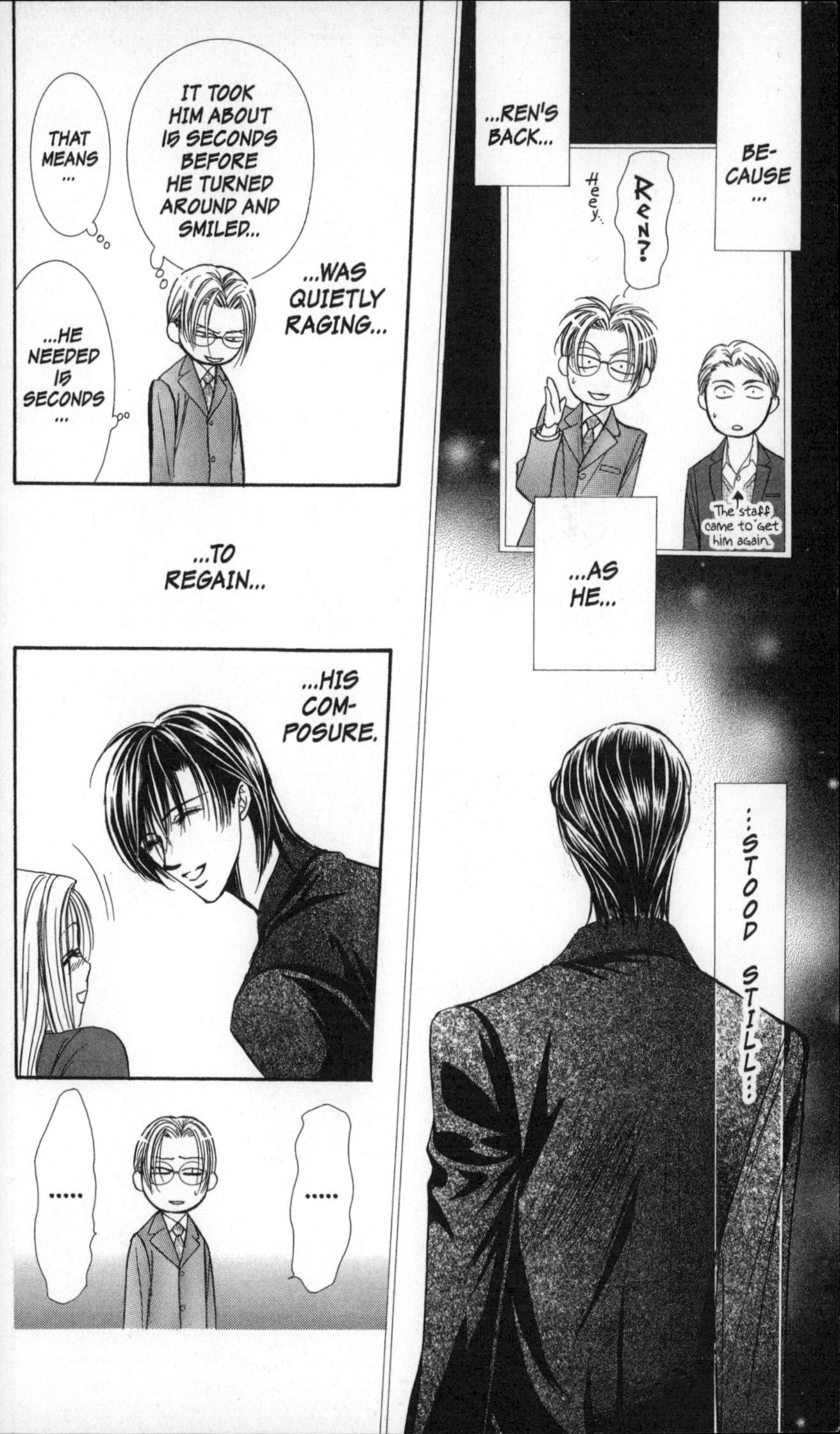
BE-CAUSE...
...REN'S BACK...
Heey...
REN?
The staff came to get him again.
...AS HE...
...STOOD STILL...
...WAS QUIETLY RAGING...
IT TOOK HIM ABOUT 15 SECONDS BEFORE HE TURNED AROUND AND SMILED...
THAT MEANS...
...HE NEEDED 15 SECONDS...
...TO REGAIN...
...HIS COM-POSURE.
.....
.....

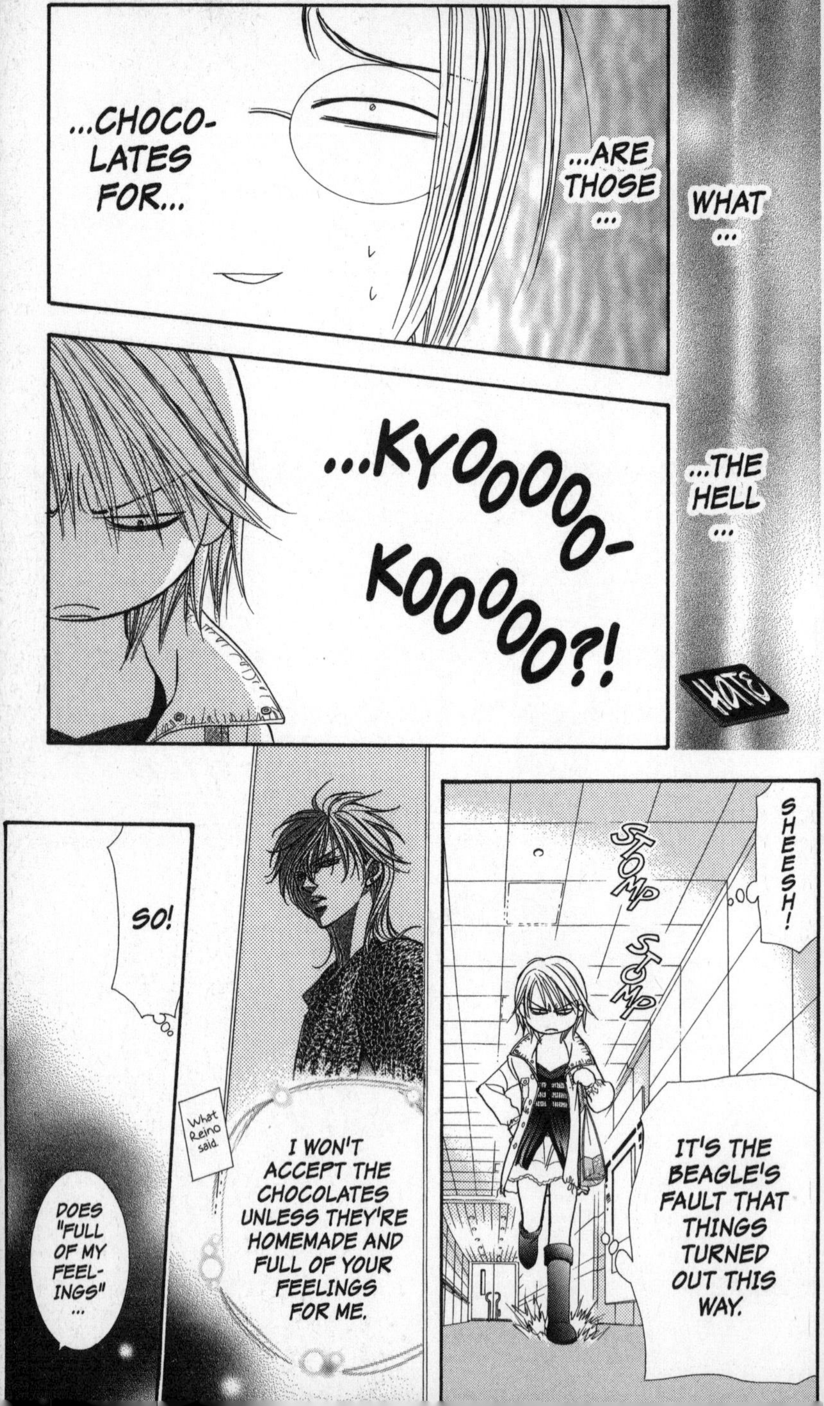
WHAT ...
...THE HELL ...
...ARE THOSE ...
...CHOCO-LATES FOR...
...KYOOOOO-KOOOOO?!
SHEESH!
STOMP STOMP
IT'S THE BEAGLE'S FAULT THAT THINGS TURNED OUT THIS WAY.
What Reino said.
I WON'T ACCEPT THE CHOCOLATES UNLESS THEY'RE HOMEMADE AND FULL OF YOUR FEELINGS FOR ME.
SO!
DOES "FULL OF MY FEEL-INGS" ...

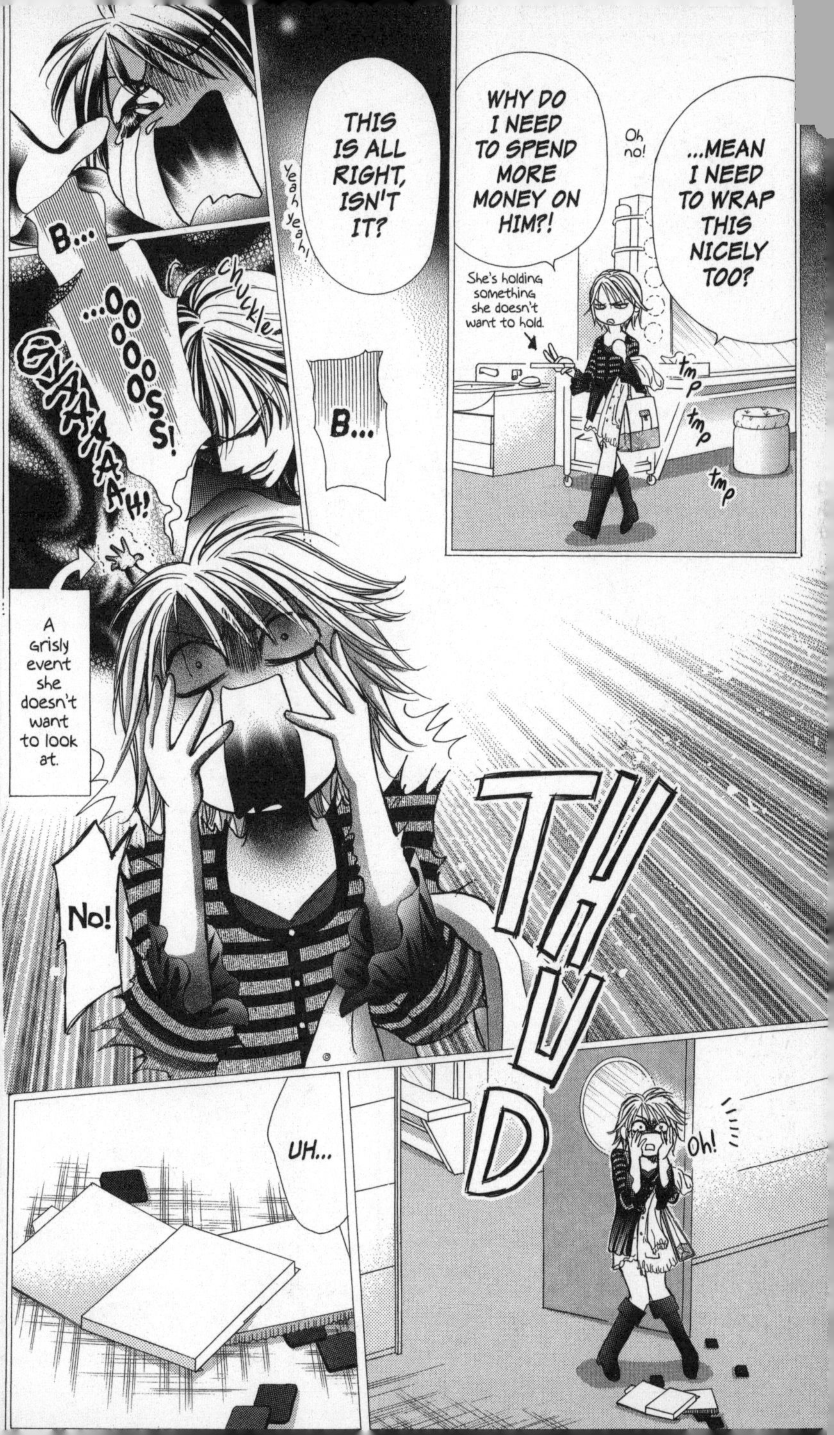
...MEAN I NEED TO WRAP THIS NICELY TOO?
Oh no!
WHY DO I NEED TO SPEND MORE MONEY ON HIM?!
She's holding something she doesn't want to hold.
tmp tmp tmp
THIS IS ALL RIGHT, ISN'T IT?
Yeah yeah!
B...
Chuckle
B... ...OOOOOOSS!
GYAAAAH!
A grisly event she doesn't want to look at.
No!
THUD
Oh!
UH...

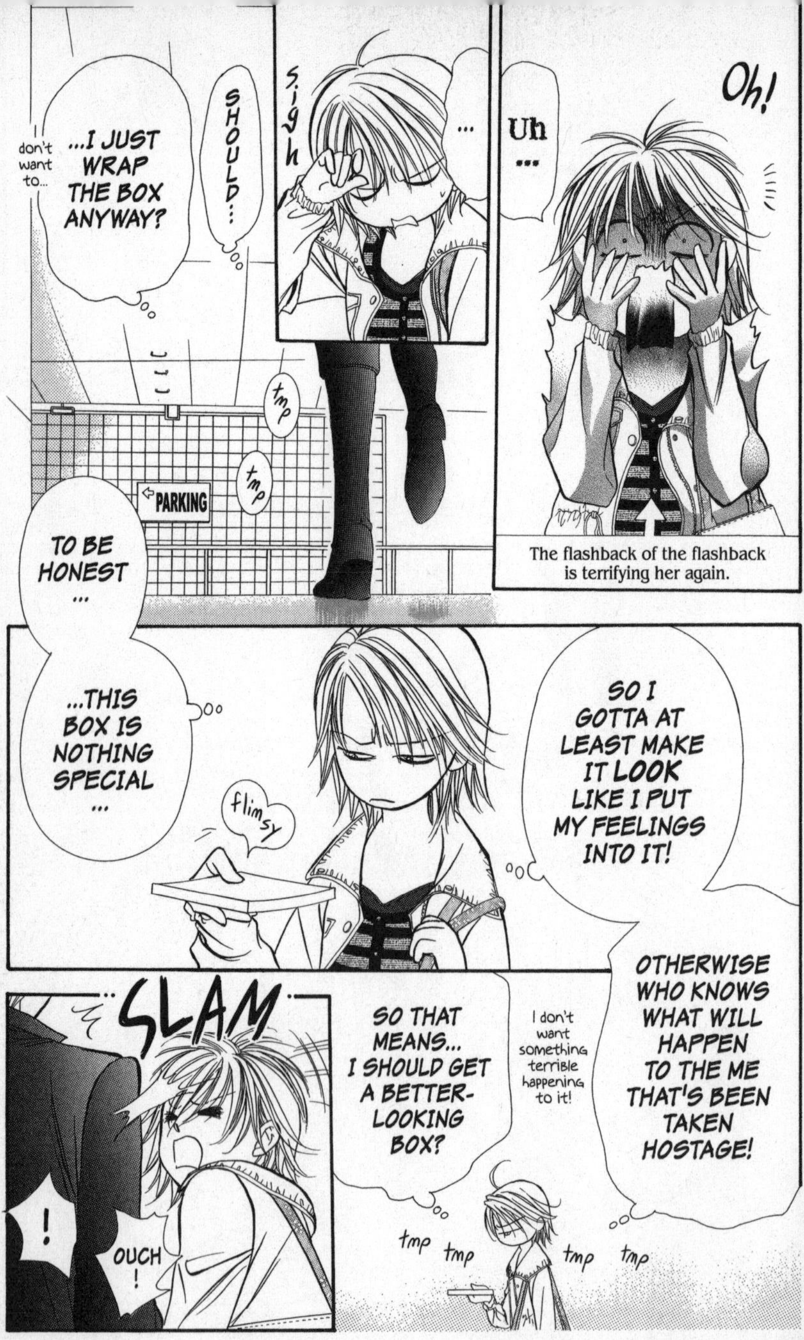
Oh!
Uh...
The flashback of the flashback is terrifying her again.
Sigh
...
SHOULD...
...I JUST WRAP THE BOX ANYWAY?
I don't want to...
tmp
tmp
PARKING
TO BE HONEST...
...THIS BOX IS NOTHING SPECIAL...
flimsy
SO I GOTTA AT LEAST MAKE IT LOOK LIKE I PUT MY FEELINGS INTO IT!
OTHERWISE WHO KNOWS WHAT WILL HAPPEN TO THE ME THAT'S BEEN TAKEN HOSTAGE!
I don't want something terrible happening to it!
SO THAT MEANS... I SHOULD GET A BETTER-LOOKING BOX?
tmp tmp tmp tmp
SLAM
!
OUCH!

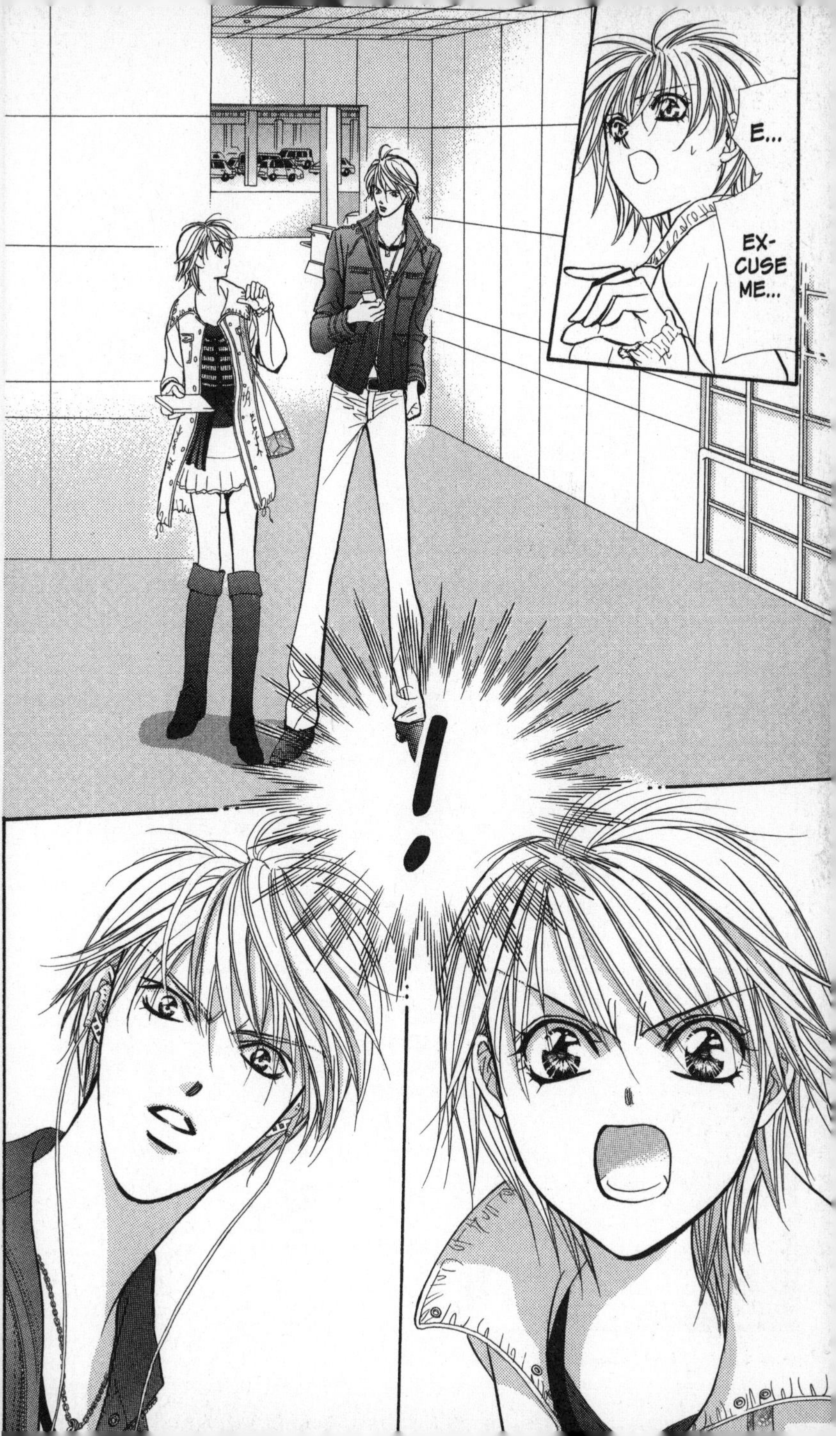
E...
EX-CUSE ME...
!

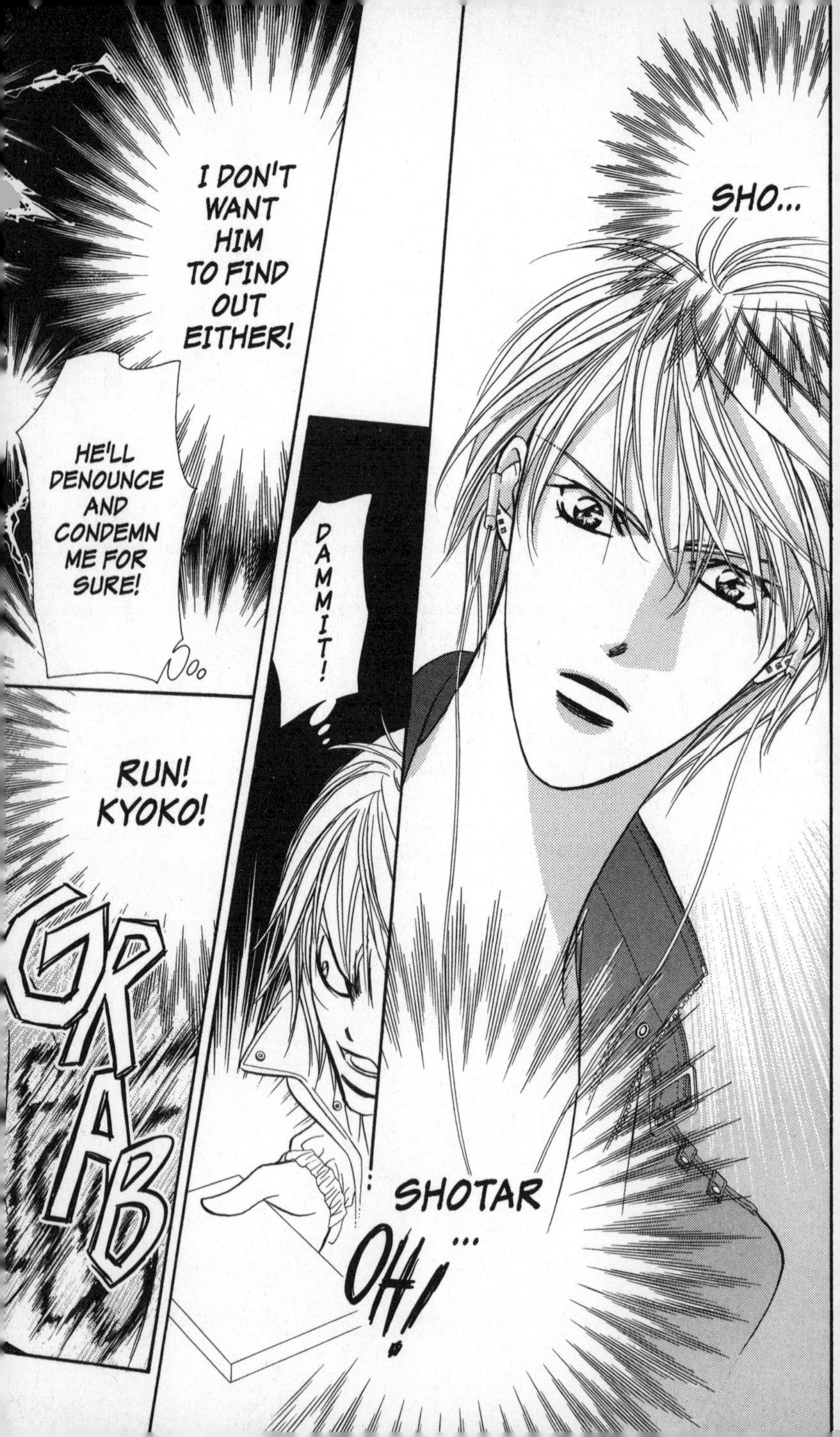
SHO...
SHOTAR...OH!
DAMMIT!
I DON'T WANT HIM TO FIND OUT EITHER!
HE'LL DENOUNCE AND CONDEMN ME FOR SURE!
RUN! KYOKO!
GRAB

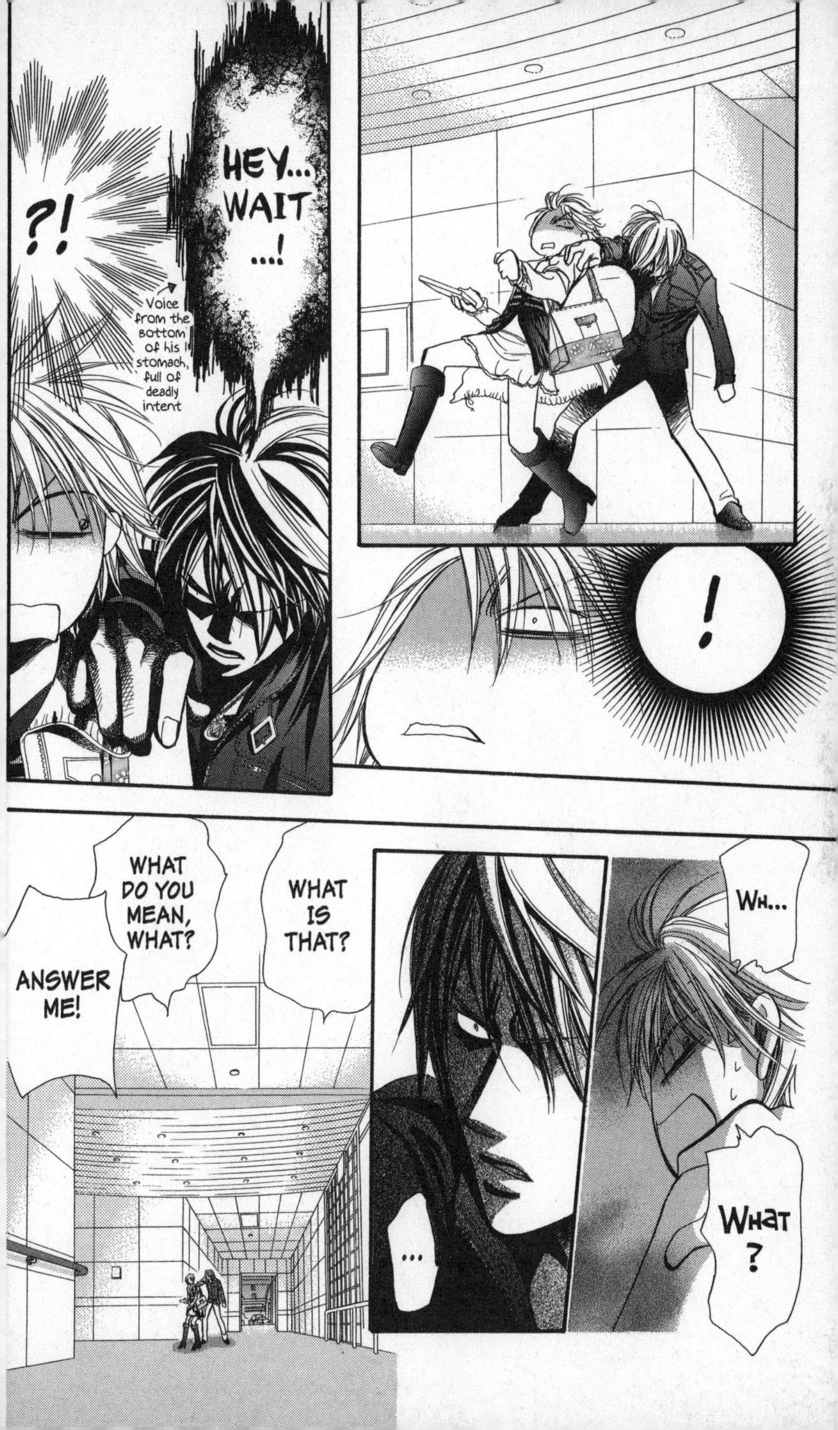
!
HEY... WAIT ...!
Voice from the bottom of his stomach, full of deadly intent
?!
Wh...
What ?
...
WHAT IS THAT?
WHAT DO YOU MEAN, WHAT?
ANSWER ME!

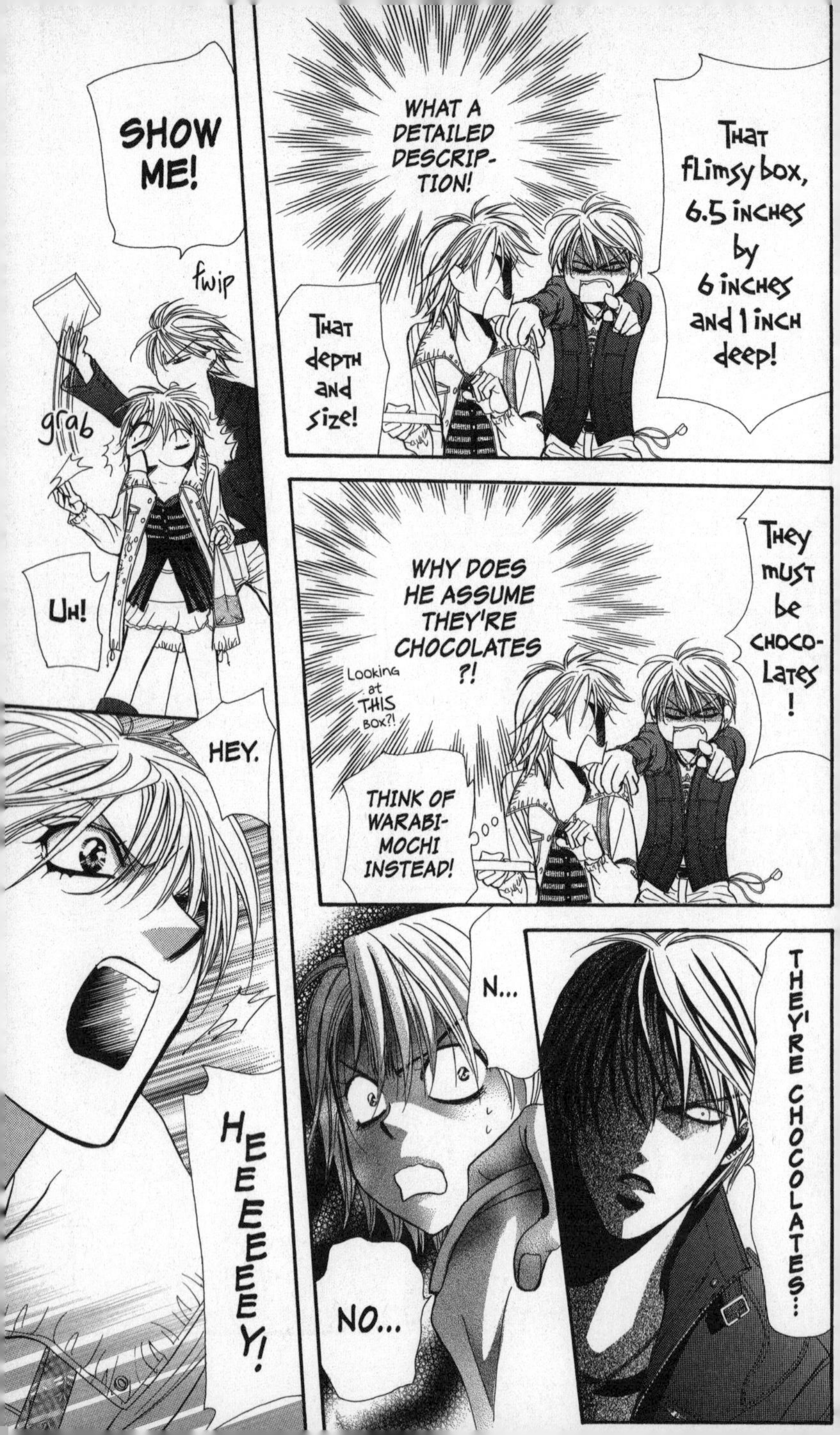
That flimsy box, 6.5 inches by 6 inches and 1 inch deep!
WHAT A DETAILED DESCRIPTION!
That depth and size!
They must be chocolates!
WHY DOES HE ASSUME THEY'RE CHOCOLATES?!
Looking at THIS box?!
THINK OF WARABI-MOCHI INSTEAD!
They're chocolates...
N...
NO...
SHOW ME!
fwip
grab
UH!
HEY.
HEEEEEEY!

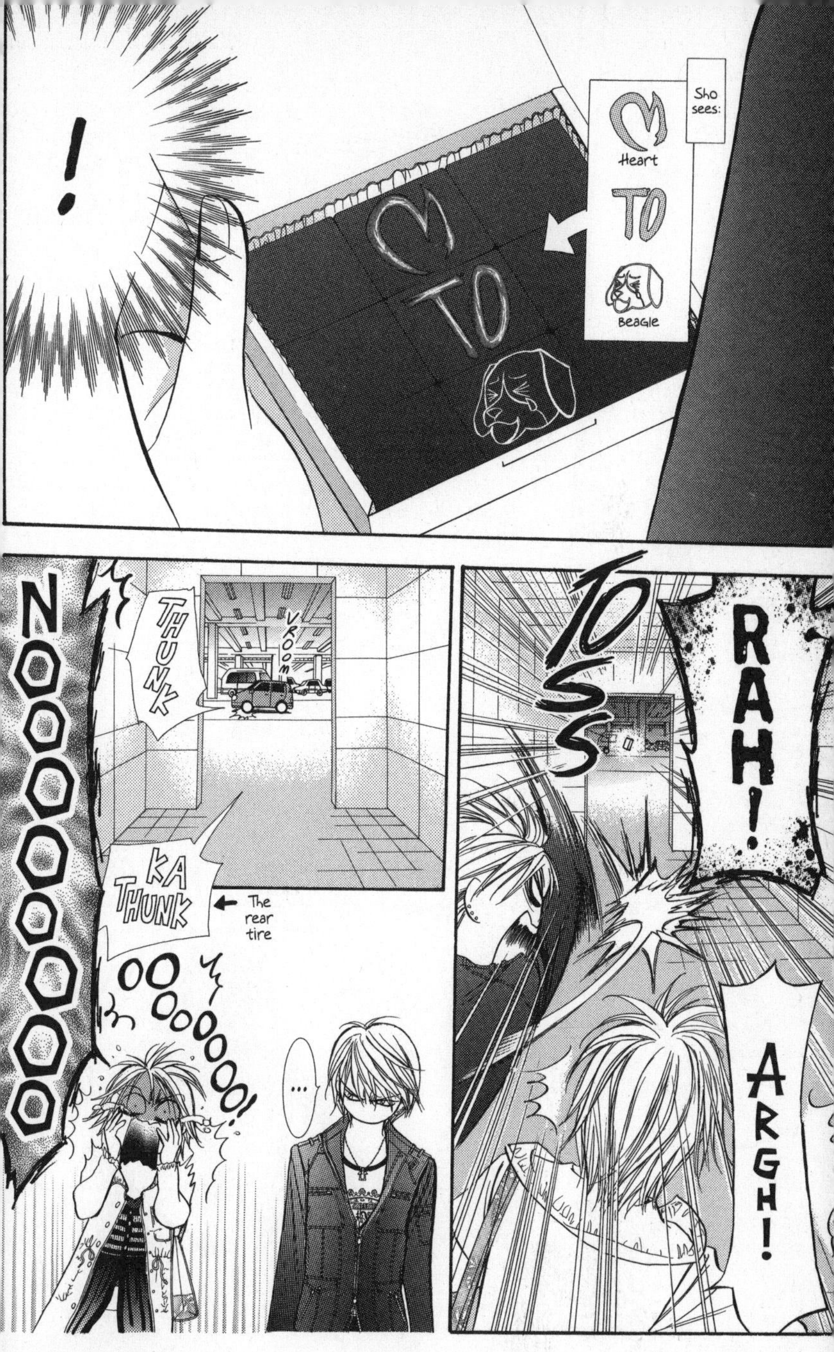
!
Sho sees:
Heart
TO
Beagle
TOSS
RAH!
ARGH!
THUNK
VROOM
KA THUNK
The rear tire
NOOOOOOOOOO
OOOOOOOOOO!
...

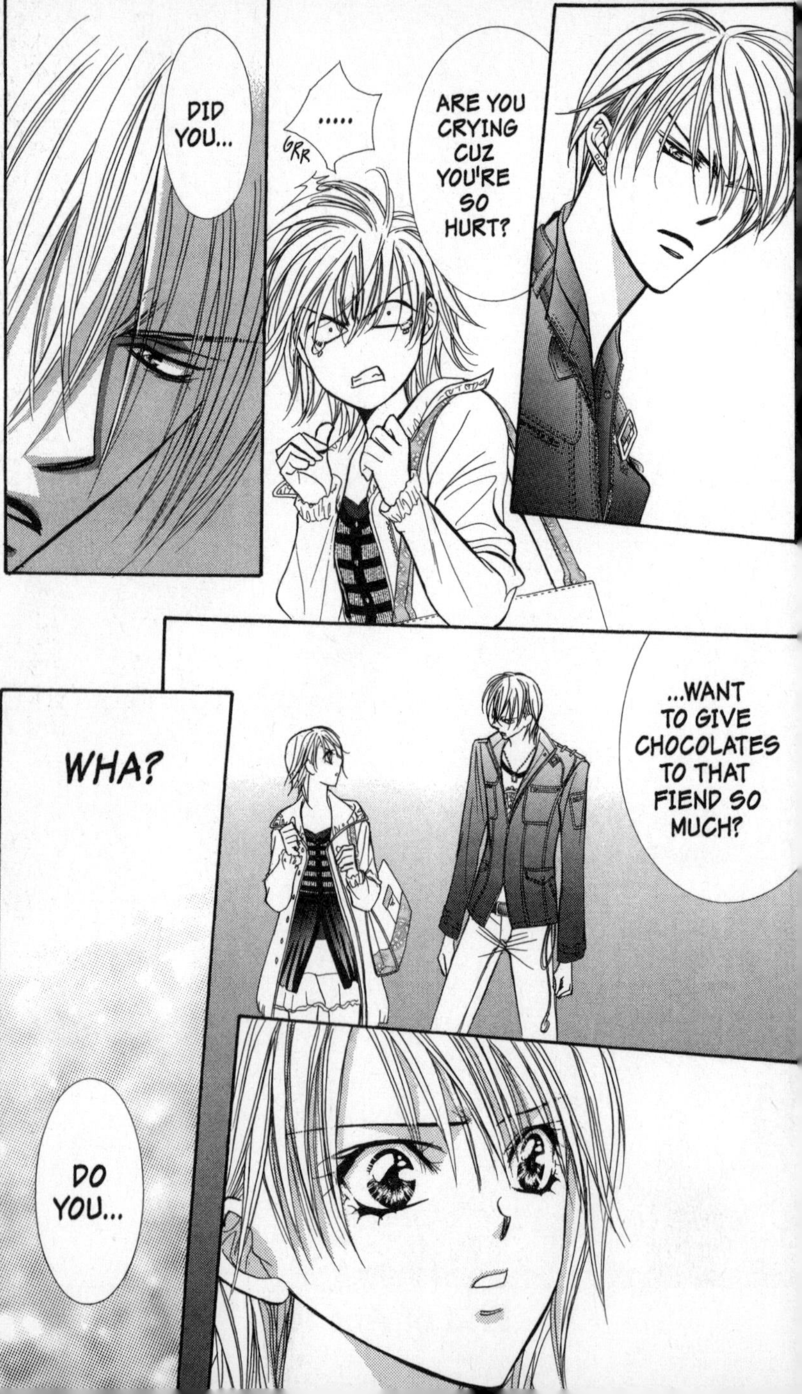
ARE YOU CRYING CUZ YOU'RE SO HURT?
GRR
.....
DID YOU...
...WANT TO GIVE CHOCOLATES TO THAT FIEND SO MUCH?
WHA?
DO YOU...

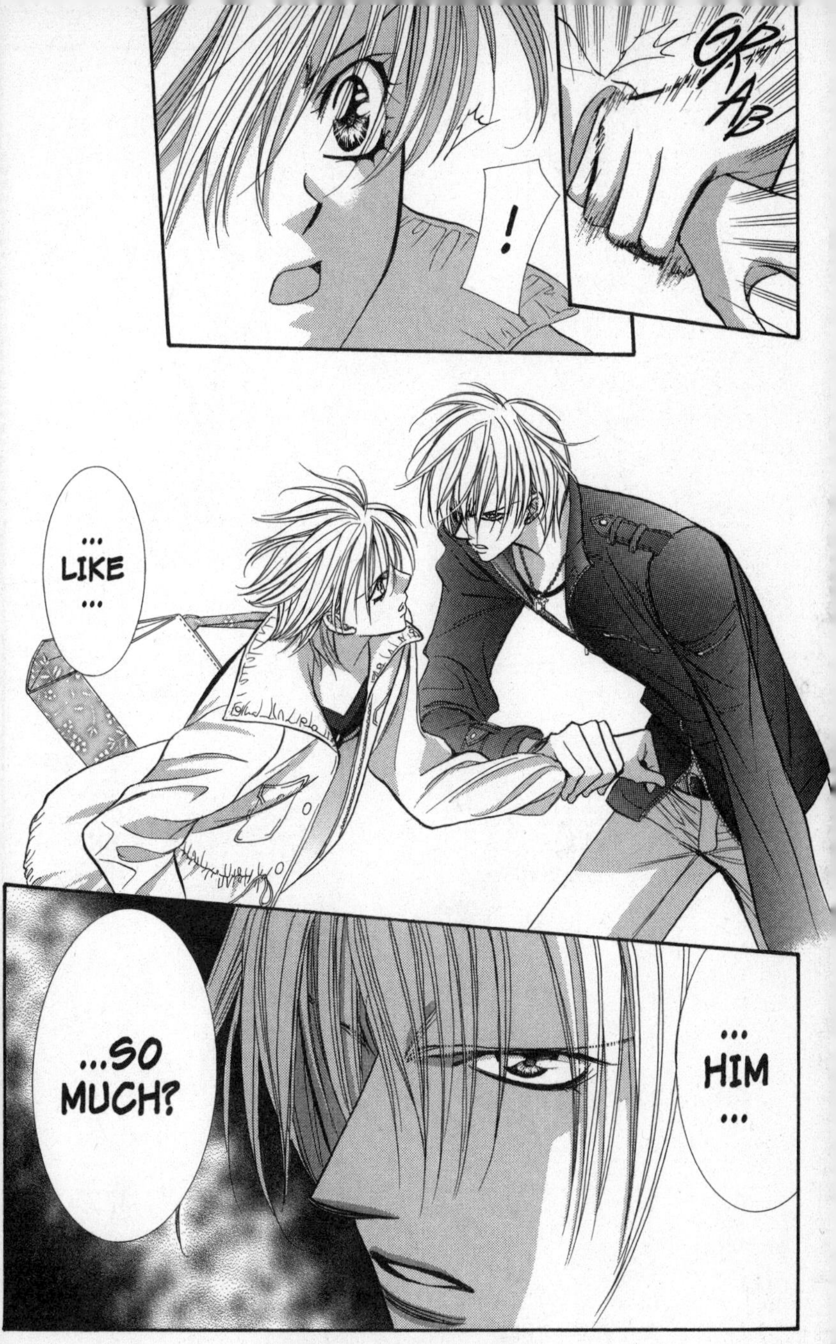
GRAB
!
...LIKE...
...HIM...
...SO MUCH?

End of Act 142

The Mystery of Valentine's Day *Yukihito Yashiro version*

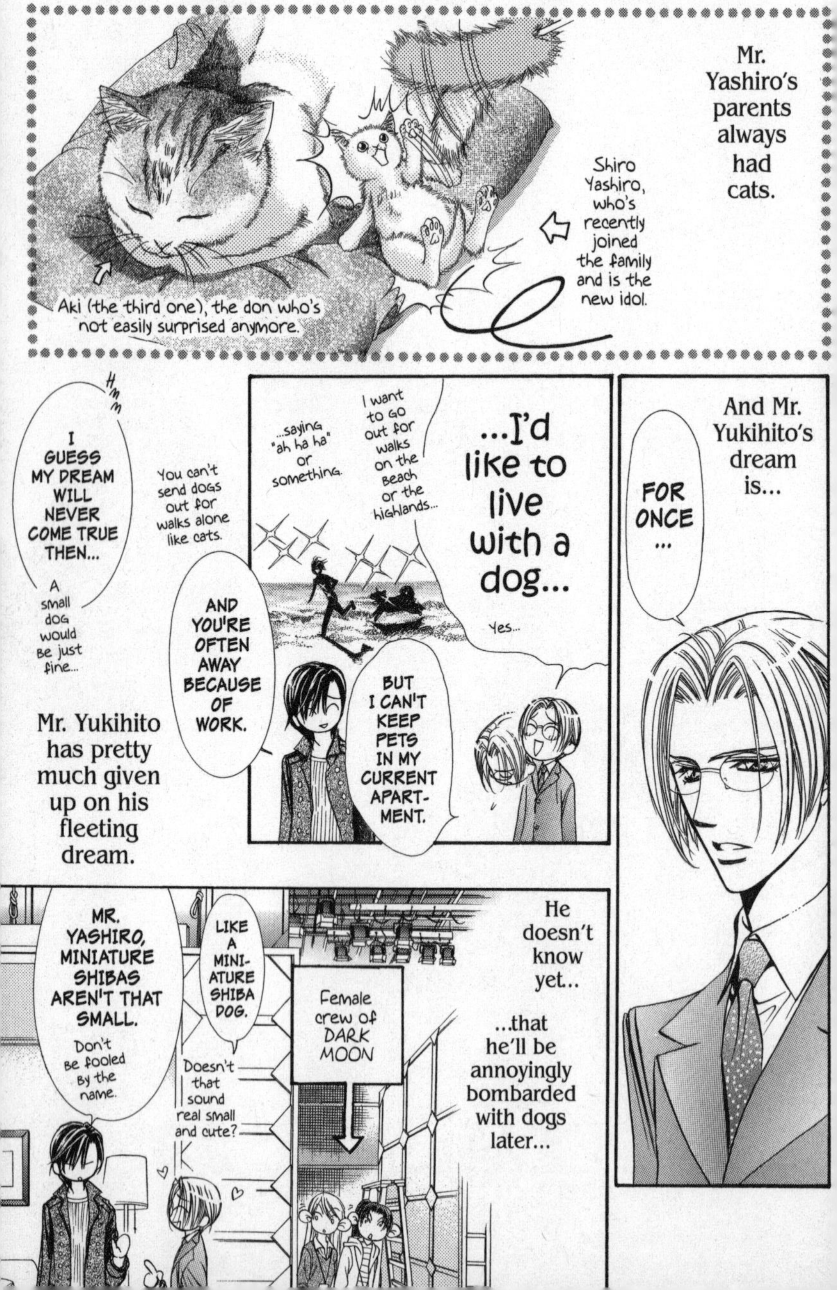
Mr. Yashiro's parents always had cats.
Shiro Yashiro, who's recently joined the family and is the new idol.
Aki (the third one), the don who's not easily surprised anymore.
And Mr. Yukihito's dream is...
FOR ONCE...
...I'd like to live with a dog...
I want to go out for walks on the beach or the highlands...
...saying "ah ha ha" or something.
Yes...
BUT I CAN'T KEEP PETS IN MY CURRENT APART-MENT.
AND YOU'RE OFTEN AWAY BECAUSE OF WORK.
You can't send dogs out for walks alone like cats.
Hmm
I GUESS MY DREAM WILL NEVER COME TRUE THEN...
A small dog would be just fine...
Mr. Yukihito has pretty much given up on his fleeting dream.
He doesn't know yet.. ...that he'll be annoyingly bombarded with dogs later...
Female crew of DARK MOON
LIKE A MINI-ATURE SHIBA DOG.
Doesn't that sound real small and cute?
MR. YASHIRO, MINIATURE SHIBAS AREN'T THAT SMALL.
Don't be fooled by the name.

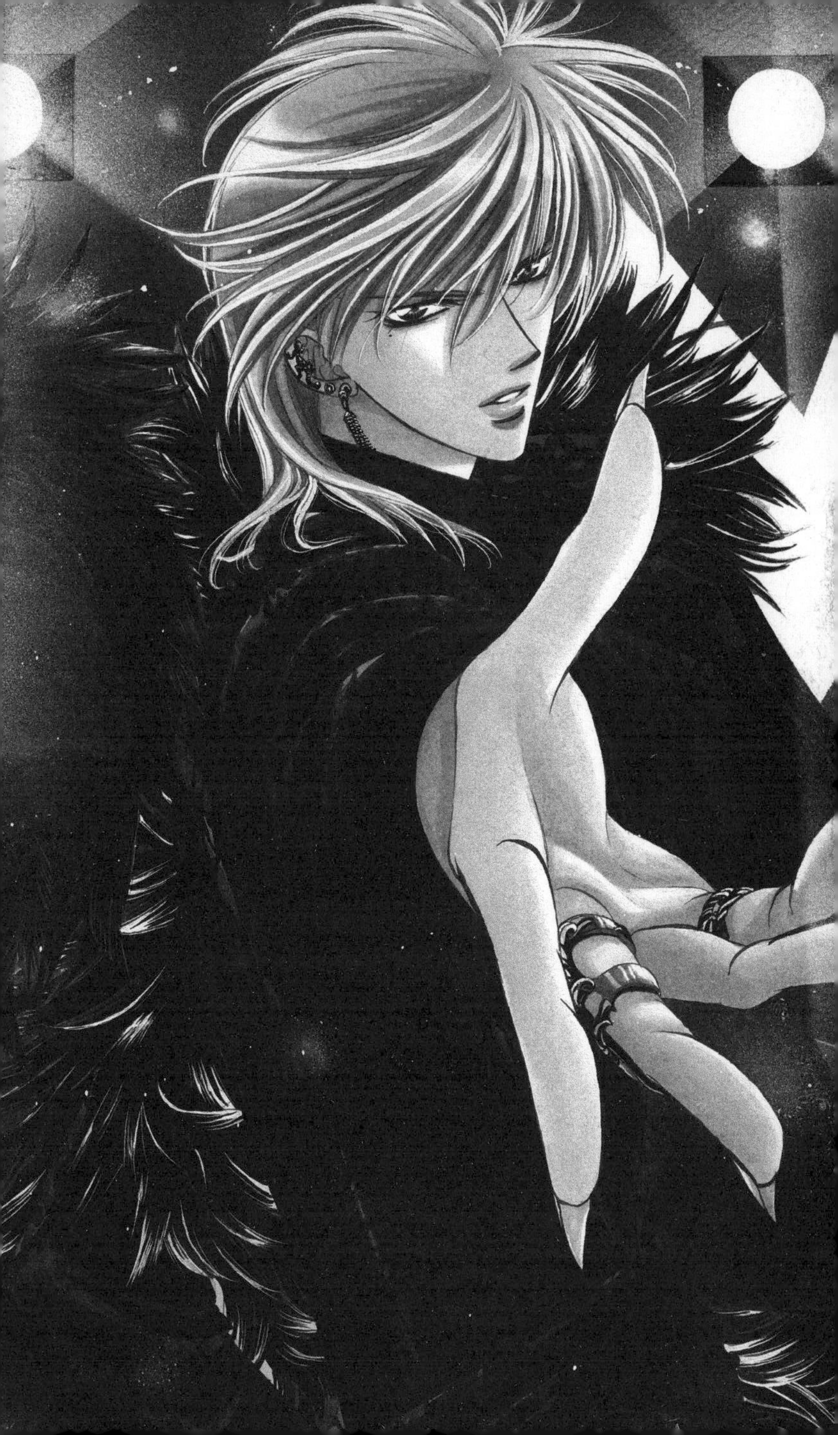

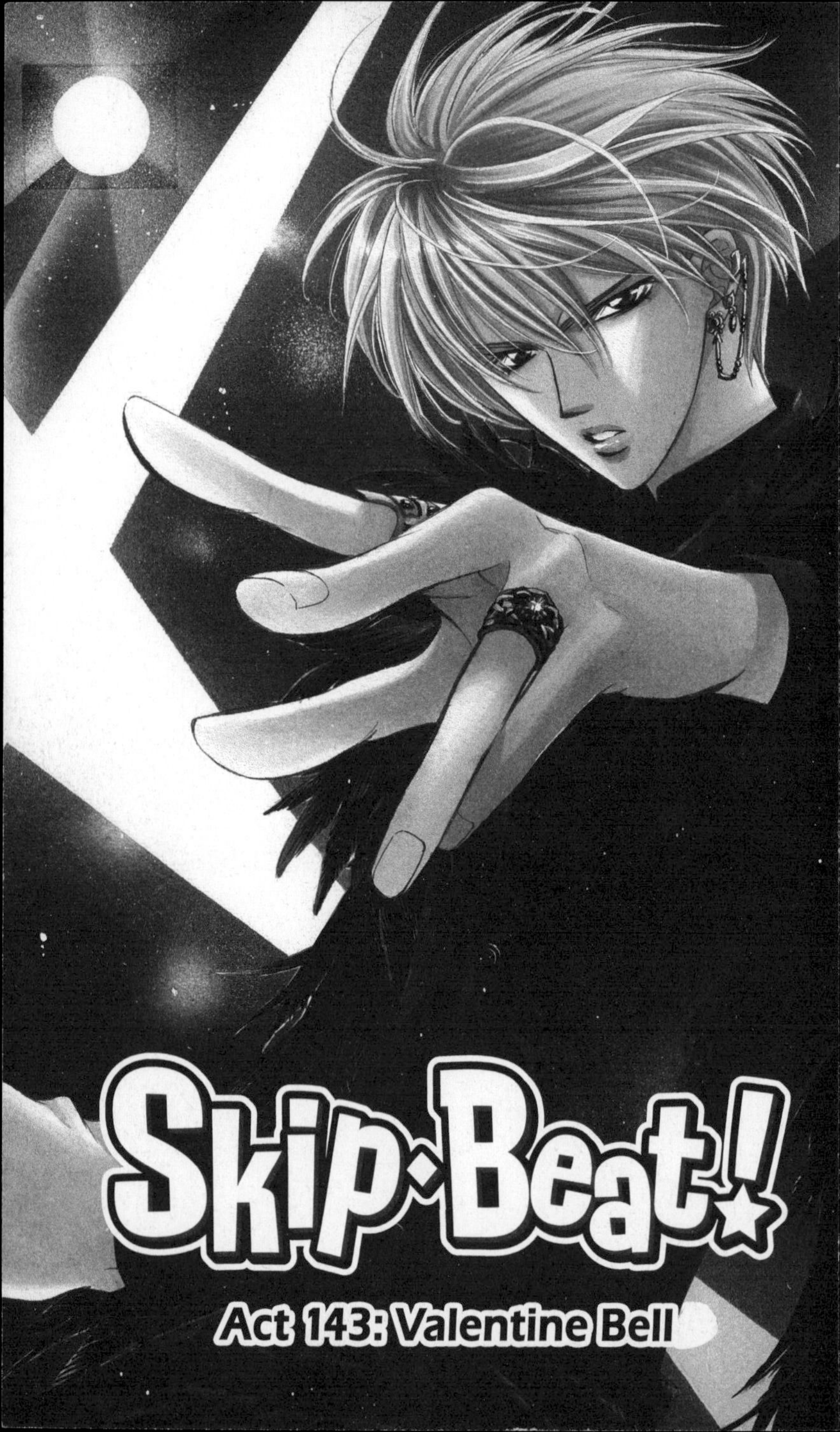
Skip·Beat!
Act 143: Valentine Bell

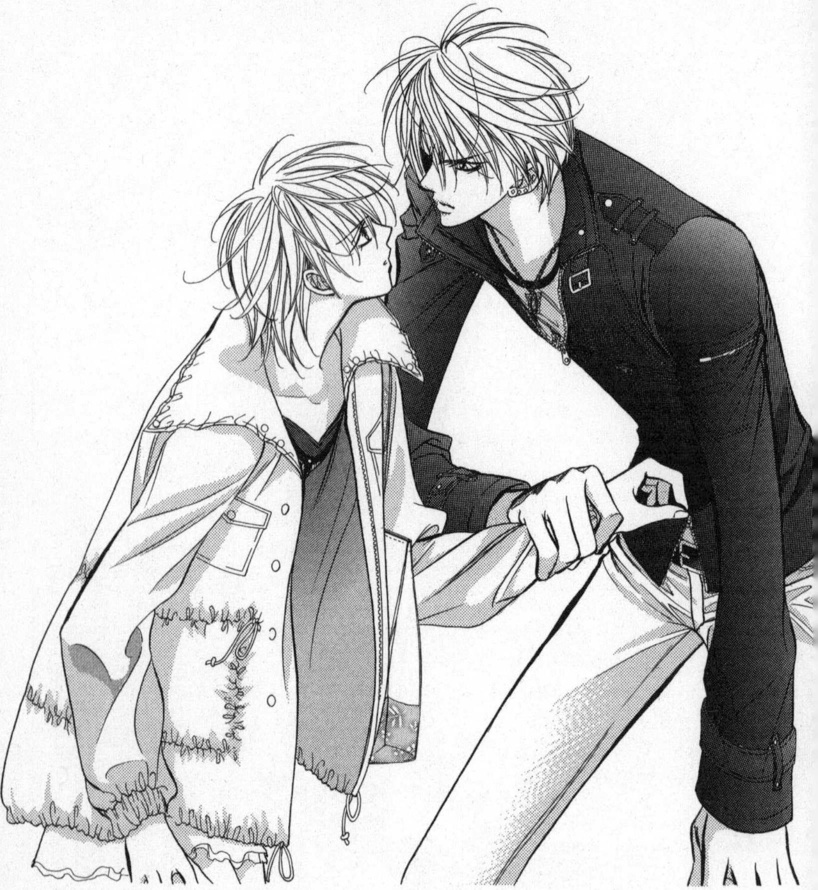

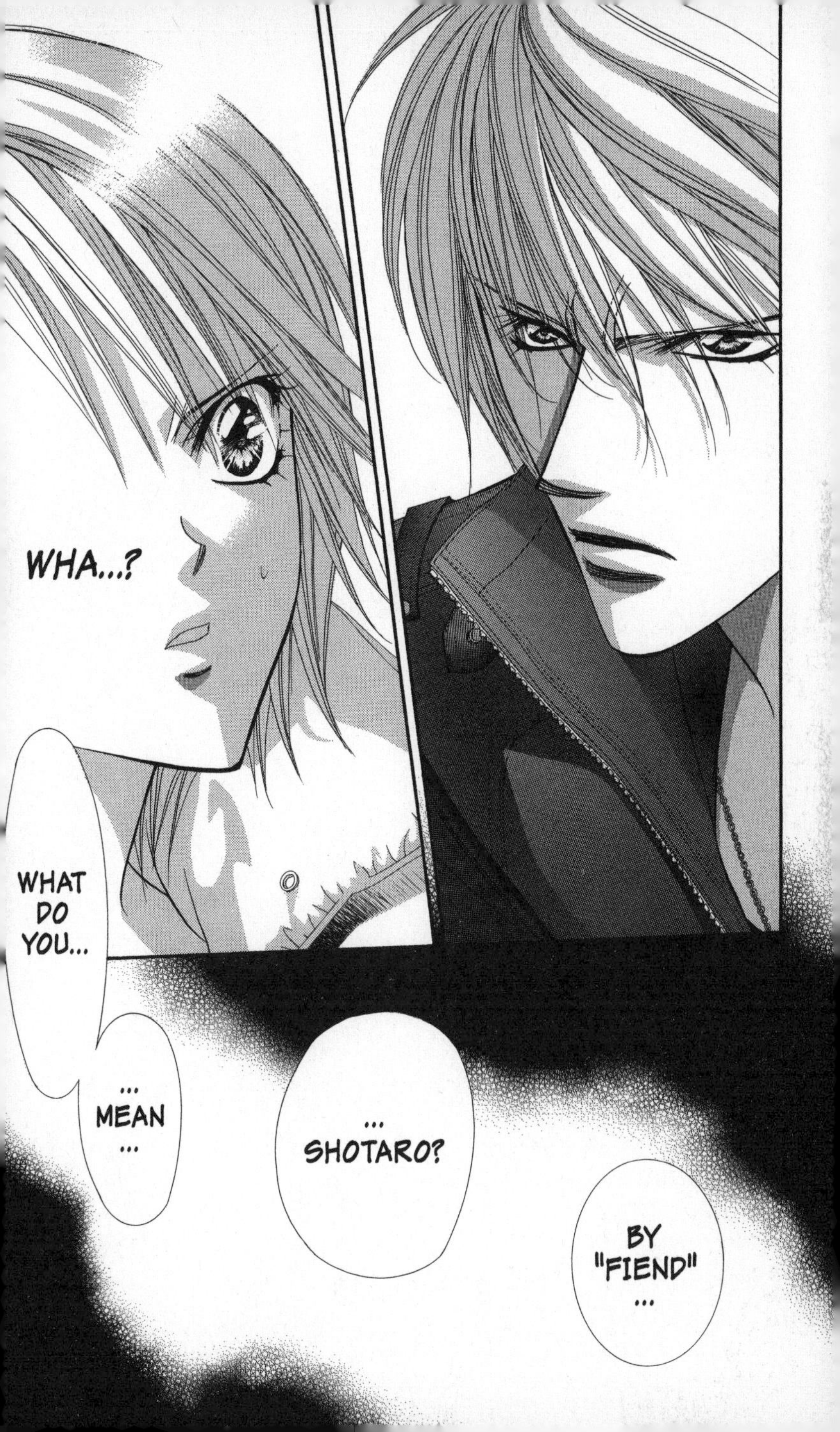
WHA...?
WHAT DO YOU...
... MEAN ...
... SHOTARO?
BY "FIEND" ...

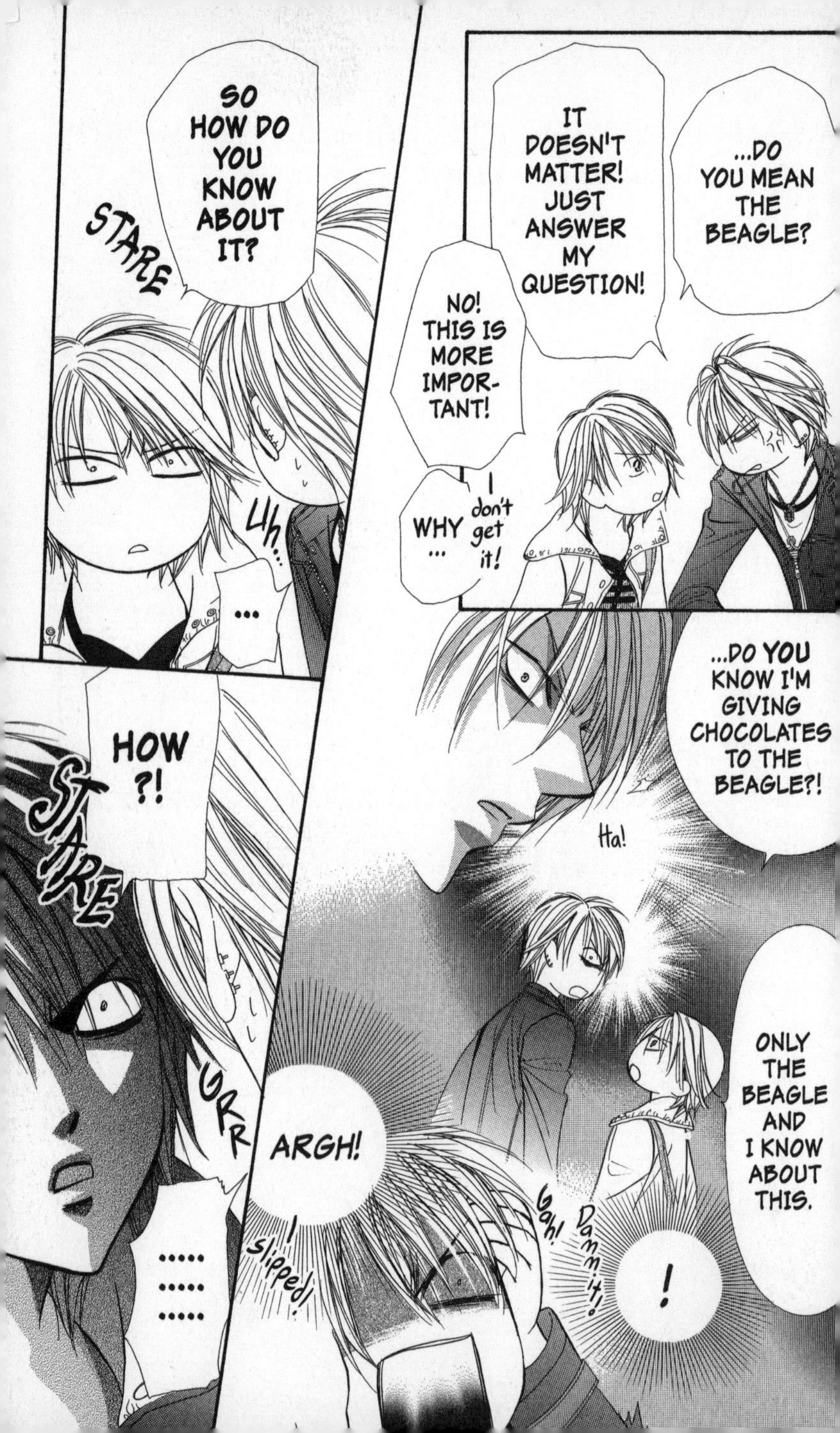
...DO YOU MEAN THE BEAGLE?
IT DOESN'T MATTER! JUST ANSWER MY QUESTION!
NO! THIS IS MORE IMPORTANT!
I don't get it!
WHY ...
SO HOW DO YOU KNOW ABOUT IT?
STARE
Uh...
...
...DO YOU KNOW I'M GIVING CHOCOLATES TO THE BEAGLE?!
Ha!
ONLY THE BEAGLE AND I KNOW ABOUT THIS.
!
Dammit!
Gah!
I slipped!
ARGH!
HOW ?!
STARE
GRR
.....
.....
.....

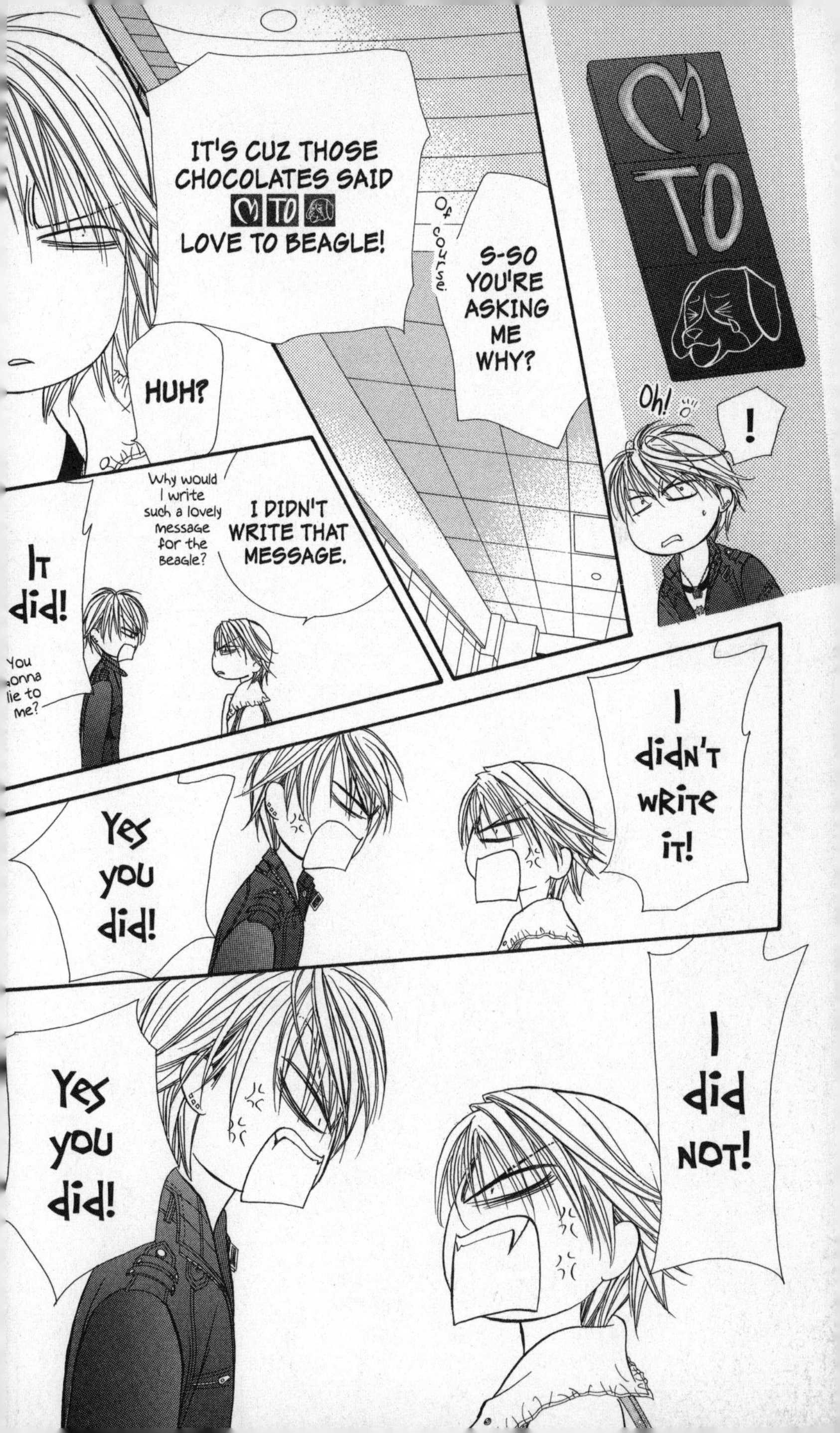
TO
Oh!
!
S-SO YOU'RE ASKING ME WHY?
Of course.
IT'S CUZ THOSE CHOCOLATES SAID
TO
LOVE TO BEAGLE!
HUH?
I DIDN'T WRITE THAT MESSAGE.
Why would I write such a lovely message for the Beagle?
It did!
You gonna lie to me?
I didn't write it!
Yes you did!
I did NOT!
Yes you did!

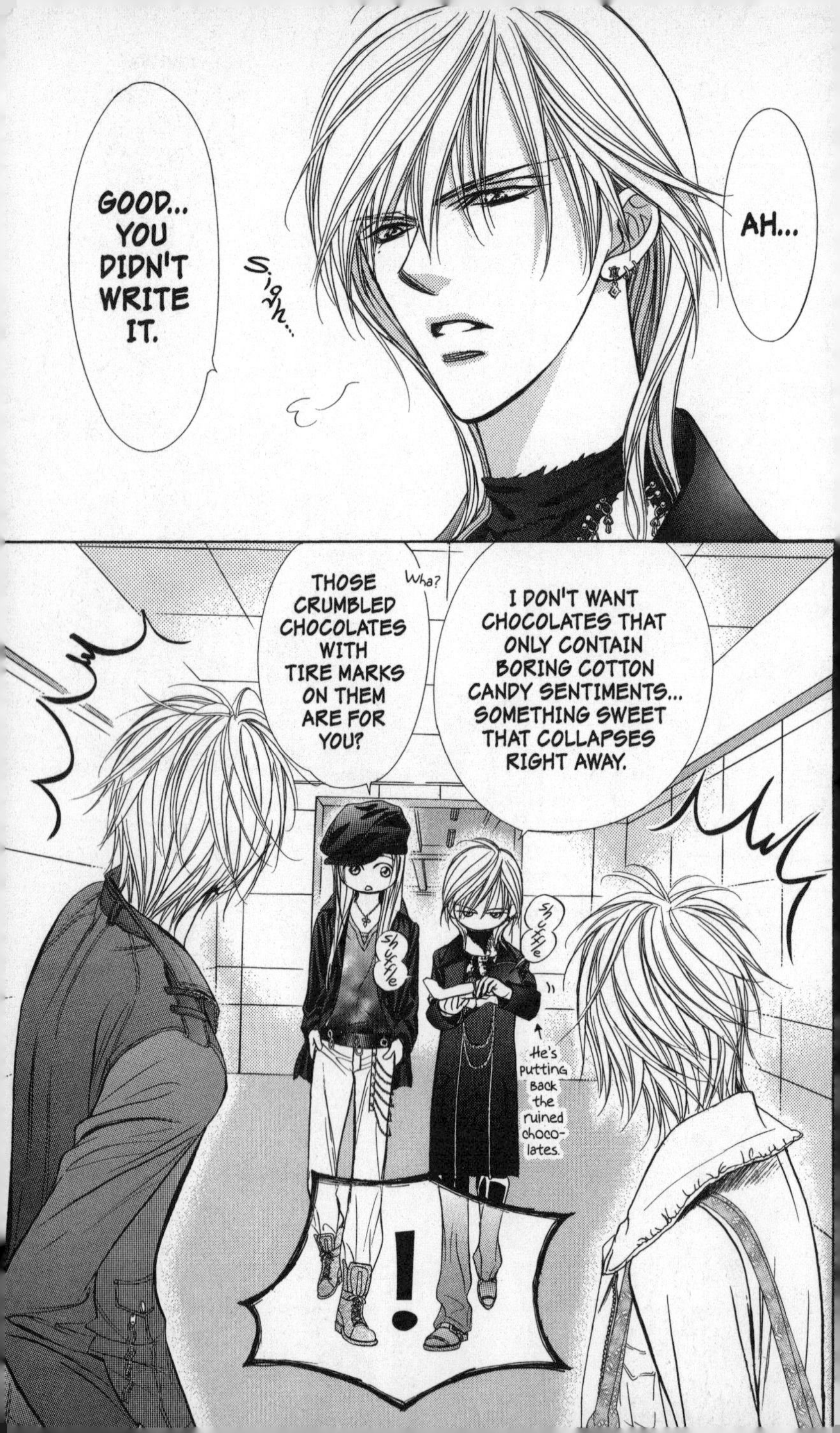
AH...
Sigh...
GOOD... YOU DIDN'T WRITE IT.
I DON'T WANT CHOCOLATES THAT ONLY CONTAIN BORING COTTON CANDY SENTIMENTS... SOMETHING SWEET THAT COLLAPSES RIGHT AWAY.
Wha?
THOSE CRUMBLED CHOCOLATES WITH TIRE MARKS ON THEM ARE FOR YOU?
shuffle
shuffle
He's putting back the ruined choco-lates.
!

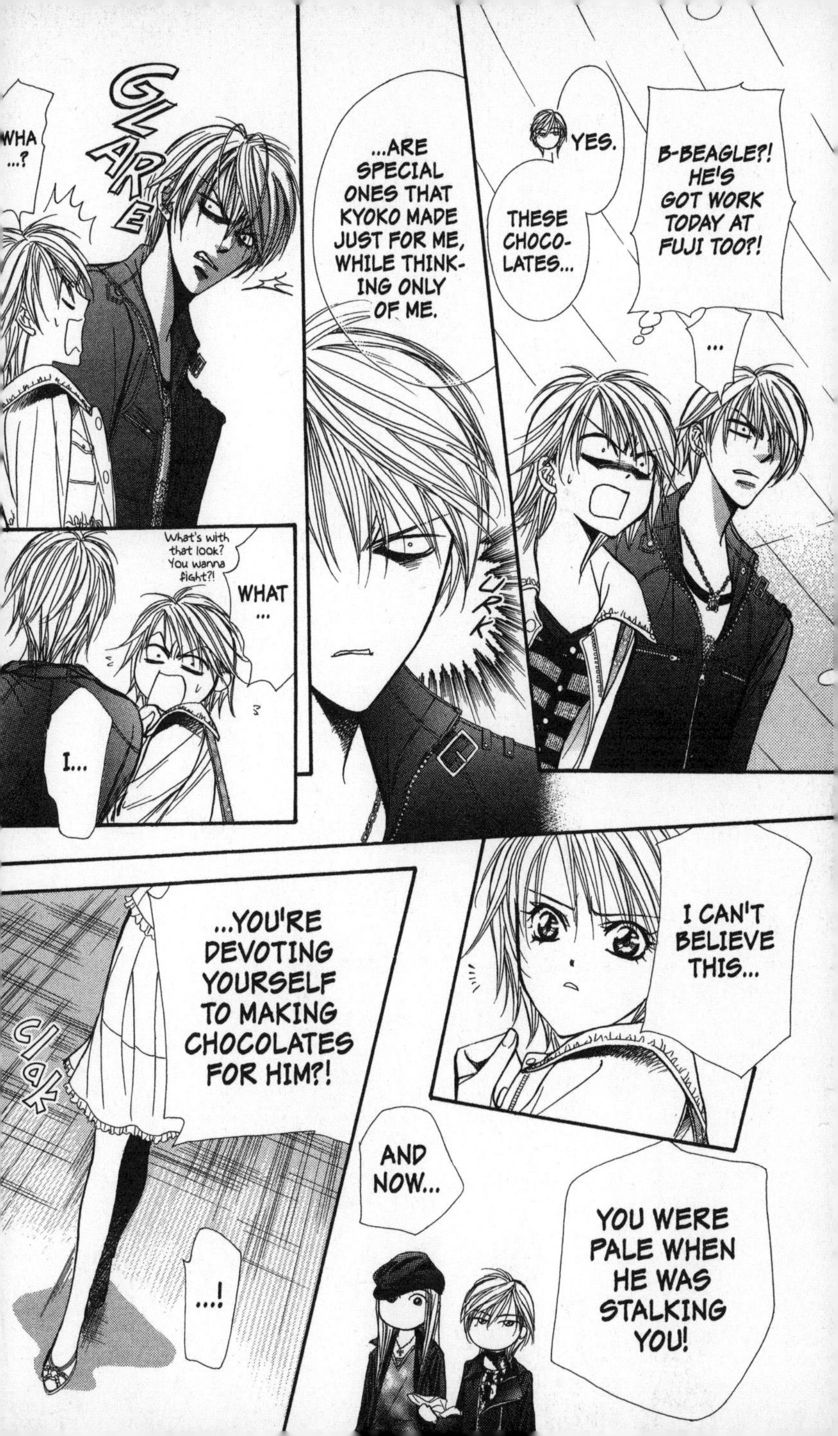
B-BEAGLE?! HE'S GOT WORK TODAY AT FUJI TOO?!
YES.
...
THESE CHOCO-LATES...
...ARE SPECIAL ONES THAT KYOKO MADE JUST FOR ME, WHILE THINK-ING ONLY OF ME.
URK
GLARE
WHA ...?
WHAT ...
What's with that look? You wanna fight?!
I...
I CAN'T BELIEVE THIS...
YOU WERE PALE WHEN HE WAS STALKING YOU!
AND NOW...
...YOU'RE DEVOTING YOURSELF TO MAKING CHOCOLATES FOR HIM?!
Clak
...!

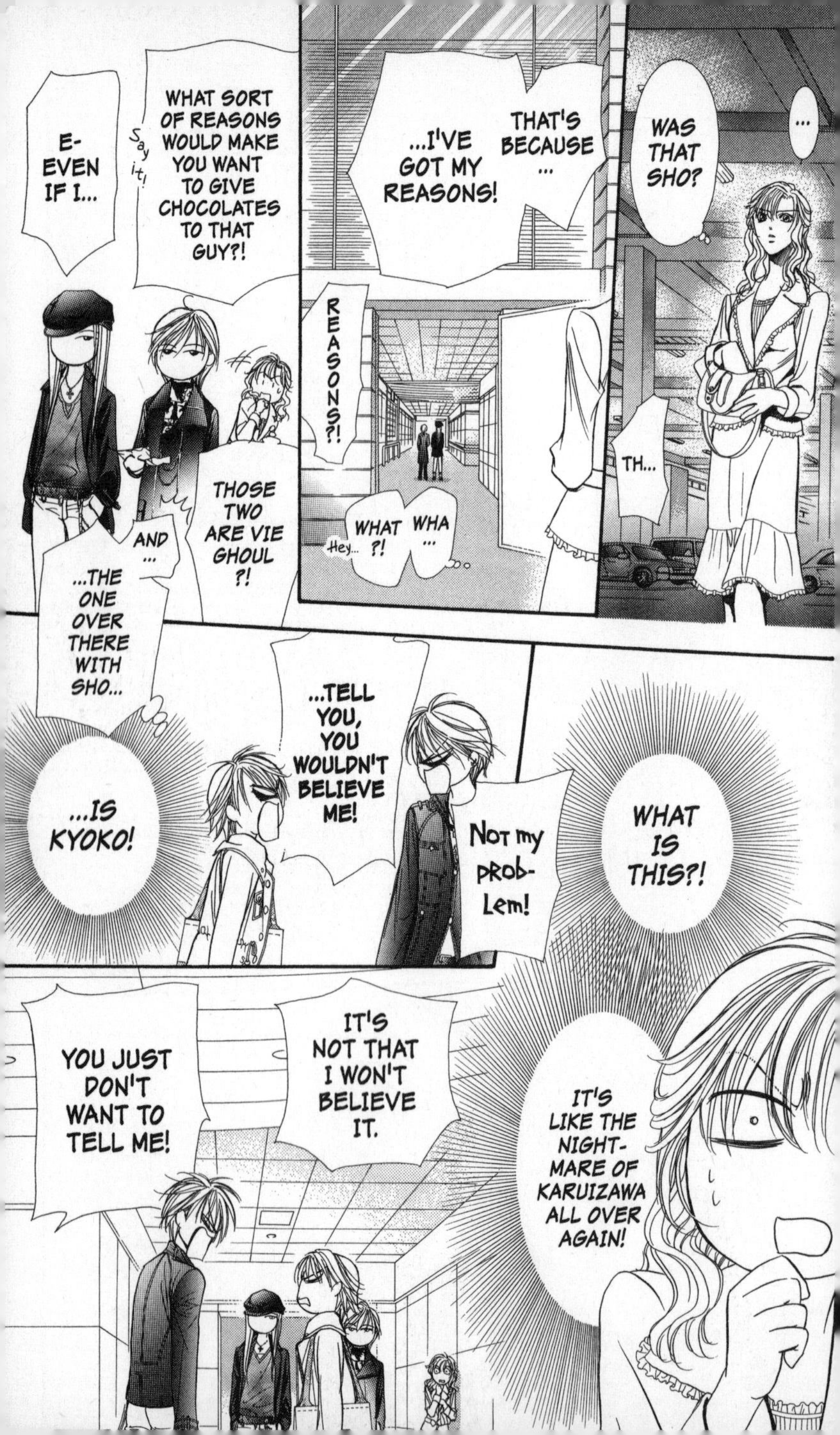
...
WAS THAT SHO?
TH...
THAT'S BECAUSE ...
...I'VE GOT MY REASONS!
REASONS?!
WHA ...
WHAT ?!
Hey...
WHAT SORT OF REASONS WOULD MAKE YOU WANT TO GIVE CHOCOLATES TO THAT GUY?!
Say it!
E-EVEN IF I...
THOSE TWO ARE VIE GHOUL ?!
AND ...
...THE ONE OVER THERE WITH SHO...
...IS KYOKO!
...TELL YOU, YOU WOULDN'T BELIEVE ME!
Not my prob-lem!
WHAT IS THIS?!
IT'S LIKE THE NIGHT-MARE OF KARUIZAWA ALL OVER AGAIN!
IT'S NOT THAT I WON'T BELIEVE IT.
YOU JUST DON'T WANT TO TELL ME!

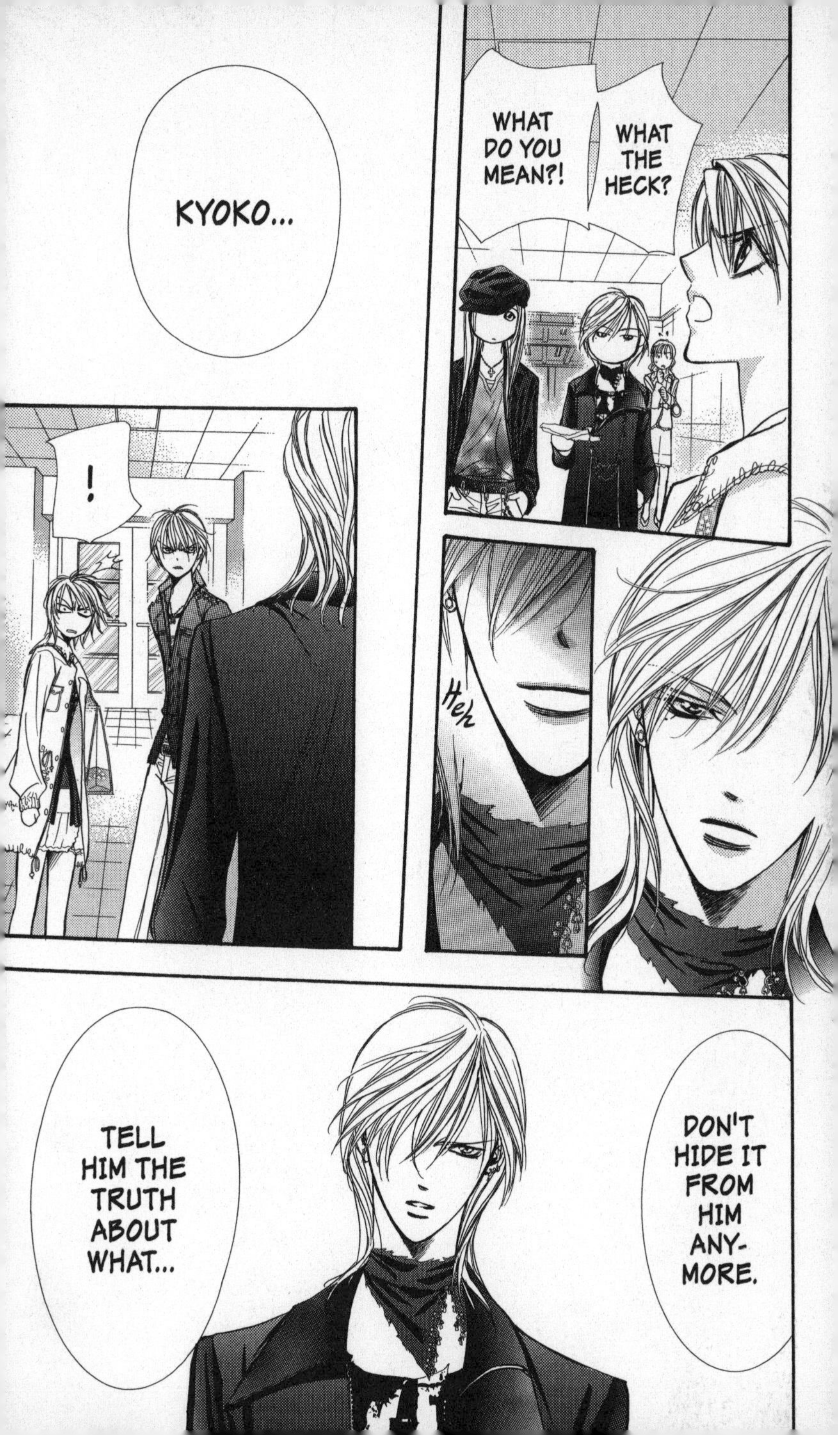
WHAT THE HECK?
WHAT DO YOU MEAN?!
KYOKO...
Heh
!
DON'T HIDE IT FROM HIM ANYMORE.
TELL HIM THE TRUTH ABOUT WHAT...

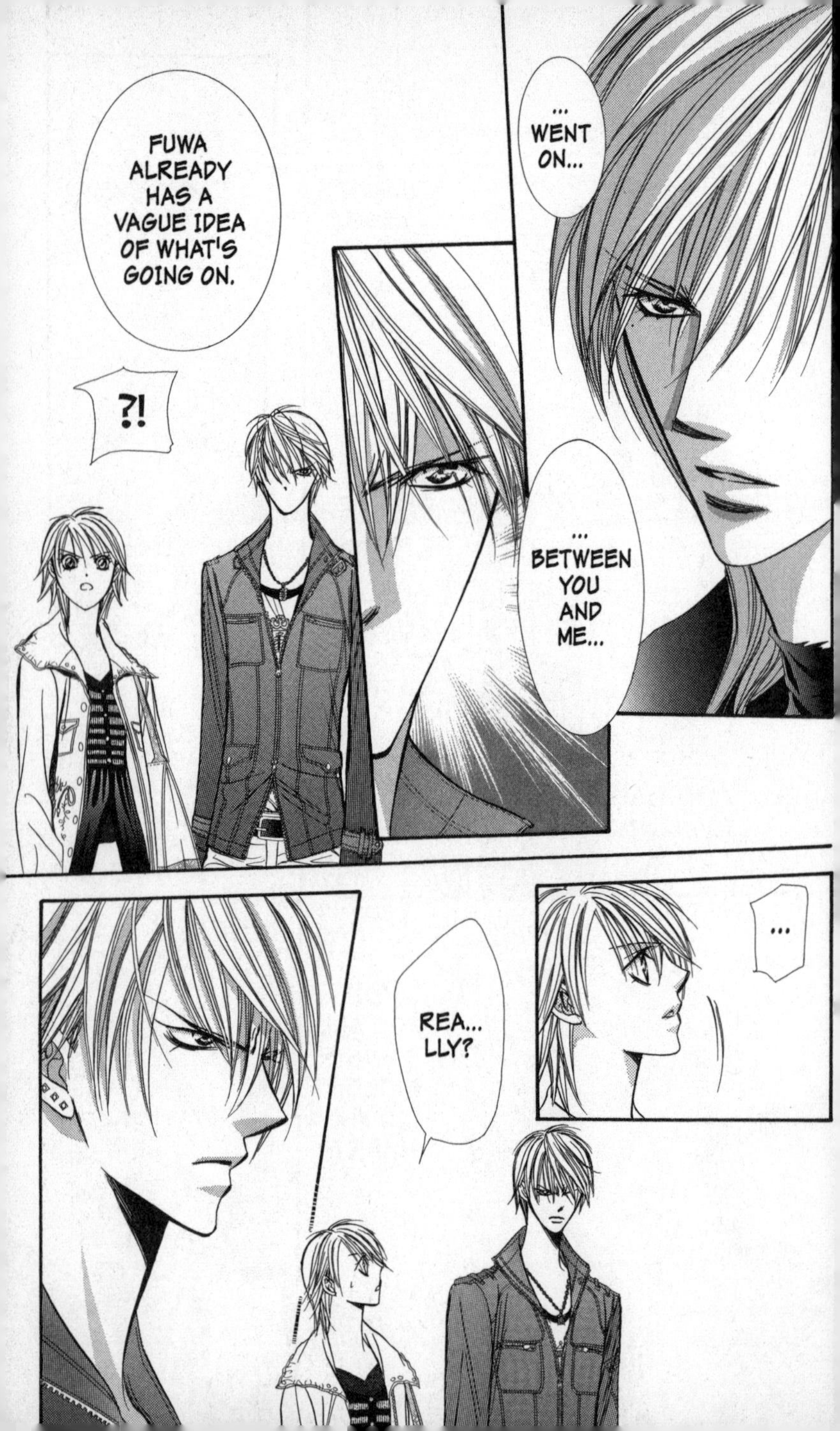

... WENT ON...
... BETWEEN YOU AND ME...
FUWA ALREADY HAS A VAGUE IDEA OF WHAT'S GOING ON.
?!
...
REA... LLY?

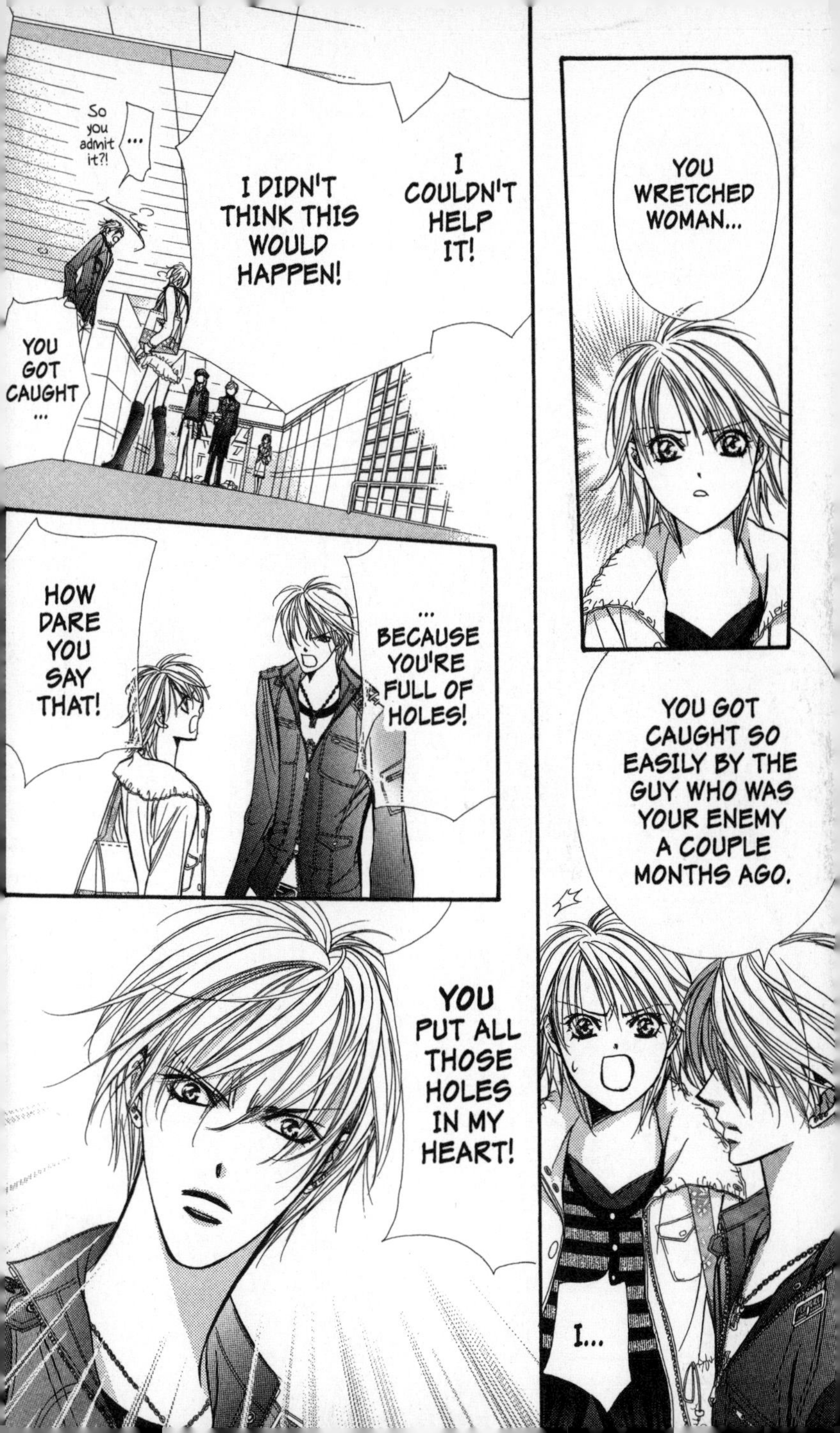
YOU WRETCHED WOMAN...
YOU GOT CAUGHT SO EASILY BY THE GUY WHO WAS YOUR ENEMY A COUPLE MONTHS AGO.
I...
I COULDN'T HELP IT!
I DIDN'T THINK THIS WOULD HAPPEN!
...
So you admit it?!
YOU GOT CAUGHT ...
... BECAUSE YOU'RE FULL OF HOLES!
HOW DARE YOU SAY THAT!
YOU PUT ALL THOSE HOLES IN MY HEART!

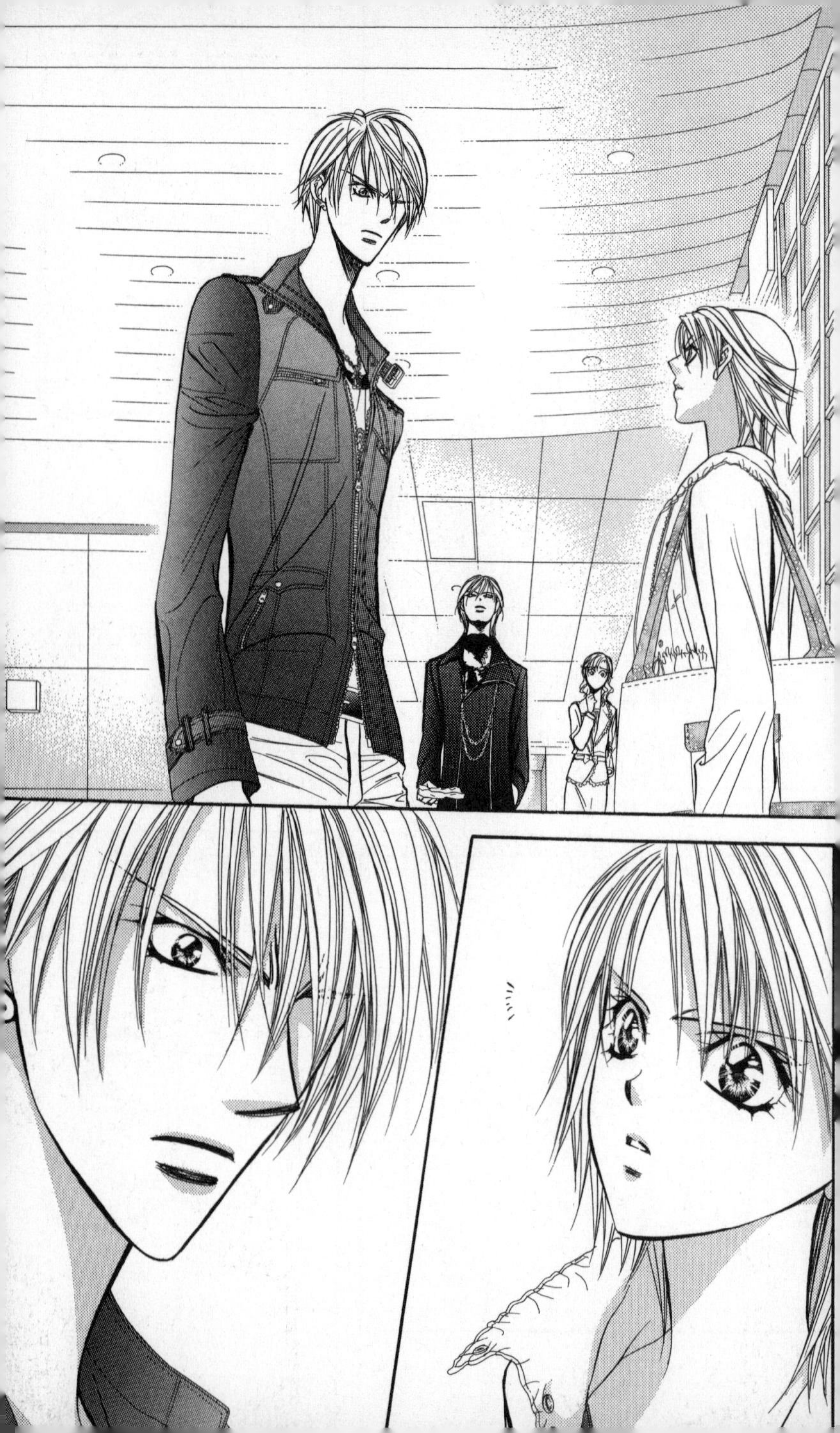

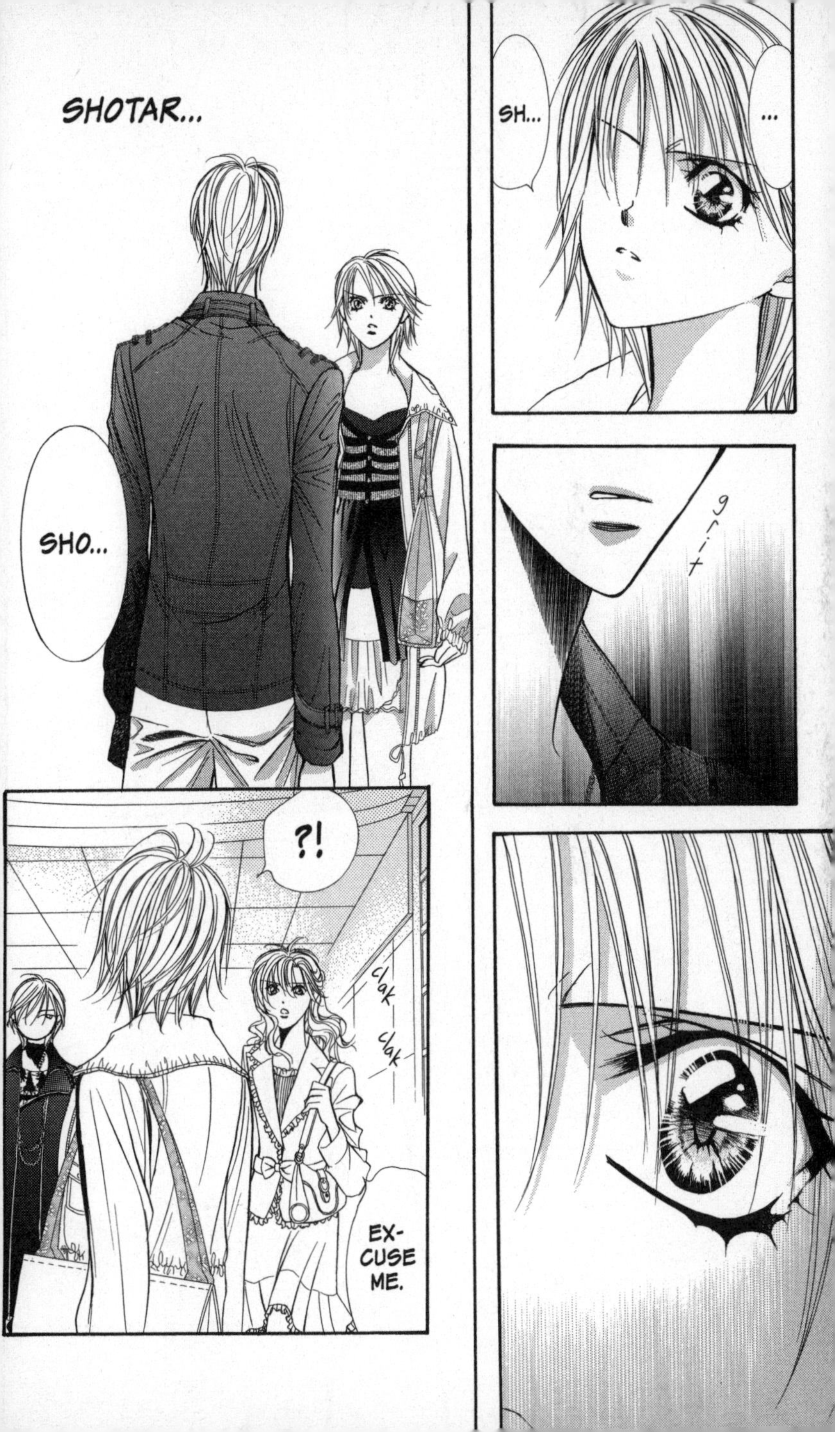
...
SH...
grit
SHOTAR...
SHO...
?!
clak
clak
EX-CUSE ME.

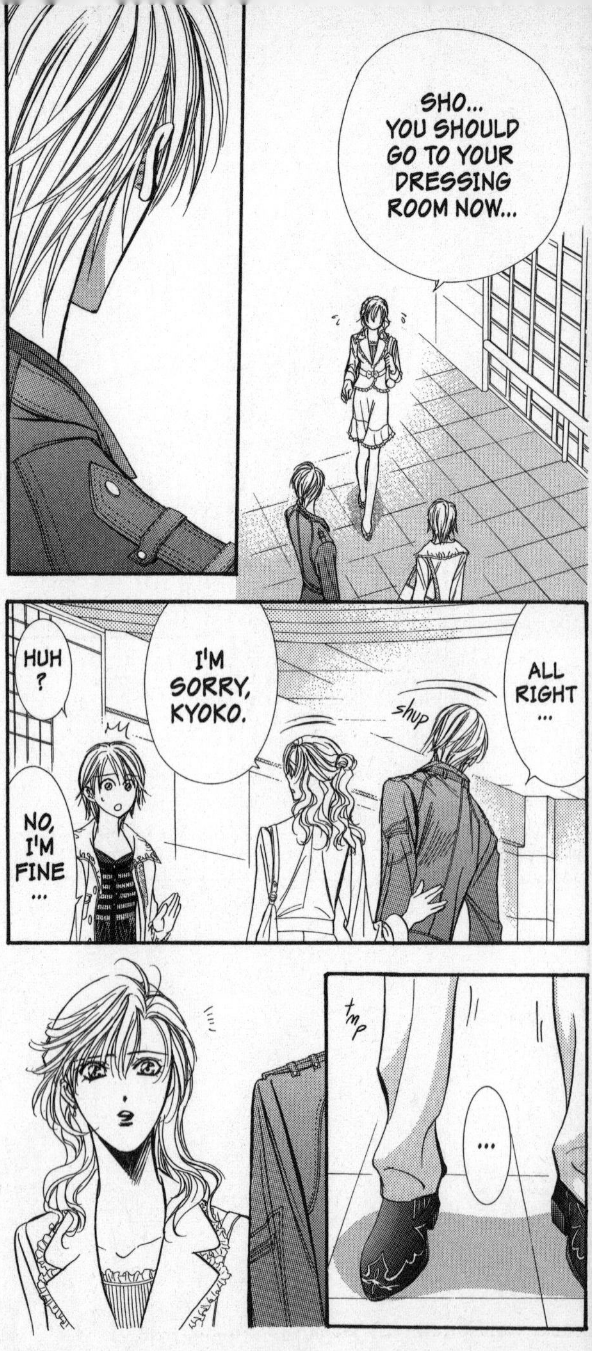
SHO... YOU SHOULD GO TO YOUR DRESSING ROOM NOW...
ALL RIGHT ...
shup
I'M SORRY, KYOKO.
HUH ?
NO, I'M FINE ...
tmp
...

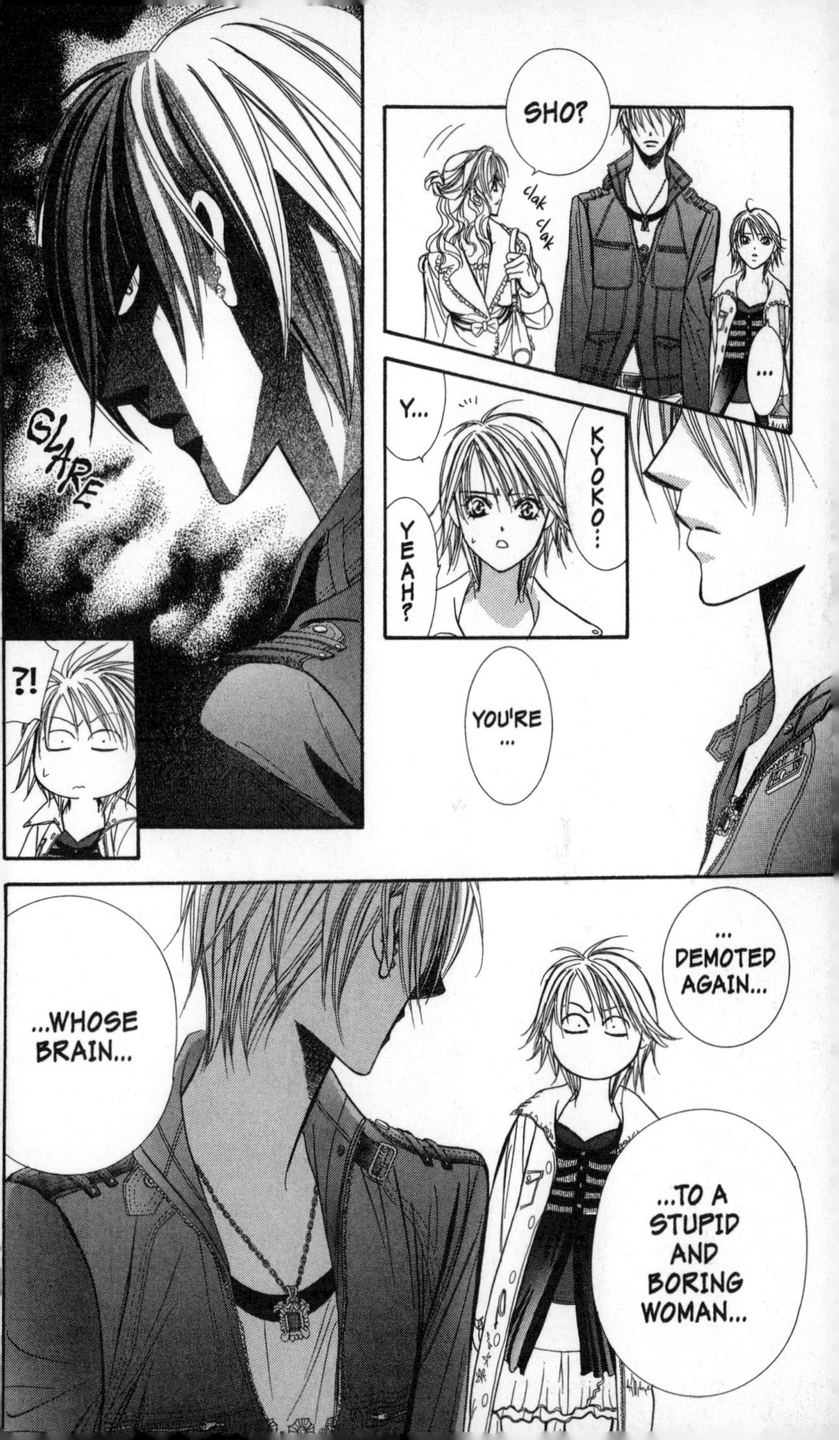
SHO?
clak clak
...
KYOKO...
Y...
YEAH?
YOU'RE ...
GLARE
?!
... DEMOTED AGAIN...
...WHOSE BRAIN...
...TO A STUPID AND BORING WOMAN...

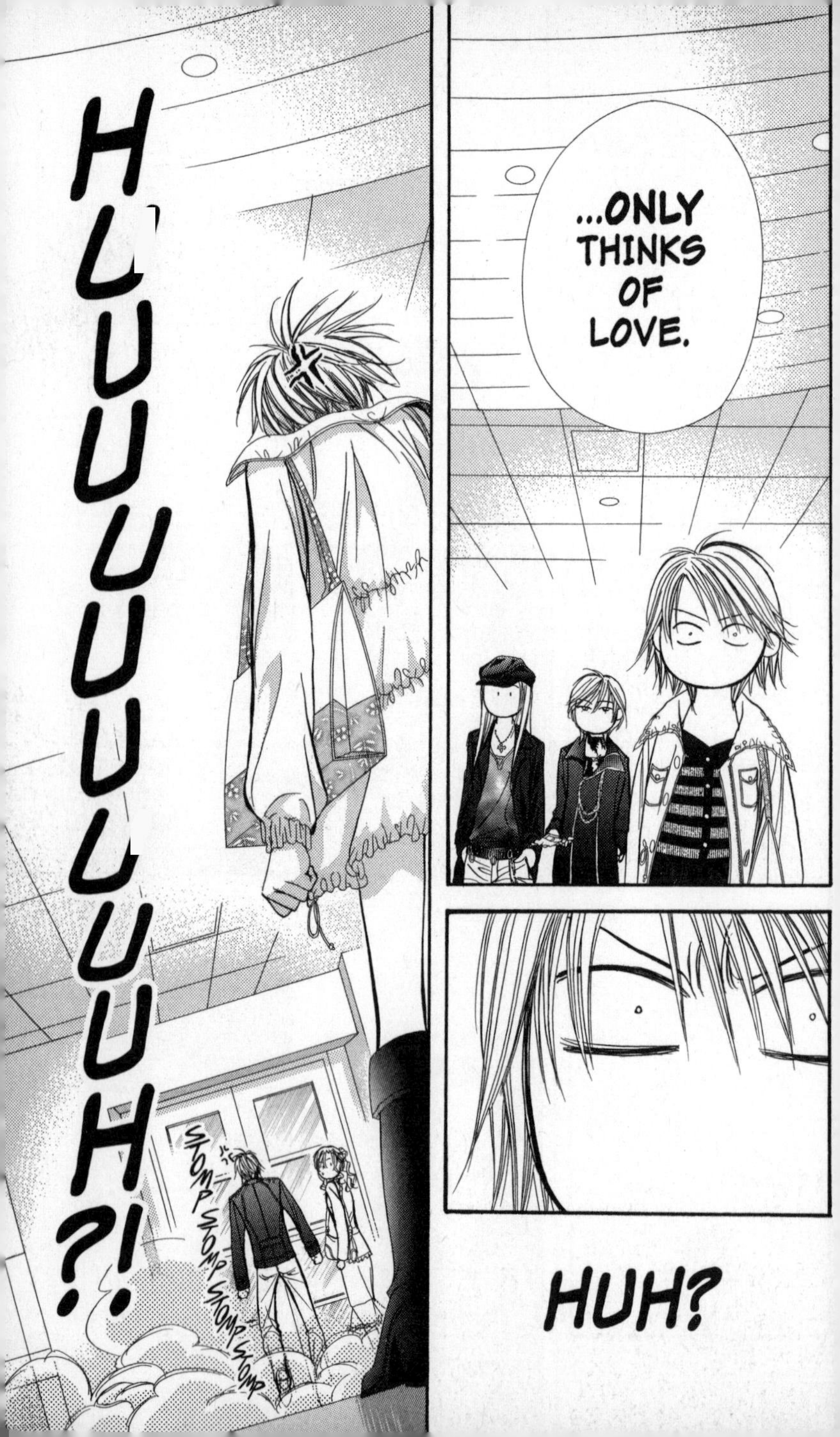
...ONLY THINKS OF LOVE.
HUH?
HUUUUUUUUUH?!
STOMP STOMP STOMP STOMP

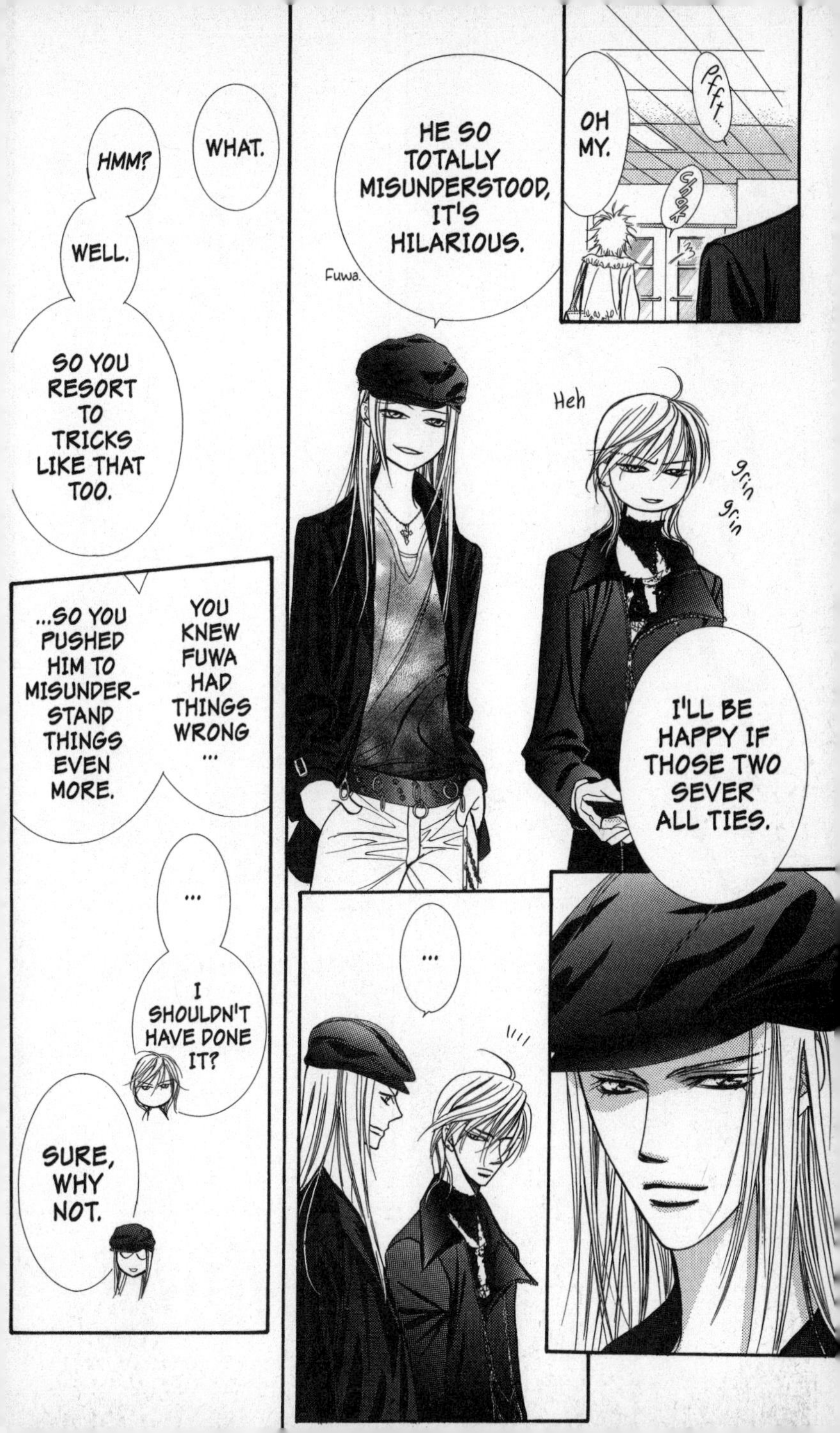
Pfft...
Chok
OH MY.
HE SO TOTALLY MISUNDERSTOOD, IT'S HILARIOUS.
Fuwa.
Heh
grin grin
I'LL BE HAPPY IF THOSE TWO SEVER ALL TIES.
...
WHAT.
HMM?
WELL.
SO YOU RESORT TO TRICKS LIKE THAT TOO.
YOU KNEW FUWA HAD THINGS WRONG ...
...SO YOU PUSHED HIM TO MISUNDERSTAND THINGS EVEN MORE.
...
I SHOULDN'T HAVE DONE IT?
SURE, WHY NOT.

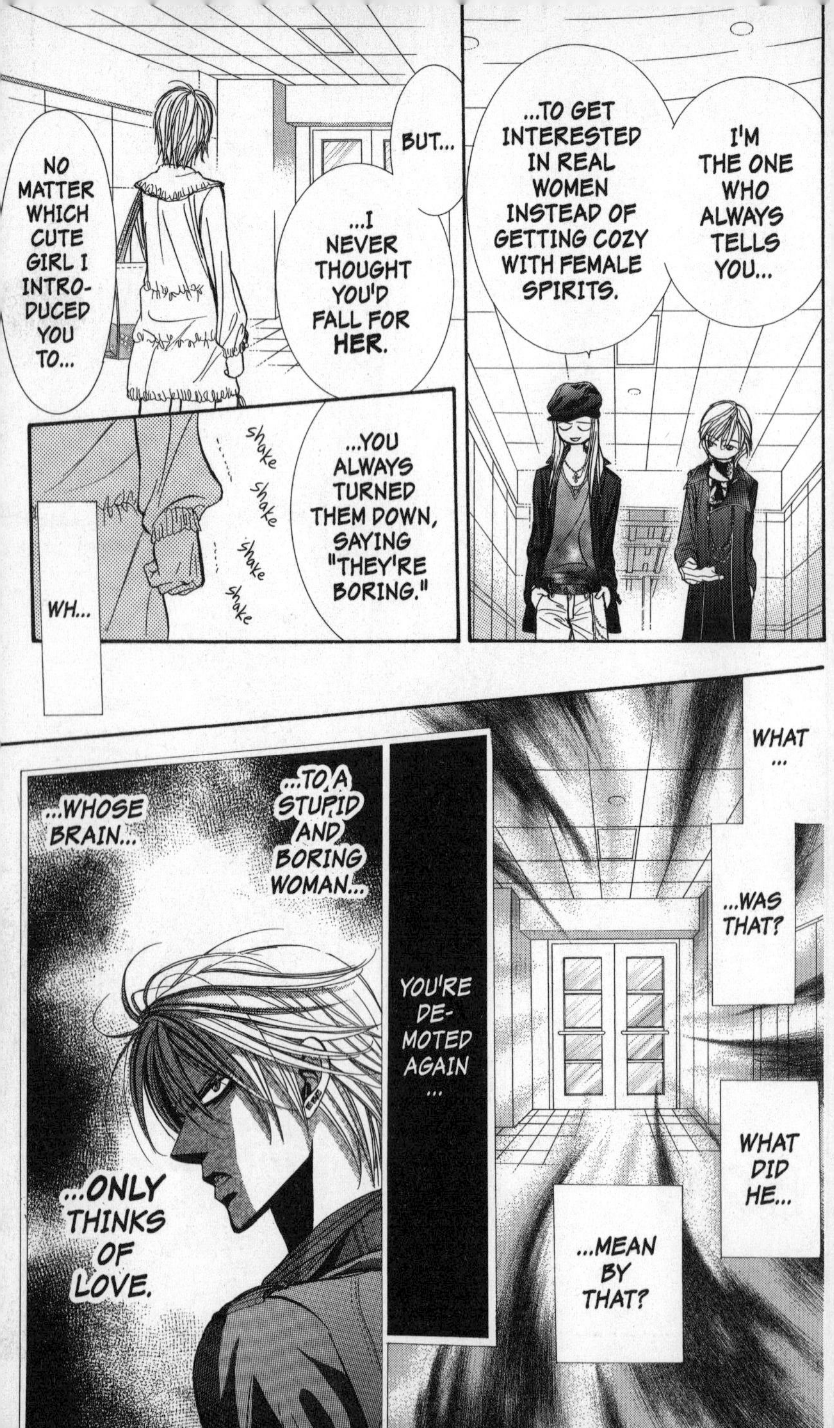
I'M THE ONE WHO ALWAYS TELLS YOU...
...TO GET INTERESTED IN REAL WOMEN INSTEAD OF GETTING COZY WITH FEMALE SPIRITS.
BUT...
...I NEVER THOUGHT YOU'D FALL FOR HER.
NO MATTER WHICH CUTE GIRL I INTRO-DUCED YOU TO...
...YOU ALWAYS TURNED THEM DOWN, SAYING "THEY'RE BORING."
shake
shake
shake
shake
WH...
WHAT ...
...WAS THAT?
WHAT DID HE...
...MEAN BY THAT?
YOU'RE DE-MOTED AGAIN ...
...TO A STUPID AND BORING WOMAN...
...WHOSE BRAIN...
...ONLY THINKS OF LOVE.

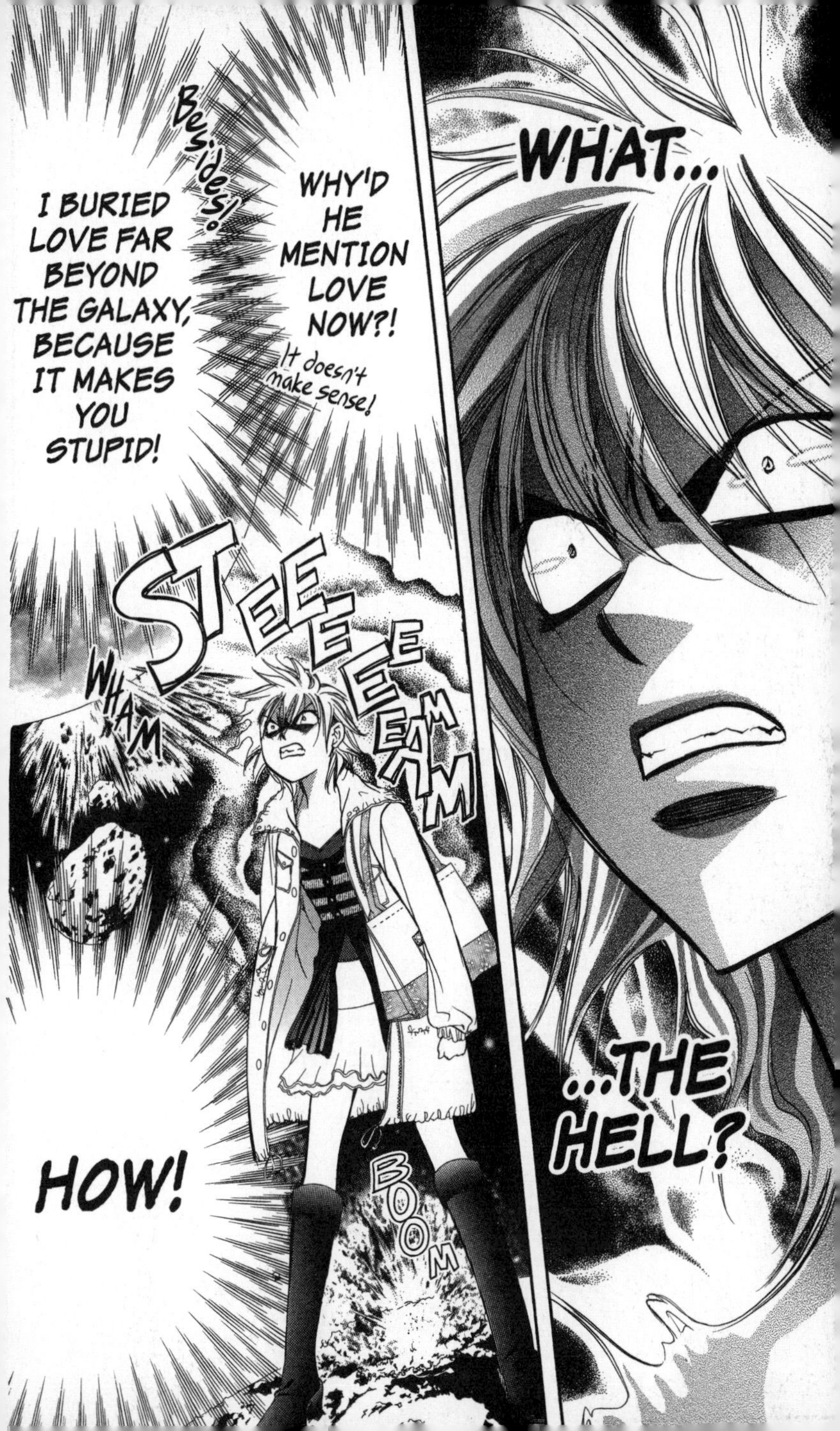
WHAT...
...THE HELL?
WHY'D HE MENTION LOVE NOW?!
It doesn't make sense!
Besides!
I BURIED LOVE FAR BEYOND THE GALAXY, BECAUSE IT MAKES YOU STUPID!
STEEEEEAM
WHAM
BOOM
HOW!

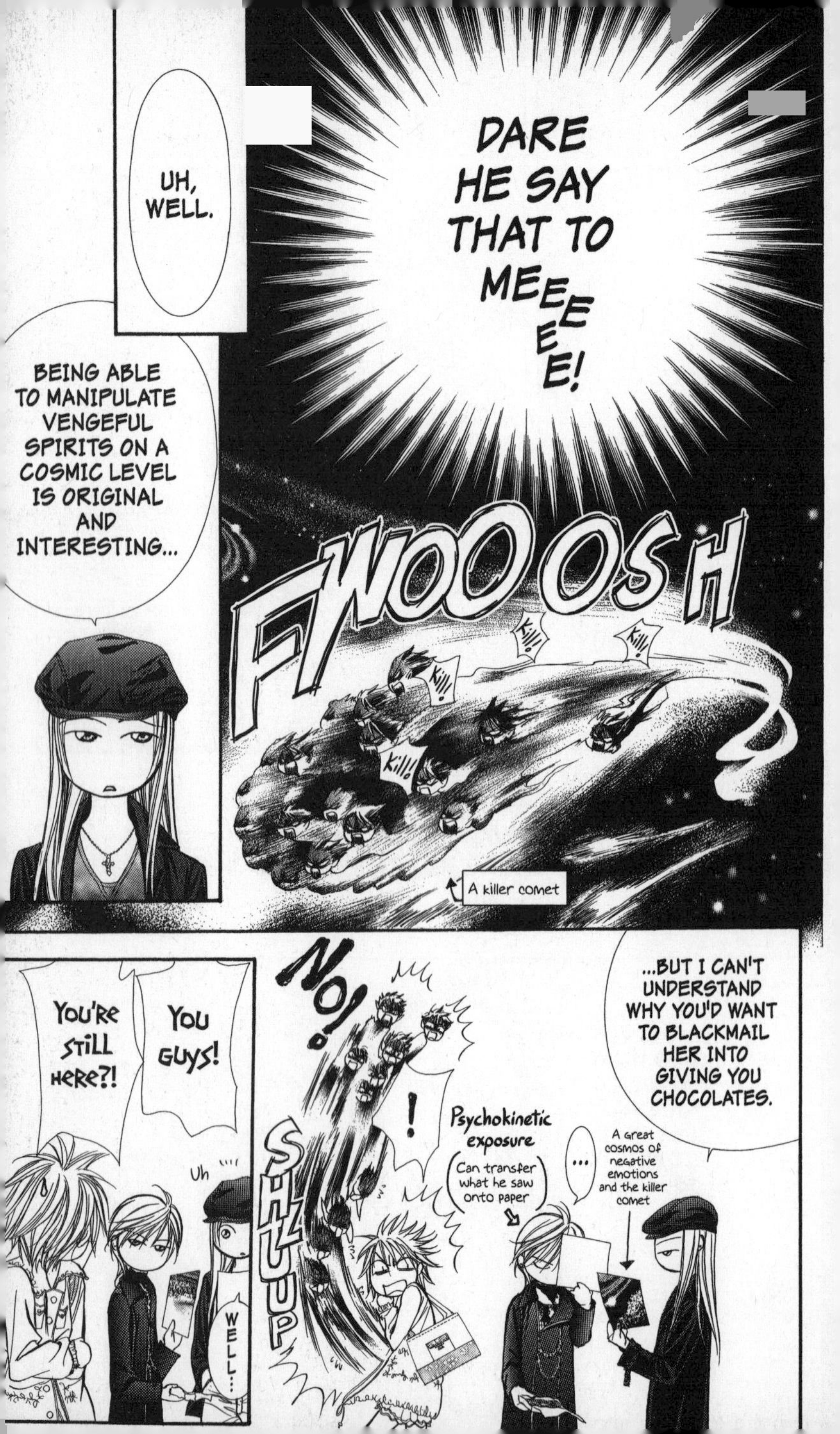
DARE HE SAY THAT TO MEEEEE!
FWOOOOSH
Kill!
Kill!
Kill!
Kill!
A killer comet
UH, WELL.
BEING ABLE TO MANIPULATE VENGEFUL SPIRITS ON A COSMIC LEVEL IS ORIGINAL AND INTERESTING...
...BUT I CAN'T UNDERSTAND WHY YOU'D WANT TO BLACKMAIL HER INTO GIVING YOU CHOCOLATES.
A great cosmos of negative emotions and the killer comet
...
Psychokinetic exposure
(Can transfer what he saw onto paper)
NO!
!
SHLUUP
You guys!
You're still here?!
Uh
WELL...

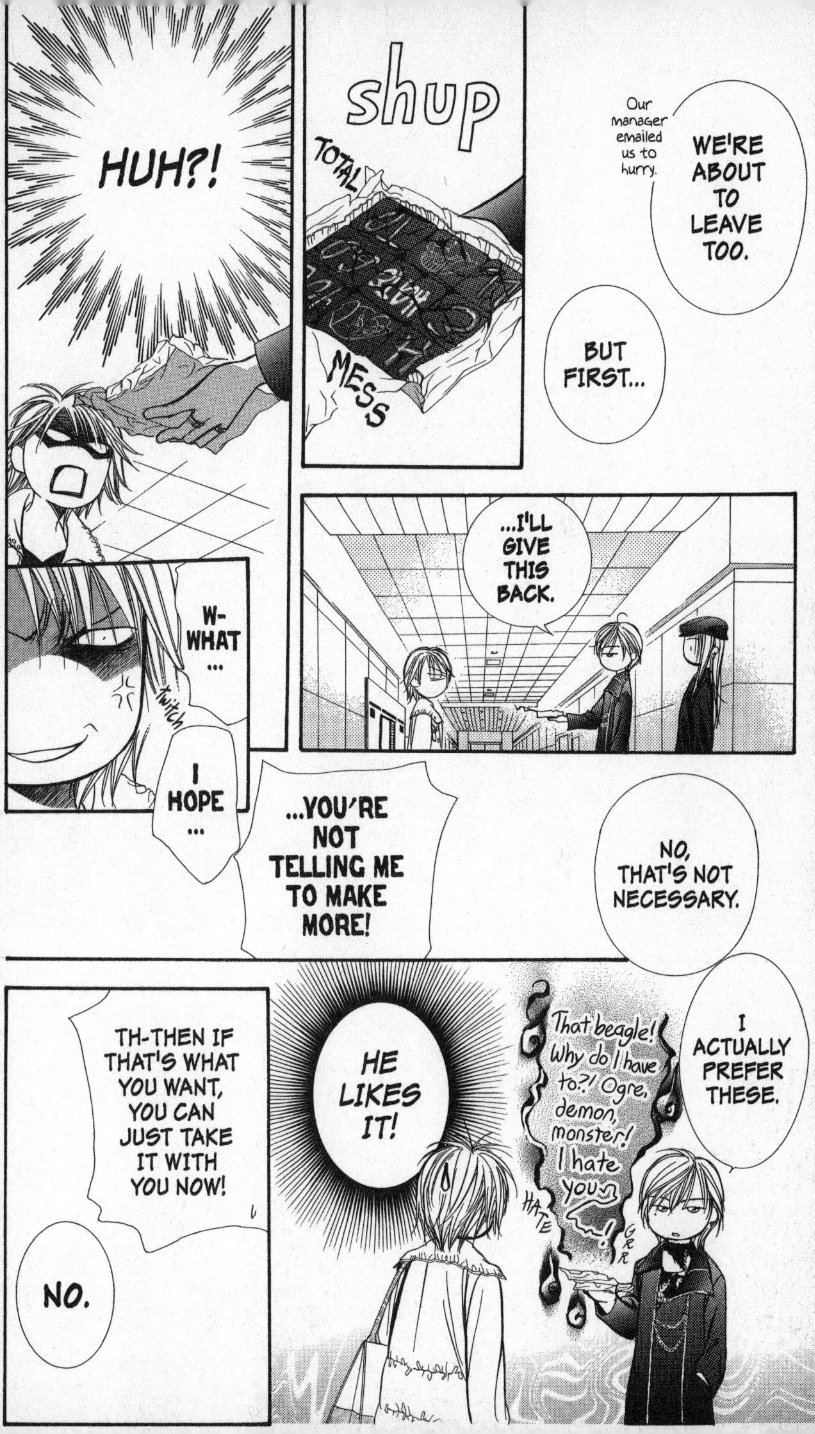
Our manager emailed us to hurry.
WE'RE ABOUT TO LEAVE TOO.
BUT FIRST...
...I'LL GIVE THIS BACK.
shup
TOTAL MESS
HUH?!
W-WHAT...
twitch
I HOPE...
...YOU'RE NOT TELLING ME TO MAKE MORE!
NO, THAT'S NOT NECESSARY.
I ACTUALLY PREFER THESE.
That beagle! Why do I have to?! Ogre, demon, monster! I hate you~!
HATE
GRR
HE LIKES IT!
TH-THEN IF THAT'S WHAT YOU WANT, YOU CAN JUST TAKE IT WITH YOU NOW!
NO.

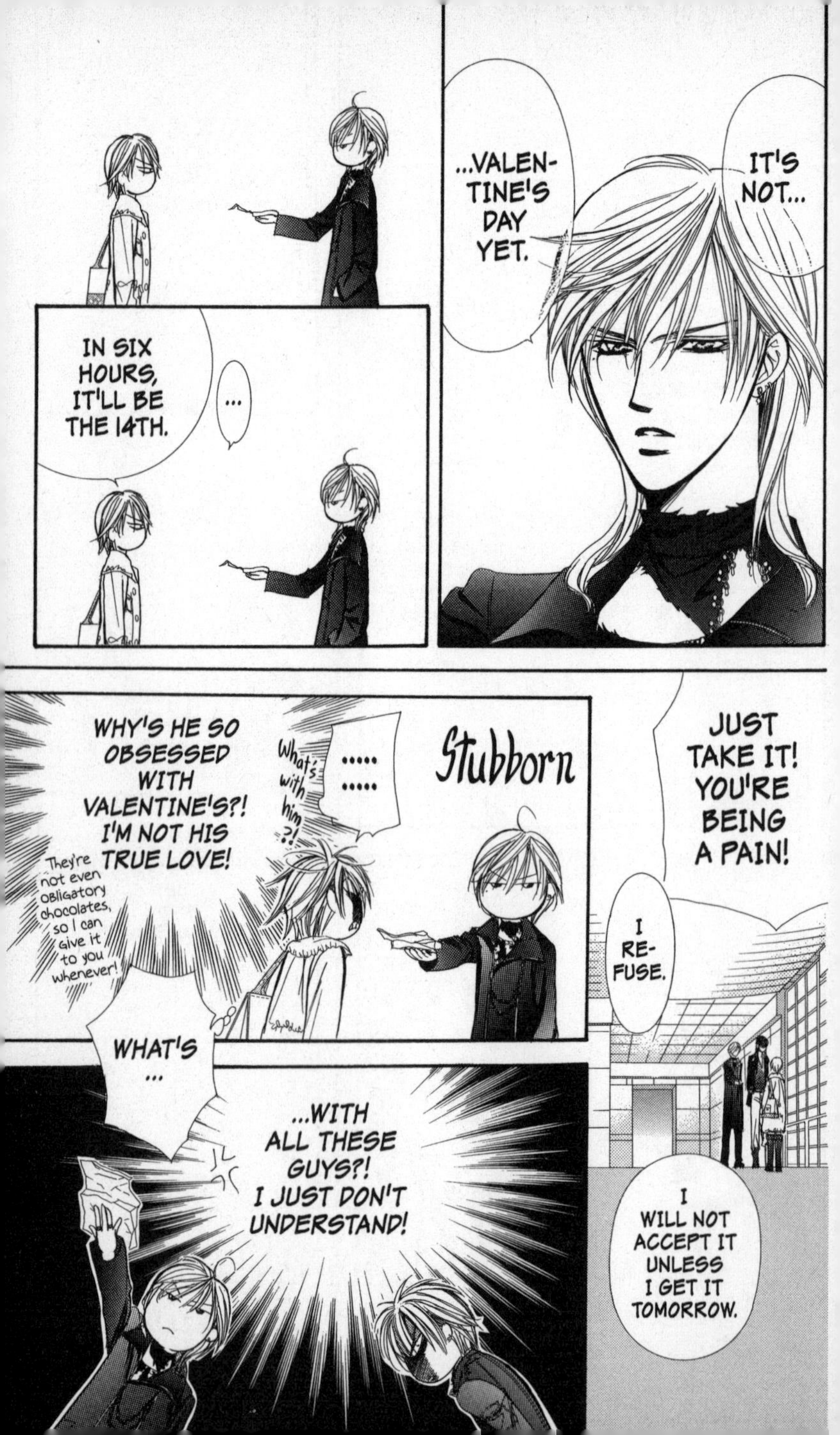
IT'S NOT...
...VALENTINE'S DAY YET.
IN SIX HOURS, IT'LL BE THE 14TH.
...
JUST TAKE IT! YOU'RE BEING A PAIN!
I REFUSE.
I WILL NOT ACCEPT IT UNLESS I GET IT TOMORROW.
Stubborn
....
What's with him?!
WHY'S HE SO OBSESSED WITH VALENTINE'S?! I'M NOT HIS TRUE LOVE!
They're not even obligatory chocolates, so I can give it to you whenever!
WHAT'S ...
...WITH ALL THESE GUYS?! I JUST DON'T UNDERSTAND!

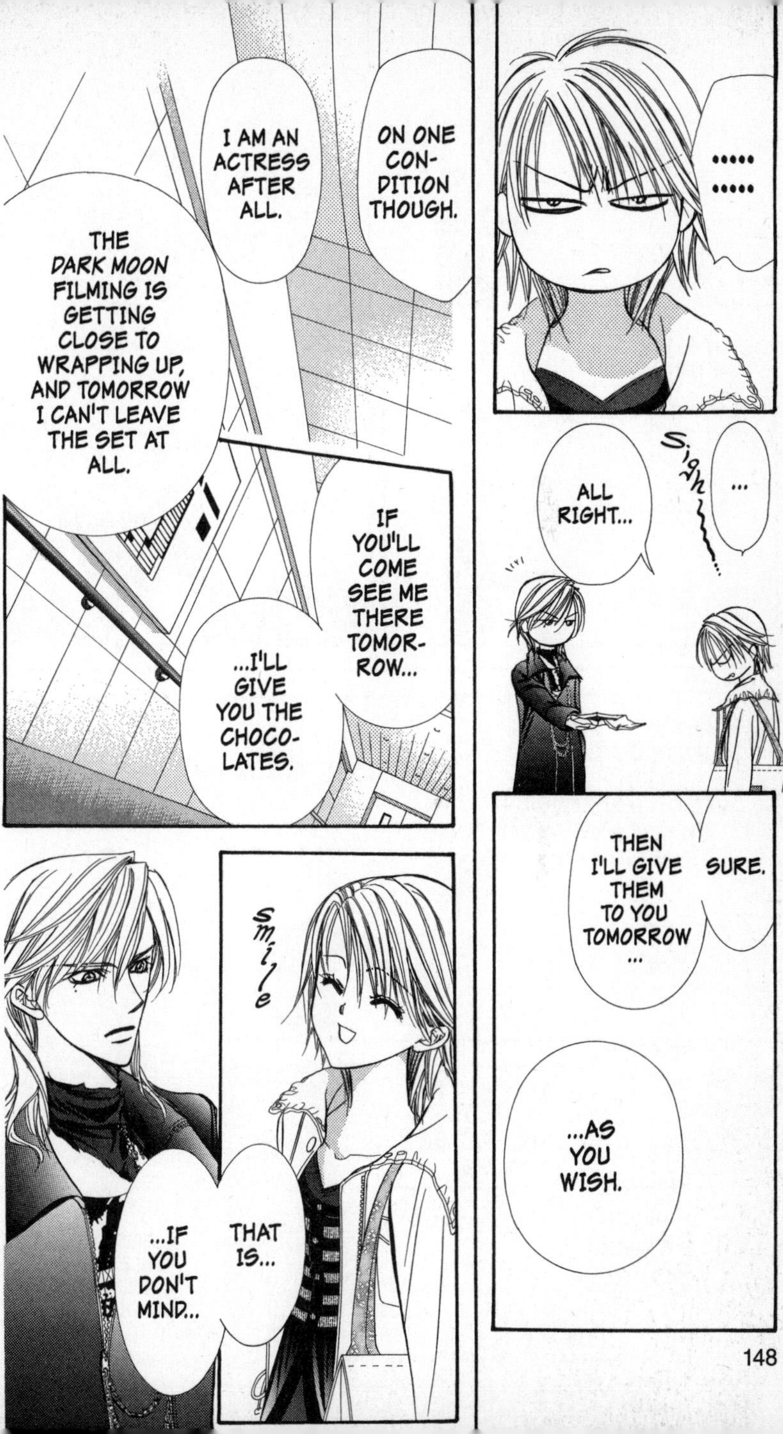
ON ONE CON-DITION THOUGH.
I AM AN ACTRESS AFTER ALL.
THE DARK MOON FILMING IS GETTING CLOSE TO WRAPPING UP, AND TOMORROW I CAN'T LEAVE THE SET AT ALL.
IF YOU'LL COME SEE ME THERE TOMOR-ROW...
...I'LL GIVE YOU THE CHOCO-LATES.
smile
THAT IS...
...IF YOU DON'T MIND...
.....
.....
...
Sigh...
ALL RIGHT...
SURE.
THEN I'LL GIVE THEM TO YOU TOMORROW...
...AS YOU WISH.

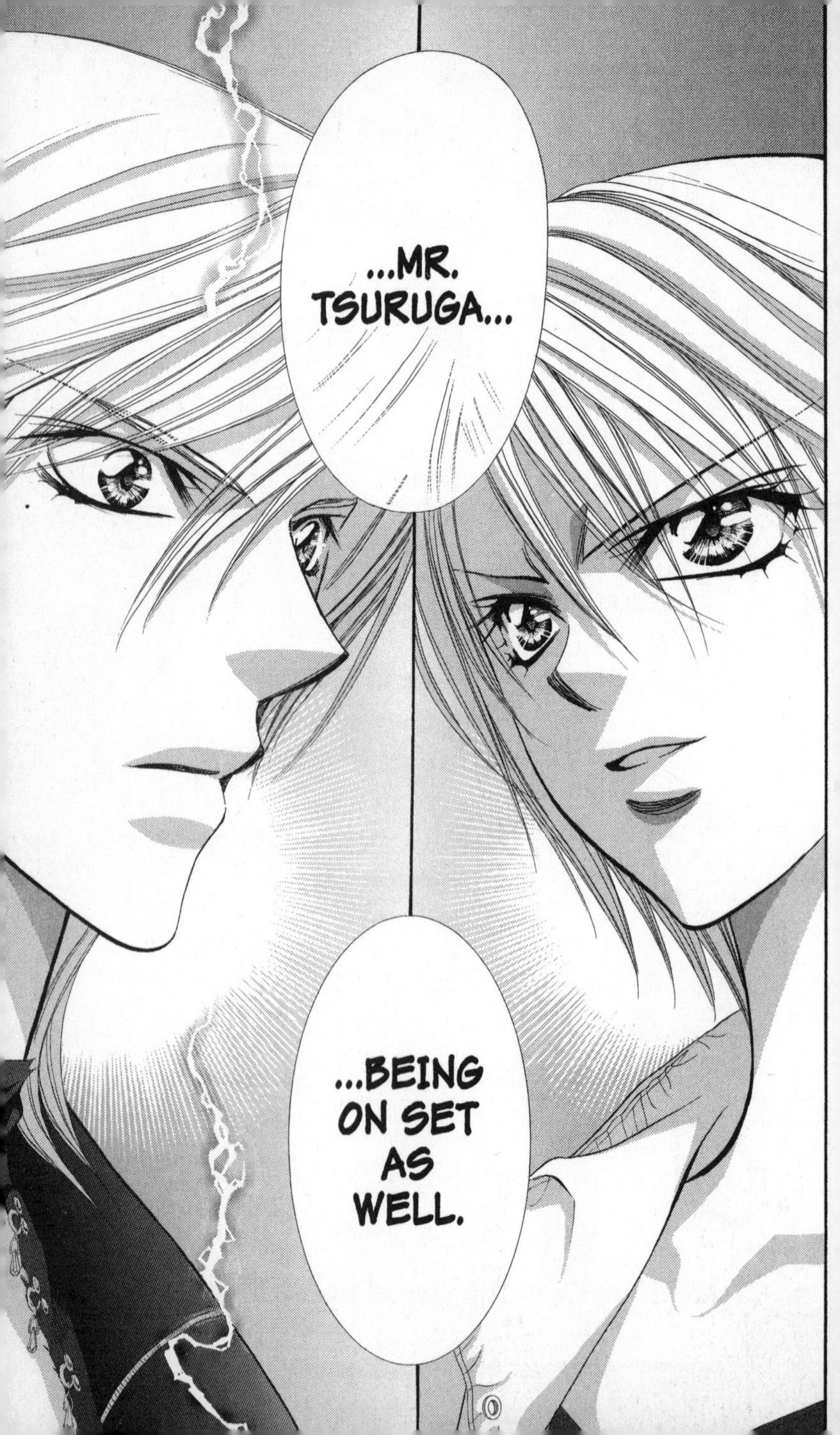
...MR. TSURUGA...
...BEING ON SET AS WELL.

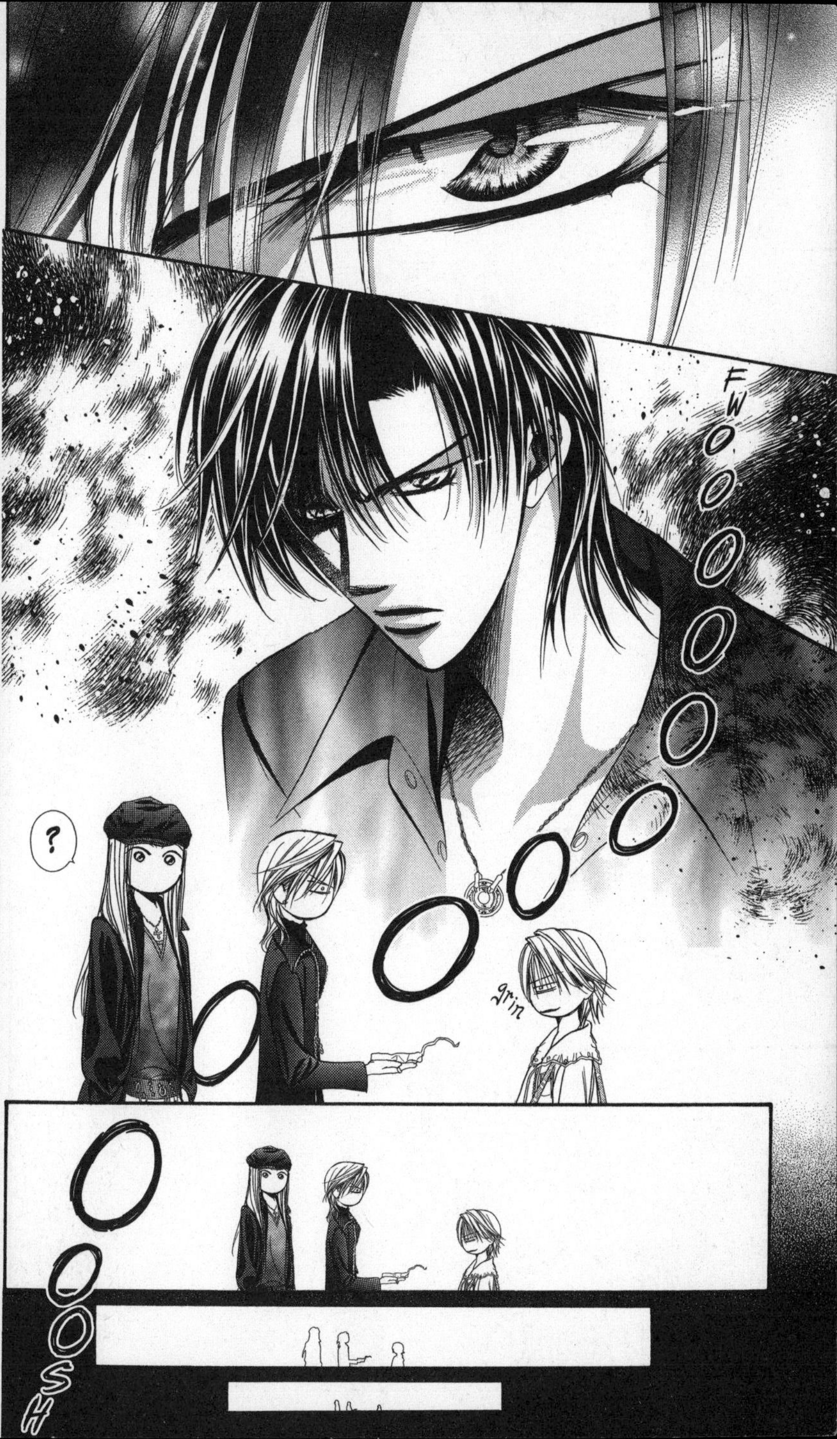
FWOOOOOOOOOOO
?
grin
OOSH

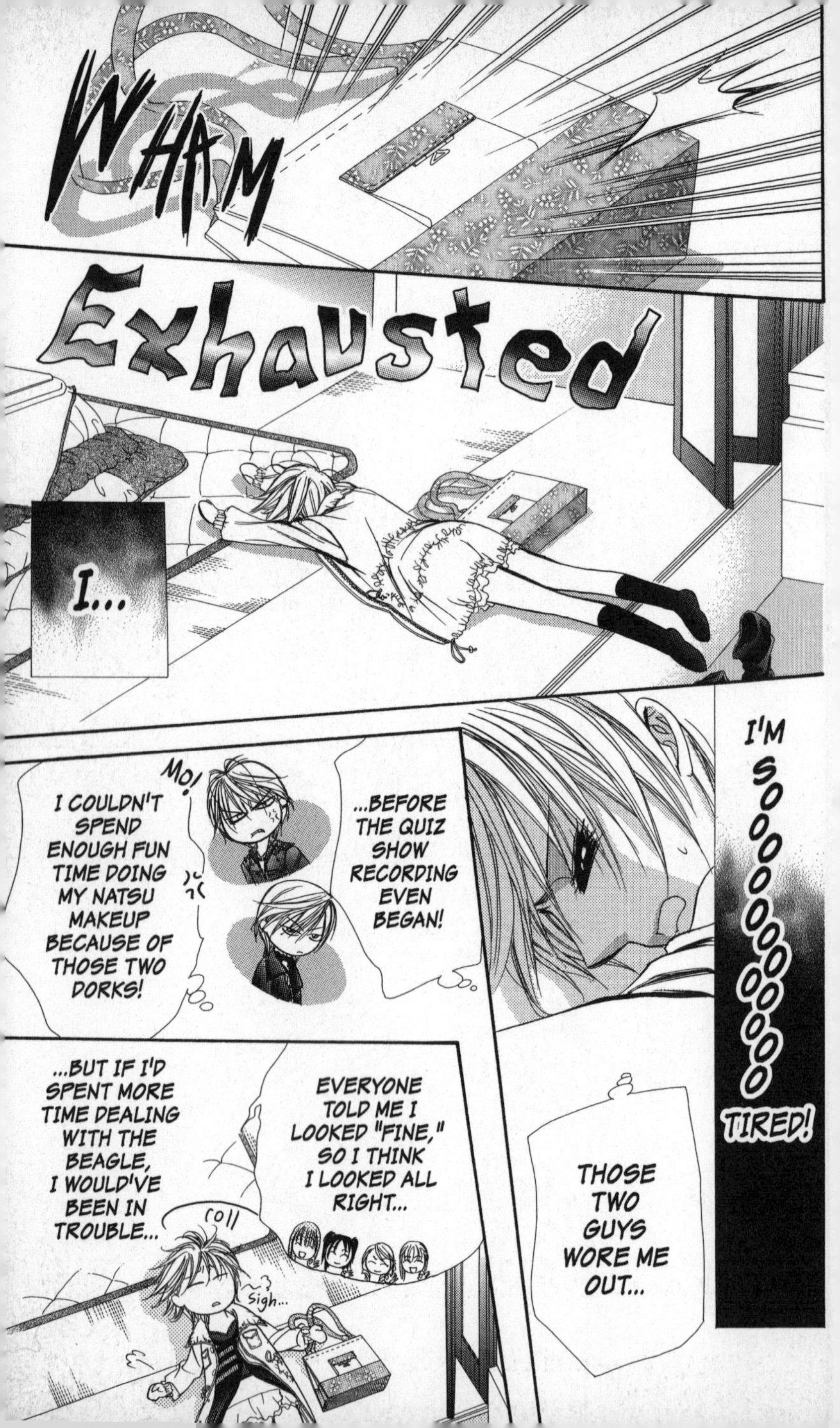

WHAM
Exhausted
I...
I'M SOOOOOOOOOOOOO TIRED!
MO!
I COULDN'T SPEND ENOUGH FUN TIME DOING MY NATSU MAKEUP BECAUSE OF THOSE TWO DORKS!
...BEFORE THE QUIZ SHOW RECORDING EVEN BEGAN!
THOSE TWO GUYS WORE ME OUT...
EVERYONE TOLD ME I LOOKED "FINE," SO I THINK I LOOKED ALL RIGHT...
...BUT IF I'D SPENT MORE TIME DEALING WITH THE BEAGLE, I WOULD'VE BEEN IN TROUBLE...
roll
Sigh...

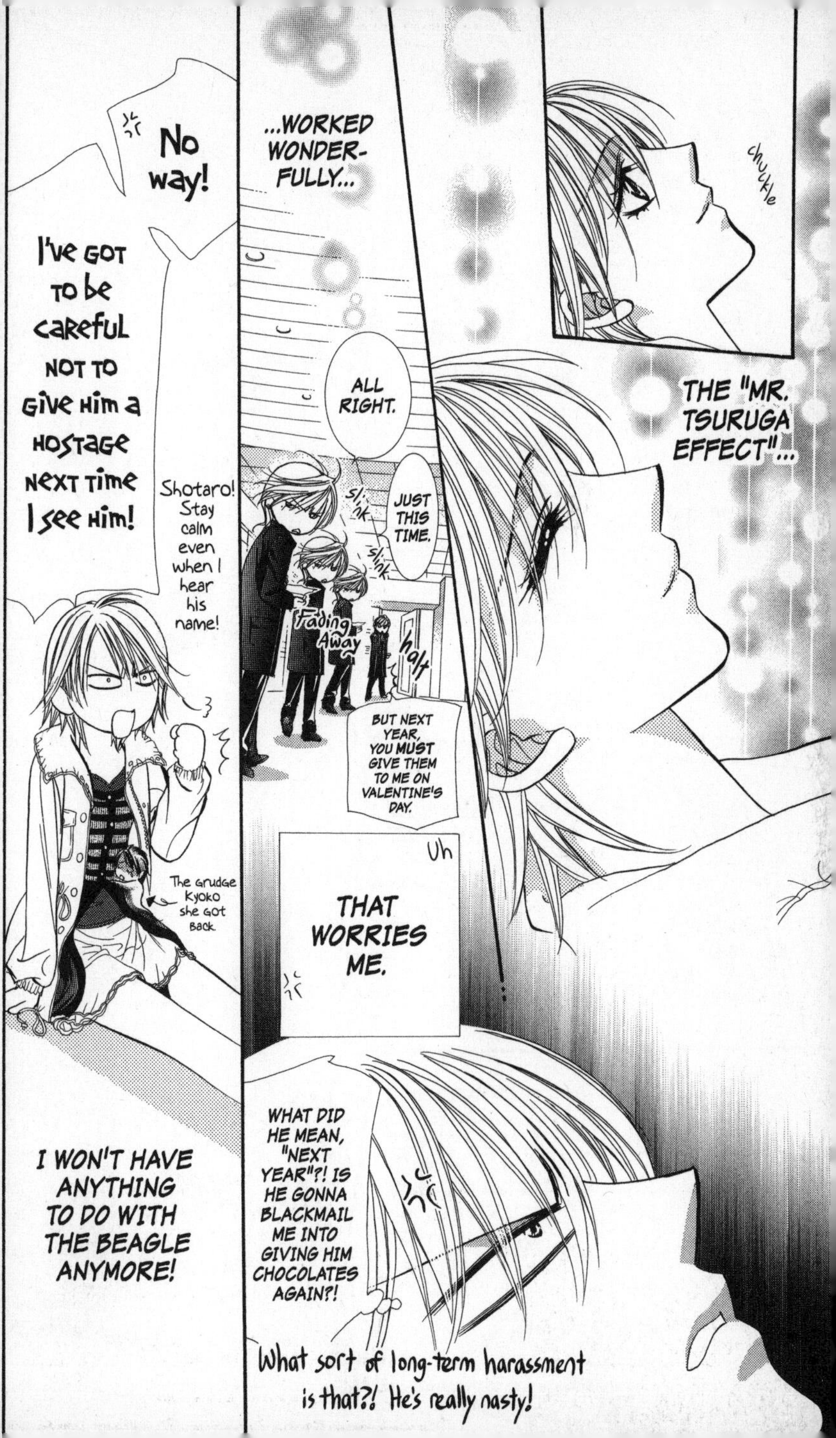
chuckle
THE "MR. TSURUGA EFFECT"...
...WORKED WONDERFULLY...
ALL RIGHT.
JUST THIS TIME.
slink
slink
Fading Away
halt
BUT NEXT YEAR, YOU MUST GIVE THEM TO ME ON VALENTINE'S DAY.
Uh
THAT WORRIES ME.
WHAT DID HE MEAN, "NEXT YEAR"?! IS HE GONNA BLACKMAIL ME INTO GIVING HIM CHOCOLATES AGAIN?!
What sort of long-term harassment is that?! He's really nasty!
No way!
I've GOT TO be careful NOT TO Give Him a HOSTage NEXT Time I see Him!
Shotaro! Stay calm even when I hear his name!
The Grudge Kyoko she Got Back
I WON'T HAVE ANYTHING TO DO WITH THE BEAGLE ANYMORE!

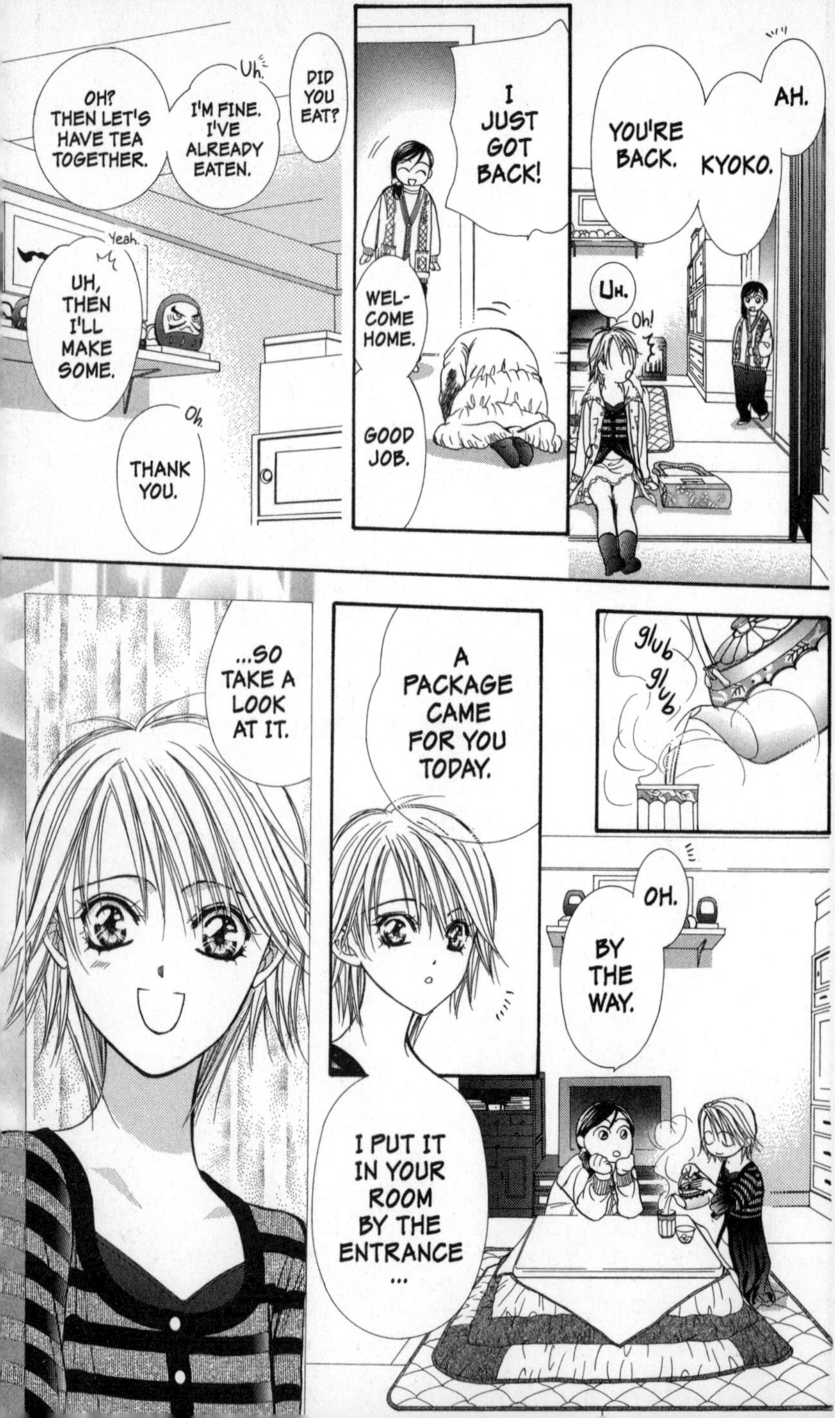
AH.
KYOKO.
YOU'RE BACK.
Uh.
Oh!
I JUST GOT BACK!
WELCOME HOME.
GOOD JOB.
DID YOU EAT?
Uh.
I'M FINE. I'VE ALREADY EATEN.
OH? THEN LET'S HAVE TEA TOGETHER.
Yeah.
UH, THEN I'LL MAKE SOME.
Oh.
THANK YOU.
glub glub
OH.
BY THE WAY.
A PACKAGE CAME FOR YOU TODAY.
I PUT IT IN YOUR ROOM BY THE ENTRANCE...
...SO TAKE A LOOK AT IT.

...that the VIE GHOUL* problem...

...was settled.

...was that even if the VIE GHOUL problem was no more...

IT LOOKS LOVELY.

Yes.

GOOD.

However...

...didn't know...

what she...

shuu

shuu

shuu

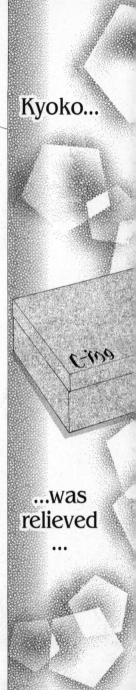

Kyoko...

C-rog

...was relieved...

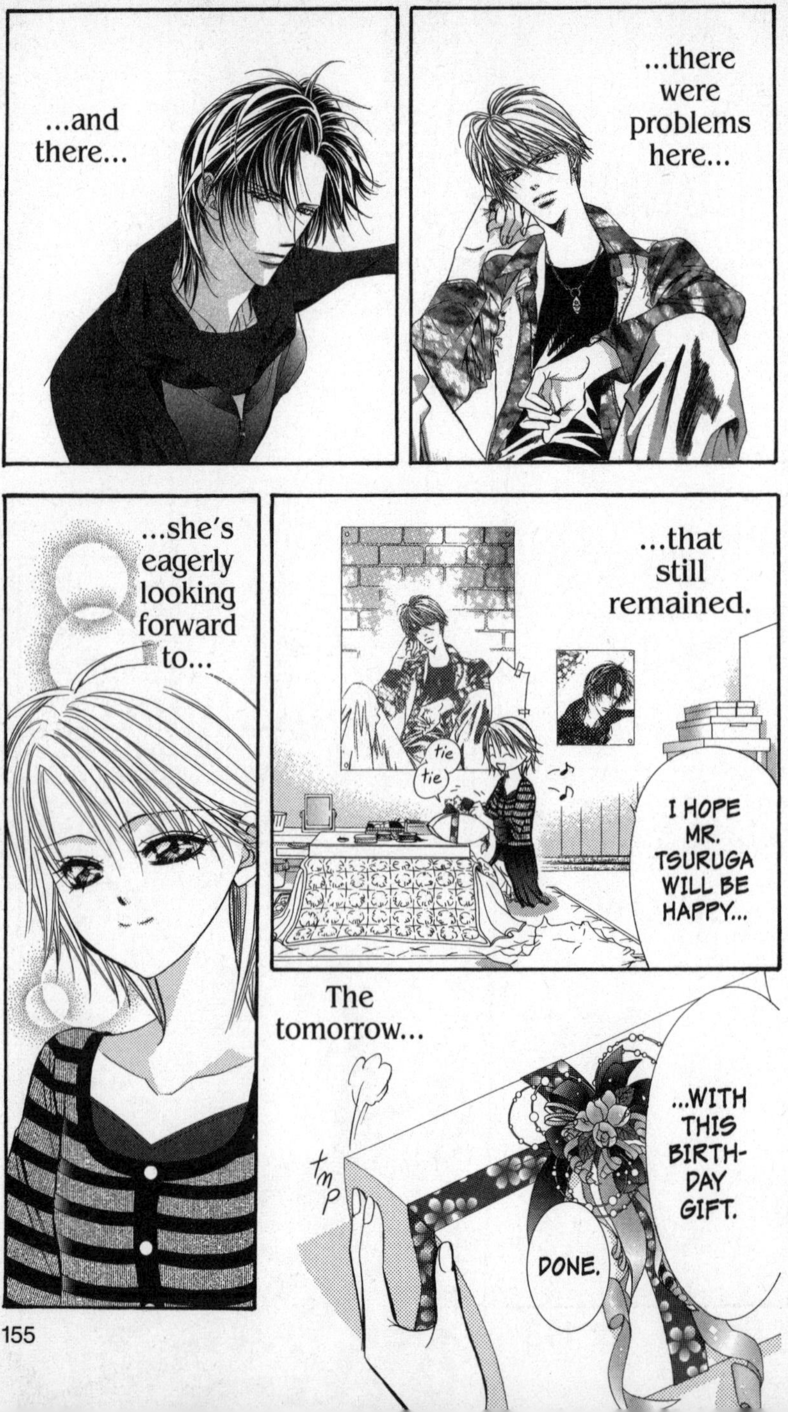
...there were problems here...
...and there...
...that still remained.
tie tie
I HOPE MR. TSURUGA WILL BE HAPPY...
...WITH THIS BIRTHDAY GIFT.
DONE.
tmp
The tomorrow...
...she's eagerly looking forward to...

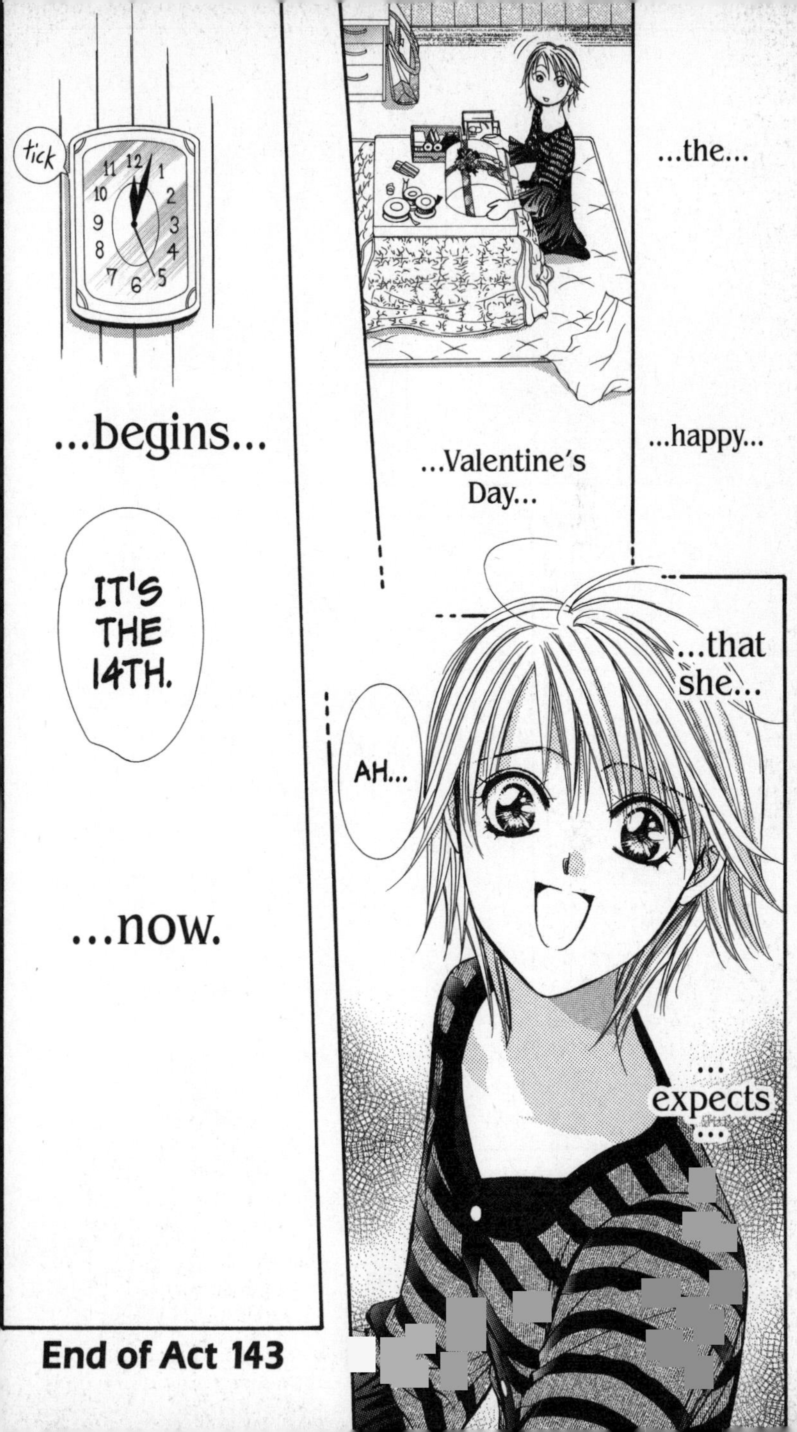
...the...
...happy...
...Valentine's Day...
...that she...
AH...
...expects...
tick
...begins...
IT'S THE 14TH.
...now.
End of Act 143

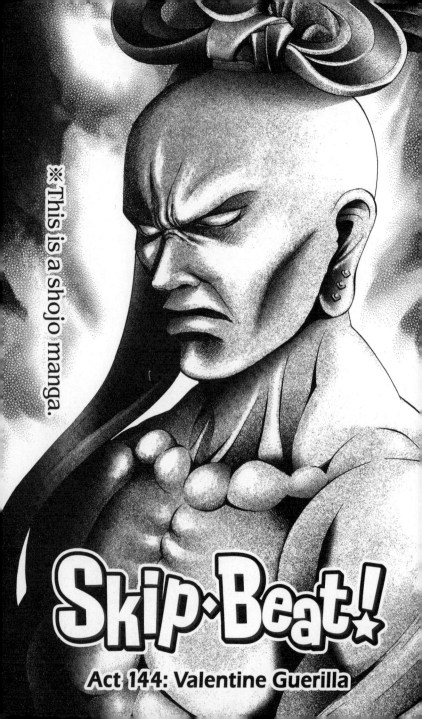

※This is a shojo manga.

Skip·Beat!

Act 144: Valentine Guerilla

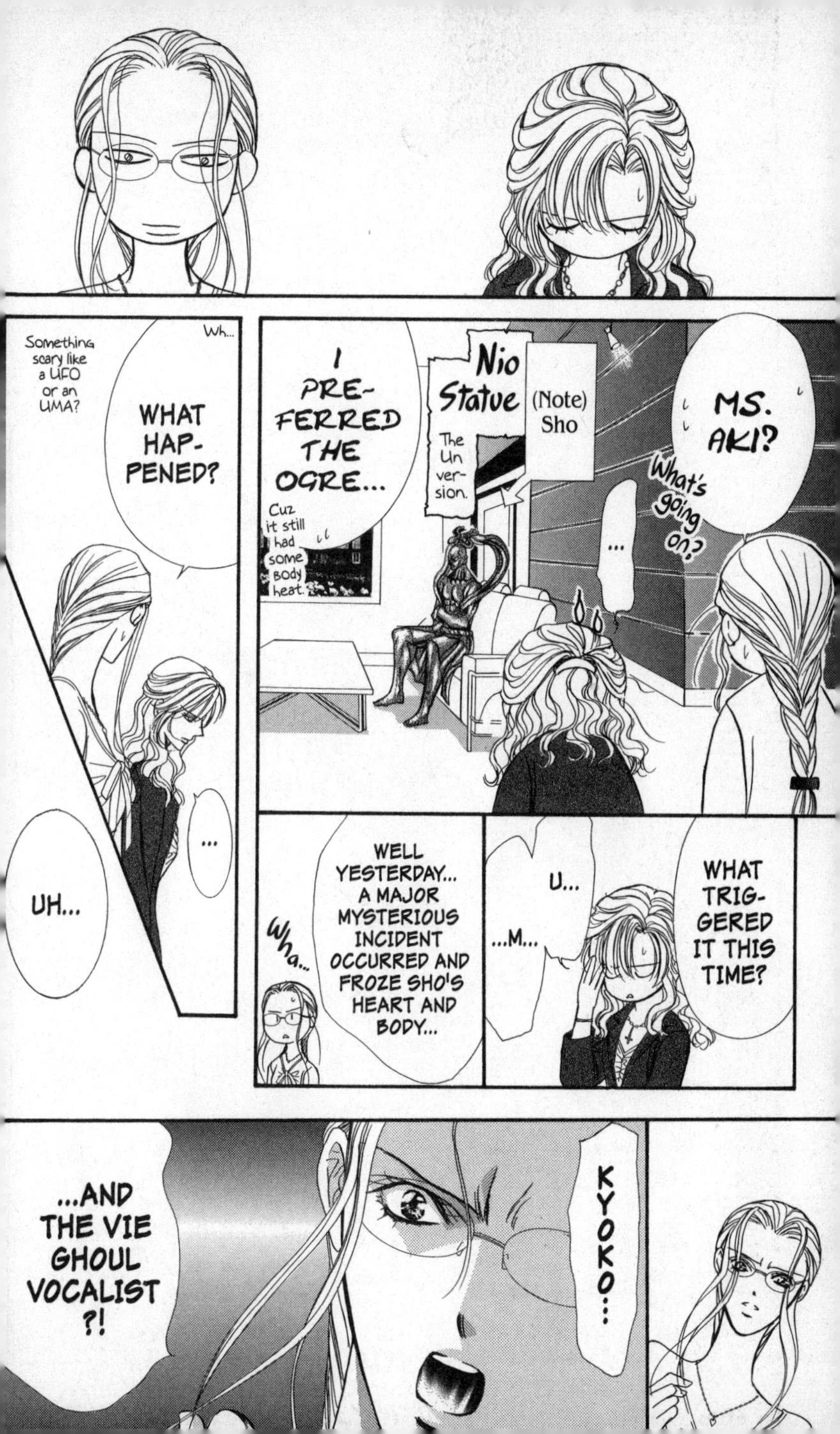
MS. AKI?
What's going on?
...
I PRE-FERRED THE OGRE...
Cuz it still had some body heat.
Nio Statue
(Note) Sho
The Un ver-sion.
WHAT TRIG-GERED IT THIS TIME?
U...
...M...
Wha...
WELL YESTERDAY... A MAJOR MYSTERIOUS INCIDENT OCCURRED AND FROZE SHO'S HEART AND BODY...
Wh...
WHAT HAP-PENED?
Something scary like a UFO or an UMA?
...
UH...
KYOKO...
...AND THE VIE GHOUL VOCALIST?!

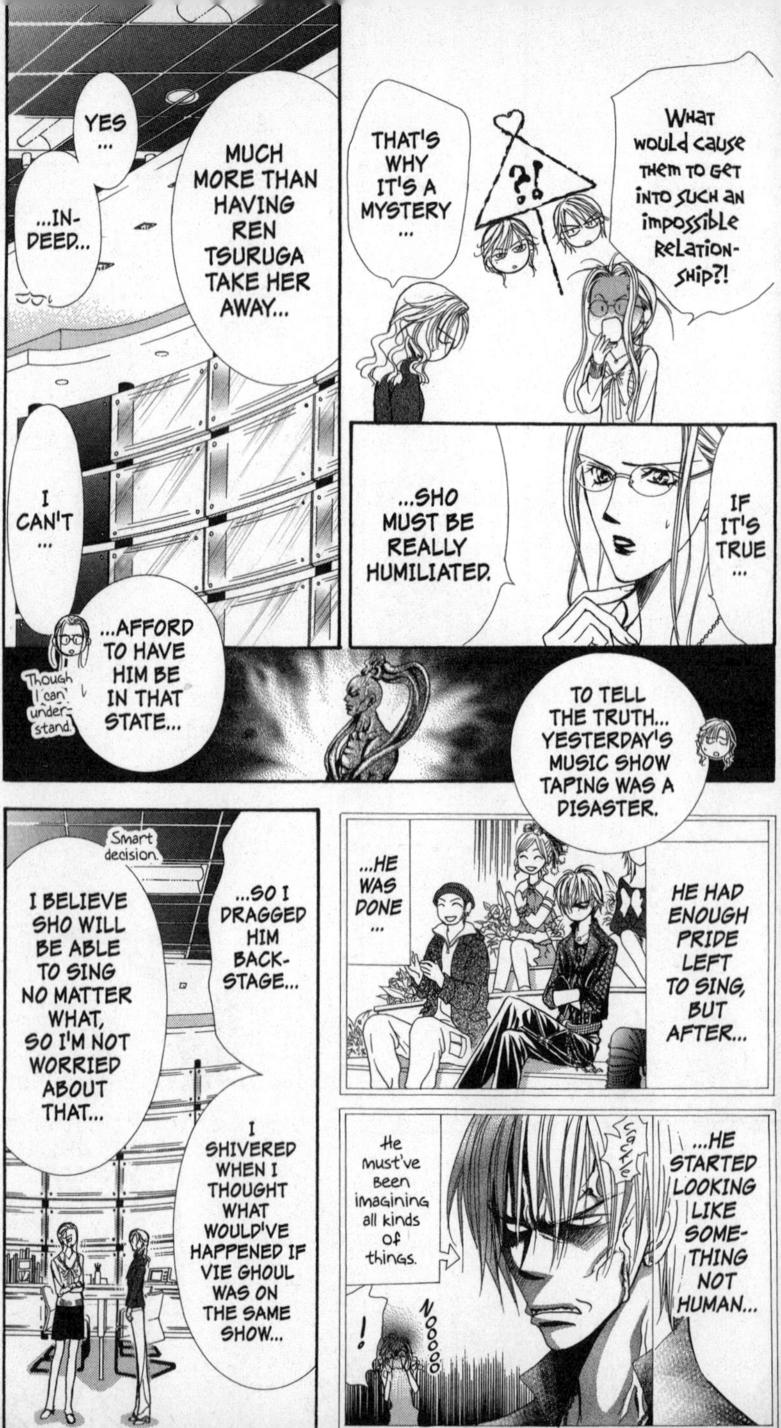

What would cause them to get into such an impossible relationship?!
?!
THAT'S WHY IT'S A MYSTERY...
IF IT'S TRUE...
...SHO MUST BE REALLY HUMILIATED.
MUCH MORE THAN HAVING REN TSURUGA TAKE HER AWAY...
YES...
...INDEED...
I CAN'T...
...AFFORD TO HAVE HIM BE IN THAT STATE...
Though I can understand.
TO TELL THE TRUTH... YESTERDAY'S MUSIC SHOW TAPING WAS A DISASTER.
HE HAD ENOUGH PRIDE LEFT TO SING, BUT AFTER...
...HE WAS DONE...
...HE STARTED LOOKING LIKE SOMETHING NOT HUMAN...
Cackle
He must've been imagining all kinds of things.
NOOOOO
!
...SO I DRAGGED HIM BACKSTAGE...
Smart decision.
I BELIEVE SHO WILL BE ABLE TO SING NO MATTER WHAT, SO I'M NOT WORRIED ABOUT THAT...
I SHIVERED WHEN I THOUGHT WHAT WOULD'VE HAPPENED IF VIE GHOUL WAS ON THE SAME SHOW...

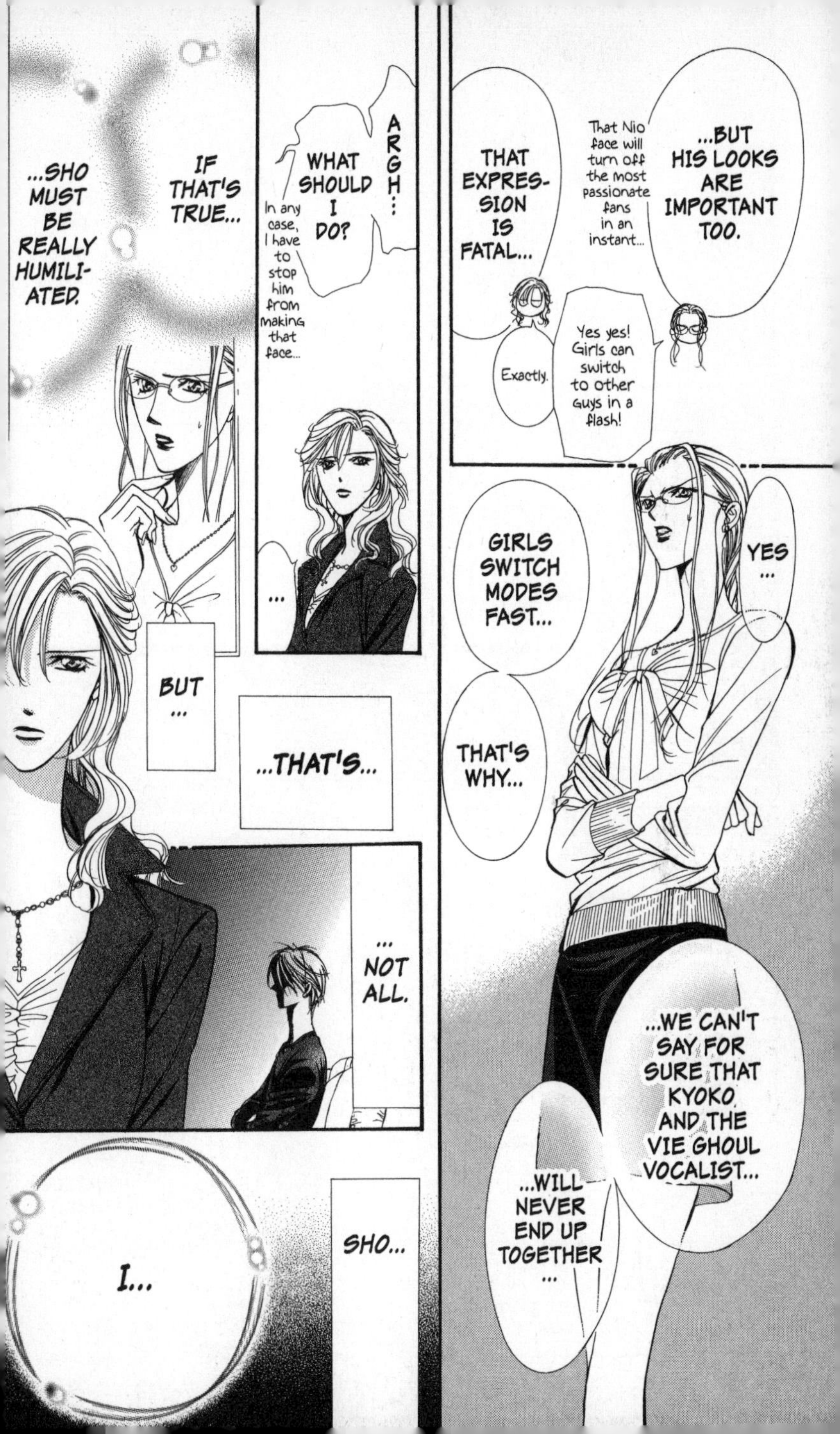
...BUT HIS LOOKS ARE IMPORTANT TOO.
That Nio face will turn off the most passionate fans in an instant...
THAT EXPRESSION IS FATAL...
Yes yes! Girls can switch to other guys in a flash!
Exactly.
YES...
GIRLS SWITCH MODES FAST...
THAT'S WHY...
...WE CAN'T SAY FOR SURE THAT KYOKO AND THE VIE GHOUL VOCALIST...
...WILL NEVER END UP TOGETHER...
ARGH...
WHAT SHOULD I DO?
In any case, I have to stop him from making that face...
...
IF THAT'S TRUE...
...SHO MUST BE REALLY HUMILIATED.
BUT...
...THAT'S...
...NOT ALL.
SHO...
I...

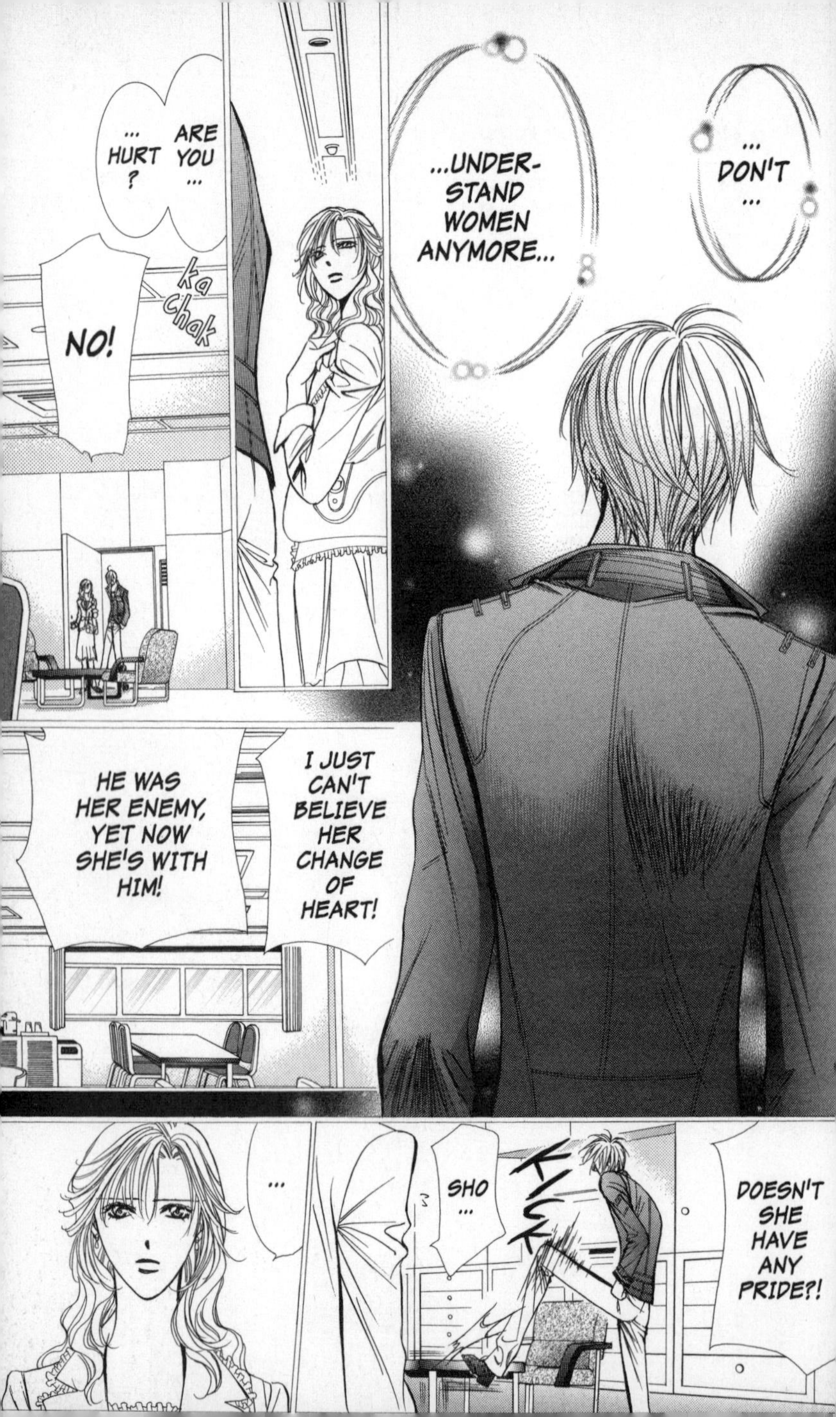
... DON'T ...
...UNDER-STAND WOMEN ANYMORE...
ARE YOU ... ... HURT ?
ka chak
NO!
I JUST CAN'T BELIEVE HER CHANGE OF HEART!
HE WAS HER ENEMY, YET NOW SHE'S WITH HIM!
DOESN'T SHE HAVE ANY PRIDE?!
KICK
SHO ...
...

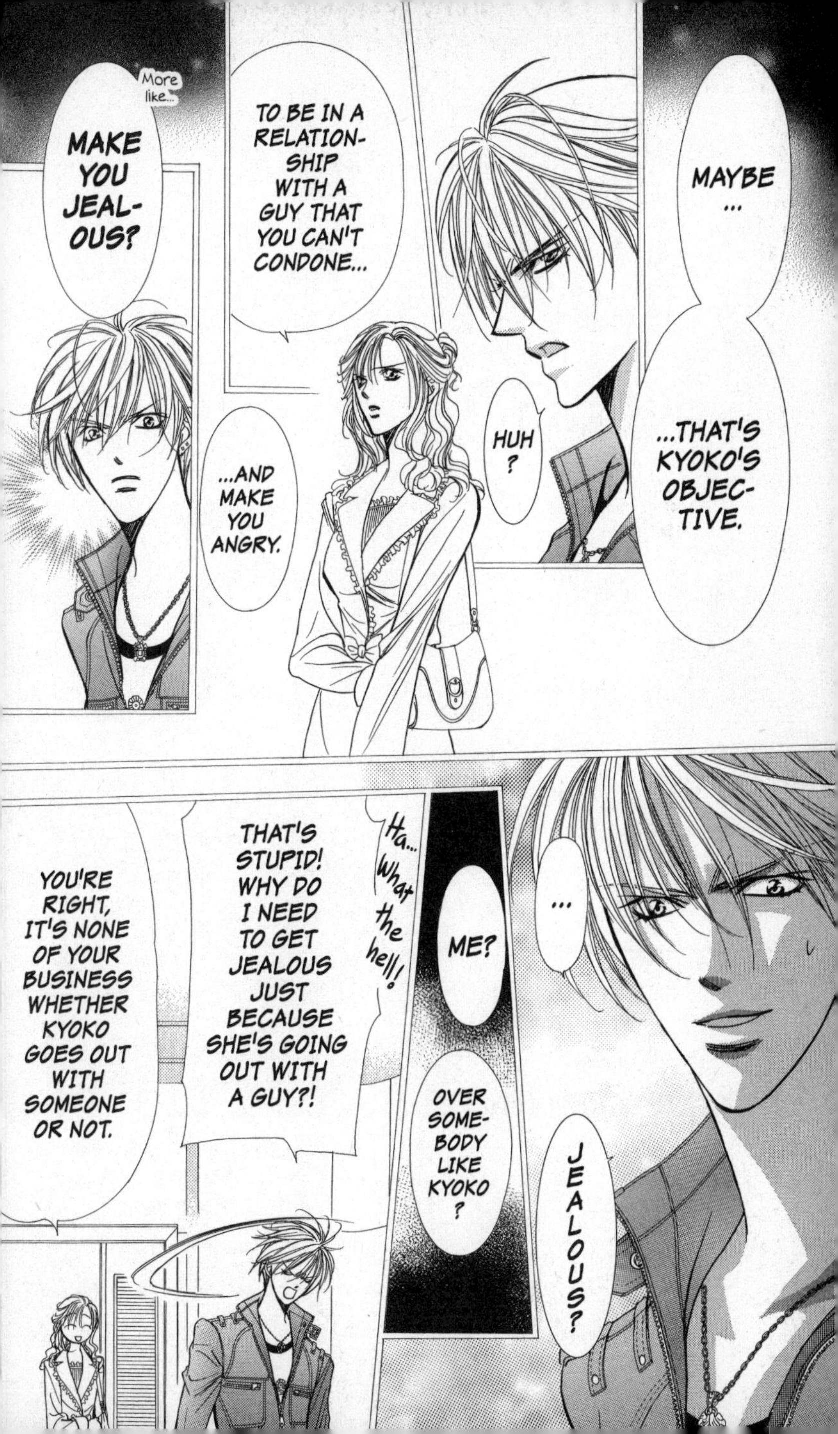
MAYBE ...
...THAT'S KYOKO'S OBJECTIVE.
HUH?
TO BE IN A RELATIONSHIP WITH A GUY THAT YOU CAN'T CONDONE...
...AND MAKE YOU ANGRY.
More like...
MAKE YOU JEALOUS?
...
JEALOUS?
ME?
OVER SOMEBODY LIKE KYOKO?
Ha... What the hell!
THAT'S STUPID! WHY DO I NEED TO GET JEALOUS JUST BECAUSE SHE'S GOING OUT WITH A GUY?!
YOU'RE RIGHT, IT'S NONE OF YOUR BUSINESS WHETHER KYOKO GOES OUT WITH SOMEONE OR NOT.

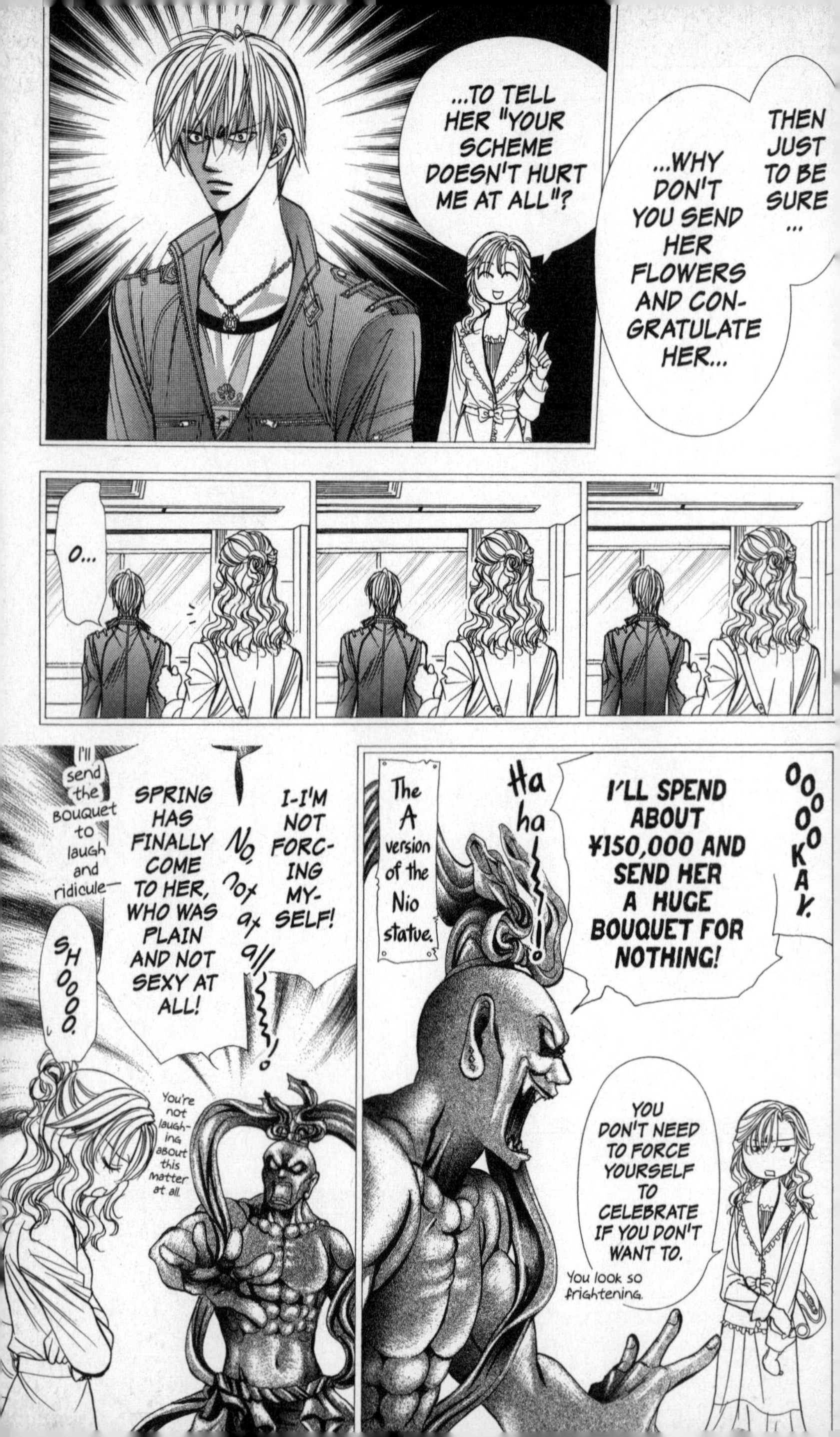
THEN JUST TO BE SURE...
...WHY DON'T YOU SEND HER FLOWERS AND CON-GRATULATE HER...
...TO TELL HER "YOUR SCHEME DOESN'T HURT ME AT ALL"?
O...
OOOOOKAY.
I'LL SPEND ABOUT ¥150,000 AND SEND HER A HUGE BOUQUET FOR NOTHING!
Ha ha!!
The A version of the Nio statue.
YOU DON'T NEED TO FORCE YOURSELF TO CELEBRATE IF YOU DON'T WANT TO.
You look so frightening.
I-I'M NOT FORC-ING MY-SELF!
No, not at all!
SPRING HAS FINALLY COME TO HER, WHO WAS PLAIN AND NOT SEXY AT ALL!
I'll send the bouquet to laugh and ridicule—
SHOOOO.
You're not laugh-ing about this matter at all.

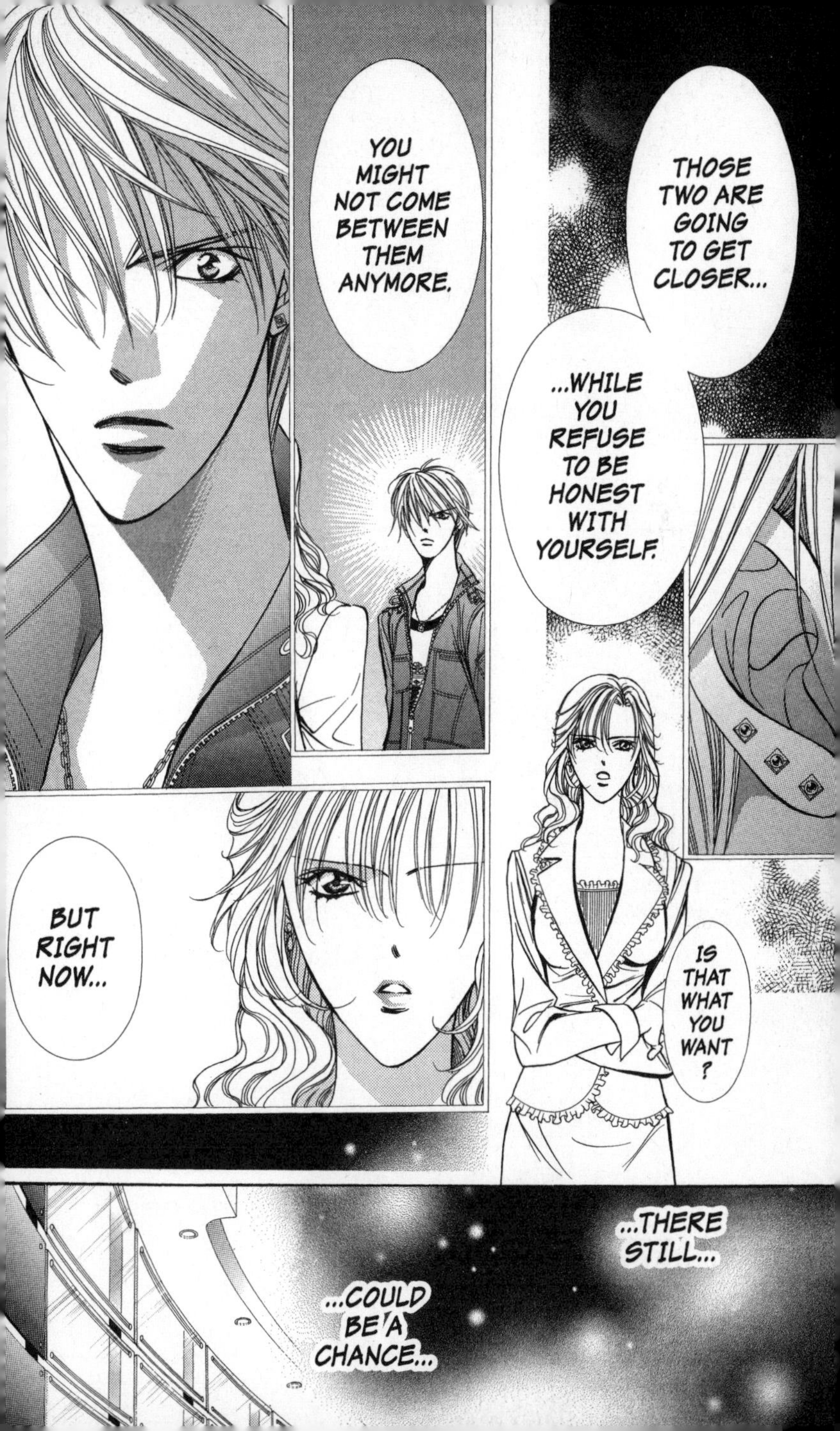
THOSE TWO ARE GOING TO GET CLOSER...
...WHILE YOU REFUSE TO BE HONEST WITH YOURSELF.
IS THAT WHAT YOU WANT?
YOU MIGHT NOT COME BETWEEN THEM ANYMORE.
BUT RIGHT NOW...
...THERE STILL...
...COULD BE A CHANCE...

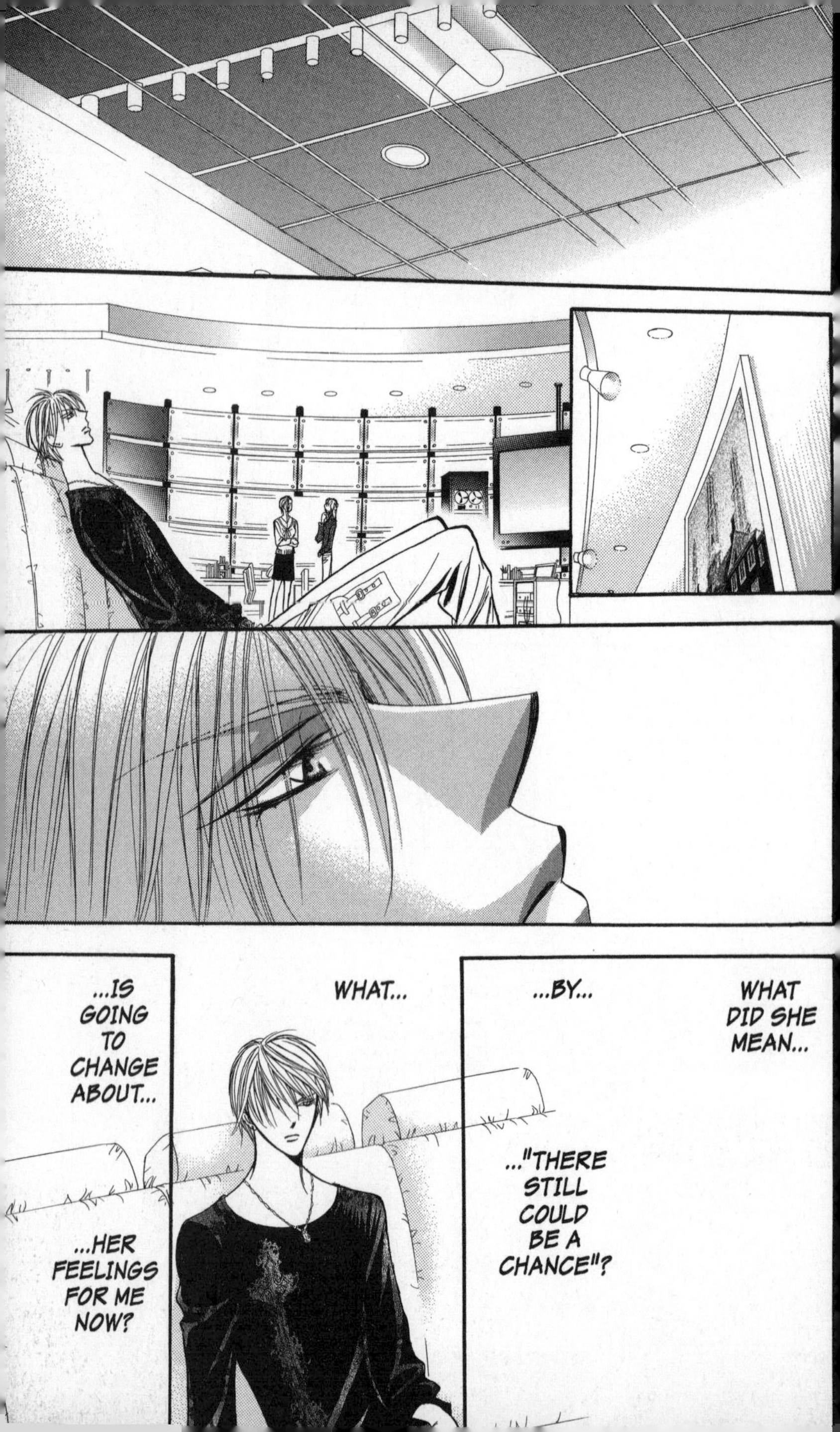
WHAT DID SHE MEAN...
...BY...
..."THERE STILL COULD BE A CHANCE"?
WHAT...
...IS GOING TO CHANGE ABOUT...
...HER FEELINGS FOR ME NOW?

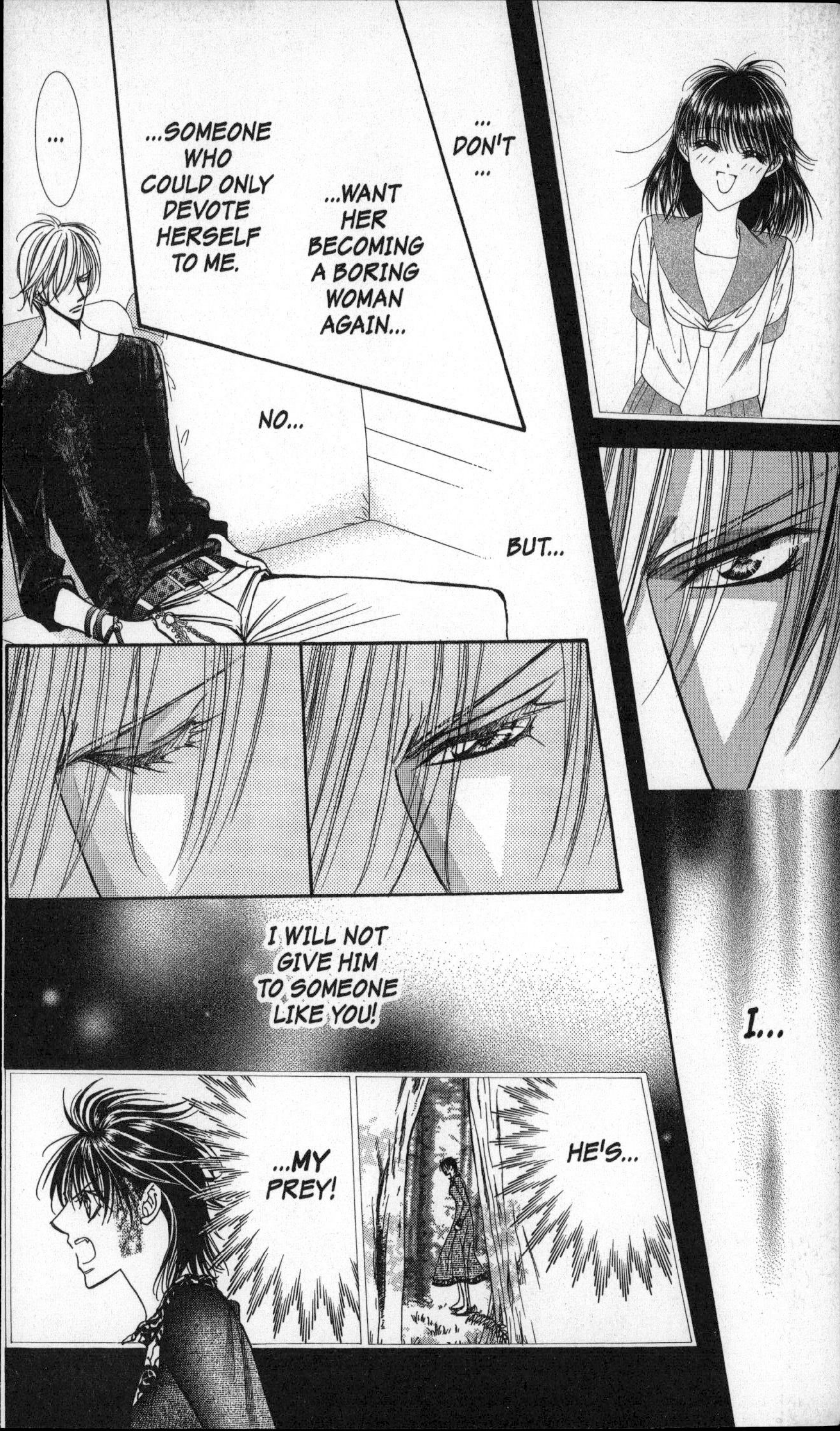
... DON'T ...
...WANT HER BECOMING A BORING WOMAN AGAIN...
...SOMEONE WHO COULD ONLY DEVOTE HERSELF TO ME.
...
NO...
BUT...
I...
I WILL NOT GIVE HIM TO SOMEONE LIKE YOU!
HE'S...
...MY PREY!

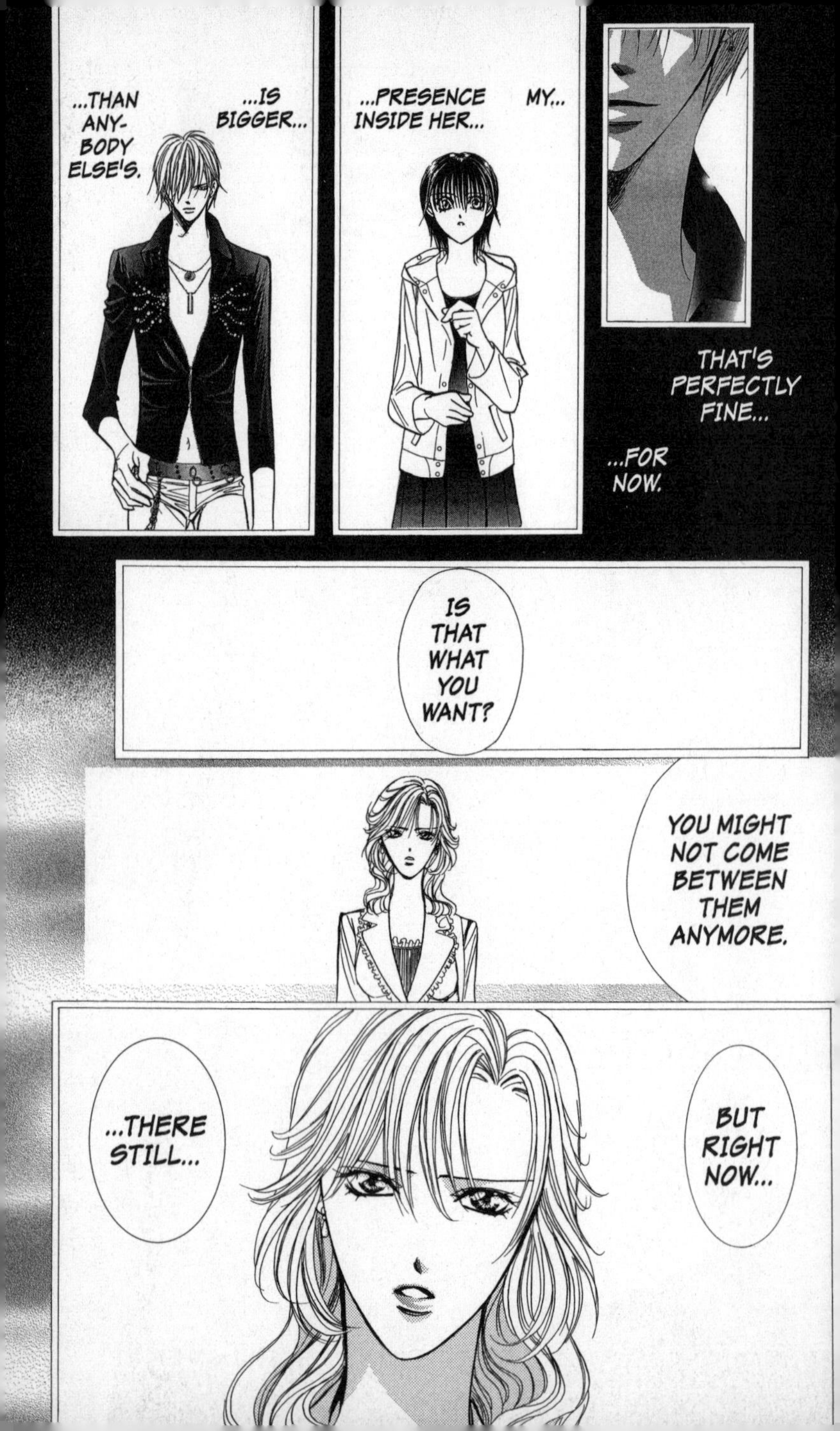
MY...
...PRESENCE INSIDE HER...
...IS BIGGER...
...THAN ANY-BODY ELSE'S.
THAT'S PERFECTLY FINE...
...FOR NOW.
IS THAT WHAT YOU WANT?
YOU MIGHT NOT COME BETWEEN THEM ANYMORE.
BUT RIGHT NOW...
...THERE STILL...

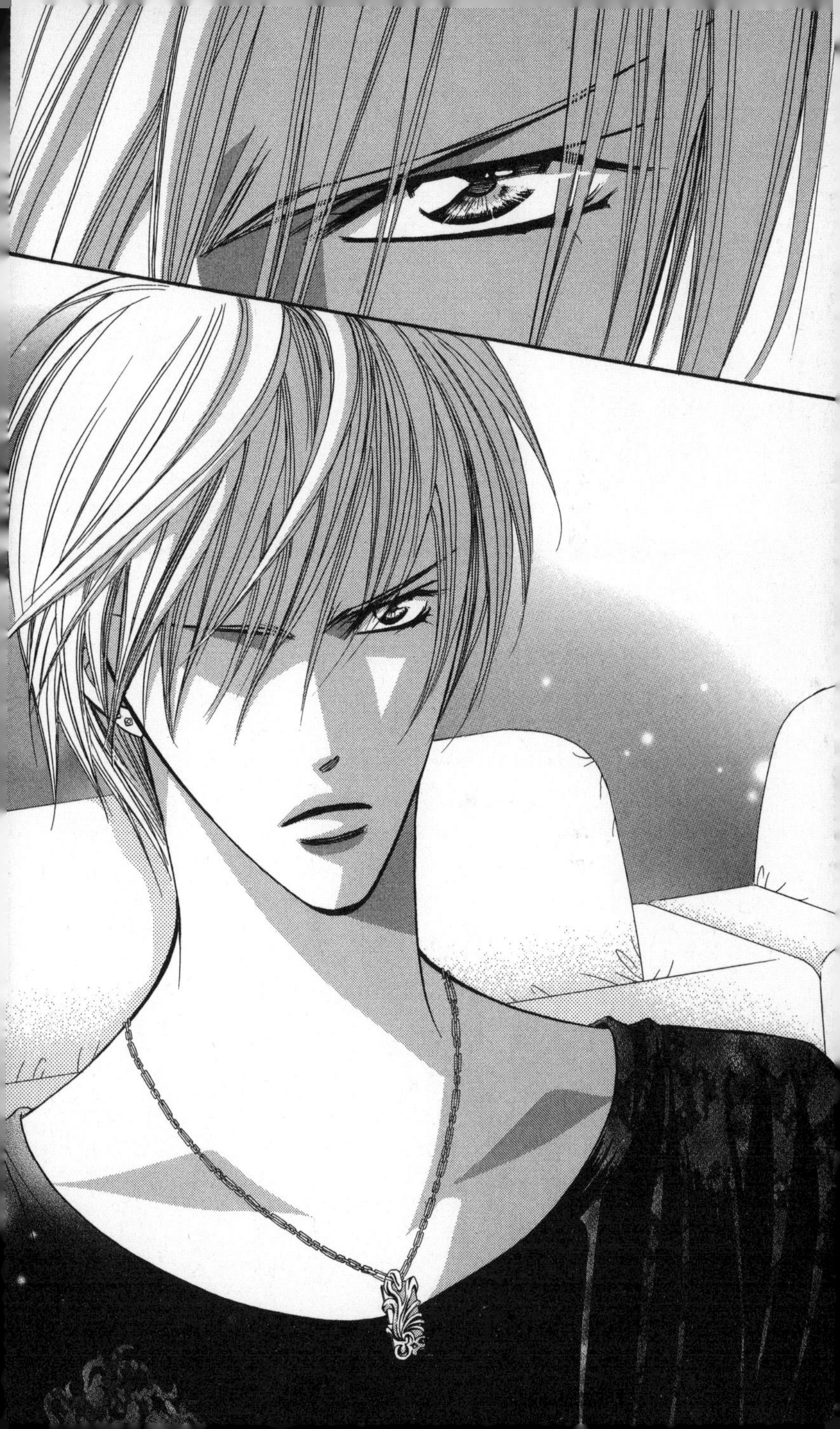

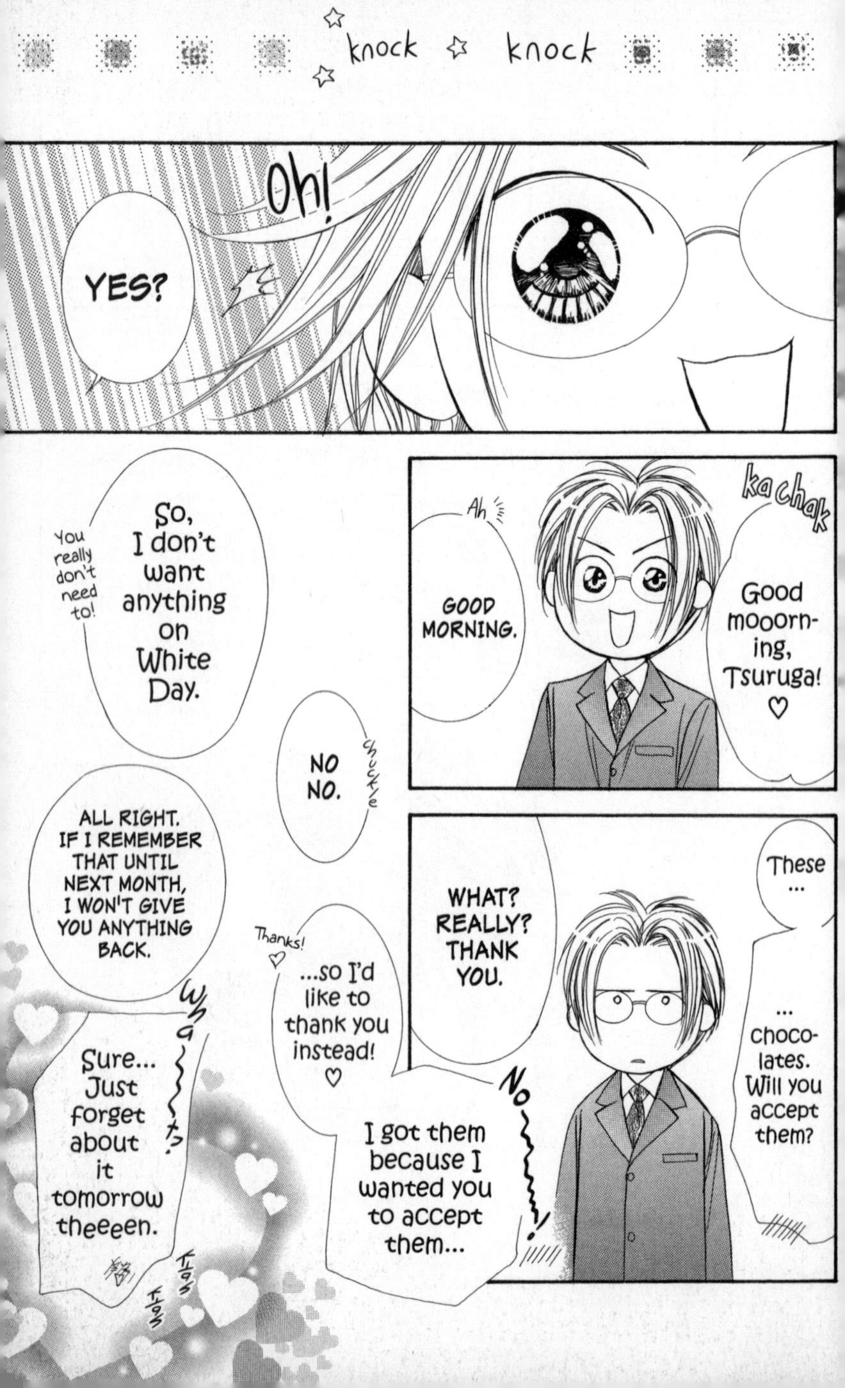
knock knock
Oh!
YES?
ka chak
Good mooorning, Tsuruga! ♡
Ah
GOOD MORNING.
These...
... chocolates. Will you accept them?
WHAT? REALLY? THANK YOU.
No~!
I got them because I wanted you to accept them...
...so I'd like to thank you instead! ♡
Thanks! ♡
So, I don't want anything on White Day.
You really don't need to!
NO NO.
chuckle
ALL RIGHT. IF I REMEMBER THAT UNTIL NEXT MONTH, I WON'T GIVE YOU ANYTHING BACK.
Wha~t?!
Sure... Just forget about it tomorrow theeeen.

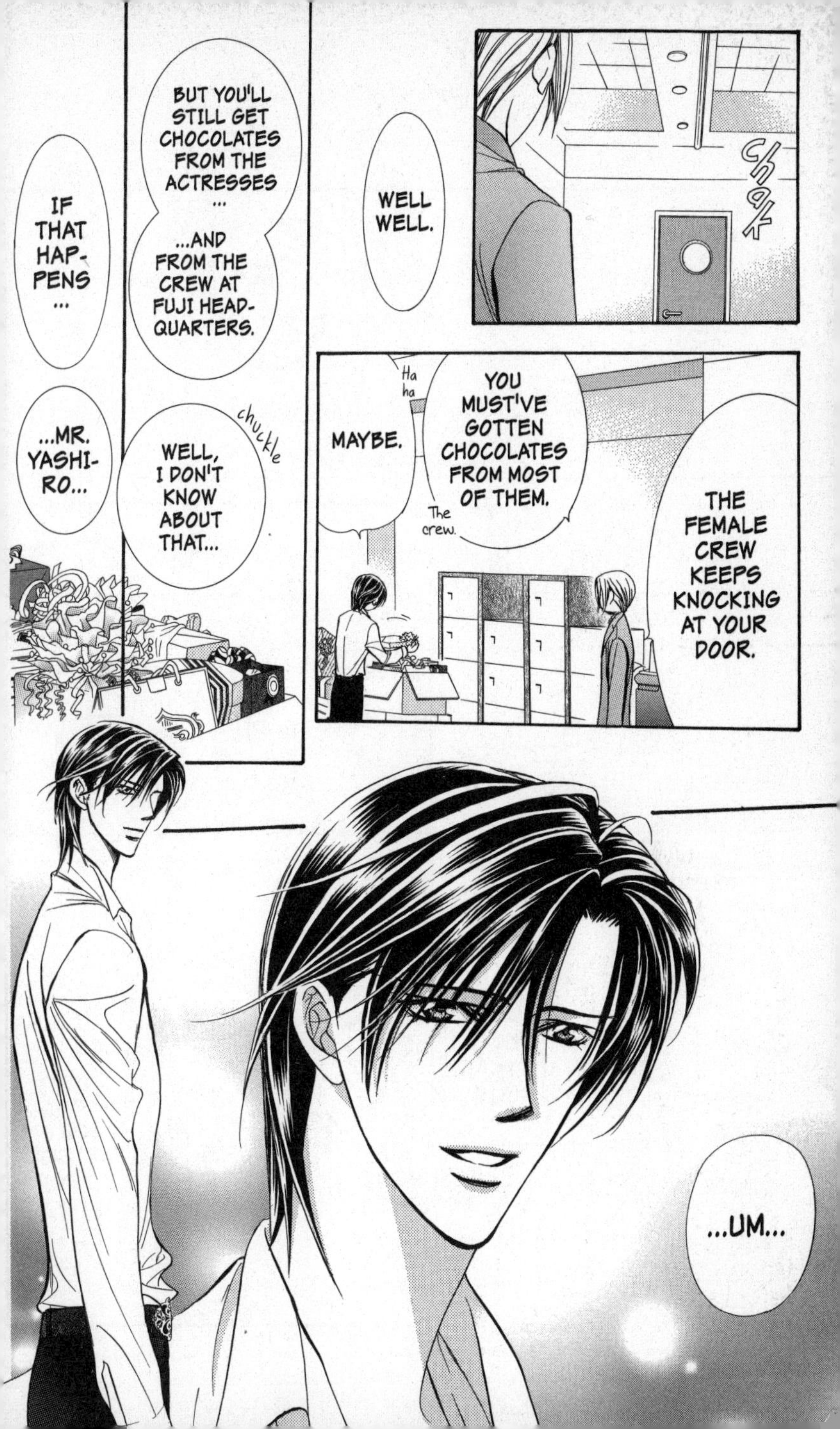
Chak
WELL WELL.
THE FEMALE CREW KEEPS KNOCKING AT YOUR DOOR.
YOU MUST'VE GOTTEN CHOCOLATES FROM MOST OF THEM.
The crew.
Ha ha
MAYBE.
BUT YOU'LL STILL GET CHOCOLATES FROM THE ACTRESSES ...
...AND FROM THE CREW AT FUJI HEAD-QUARTERS.
chuckle
WELL, I DON'T KNOW ABOUT THAT...
IF THAT HAP-PENS ...
...MR. YASHI-RO...
...UM...

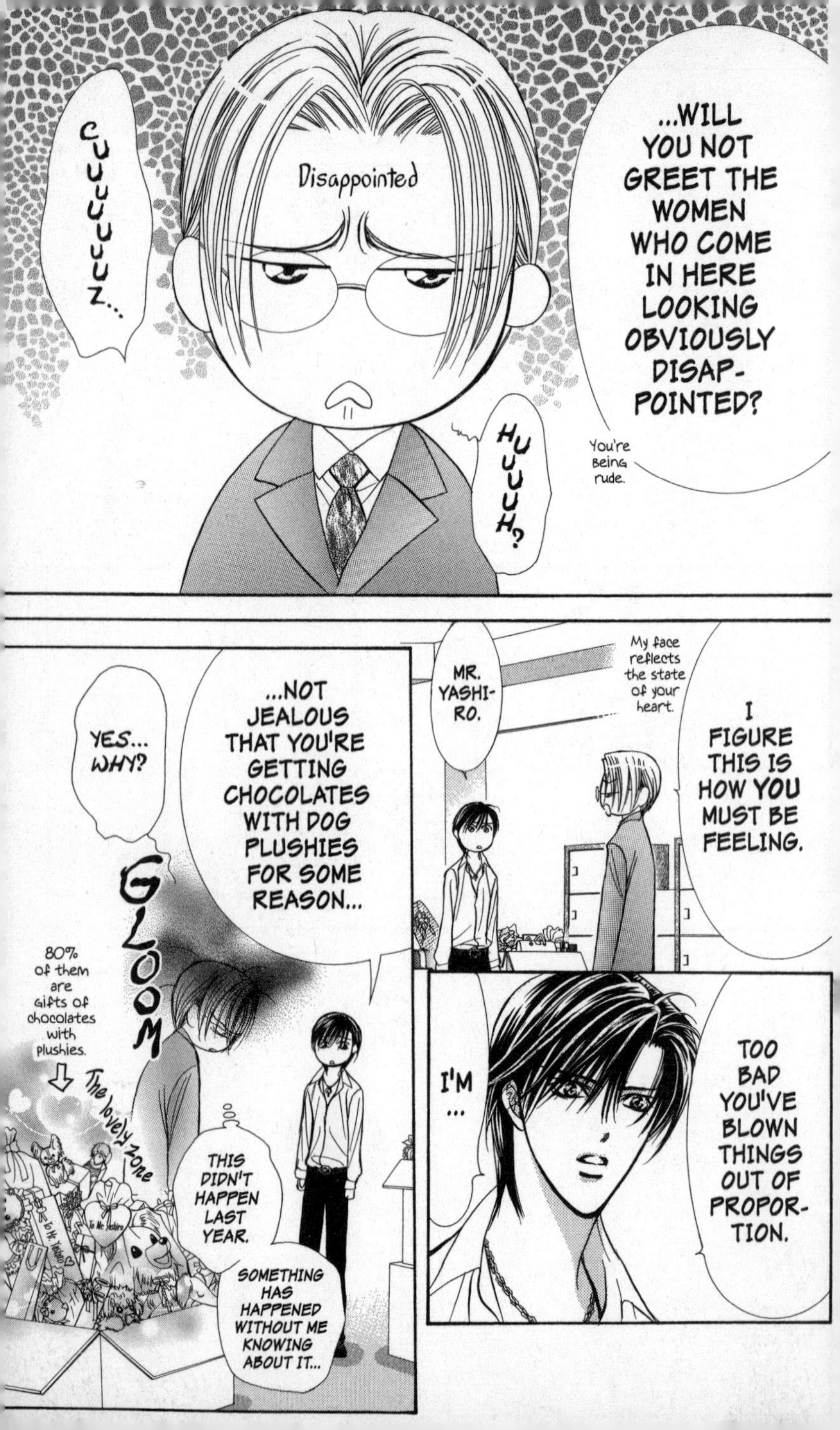
...WILL YOU NOT GREET THE WOMEN WHO COME IN HERE LOOKING OBVIOUSLY DISAP-POINTED?
You're being rude.
Disappointed
CUUUUUUUZ...
HUUUUH?
I FIGURE THIS IS HOW YOU MUST BE FEELING.
My face reflects the state of your heart.
MR. YASHI-RO.
TOO BAD YOU'VE BLOWN THINGS OUT OF PROPOR-TION.
I'M ...
...NOT JEALOUS THAT YOU'RE GETTING CHOCOLATES WITH DOG PLUSHIES FOR SOME REASON...
YES... WHY?
GLOOM
80% of them are gifts of chocolates with plushies.
The lovely zone
THIS DIDN'T HAPPEN LAST YEAR.
SOMETHING HAS HAPPENED WITHOUT ME KNOWING ABOUT IT...

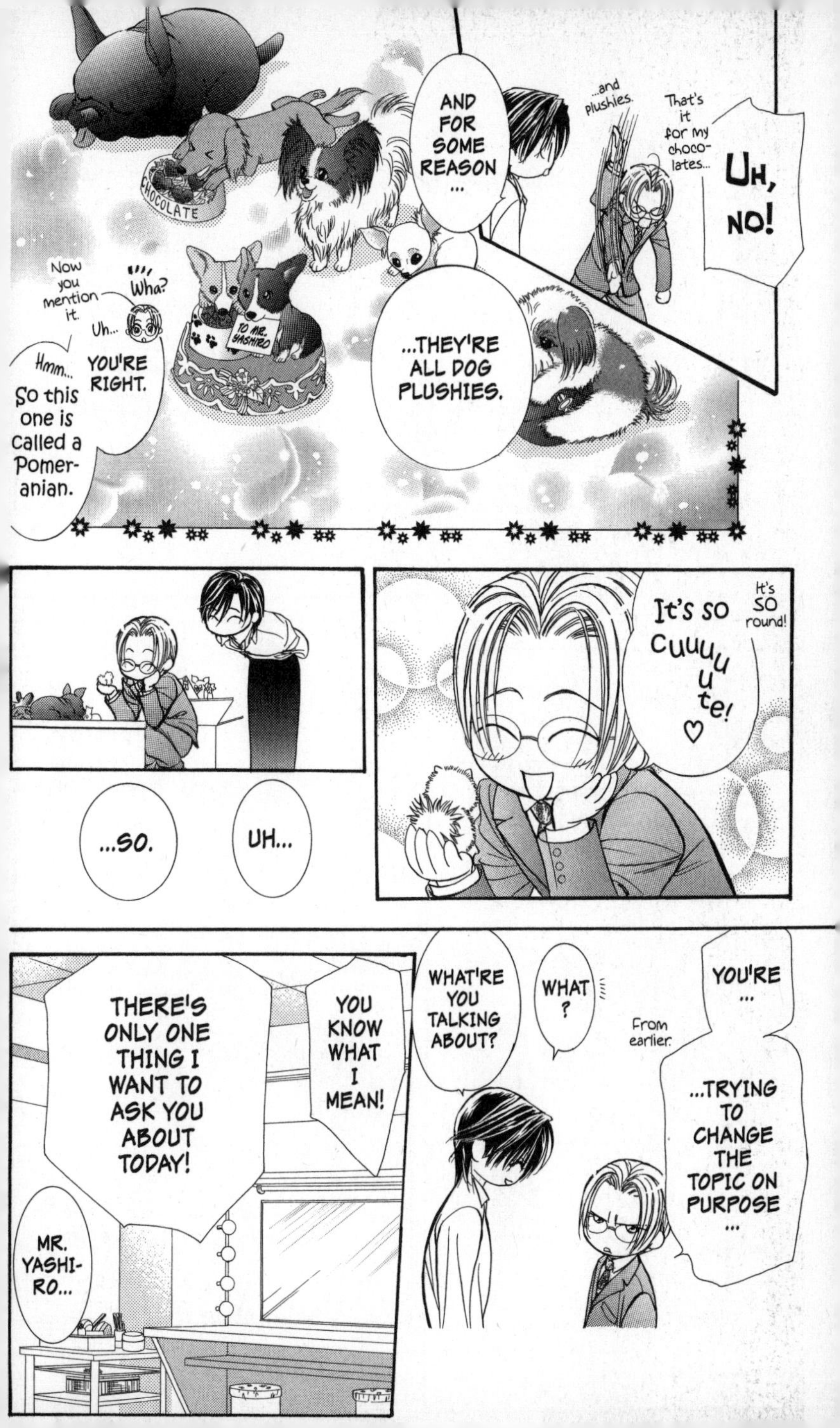
UH, NO!
That's it for my chocolates...
...and plushies.
AND FOR SOME REASON...
...THEY'RE ALL DOG PLUSHIES.
TO MR. YASHIRO
CHOCOLATE
Now you mention it.
Wha?
Uh...
YOU'RE RIGHT.
Hmm...
So this one is called a Pomeranian.
It's so cuuuuute! ♡
It's SO round!
UH...
...SO.
YOU'RE...
...TRYING TO CHANGE THE TOPIC ON PURPOSE...
From earlier.
WHAT?
WHAT'RE YOU TALKING ABOUT?
YOU KNOW WHAT I MEAN!
THERE'S ONLY ONE THING I WANT TO ASK YOU ABOUT TODAY!
MR. YASHIRO...

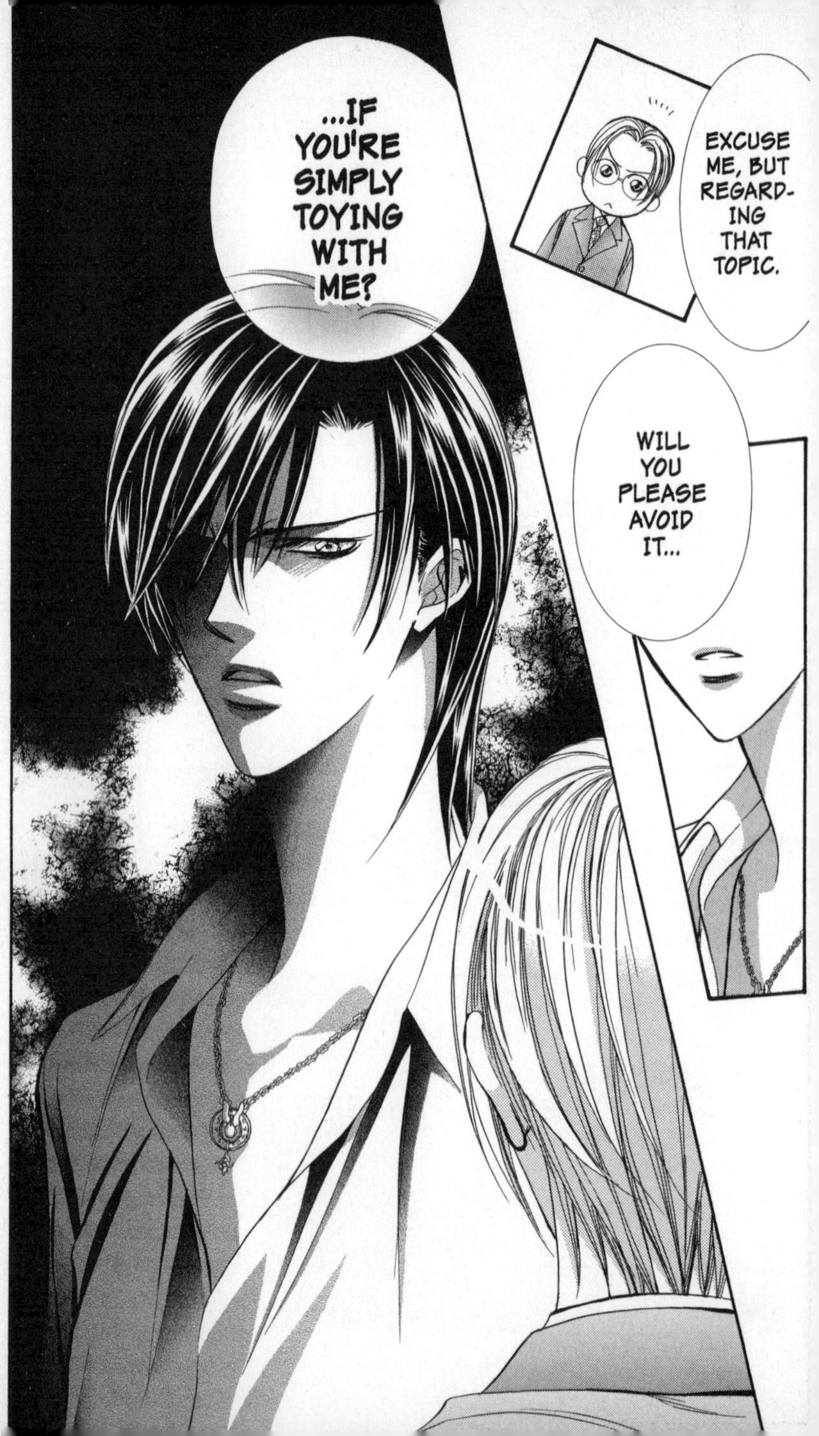
EXCUSE ME, BUT REGARDING THAT TOPIC.
WILL YOU PLEASE AVOID IT...
...IF YOU'RE SIMPLY TOYING WITH ME?

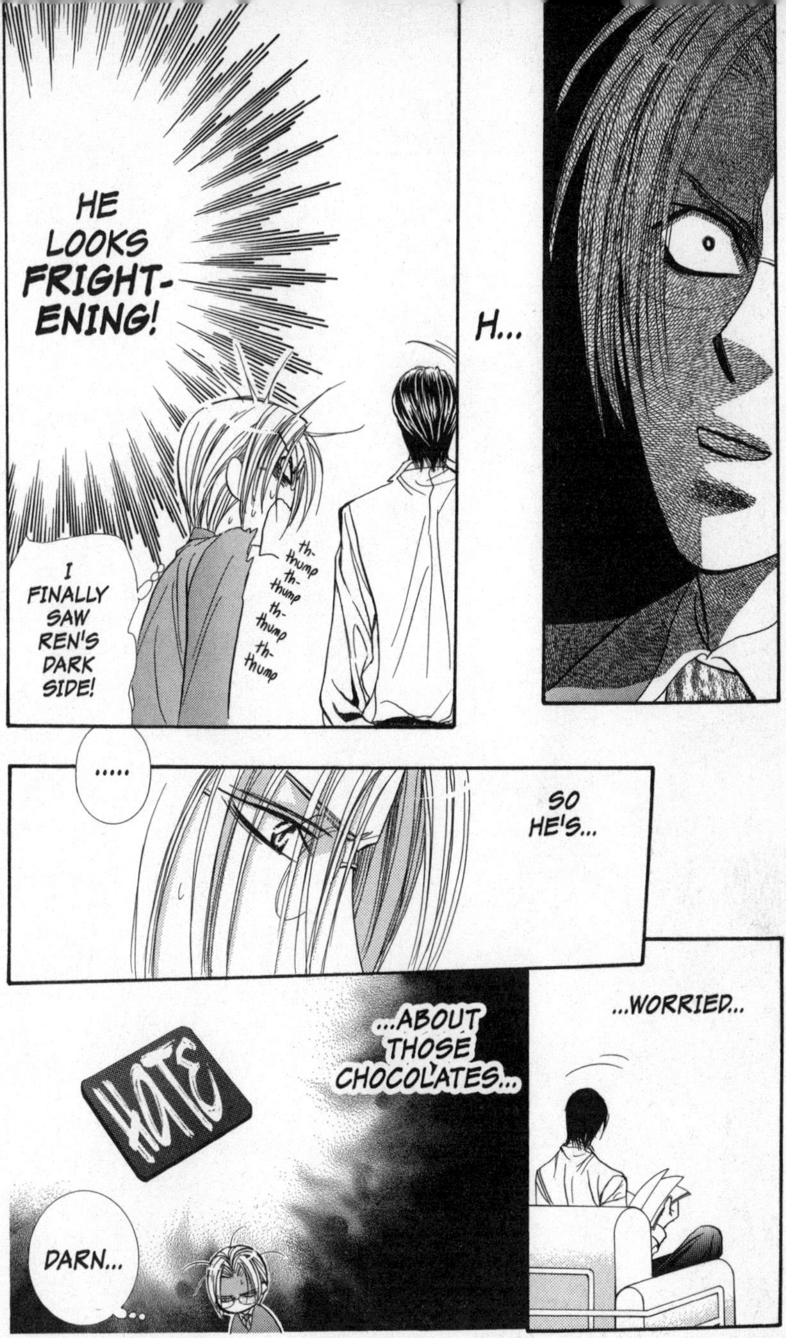
H...
HE LOOKS FRIGHT-ENING!
th-thump th-thump th-thump th-thump
I FINALLY SAW REN'S DARK SIDE!
.....
SO HE'S...
...WORRIED...
...ABOUT THOSE CHOCOLATES...
HATE
DARN...

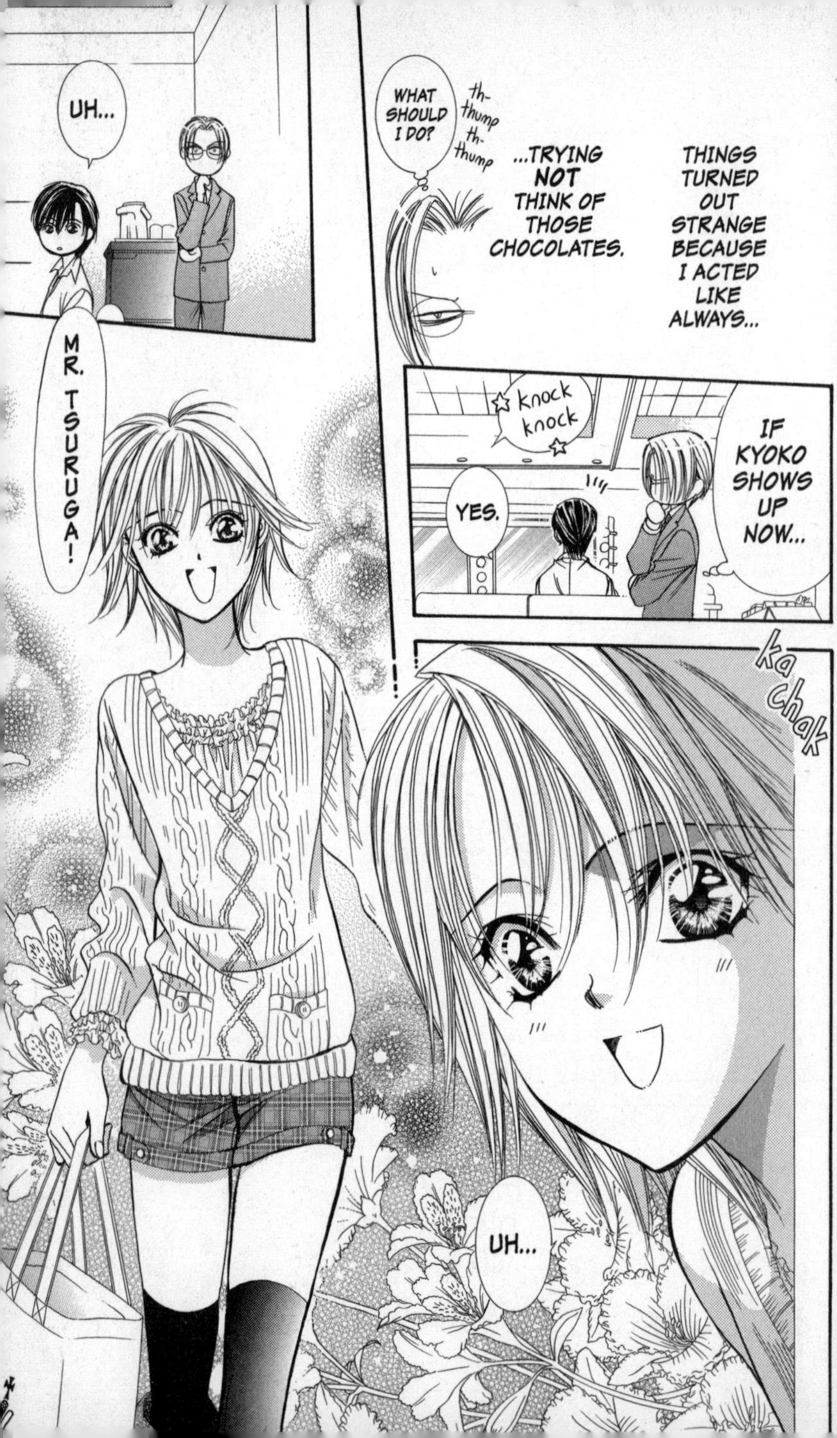
THINGS TURNED OUT STRANGE BECAUSE I ACTED LIKE ALWAYS...
...TRYING NOT THINK OF THOSE CHOCOLATES.
WHAT SHOULD I DO?
th-thump th-thump
UH...
IF KYOKO SHOWS UP NOW...
knock knock
YES.
ka chak
UH...
MR. TSURUGA!

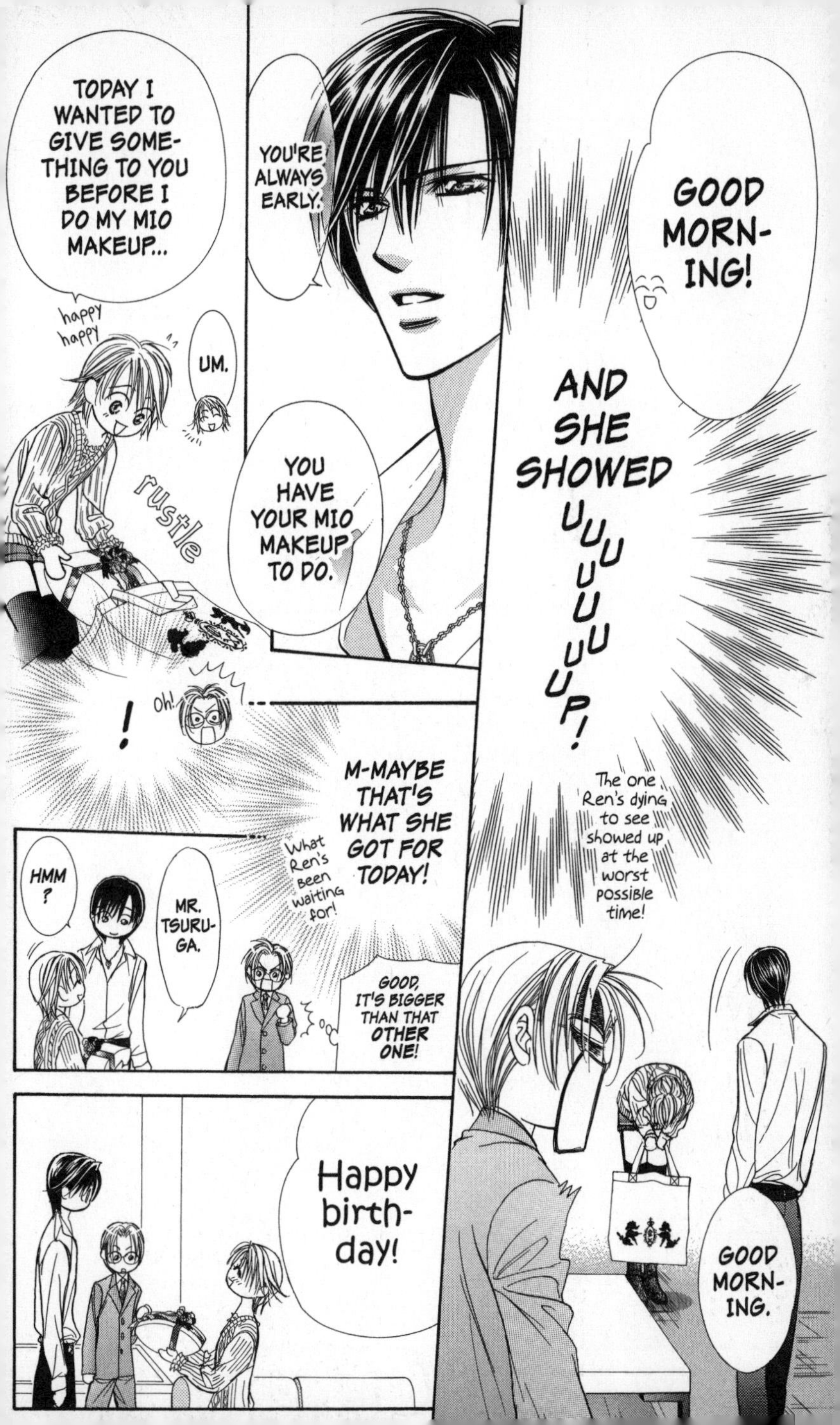

GOOD MORNING!
AND SHE SHOWED UUUUUUUUP!
The one Ren's dying to see showed up at the worst possible time!
GOOD MORNING.
YOU'RE ALWAYS EARLY.
YOU HAVE YOUR MIO MAKEUP TO DO.
TODAY I WANTED TO GIVE SOMETHING TO YOU BEFORE I DO MY MIO MAKEUP...
happy happy
UM.
rustle
M-MAYBE THAT'S WHAT SHE GOT FOR TODAY!
What Ren's been waiting for!
Oh!
!
MR. TSURUGA.
HMM?
GOOD, IT'S BIGGER THAN THAT OTHER ONE!
Happy birthday!

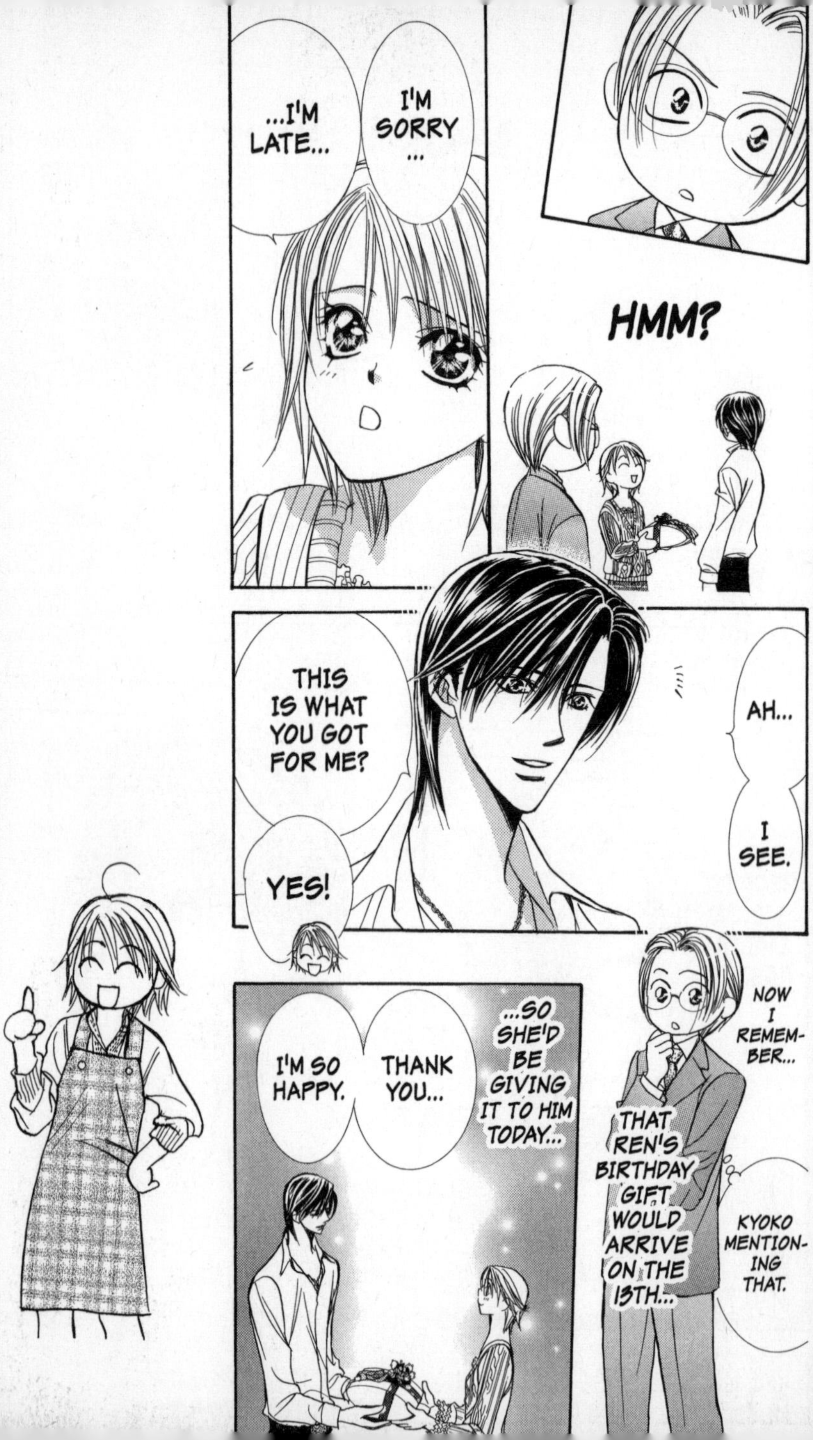
I'M SORRY ...
...I'M LATE...
HMM?
AH...
I SEE.
THIS IS WHAT YOU GOT FOR ME?
YES!
NOW I REMEMBER...
THAT REN'S BIRTHDAY GIFT WOULD ARRIVE ON THE 13TH...
KYOKO MENTIONING THAT.
...SO SHE'D BE GIVING IT TO HIM TODAY...
THANK YOU...
I'M SO HAPPY.

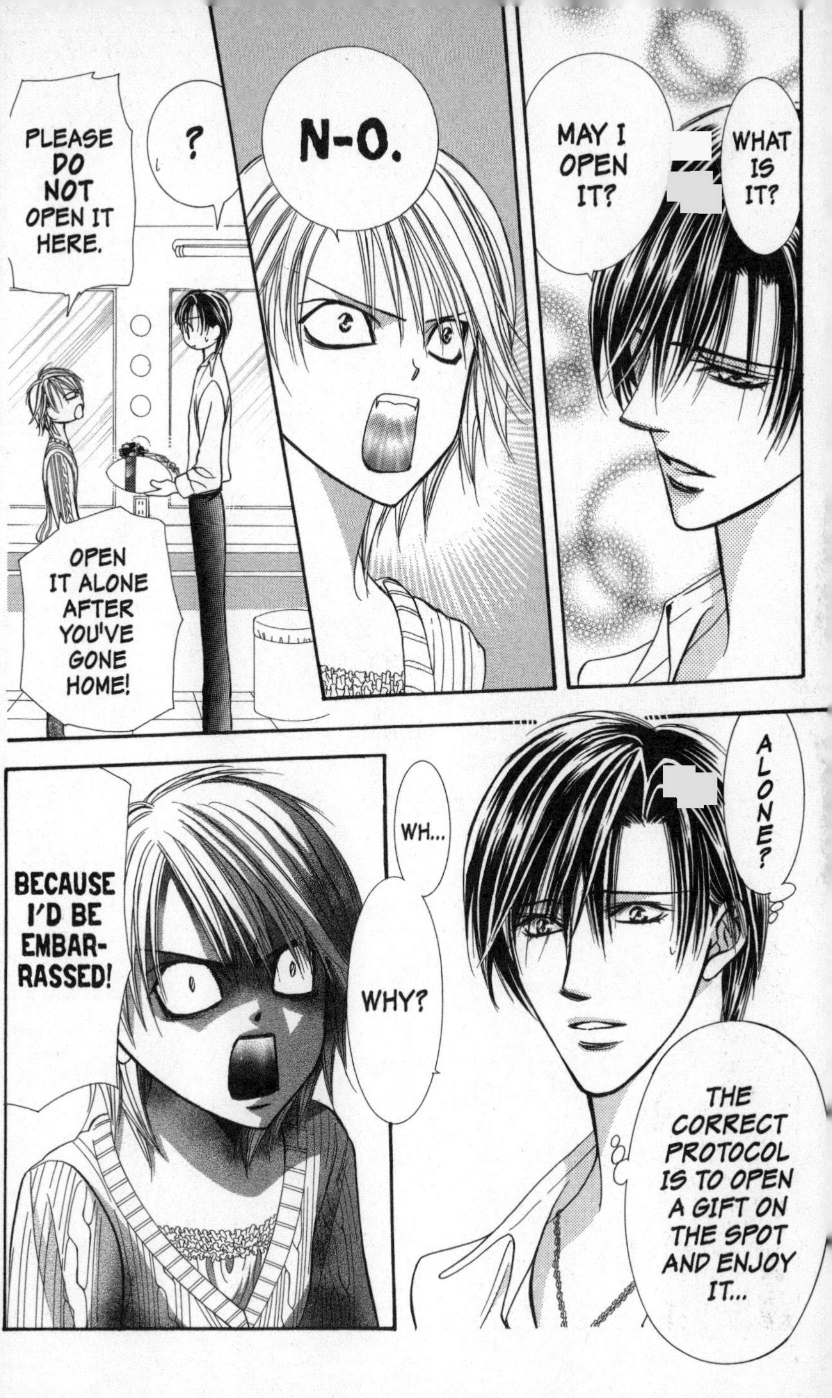
WHAT IS IT?
MAY I OPEN IT?
N-O.
?
PLEASE DO NOT OPEN IT HERE.
OPEN IT ALONE AFTER YOU'VE GONE HOME!
ALONE?
THE CORRECT PROTOCOL IS TO OPEN A GIFT ON THE SPOT AND ENJOY IT...
WH...
WHY?
BECAUSE I'D BE EMBARRASSED!

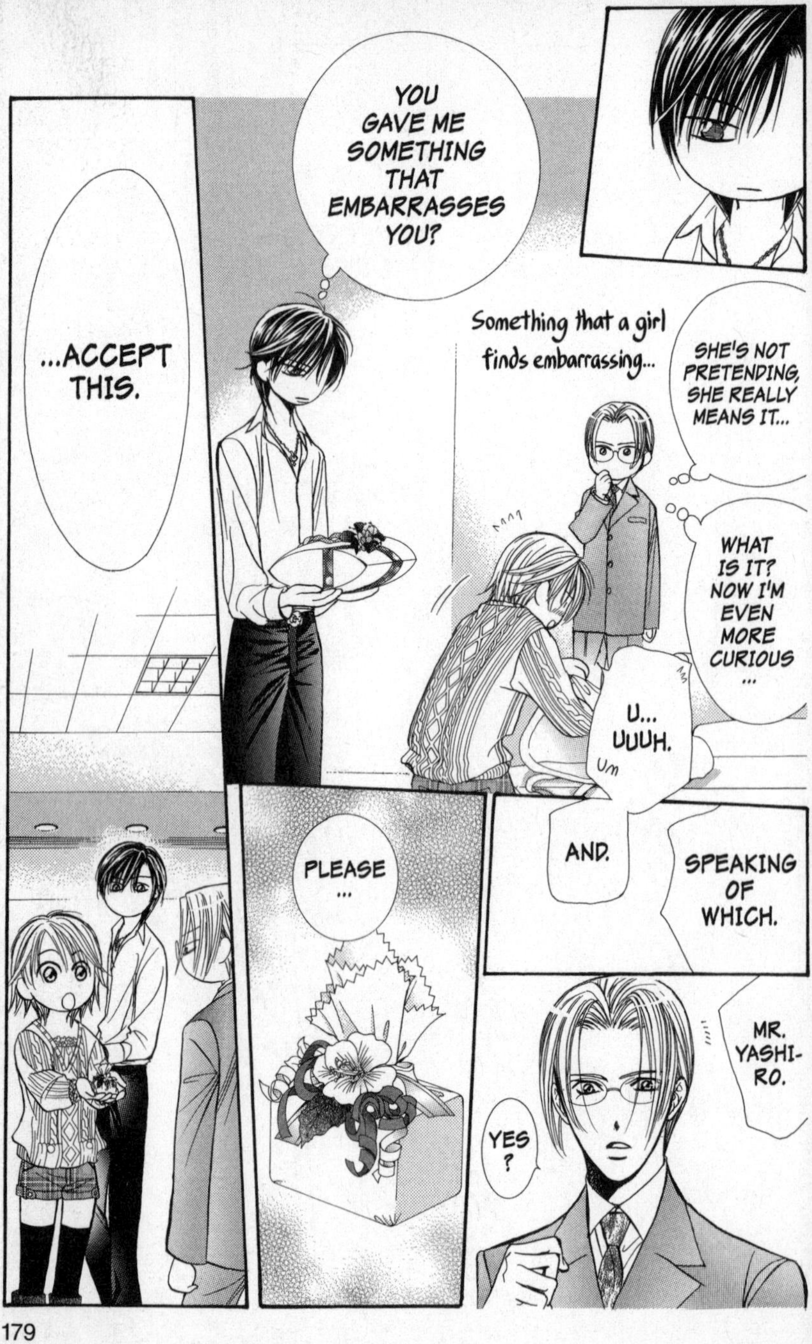
Something that a girl finds embarrassing...
SHE'S NOT PRETENDING, SHE REALLY MEANS IT...
WHAT IS IT? NOW I'M EVEN MORE CURIOUS...
U... UUUH.
Um
YOU GAVE ME SOMETHING THAT EMBARRASSES YOU?
...ACCEPT THIS.
AND.
SPEAKING OF WHICH.
MR. YASHIRO.
YES?
PLEASE...

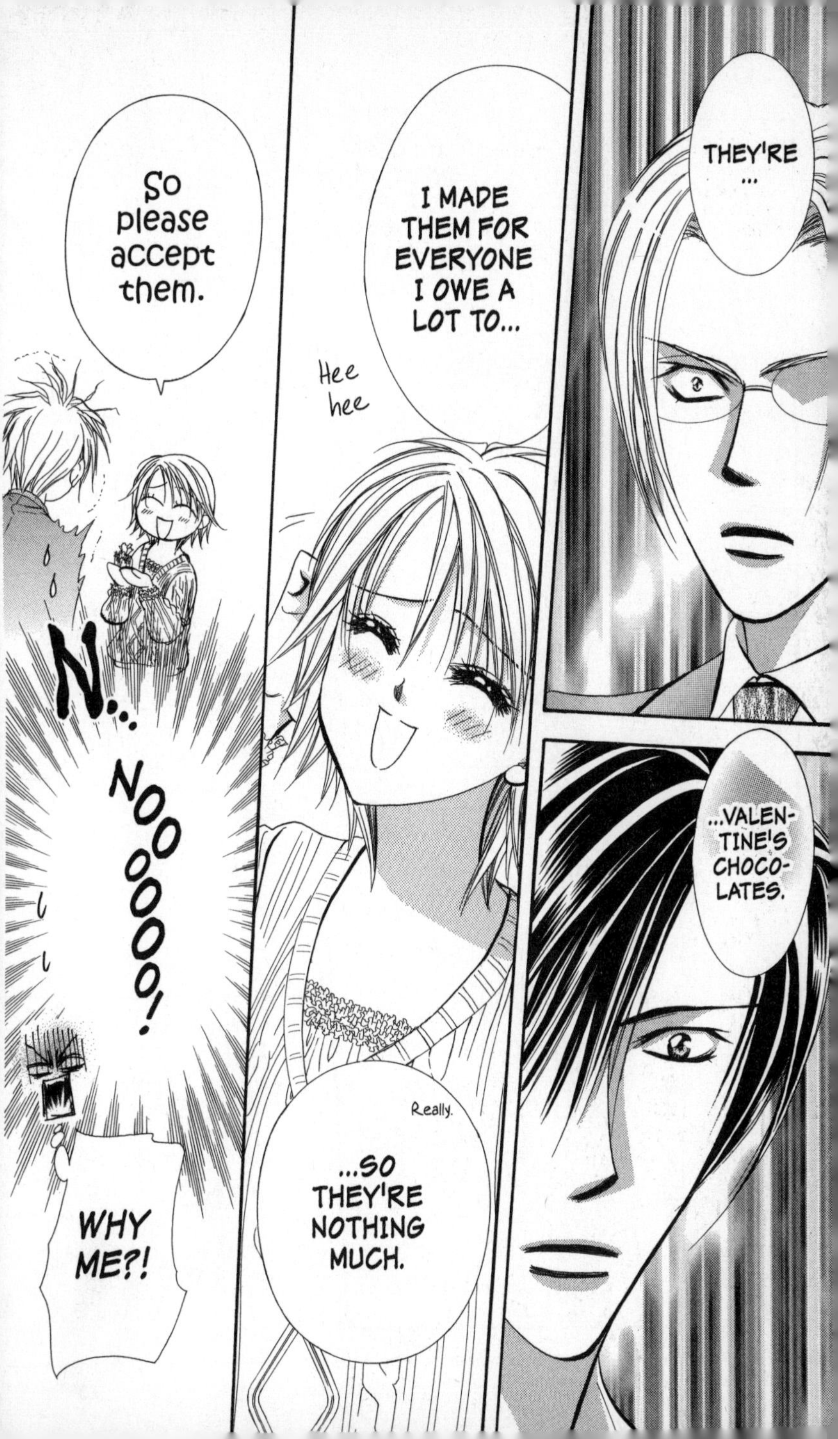
THEY'RE ...
...VALEN-TINE'S CHOCO-LATES.
I MADE THEM FOR EVERYONE I OWE A LOT TO...
Hee hee
...SO THEY'RE NOTHING MUCH.
Really.
So please accept them.
N...
NOOOOOOO!
WHY ME?!

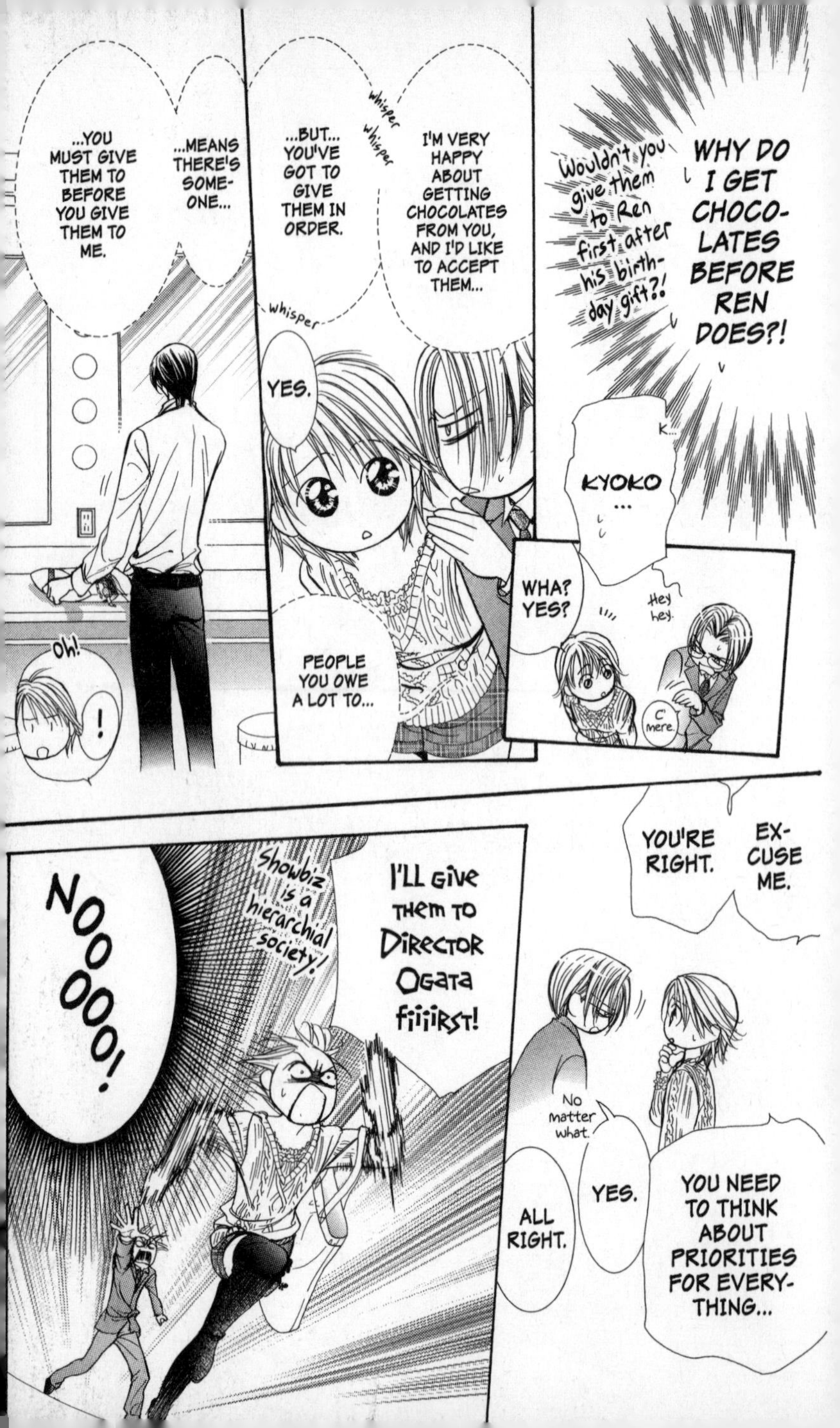
WHY DO I GET CHOCOLATES BEFORE REN DOES?!
Wouldn't you give them to Ren first after his birthday gift?!
K...
KYOKO...
WHA? YES?
Hey hey.
C'mere.
I'M VERY HAPPY ABOUT GETTING CHOCOLATES FROM YOU, AND I'D LIKE TO ACCEPT THEM...
whisper
whisper
...BUT... YOU'VE GOT TO GIVE THEM IN ORDER.
whisper
YES.
PEOPLE YOU OWE A LOT TO...
...MEANS THERE'S SOMEONE...
...YOU MUST GIVE THEM TO BEFORE YOU GIVE THEM TO ME.
Oh!
!
EXCUSE ME.
YOU'RE RIGHT.
YOU NEED TO THINK ABOUT PRIORITIES FOR EVERYTHING...
No matter what.
YES.
ALL RIGHT.
I'LL GIVE THEM TO DIRECTOR OGATA FIIIRST!
Showbiz is a hierarchial society!
NOOOOO!

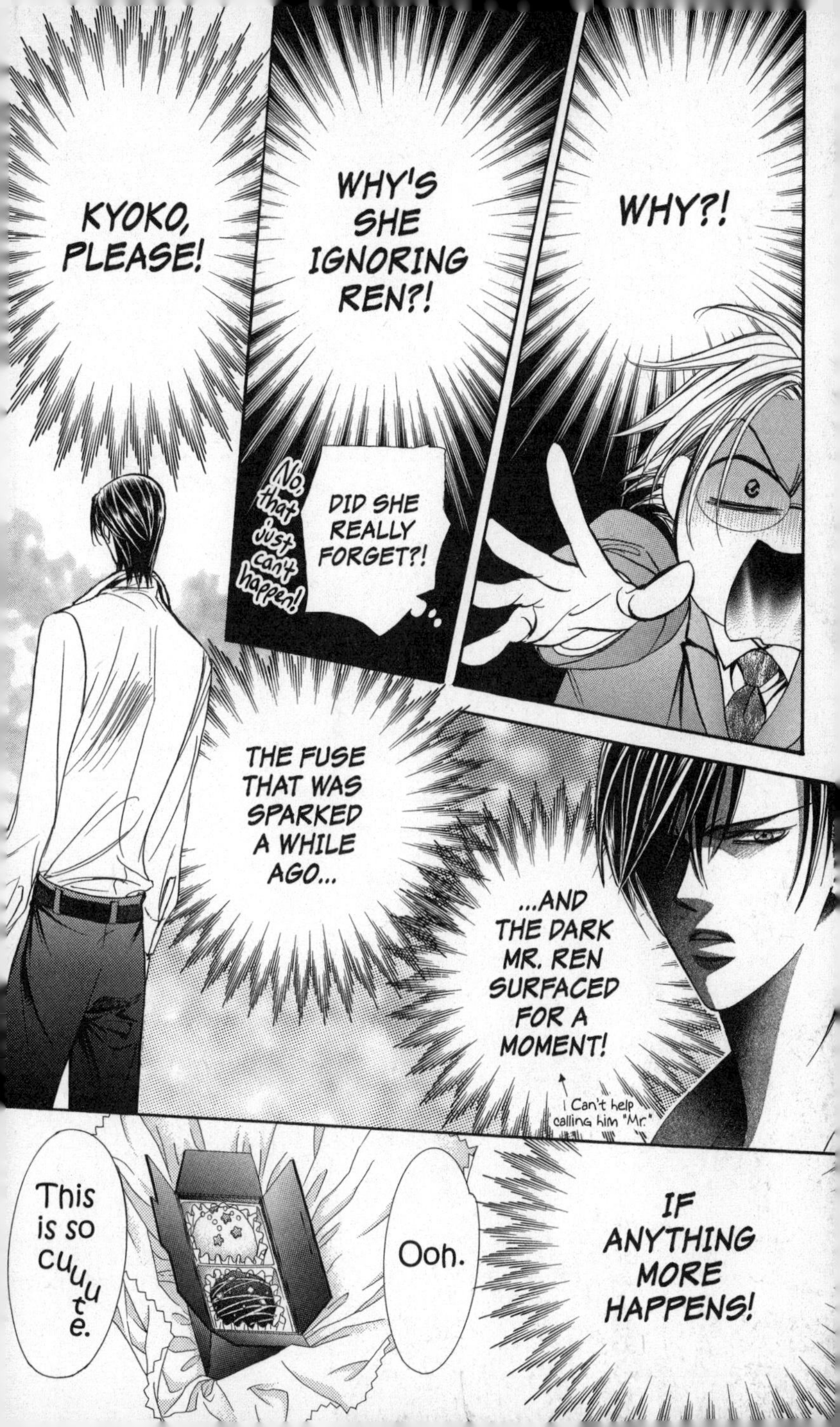
WHY?!
WHY'S SHE IGNORING REN?!
DID SHE REALLY FORGET?!
No, that just can't happen!
THE FUSE THAT WAS SPARKED A WHILE AGO...
...AND THE DARK MR. REN SURFACED FOR A MOMENT!
I Can't help calling him "Mr."
KYOKO, PLEASE!
IF ANYTHING MORE HAPPENS!
Ooh.
This is so cuuuute.

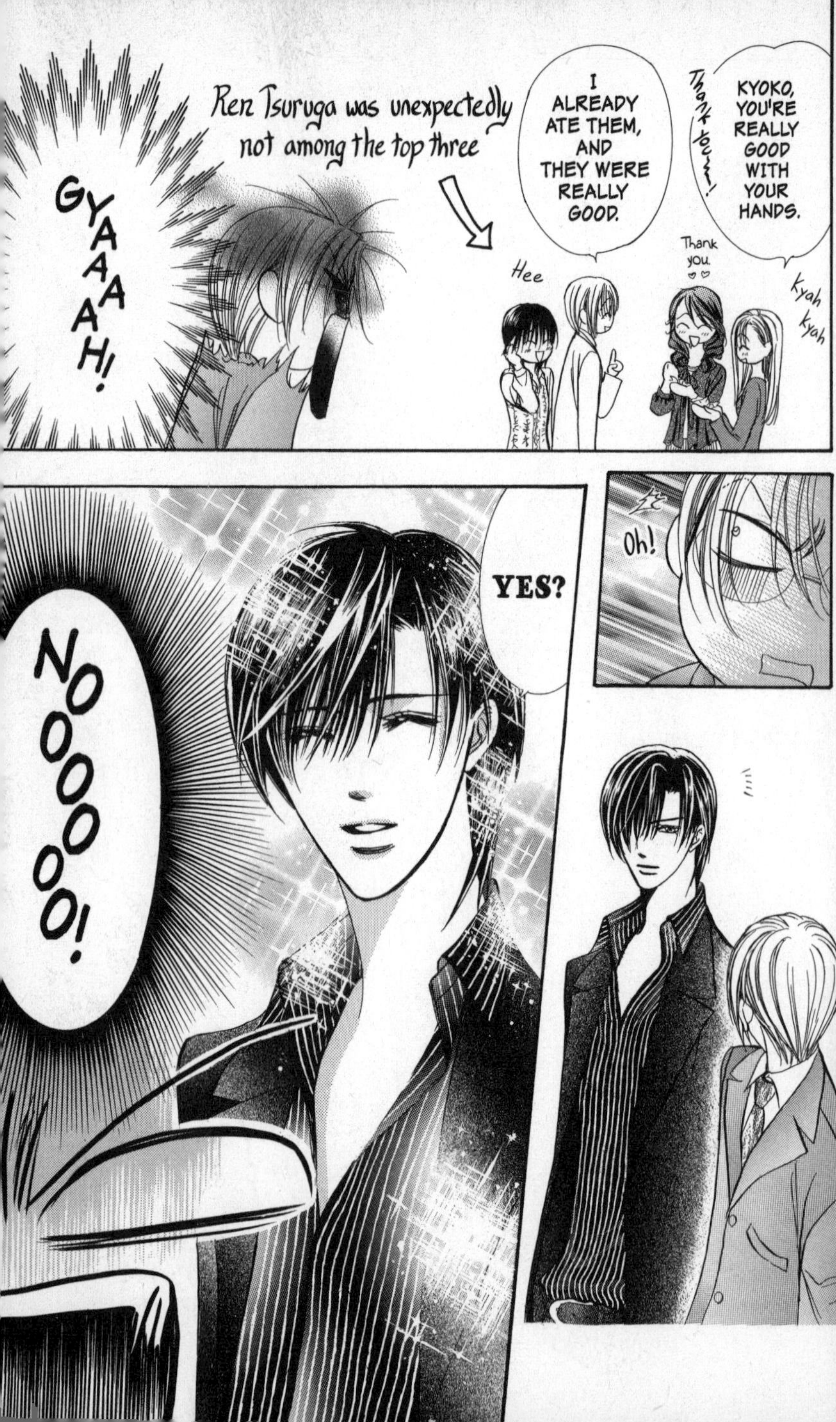
KYOKO, YOU'RE REALLY GOOD WITH YOUR HANDS.
Thank you~~!
Kyah kyah
Thank you. ♡♡
I ALREADY ATE THEM, AND THEY WERE REALLY GOOD.
Hee
Ren Tsuruga was unexpectedly not among the top three
GYAAAAH!
Oh!
YES?
NOOOOOOO!

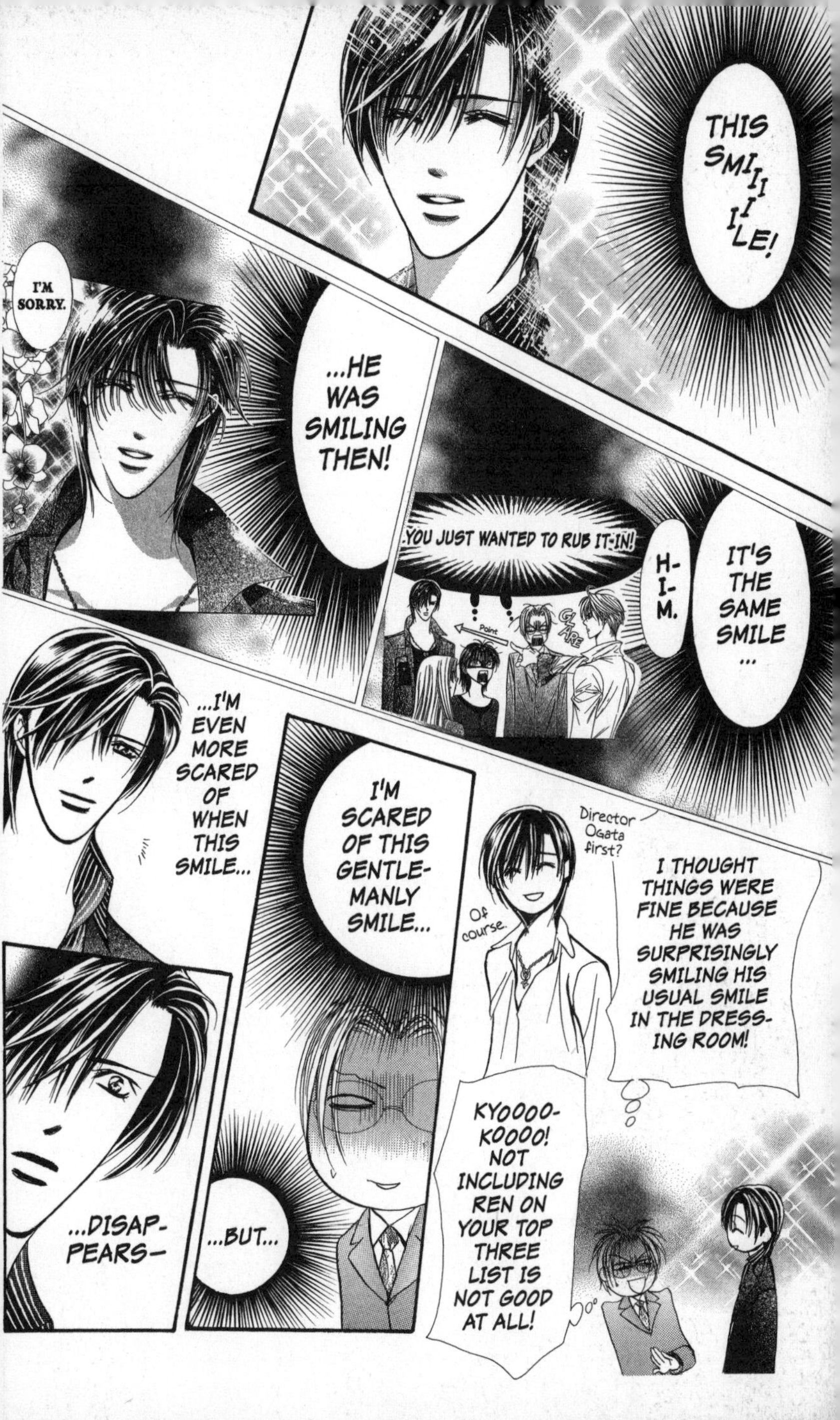
THIS SMIIIIILE!
IT'S THE SAME SMILE...
H-I-M.
...YOU JUST WANTED TO RUB IT IN!
GLARE
Point
...HE WAS SMILING THEN!
I'M SORRY.
I THOUGHT THINGS WERE FINE BECAUSE HE WAS SURPRISINGLY SMILING HIS USUAL SMILE IN THE DRESSING ROOM!
Director Ogata first?
Of course.
KYOOOO-KOOOO! NOT INCLUDING REN ON YOUR TOP THREE LIST IS NOT GOOD AT ALL!
I'M SCARED OF THIS GENTLE-MANLY SMILE...
...BUT...
...I'M EVEN MORE SCARED OF WHEN THIS SMILE...
...DISAP-PEARS-

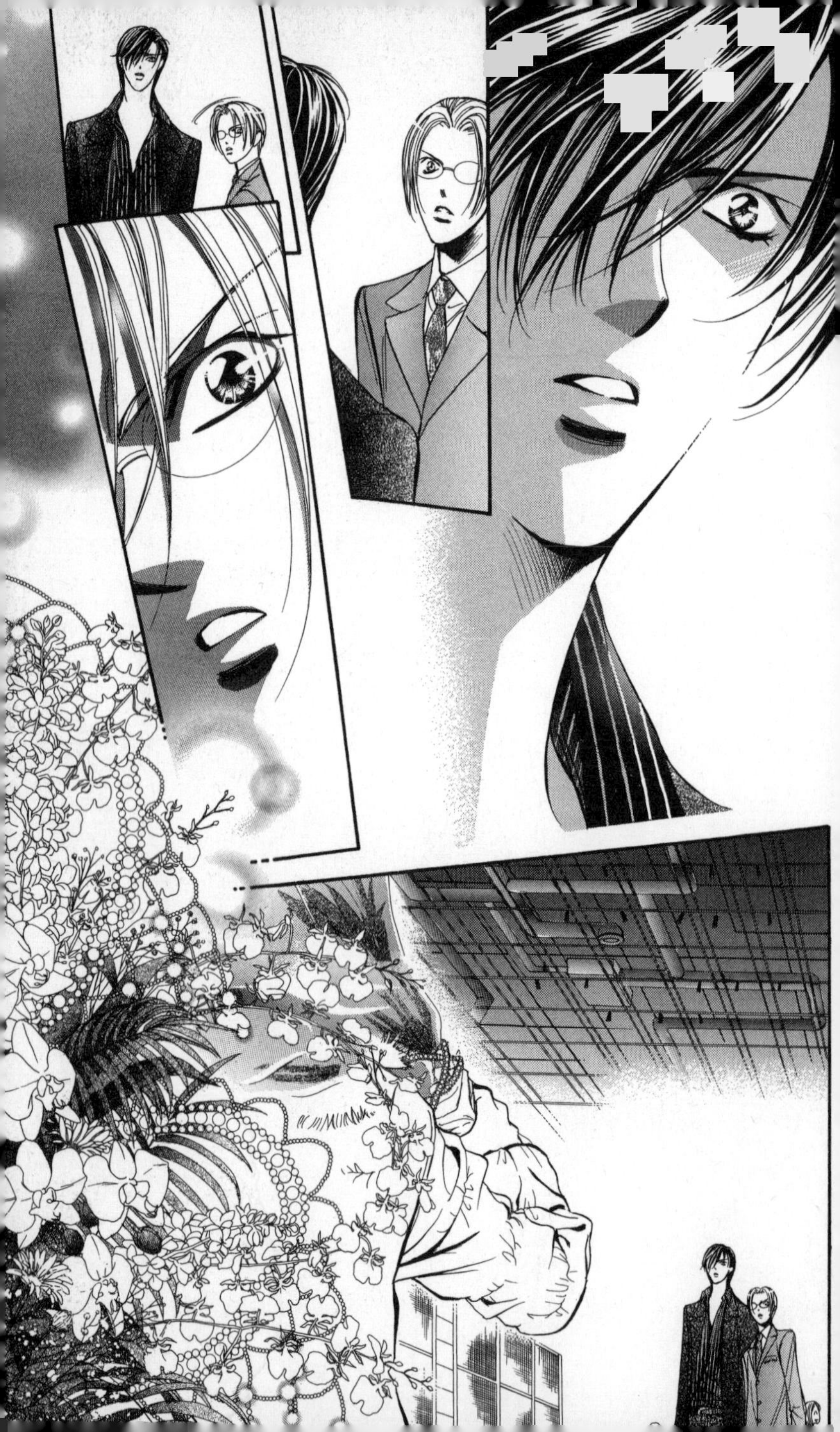

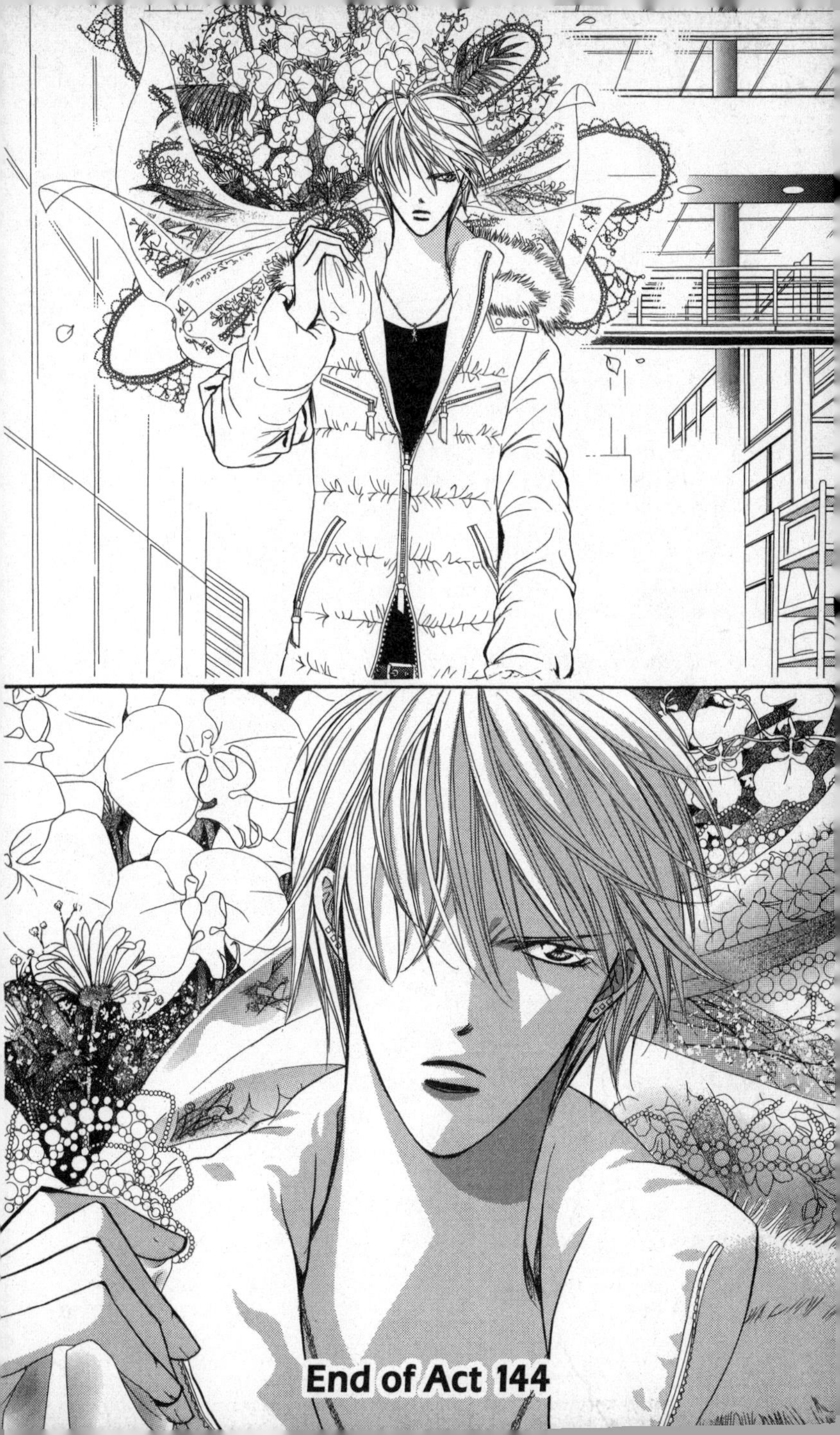
End of Act 144

Skip·Beat! End Notes

Everyone knows how to be a fan, but sometimes cool things from other cultures need a little help crossing the language barrier.

Page 8, panel 3: Talento
A "talento" in Japan usually appears on various TV shows and other mass media outlets. They often sing, star in commercials, and write for print media as well.

Page 30, panel 1: Taisho and Okamisan
Taisho is the term used for the proprietor of a traditional Japanese restaurant and *Okamisan* is the term used for the proprietress.

Page 36, panel 5: Genji Hikaru
The protagonist of the novel *Tale of Genji*. In the story, Genji helps to raise the girl who later becomes his lover.

Page 60, panel 2: Apollo chocolate
An inexpensive type of chocolate available at convenience stores.

Page 84, panel 4: White Day
The day when boys and men give small presents to the women who gave them something on Valentine's.

Page 95, panel 2: Onabira unken bazaradadoban
This is a mantra to the *Dainichi* (Great Sun) Buddha and it means "Dainichi Buddha, who possesses eternal and indestructible light, please lead me to the world of spiritual enlightenment."

Page 119, panel 2: Warabi-mochi
A sticky, gelatinous confection made from bracken starch and dusted with *kinako* (toasted soybean flour).

Page 147, panel 5: Obligatory chocolates
Giri choco are chocolates given out to coworkers and casual acquaintances, and don't have the romantic connotation of *honmei choco* (true feelings chocolate).

Page 158, panel 2: Nio statues
Statues of guardian gods that are placed at temple gates. One is the Agyo (with its mouth open), and the other is the Ungyo (with its mouth closed).

Page 163, panel 6: 150,000 yen
Around $1,790.

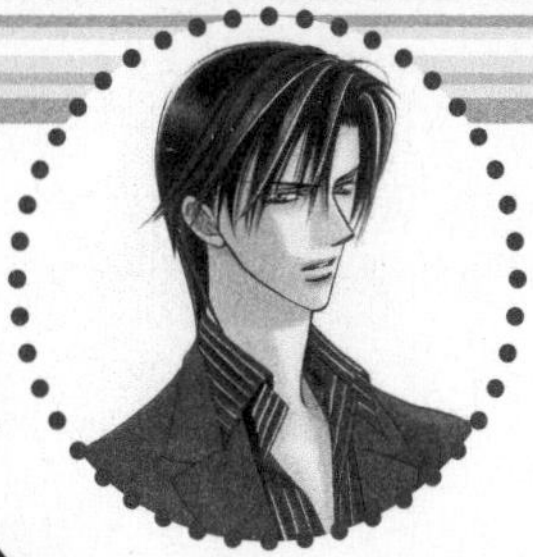

Yoshiki Nakamura is originally from Tokushima Prefecture. She started drawing manga in elementary school, which eventually led to her 1993 debut of *Yume de Au yori Suteki* (Better than Seeing in a Dream) in *Hana to Yume* magazine. Her other works include the basketball series *Saint Love*, *MVP wa Yuzurenai* (Can't Give Up MVP), *Blue Wars* and *Tokyo Crazy Paradise*, a series about a female bodyguard in 2020 Tokyo.

SKIP·BEAT!
Vol. 24
Shojo Beat Edition

STORY AND ART BY YOSHIKI NAKAMURA

English Translation & Adaptation/Tomo Kimura
Touch-up Art & Lettering/Sabrina Heep
Design/Ronnie Casson
Editor/Pancha Diaz

Printed in the U.S.A.

Published by VIZ Media, LLC
P.O. Box 77010
San Francisco, CA 94107

www.viz.com

www.shojobeat.com

10 9 8 7 6 5 4 3 2
First printing, July 2011
Second printing, September 2013

RATED T FOR TEEN

PARENTAL ADVISORY
SKIP·BEAT! is rated T for Teen and is recommended for ages 13 and up. This volume contains a grudge.

ratings.viz.com

Don't Hide What's *Inside*

SURPRISE!

You may be reading the wrong way!

It's true: In keeping with the original
Japanese comic format, this book
reads from
sound effe
are comple
preserves t
original art
Check out
here to get the hang of things,
and then turn to the other side
of the book to get started!

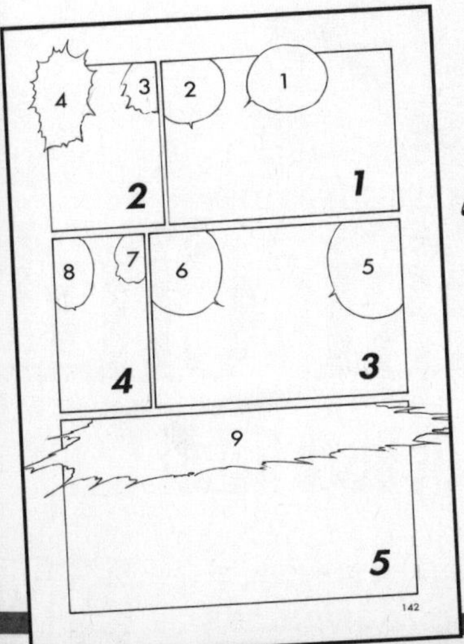

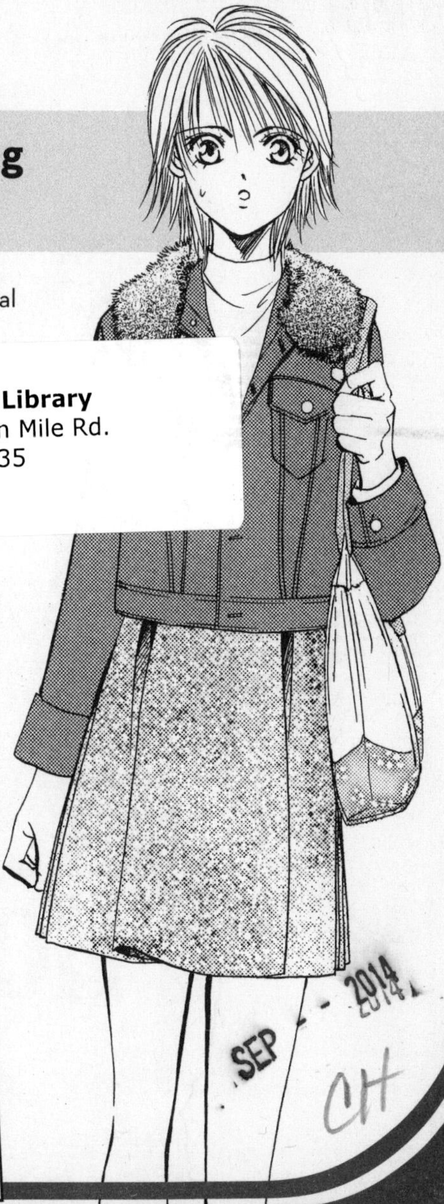